# ESSAYS

## ON

# OTHER MINDS

EDITED BY

THOMAS O. BUFORD

UNIVERSITY OF ILLINOIS PRESS

URBANA CHICAGO LONDON

# PREFACE

The other minds problem has occupied the attention of some of the best of our philosophical colleagues. For whatever reasons they have become interested in this problem, they have approached it with imagination, clarity, rigor, and sometimes humor. Indeed, the dialectic carried on has been and continues to be lively and exemplary of a community of scholars at work on a philosophical problem. It is hoped that this collection of essays will make this dialogue available to a wider audience and will facilitate the reader's own work in this area by articulating the major questions and primary lines of argument which have been developed. No doubt this work will prove most valuable to students in courses in epistemology and analytic philosophy. However, it may be useful to those of my colleagues who, for reasons of their own, have not spent much time with this problem and would like some help in orienting themselves to the issues raised in the debate about other minds.

Special thanks go to those who have provoked me to take seriously the other minds problem, who have criticized my own views with their cogent analysis, who have devised in-

v

genious arguments to support their equally fascinating views, and who have with their good-humored dialectic provided an example of "good philosophy": the authors included in this work.

*Thomas O. Buford*

MARCH, 1970
GREENVILLE, SOUTH CAROLINA

# CONTENTS

vii

# INTRODUCTION

THE OTHER MINDS PROBLEM received its first clear formulation by John Stuart Mill in the nineteenth century. Since that time philosophers of varying persuasions have sought to find satisfactory ways of justifying knowledge claims that other minds *exist*. However, some feel that the problem itself needs to be restated. The issue, they suggest, is not whether other minds exist; unquestionably they do. Rather the issue is justifying knowledge claims about the *feelings, intensions,* and *cognitive style* of other minds. Still others contend that the central question is that of *justifying* these knowledge claims. As a result of such investigations it may be said that there is not one other minds problem; rather, there is a cluster of issues which can be subsumed under the topic, "the problem of other minds."

It is the purpose of this introduction to map this topic by stating the problems which are now generally recognized as central to the other minds problem and by outlining the major lines of argument and counterargument employed in attempts to deal effectively with them. Of course, like most other important philosophical problems, the issues included in the other minds question impinge on other topics of philosophical interest such as the mind-body relation, private language, and phenomenalism. These subsidiary but relevant issues will be discussed to the degree that they are important in understanding the central problems. The approach taken here is, first, to formulate a position which a skeptic might offer and against which those who write on the other minds problem are arguing, and then to outline the kinds of arguments used in attacking the skeptic's position. As Chappell found a similar approach helpful in tackling the more general topic of philosophy of mind, I have found it useful, if not required, in outlining the other minds problem. As a result of this procedure the reader should be equipped to work his way through some interesting and innovative approaches to the issues in this problem, to follow the dialectic as thinkers of opposing persuasions grapple with the questions, and to begin to decide for himself which of the approaches, if any, is the most acceptable.

The position of the skeptic formulated below is taken primarily from the writings of the authors included in this anthology. As this position is examined it is important to recognize that it is based on Cartesian presuppositions. The reason for stating the skeptic's argument in this manner is that while each philosopher is attacking some aspect of skepticism, many are also attacking the Cartesian framework in which the skeptic's argument is stated. These insist that if such an argument for skepticism is accepted, the main tenets of Cartesianism must also be accepted, and this they do not want to do. Other writers, however, do not accept the converse of this statement. One may accept many aspects of Cartesianism, they claim, without necessarily adopting or falling into skepticism. This issue, which is a central one for much of contemporary work in epistemology, is also central to the readings included. Careful attention to this discussion will be profitable. The main tenets of the skeptic's argument can be stated in the following manner:

(1) Any conscious undergoing of an experience is an idea. This means that seeing red, tasting sweet, feeling a twinge of

pain, being joyful, hoping, needing, choosing, etc., are all ideas. They are data present for a conscious subject and may be called mental events.

(2) As mental events they are modifications of an individual mind and, consequently, subjective.

(3) Also, mental events are because an individual mind has them. It is correct, then, to say about mental events, *esse est percipi*.

(4) Mental events and physical behavior are different things. I know this because I can have a headache and successfully pretend not to have one, or I can not have a headache and successfully pretend to have one. Indeed, other persons can be successful in their pretense of having or not having pain or other sensations.

(5) Mental events and physical behavior are contingently related, not logically or causally related.

(6) Every act of knowing begins and terminates with experience, that is, with the kind of subjective data identified in proposition 1.

(7) A necessary condition for knowing either that another person exists or what he experiences is either that I experience his experiences directly or that I infer by some reliable method that he exists and that he is having certain kinds of experiences. It is logically impossible directly to apprehend another's experience. If I did, it would then be mine and not his and his would be his and not mine. Furthermore, there is no method that is perfectly reliable by which I can make correct knowledge claims about other minds.

(8) Therefore, I can know neither that another person exists nor what another person experiences.

## Analogy

The argument from analogy is the oldest of other minds arguments against skepticism. During its history it has produced varied statements, each attempting to find a strategy which would circumvent difficulties in earlier formulations. Those who accept one form of the analogical argument reject proposition 7. It is not a necessary condition for knowing that another mind exists or what another mind is feeling that I be able to feel his feelings as he feels them, and it is not the case that there is no perfectly reliable method by which inferences about other minds can be made. Furthermore, some adherents to the analogical argument reject proposition 5 and claim that on the basis of an observed causal relation between certain feelings and bodily behavior it is legitimate to infer both that other minds exist and they have certain feelings.

Russell, who rejects both propositions 7 and 5, argues that I know from observation that a specific thought or feeling of mine always causes my body to act in a particular way. Given a particular movement of my body, I always know its cause. If I observe another body like mine moving in the same way, I conclude that the cause was a definite thought or feeling. Further, the thought or feeling is not mine. It must be a thought or feeling causing that body to behave in the way it does. Therefore, another mind exists and has this particular thought or feeling. For example, I observe that when I am thirsty my body moves in particular ways. It goes to a water fountain or in some way seeks to satisfy the thirst. Another body is observed in a hot desert drinking water. There must be a cause for this bodily movement. I am not now thirsty. There must, then, be a thirst in that body moving it to drink. Hence, another mind exists and feels thirst.

This classical form of the analogical argument has been generally rejected by most thinkers. The major difficulty lies in the problematical character of the privately observed causal connection between a particular feeling and a particular movement of the body. The crux of the problem is how causality is to be understood and how the claim can be justified that such a connection exists between particular feelings and particular movements of the body.

Some thinkers who want to maintain some form of the argument from analogy but without the weight of the problems arising from the claim of a causal connection between feeling and bodily movement reformulate the argument in inductive terms. Adherents to this approach are willing to forego rejection of proposition 5 and direct their attack to the skeptic's proposition (in number 7) that there are no reliable methods by which one can make inferences about other minds. Hampshire argues that other persons sometimes infer from my behavior that I am in pain. I am in a unique position to check their claim and to determine the reliability of the method they use to draw this inference. When I have determined the reliability of their method of inference and have found it satisfactory in my own instance, I am justified in using it with modest confidence in making claims about other minds. The analogy here is not between mental events and physical behavior, a relation the character of which is problematical. Rather, the analogy is between use of the same method by different people on different occasions. However, Plantinga points out that one step in inductive arguments (a step implicit to Hampshire's position) is that probably every case of pain behavior is accompanied by pain in the body displaying it. It is generally agreed that for an inductive argument to be sound the method of sampling must be fair and unbiased. But if that step is taken, the sampling is not fair. If one is observing feelings of pain and pain behavior and finds they are always associated, and one also knows that because of the method of sampling all feelings of pain will accompany pain behavior, then one knows that the sampling is biased and unfair. Hence, the analogical-inductive argument must be rejected.

Another statement of the inductive argument which does not depend on causal relations between feelings and physical behavior and attempts to overcome Plantinga's objection emphasizes the legitimacy of the inference from my own case to what must be the case about another mind. Slote puts his argument in the following form:

(a) Every case of (full-blown) pain behavior on the part of my (human) body (that I can remember) has been accompanied by pain or the pretense of pain (namely, on my part). So (b) (it is reasonable for me to believe that) every case of

ESSAYS ON OTHER MINDS

(full-blown) pain behavior (on the part of any human body) is accompanied by pain or the pretense of pain. But (c) that (human) body over there is displaying (full-blown) pain behavior. So (d) (it is reasonable for me to believe that) someone is feeling pain, or else pretending to be in pain. But (e) I am not feeling pain, nor pretending to be in pain. So (f) (it is reasonable for me to believe that) someone else (or something else) is either feeling pain or pretending to be in pain, and therefore there is at least one other mind.

This argument, according to Slote, is based on two principles: (1) "If all the $x$'s one has sampled have been found to be $f$ (and one has sampled numerous $x$'s), and if one has after careful, rational, thorough examination of one's evidence discovered no reason to think that one's sample is unfair or biased, then it is reasonable to believe that all $x$'s are $f$," and (2) one has no reason to believe that he is biased or unfair in sampling pain behavior "as far as the property of being accompanied by pain or the pretense of pain is concerned." Obviously, the inductive character of this argument lies in the inference from what is true of observed $x$'s to what is true of all $x$'s. Its strength comes from employing a method which has proved reliable in other areas of investigation such as the sciences. If the method is used correctly and the sampling is neither biased nor unfair, then one should be able to have confidence in its results. On this basis some thinkers believe they have found a strategy which will allow them to argue successfully against the skeptic's position. Other philosophers (Malcolm, Strawson, Austin, Zemach, Gallagher) are quick to point out, however, that the argument from analogy, whatever strategy those holding it might take, suffers from fundamental defects which preclude any successful defense of it. Indeed, the only way to deal with the other minds problem is to reject the Cartesian assumptions underlying not only the skeptic's position but also the analogical position. This kind of statement has also been made by those who can be called behaviorists.

xiv

## *Behaviorism*

Behaviorism has had many formulations. Its strategists have devised arguments ranging from what can be called logical behaviorism to modified behaviorism. The logical behaviorist claims that proposition 4 of the skeptic's position is mistaken. It is the case, according to Carnap, that sensation or mental event words have meaning only if they can be translated into a physical language which is empirically verifiable. Words referring to a private mental state are, in principle, unverifiable and are consequently meaningless; they must be translated into physical terms before any meaning can be attached to them. On these grounds the logical behaviorist proceeds to argue in the following way: (1) Mr. Jones is behaving in certain ways; he has facial expressions, gestures, or physical effects of his behavior such as handwriting. (2) When a person is perceived to have these facial expressions, or gestures in such a manner, or his handwriting is such and such, he usually turns out to be excited. (3) Therefore, Mr. Jones is excited. No doubt the logical behaviorist has something to say for his position. It does allow one to explain how it is the case that we do sometimes know that another person is angry or has a toothache. Further, on the basis of the empiricist criterion one can determine the correctness or incorrectness of one's assertions about other minds. However, powerful arguments have been lodged against this brand of behaviorism not only by thinkers who take a position other than either analogy or behaviorism but also by thinkers who adopt a modified behaviorism.

Ziff, who accepts modified behaviorism, argues that logical behaviorism must be rejected on at least two counts: (1) if logical behaviorism is correct, then I must observe my behavior in order to determine whether or not I am angry; but surely this is not the case. I know if I am angry or not quite apart from inspection of my physical behavior. (2) If logical behaviorism is correct, I can in principle always find out whether or not another person is angry. But I cannot always find this out. Even though it is in principle possible for me to observe the behavior of another person, this person may not behave in a pain manner even though he is in pain. Therefore, logical behaviorism, if not completely rejected, must be at least modified to a more defensible form.

One modification behaviorists such as Ziff insist on is that physical behavior must be understood not just in terms of bodily movement but also in terms of the total behavior of the person in his social, physical, and cultural context. This means that behavior must include verbal behavior. Indeed, for Ziff, verbal behavior has a privileged status in any judgment regarding the mental state of another person. This can be seen in the fact that persons often behave in nonpain ways yet say that they are in pain. A behaviorist who would hold to this more sophisticated form of behaviorism would contend that even though some kind of behavior is required if one is to determine when and if another person is in pain, verbal behavior is crucial to any judgment of this kind.

Although this modified form of behaviorism is not open to the same kinds of attacks which were made on logical behaviorism, it does have its difficulties. Can it not be the case that a person may not act as if he is in pain, say that he is in pain, and yet not be in pain? Or that he may act as if he is in pain, say that he is not in pain, and yet be in pain? The modified behaviorist might answer that by examining the relevant context and total pattern of behavior of the individual such difficulties could be resolved and correct judgments about other minds could be made. But if successful pretense is possible, how is it legitimate to appeal to behavior to determine successful pretense? Such questions as these (raised by Wisdom and others), in addition to the already noted attacks made on logical behaviorism, have led many thinkers to seek a line of argument which would avoid the extremes of either analogy or behaviorism.

## *Identity*

One attempt to steer a course between the analogical and the behaviorist argument is made by the identity theorist. His attack on the skeptic's position is not directed at propositions 4 and 5. Mental events and physical behavior are different kinds of things, and they are only contingently related at best. What is rejected is proposition 7, that there is no reliable method for determining what other minds feel. The best way to "exorcise the ghost of the machine," according to Feigl, is to speak of central states which are manifested or indicated in subjective terms. The point of his position is that we may legitimately identify mental events such as sensations and central states. It can be argued that if one has a sufficiently well-developed theory regarding the neurophysiological characteristics of central states, then one could translate all statements describing mental events into neurophysiological language. To determine the correctness of claims about the mental events of another person, all that would be required would be a reading of his brain processes. If his brain processes confirm the claim, then it could be said with confidence that his mental state has been correctly described. But, it may be asked, how is one to determine if an identity has been established? What evidence would support such a claim? Feigl is willing to admit as evidence first-person, direct confirmation of mental states to establish the identity in one's own case, and also to admit as part of the method of testing claims about other minds an analogy between my mental states and cerebral processes and another person's mental states and cerebral processes. Indeed, he insists, if all one can expect from most theories is confirmation, why should one expect more regarding this theory? It can be said, however, that this statement of the identity theory not only suffers from the difficulty of establishing the analogy but also carries the difficult responsibility of establishing one-to-one correspondences between central states and mental states.

Though the latter may not be a logical impossibility, it does seem to many a practically ambitious undertaking.

## Hypothesis

Many thinkers who attempt to answer the skeptic and who seek to avoid the difficulties of both the analogical argument and behaviorism suggest that knowledge claims about other minds, that is, that other minds exist and have feelings, are best understood as hypotheses to explain certain phenomena. Two representative "hypothesis" theories are those advanced by H. H. Price and Paul Ziff.

Price contends that the best way to deal with the other minds problem is to understand language and communication. We hear noises like "That is a bus." How is one to explain such noises as this? This can be done on the hypothesis that they come from another mind. However, in order to justify this hypothesis three criteria must be fulfilled: "(1) Noises (must) have symbolic character for me, (2) symbolize something true or false, (3) must give me new information." He continues, "I know from introspection that noises of this sort frequently function as instruments to a certain sort of mental act. (Hence) they are probably functioning as instruments to an act of that sort in the present case. But in the present case that act is not mine." According to this argument, if I hear noises such as "I am in pain," they can best be explained by advancing the hypothesis that another mind exists and feels pain. This hypothesis can be verified by appealing to the criteria and to one's own understanding, gained introspectively, that noises of this sort are instrumental in one's own mental acts and that they are probably functioning this way in the present case. In this case, however, the act is not mine and must be someone else's mental act. Therefore, another mind exists and has "pain" kinds of feelings.

On the basis of this account it is clear that Price does not reject propositions 1–6. In fact, his proposition is stated in a

Cartesian framework. However, he does reject the skeptic's
claim in proposition 7 that there is no reliable method for
determining whether or not other minds exist and that one
can know that another mind exists and what that other mind
is feeling only if one experiences directly the experiences of
that other mind. Though Price construes his argument along the
lines of a hypothesis which best explains the data he is seeking to understand, Malcolm contends that Price's argument is
based not only on questionable presuppositions but also on the
argument from analogy, an argument which is open to devas-
tating charges. In particular, to maintain his line of argument,
Price must admit a private use of language and must develop
a criterion of "same" on the basis of which one can determine
that another person is having the same experiences I have.
Malcolm contends that a criterion for "same" cannot be supplied to undergird the analogy. Furthermore, if one allows a
private language, one can neither make warranted judgments
about other minds nor have justified opinions about one's own.
This point will be developed later in the discussion of the
criteriological argument.

Ziff develops his position somewhat differently than does
Price. He attempts to make the point that "if I had a mindless
double, I would be unable to provide a sound (i.e., coherent,
complete, and simple) theory explaining this fact." One way
to support this hypothesis is by seeking to establish a counterthesis: "Could the other one and I relevantly differ only in
this: I do and he does not have a mind?" Finding the counterthesis unsupportable, Ziff turns to the hypothesis that other
minds do exist. This hypothesis is supported by a wide range of
other hypotheses which are in turn supported by a vast array
of observations and experiments. His point is not that this
hypothesis is just a single one standing alone; rather, it is part
of a wider, complex conceptual scheme. Hence, the most coherent, simple, and complete theory is that other minds exist.
This position, however, is open to a number of attacks, not the
least of which is that made by Plantinga. He offers what he

believes to be a theory which is coherent, simple, and complete which does explain that I have a mindless double. Descartes' "Evil Genius" created me to play a practical joke. In addition, he created many "mindless human bodies (among them my mindless double) that behave pretty much the way one might expect minded human bodies to behave." It can cogently be claimed for this hypothesis that it is coherent, simple, and complete. At this point Plantinga asks, "How does it follow that, on my total evidence, it is unlikely that I am unique in having a mind?"

## Criteriological Argument

Proponents of the criteriological argument agree with the "identity" and hypothesis theorists in contending that neither skepticism nor the analogical and behaviorist arguments are acceptable. They insist that any position on the other minds problem, such as the analogical argument, which admits the legitimacy of a private access to mental states, faces the insoluble problem of providing a criterion to determine when correct identifications have been made. They also claim that logical behaviorism is untenable. It is not the case that all talk about mental events must be couched in physical language. Finally, those who accept this position contend that proposition 5 of the skeptic's position must be rejected. Even though mental events and physical behavior are related in neither a contingent nor a causal manner, they are related logically. The reasoning for this position can be seen by examining, first, some of the arguments against the analogical and behaviorist positions.

A major difficulty of the analogical argument, according to those who advance the criteriological argument (Malcolm, Strawson, and Austin), is its adherence to the Cartesian presupposition that a private access to mental events is legitimate. This view has it that all talk about mental events must start with "one's own case." However, this presupposition leads to grave problems. For example, suppose one starts with "one's own case" and identifies a particular sensation such as pain. Later, he has another sensation which he also identifies as pain. If he were then asked if he had made a correct identification, he would be hard put to answer the question. Indeed, he has no criterion on the basis of which he can justify such identification. He has, as Malcolm says, "no standard, no examples, no customary practice, with which to compare (his) inner recognitions." But the analogical argument is not only based on questionable assumptions; it is also beset with problems in establishing the analogy. On the basis of the analogy of physical movement the analogy theorist suggests that I may infer there is another mind which has the same kinds of feelings I am having and that these feelings are causing or are associated with the physical movement being observed. But, it may be asked, what criterion does one have that the other person is having the "same" feelings I am having? As Malcolm pointedly states, "If you can (supply this criterion) you will have no use for the argument from analogy; and if you cannot then you do not understand the supposed conclusion of that argument."

Malcolm and others who accept the criteriological argument not only reject the analogical position but they also reject logical behaviorism. It is clearly the case that I do not know my sensations by appealing to my behavior. I can know that I am in pain immediately and directly. Indeed, such expressions as "I am in pain" are best understood as similar to "the natural, nonverbal, behavioral expressions of psychological states" such as crying, limping, or grimacing. The correct way to understand how these expressions are used is to see them as replacing behavioral expressions. Another criticism of the behaviorist argument (one made by Wisdom) is that the central difficulty of logical behaviorism is that even though we may know the behavior of another person, we may be in doubt about how he felt, in the same way we may be in doubt about the inner workings of a machine even though we know what is happening outside. Wisdom sees an important difference between mental events and physical behavior and denies that they can be considered one. An additional reason for rejecting the logical behaviorist position is that its meaning of behavior is much too narrow. Behavior is not only physical but also verbal movement and always takes place in a context of life. According to Austin, saying that a person has the sensation of pain, for example, is best understood as something like saying that a person has the mumps. One cannot identify any one item as the sufficient criterion of having "mumps"; rather, one must point to a complex situation and indicate that all the elements in it are the signs of mumps. The same is the case for saying that another person is experiencing pain. One cannot point to the physical movement of a body only and claim that this is a sufficient criterion for justifying the statement, "He is experiencing pain." Rather, one must point to the whole complex behavioral situation in which the claim is made.

On the basis of arguments such as those made against the analogist and the logical behaviorist, those who adhere to the criteriological argument believe that they have laid the groundwork for justifying knowledge claims about other minds. By implication the above arguments are also arguments against the skeptic's position in propositions 5 and 7. Mental events and physical behavior are related in a way other than causally and contingently, and there is a reliable method of inference by which one can justify claims about minds other than one's own. As Strawson says, behavior is "a logically adequate criterion" for determining the correctness of other minds statements. If one satisfies the criterion, then it must be concluded that that of which it is the criterion exists. The argument for this position can be put in the following manner: words such as "pain" have a public meaning only and we learn their meaning and correct use by appealing to the public meaning of words used in contexts and associated with the behavior, beliefs, and attitudes on the part of the users and those of whom the words are ascribed. I can know that another person is experiencing pain by determining if he is using his words correctly, that is, according to the criterion of correct use of such words. If a person claims that he is in pain and is not behaving in a pain manner, then we would have to say something like "he is lying or pretending." If he is actually in pain and only pretending, we can know by the situation in which the word is being used whether or not the user or that one to whom pain is ascribed is pretending. The same can be said for lying. The point is that the sensation of pain and overt behavior are logically related, and one can know when another is in pain by appealing to his behavior to determine the correctness of the claim.

No doubt the proponents of this theory are correct that at least behavior is a criterion of pain. But it can be asked what is to be understood by the statement, "Mental events and physical behavior are logically related." As we have seen, Strawson's answer is that the relation is that which obtains between a criterion and that of which it is a criterion. Yet what is the nature of this relation? Clearly it is neither a causal nor a contingent relation. If it is a logical one, does this mean that the relation is one of logical entailment (that is, from behavior in certain contexts the existence of a particular sensation can validly be inferred)? Malcolm rejects this option and is no doubt correct in doing so. But then the question presses even harder: if the relation is a logical one and is not logical entailment, then what kind of logical relation is it? This question has been dealt with by Rogers Albritton and Carl Wellman (see Bibliography), but the nature of this relation has not been fully articulated to some philosophers' way of thinking. Nevertheless, the criteriological argument is a powerful one and is accepted rather widely by those who work with the other minds problem.

## Direct Access

Each of the foregoing arguments, according to some philosophers (Zemach and Gallagher), may be characterized as indirect approaches to the other minds problem (except, possibly, logical behaviorism). Each accepts the distinction be-tween mind and body and accepts that part of proposition 7 which asserts that it is logically impossible to apprehend di-rectly another person's experiences. Once this position is adopted all knowledge of other minds must be achieved through inference, that is, indirectly. However, if this approach is taken, one is never able to justify fully such knowledge claims; indeed, it is difficult to see how skepticism and solip-sism can be avoided. To avoid the implications of the indirect approach to the other minds problems, one must take the op-posite strategy and take the direct approach.

Zemach contends that it is possible to know other minds directly, that we do have in fact "first hand knowledge of the sensations of other persons." Though this may seem strange on first hearing, what makes it strange is that we assume an atomistic view of personal identity such as that held by Straw-son. If the atomist position is correct and personal identity is established by appealing to physical organization, then one is prohibited from taking any approach to other minds other than the indirect one. Yet if this tends to lead to solipsism and skepticism and if we do believe that we sometimes know other minds, it is legitimate to question the assumption on which, at least in part, the indirect approach is based. One way to show that the atomist position is incorrect is to indicate how it is possible to identify persons in ways other than by appeal-ing to some kind of physical structure. What is to prohibit identifying persons by distinguishing minds? It is plausible, Zemach suggests, to assert that persons can be identified in principle by determining the cognitive style of their minds. Who has not said with confidence and credibility that the style of thinking of one person is quite different from the style of thinking of another? But does this mean that one can identify a bodiless entity? Zemach contends that in principle it can be done and that if this is logically possible, then there is no logical difficulty in two persons experiencing the same sensa-tion.

Another approach taken in developing the direct access argument is that of Gallagher. He contends that one can know other minds directly through the I-Thou relation. The cornerstone of this view is that the self is essentially social. Accordingly, it is unintelligible to contend that the understanding of the "I" is prior to the understanding of the "Thou." Such a view is inconsistent with the development of the self (which requires society) and with the growth of "rational consciousness" (which also requires society). If this is the case, then it is also inconsistent to raise the question of the existence of other selves. But, if may be asked, in what way can the experiences of other minds be known directly? Such knowledge is gained in the I-Thou relation, a relation characterized by the undergoing of the "full experience of presence" of another. Gallagher pithily puts his point by saying that "self-presence and the presence of a thou are two sides of one coming-to-presence which is the creative achievement of human communion." Nevertheless, one may ask, in what sense is this apprehension of another mind in the relation of communion to be understood as knowledge? The answer is that the hallmark of knowledge is expressibility. Since this kind of knowledge is expressible, one can claim that one has direct knowledge of another mind.

One line of critique which may be taken regarding the direct access view of other minds is to ask on what conditions am I able to determine when I correctly identify the experiences I have of another mind? That is, if I were to claim that I can identify your pain experience which I am directly apprehending, on what basis could I justify my identification? It seems that one could say that I can identify this kind of experience in the same way that identification of my own pain is established, that is, directly, by appealing directly to my own case. However, this will not do. It has been pointed out by Malcolm that any attempt to justify knowledge claims which start with "one's own case" can appeal only to "one's own case" to establish correct identification of experiences such as pain. Yet if one does this, one has no standard or "customary practice" to appeal to in establishing the claim. Does not the direct access view start with "our own case"? To what can one appeal as a criterion if this starting place is accepted? Again, there is no standard or usual practice to look to in justifying the knowledge claim that I correctly identify your pain experience I apprehend directly. The other side of the issue is the difficulty of establishing the difference between your experience and mine. Indeed, what could establish this? Though the direct access view is an imaginative and interesting approach to the other minds problem, it is faced with issues such as this one which it must settle if it is to claim more general acceptance than it now enjoys.

## Conclusion

The purpose of the foregoing outline is to provide some perspective by which the issues in the other minds problem can be seen and to indicate the major lines of argument which have been developed to deal with those issues. Of course, no attempt has been made to be exhaustive. Only a careful reading of the selections themselves will allow one to gain a detailed understanding of the development of each position. Furthermore, it should be obvious that no "final answer" has been given to the other minds problem. Hopefully, the preceding discussion and the selections included in this anthology will aid in the continuing search for understanding in this interesting and exciting topic. Indeed, such a search is the "fun" of philosophy.

# I

*Analogy*

# ANALOGY

## BERTRAND RUSSELL

THE POSTULATES hitherto considered have been such as are required for knowledge of the physical world. Broadly speaking, they have led us to admit a certain degree of knowledge as to the space-time structure of the physical world, while leaving us completely agnostic as regards its qualitative character. But where other human beings are concerned, we feel that we know more than this; we are convinced that other people have thoughts and feelings that are qualitatively fairly similar to our own. We are not content to think that we know only the space-time structure of our friends' minds, or their capacity for initiating causal chains that end in sensations of our own. A philosopher might pretend to think that he knew only this, but let him get cross with his wife and you will see that he does not regard her as a mere spatio-temporal edifice of which he knows the logical properties but not a glimmer of the intrinsic character. We are therefore justified in inferring that his skepticism is professional rather than sincere.

The problem with which we are concerned is the following.

Reprinted by permission of George Allen and Unwin and Simon and Schuster, from *Human Knowledge: Its Scope and Limits*. Copyright 1948 by Bertrand Russell.

3

We observe in ourselves such occurrences as remembering, reasoning, feeling pleasure, and feeling pain. We think that sticks and stones do not have these experiences, but that other people do. Most of us have no doubt that the higher animals feel pleasure and pain, though I was once assured by a fisherman that "Fish have no sense nor feeling." I failed to find out how he had acquired this knowledge. Most people would disagree with him, but would be doubtful about oysters and starfish. However this may be, common sense admits an increasing doubtfulness as we descend in the animal kingdom, but as regards human beings it admits no doubt.

It is clear that belief in the minds of others requires some postulate that is not required in physics, since physics can be content with a knowledge of structure. My present purpose is to suggest what this further postulate may be.

It is clear that we must appeal to something that may be vaguely called "analogy." The behavior of other people is in many ways analogous to our own, and we suppose that it must have analogous causes. What people say is what we should say if we had certain thoughts, and so we infer that they probably have these thoughts. They give us information which we can sometimes subsequently verify. They behave in ways in which we behave when we are pleased (or displeased) in circumstances in which we should be pleased (or displeased). We may talk over with a friend some incident which we have both experienced, and find that his reminiscences dovetail with our own; this is particularly convincing when he remembers something that we have forgotten but that he recalls to our thoughts. Or again: you set your boy a problem in arithmetic, and with luck he gets the right answer; this persuades you that he is capable of arithmetical reasoning. There are, in short, very many ways in which my responses to stimuli differ from those of "dead" matter, and in all these ways other people resemble me. As it is clear to me that the causal laws governing my behavior have to do with "thoughts," it is natural to infer that the same is true of the analogous behavior of my friends.

4

*Analogy*

The inference with which we are at present concerned is not merely that which takes us beyond solipsism, by maintaining that sensations have causes about which *something* can be known. This kind of inference, which suffices for physics, has already been considered. We are concerned now with a much more specific kind of inference, the kind that is involved in our knowledge of the thoughts and feelings of others—assuming that we have such knowledge. It is of course obvious that such knowledge is more or less doubtful. There is not only the general argument that we may be dreaming; there is also the possibility of ingenious automata. There are calculating machines that do sums much better than our schoolboy sons; there are gramophone records that remember impeccably what So-and-so said on such-and-such an occasion; there are people in the cinema who, though copies of real people, are not themselves alive. There is no theoretical limit to what ingenuity could achieve in the way of producing the illusion of life where in fact life is absent.

But, you will say, in all such cases it was the thoughts of human beings that produced the ingenious mechanism. Yes, but how do you know this? And how do you know that the gramophone does *not* "think"?

There is, in the first place, a difference in the causal laws of observable behavior. If I say to a student, "Write me a paper on Descartes' reasons for believing in the existence of matter," I shall, if he is industrious, cause a certain response. A gramophone record might be so constructed as to respond to this stimulus, perhaps better than the student, but if so it would be incapable of telling me anything about any other philosopher, even if I threatened to refuse to give it a degree. One of the most notable peculiarities of human behavior is change of response to a given stimulus. An ingenious person could construct an automaton which would always laugh at his jokes, however often it heard them; but a human being, after laughing a few times, will yawn, and end by saying, "How I laughed the first time I heard that joke."

5

But the differences in observable behavior between living and dead matter do not suffice to prove that there are "thoughts" connected with living bodies other than my own. It is probably possible theoretically to account for the behavior of living bodies by purely physical causal laws, and it is probably impossible to refute materialism by external observation alone. If we are to believe that there are thoughts and feelings other than our own, that must be in virtue of some inference in which our own thoughts and feelings are relevant, and such an inference must go beyond what is needed in physics.

I am, of course, not discussing the history of how we come to believe in other minds. We find ourselves believing in them when we first begin to reflect; the thought that Mother may be angry or pleased is one which arises in early infancy. What I am discussing is the possibility of a postulate which shall establish a rational connection between this belief and data, e.g., between the belief "Mother is angry" and the hearing of a loud voice.

The abstract schema seems to be as follows. We know, from observation of ourselves, a causal law of the form "$A$ causes $B$," where $A$ is a "thought" and $B$ a physical occurrence. We sometimes observe a $B$ when we cannot observe any $A$; we then infer an unobserved $A$. For example: I know that when I say, "I'm thirsty," I say so, usually, because I am thirsty, and therefore, when I hear the sentence "I'm thirsty" at a time when I am not thirsty, I assume that someone else is thirsty. I assume this the more readily if I see before me a hot, drooping body which goes on to say, "I have walked twenty desert miles in this heat with never a drop to drink." It is evident that my confidence in the "inference" is increased by increased complexity in the datum and also by increased certainty of the causal law derived from subjective observation, provided the causal law is such as to account for the complexities of the datum.

It is clear that in so far as plurality of causes is to be suspected, the kind of inference we have been considering is not valid. We are supposed to know "$A$ causes $B$," and also to know

6

that *B* has occurred; if this is to justify us in inferring *A*, we must know that *only A* causes *B*. Or, if we are content to infer that *A* is probable, it will suffice if we can know that in most cases it is *A* that causes *B*. If you hear thunder without having seen lightning, you confidently infer that there was lightning, because you are convinced that the sort of noise you heard is seldom caused by anything except lightning. As this example shows, our principle is not only employed to establish the existence of other minds but is habitually assumed, though in a less concrete form, in physics. I say "a less concrete form" because unseen lightning is only abstractly similar to seen lightning, whereas we suppose the similarity of other minds to our own to be by no means purely abstract.

Complexity in the observed behavior of another person, when this can all be accounted for by a simple cause such as thirst, increases the probability of the inference by diminishing the probability of some other cause. I think that in ideally favorable circumstances the argument would be formally as follows:

From subjective observation I know that *A*, which is a thought or feeling, causes *B*, which is a bodily act, e.g., a statement. I know also that, whenever *B* is an act of my own body, *A* is its cause. I now observe an act of the kind *B* in a body not my own, and I am having no thought or feeling of the kind *A*. But I still believe, on the basis of self-observation, that only *A* can cause *B*; I therefore infer that there was an *A* which caused *B*, though it was not an *A* that I could observe. On this ground I infer that other people's bodies are associated with minds, which resemble mine in proportion as their bodily behavior resembles my own.

In practice, the exactness and certainty of the above statement must be softened. We cannot be sure that, in our subjective experience, *A* is the only cause of *B*. And even if *A* is the only cause of *B* in our experience, how can we know that this holds outside our experience? It is not necessary that we should know this with any certainty; it is enough if it is highly probable. It is the assumption of probability in such cases that is our postulate. The postulate may therefore be stated as follows:

*If, whenever we can observe whether A and B are present or absent, we find that every case of B has an A as a causal antecedent, then it is probable that most B's have A's as causal antecedents, even in cases where observation does not enable us to know whether A is present or not.*

This postulate, if accepted, justifies the inference to other minds, as well as many other inferences that are made unreflectingly by common sense.

8

# THE ANALOGY OF FEELING

STUART HAMPSHIRE

1. I am concerned in this paper with only one source of one of the many puzzles associated with our knowledge of other minds. It is often said that statements about other people's feelings and sensations cannot be justified as being based upon inductive arguments of any ordinary pattern, that is, as being inferences from the observed to the unobserved of a familiar and accepted form; I shall argue that they can be so justified. I will not deny that such inferences are difficult; everyone has always known, apart altogether from philosophical theory, that they are difficult; but I will deny that they are *logically* peculiar or invalid, when considered simply as inductive arguments. I believe that modern philosophers have found something logically peculiar and problematical about our inferences to other minds, and have even denied the possibility of such inferences, at least in part because of an incomplete understanding of the functions of pronouns and of other contextual expressions in our language; in particular they have misunderstood the proper use of these expressions in combination with words like "know," "certain," "verify," "evidence." If I am right, it becomes easier to explain why what the solipsist wants to say cannot properly

Reprinted by permission of the editor, from *Mind*, LXI (January, 1952), 1–12.

be said, why solipsism is a *linguistically* absurd thesis, and at the same time to explain why it is a thesis which tempts those who confuse epistemological distinctions with logical distinctions.

2. For reasons which will become clear later, I shall introduce two quasi-technical terms. As specimens of the type of sentence, the status of which, as normally used, is in dispute, I shall take the sentences "I feel giddy," "you feel giddy," "he feels giddy," and so on through the other cases of the verb "feel." Any normal use of the sentence "I feel giddy" will be, in my invented terminology, a specimen of an autobiographical statement, where this phrase is simply shorthand for "a statement describing somebody's momentary feelings or sensations which is expressed in the first person singular." Any normal use of the sentences "he feels giddy," "you feel giddy," or "they feel giddy" will be specimens of heterobiographical statements— that is, statements describing somebody's feelings which are not expressed in the first person singular; "we feel giddy," as normally used, would be a statement which is partly autobiographical and partly heterobiographical in my sense. It may sometimes happen that someone chooses to tell the story of his own inner life, using not the first person singular, but the third person or some fictitious or other name; it is actually possible to write one's own obituary notice, using the third person and including within it descriptions which are intended as descriptions of one's own feelings and sensations. But on such occasions the pronouns (or verb-cases for an inflected language) are misleadingly used, and deliberately so. The ordinary function of the word "I" (or of the corresponding verb-case in inflected languages) is to indicate explicitly that the author of the statement is also the designated subject of the statement; the exceptional, deliberately misleading uses mentioned above consciously take advantage of this fact. By "an autobiographical statement" I shall mean a statement describing someone's feelings or sensations which explicitly shows, in the actual form of its expression, that the author of the statement is also its

designated subject. A statement, e.g., in a novel, about which we can argue, by reference to evidence external to the verbal form of the statement itself, whether it is, as a matter of fact, an autobiographical statement, will not therefore be an autobiographical statement in my artificial and restricted sense.

It has often been noticed that there are certain peculiarities about these first person singular statements about feelings and sensations, particularly when the main verb is in the present tense; these peculiarities have led some philosophers to characterize them as incorrigible statements and have led others to deny them the title of "statement" altogether; the peculiarities emerge in the use of words like "know," "believe," and "certain" in combination with these sentences, or rather in their lack of use. In respect of most statements, "I think that *P* is true but I may be mistaken" and "I have established that *P* is true beyond all reasonable doubt" are sentences having a normal use, whatever *P* may be; but there are no normal circumstances in which one would say "I think that I feel giddy but I may be mistaken" or "I have established beyond reasonable doubt that I feel giddy," and consequently there are no normal circumstances in which it would be in place to say "I am absolutely certain that I feel giddy." By contrast the sentences "you feel giddy" or "he feels giddy" do normally occur in statements of the form "I believe that he feels giddy but I am not certain" or "it is known that he feels giddy" and so on; but again, "he believes that he feels giddy" or "he is certain that he feels giddy" have no normal use. It is the corollary of this that the questions "how do you know?" or "what is your evidence?" are out of place in respect of statements about momentary feelings and sensations, when addressed to the author of the statement, if he is also explicitly shown to be the designated subject of it.

One inference which might be drawn from these facts is that heterobiographical statements about feelings can never be known to be true directly, where "known directly" means that no question arises of how the statement is known to be true and no question arises of any evidence being required to support the statement. But this, as it stands, would be a plainly false conclusion, since the person who is the designated subject of such a heterobiographical statement does generally know directly, without need of evidence, whether the statement made about him is true or false. The proper conclusion is only that the *author* of a heterobiographical statement of this kind can never know directly, in the sense indicated, whether the statement he has made is true or false; the author can always properly be asked how he knows, or on what grounds he believes, his heterobiographical statement to be true; he is required to produce his evidence. So the so-called asymmetry is not a matter of statements expressed in the first person singular, *as such*, being different in respect of the evidence which they require from statements expressed in the second or third person singular; both descriptions of feelings in the first person singular, and those in the second and third person, may be challenged either by reference to indirect evidence (e.g., "I am sure you are lying; you have obvious motives for lying, and you show none of the symptoms which usually go with feeling giddy") or by a proper claim to direct knowledge (e.g., "I can tell you quite definitely that I do feel giddy, in spite of the evidence to the contrary").

This point is obvious, but it is apt to be dangerously slurred over when philosophers talk in general of "statements about other minds" and then go on to inquire into *the* methods appropriate to confirming or confuting such statements. They may be thought to mean by "statements about other minds" what I have called heterobiographical statements—that is, statements describing feelings and sensations which are not expressed in the first person singular; but the so-called problem of other minds, which is sometimes presented as a problem of how a *certain kind of statement* can be tested, does not attach to *a class of statements of any one particular form;* it arises equally for first person singular statements, if in this case the position of the audience is considered instead of that of the author. The problem of other minds is properly the problem of what tests and verifications are ever possible for anyone who is not in fact the designated subject of a statement about thoughts and feelings; it arises equally for any statement about feelings, whether the statement begins with the word "I" or with the word "you" or "we" or "they."

3. The commonsense answer to the question, so reformulated, seems obvious—indeed, so obvious that simply to give it cannot possibly satisfy philosophers; something more is required to explain why it has been thought inadequate. The commonsense answer is: each one of us is sometimes the designated subject of an autobiographical statement and sometimes the subject of heterobiographical statements; each one of us sometimes makes, or is in a position to make, statements about feelings which are not inferential and do not require supporting evidence, and also makes, or is in a position to make, statements about feelings which are inferential and do require supporting evidence. All that is required for testing the validity of any method of factual inference is that each one of us should sometimes be in a position to confront the conclusions of the doubtful method of inference with what is known by him to be true independently of the method of inference in question. Each one of us is certainly in this position in respect of our common methods of inference about the feelings of persons other than ourselves, in virtue of the fact that each one of us is constantly able to compare the results of this type of inference with what he knows to be true directly and noninferentially; each one of us is in the position to make this testing comparison, whenever he is the designated subject of a statement about feelings and sensations. I, Hampshire, know by what sort of signs I may be misled in inferring Jones's and Smith's feelings, because I have implicitly noticed (though probably not formulated) where Jones, Smith, and others generally go wrong in inferring my feelings. We all as children learn by experiment how to conceal and deceive, to pose and suppress; concurrently we are learning in this very process how

to detect the poses and suppressions of others; we learn the signs and occasions of concealment at first hand, and we are constantly revising our canons of duplicity as our own direct experience of its forms and occasions widens.

These are the commonsense considerations which seem at first glance to allow us to regard any heterobiographical statement, made by any one of us, as the conclusion of a valid inductive inference, the reliability of the method of inference used in any particular case being in principle testable by each one of us in confrontation with direct experience, that is, with noninferential knowledge about the successes and failures of this particular method; and I think that, as is usual in these questions, the third glance will confirm the first. But before going further, it is worth noticing how the argument from analogy, as stated by philosophers, approaches what I have called the commonsense position, but also misrepresents and oversimplifies it. There is a sense of "analogy" in which it is true that I could justify my inference that Smith is now feeling giddy by an analogy between the particular method of inference which I am now using and other uses of the same methods of inference by other people in discussing my feelings and sensations; I know by direct experience how such feelings as giddiness are concealed and revealed; both I and Smith have been in a position to test the reliability of those methods of indirect inference about giddiness and cognate sensations which we from time to time use in talking about other people. The argument from analogy, as commonly stated by philosophers, only fails because the analogy has been looked for in the wrong place. What is required is not some simple analogy between my feelings and my external symptoms on the one hand and someone else's external symptoms, and so someone else's giddiness-feeling, on the other; what is needed, and is also available, is an *analogy between different uses of the same methods of argument by different people on different occasions.* The inductive argument, the reliability of which is to be tested by each one of us, attaches both to the sentence "I feel giddy" and to the sentences "you feel giddy," "he feels giddy," etc.; it attaches to any sentence of the form "X feels giddy"; anyone hearing or using any sentence of this form, and anyone needing to test the statement conveyed on a particular occasion, can find such confirmation by looking for an analogy with occasions of its use when he was not in need of such inductive confirmation. To anyone entertaining a doubt about the justification of a particular method of inference about feelings and sensations, the reassuring analogy is between the different occasions of use of the sentence in question; for on some of these occasions the doubter, whoever he may be, was in a position to know noninferentially that the method of inference now in question led to a correct or incorrect conclusion. Each of us is in a position to learn from his own experience that certain methods of inference to conclusions of the kind "X feels giddy" are generally successful. Of course, if I, Hampshire, have never felt giddy myself, or had any sensation which is even remotely like this one, I would to that extent be at a loss to know whether other people are speaking the truth when they describe autobiographically this utterly unknown kind of sensation. In certain extreme cases this total failure of testability, and therefore failure of communication, does in fact happen; in such cases I am in fact content to admit that I personally have no means of knowing whether what is said by others is pure invention or not; I simply do not know what they are talking about. But over the normal range of statements about feelings and sensations of which I am either the author or audience, I can generally point to occasions on which I was the subject of the particular statement in question and other people had to use the now questionable method of inference. Suppose that Smith and I each suspect the other of deceiving and of encouraging the other to use unreliable methods of inference. This again is a testable and empirical doubt, because we each of us know how we ourselves proceed when we are trying to deceive in this particular manner. We each base our devices of deception on our observations of other people's methods of inference about us. We each know that there is something in common to our different methods of deception, since we each sometimes know that we have failed to deceive and so we each know from our own experience how such deception may be detected. But no common psychological language could be established with beings, outwardly human and sensitive, who never tried openly and in words to infer our feelings and who never acknowledged in words our success in inferring theirs, using the one to guide them in the other in a circle of mutual correction. We would have no good inductive grounds for speculating about the feelings of utterly silent people, or of people who did not betray themselves in speculating about us. It is merely a matter of natural history, and not of logic, that total failures of communication and understanding do not occur more frequently, and that in fact we are each generally in a position to reassure ourselves about our methods of inference to the feelings of others by confrontation with the successes and failures of others in talking about us.

It has been necessary first to insist on the truism that all statements about feelings and sensations, including such statements expressed in the first person singular, are "statements about other minds" for some people but not "statements about other minds" for other people; for it is precisely this feature of them which allows any one of us to test in direct experience the reliability of the numerous specific methods of inference which he uses when talking about the feelings of others. The importance of the truism can be brought out in the analogous case of "statements about the past"; philosophers have sometimes invented perplexities by writing as if we could pick out a class of statements as "statements about the past" and could then inquire how such statements can possibly be established as true by inductive argument; for how—it is asked—can we ever in principle confirm the validity of our inferences about the past? The mistakes which lead to this question are the same as in the "other minds" case. We cannot pick out a class of statements as statements about the past, unless we mean merely statements expressed in the past tenses. But the tenses, like the pronouns and cases of verbs, serve (among other functions) to relate a statement to the particular context or occasion of its utterance or of its consideration; clearly the *same* statement may be a statement about past, present, or future when considered, accepted, or rejected by different people in different contexts; similarly, the *same* statement may be made either heterobiographically or autobiographically. A statement in the present tense, which is in this artificial sense a statement about the present, when verified and reaffirmed, may be reaffirmed as a statement about the past, and equally a statement about the future, when finally confirmed, may be reaffirmed as a statement about the present. *The very notion of confirmation involves this possibility of comparing the different contexts of utterance of the same statement.* It does not in general lie *within* the statement itself, or in its grammatical form of expression, that it is a statement about the mind of another, or that it is a statement about the past; these are features of the circumstances of the utterance or consideration of the statement, features which are partially indicated (but not stated) by pronouns, by tenses, and by other contextual expressions, whenever and by whomever the statement is asserted, reasserted, or denied. Strictly speaking, there can be no class of statements about the past, standing in hopeless need of confirmation, any more than there can be a class of past events; similarly there can be no class of minds which are other minds, or class of statements about them. This confusion of contextual idioms such as "other," "past," with class-terms has its roots in an unnoticed double use of the idioms, which must now be explained.

4. It is often suggested that the functions of pronouns and other contextual expressions ("this," "that," "here," "now," etc.) is to designate or to refer uniquely to some person, thing, time, place, event, etc. Mr. Strawson (*Mind*, October, 1950) has suggested the appropriate label, "uniquely referring expressions"; certainly one of the ways in which pronouns and

these other contextual expressions are used is in this uniquely referring way—that is, to indicate, in a particular context of utterance, a particular person, thing, event. But it is characteristic of the contextual expressions that they are not always or solely used to refer uniquely or to designate a particular person, thing, event; they also have an important *generalized* use, in which they make no reference to a particular individual and in which they can be interpreted without any reference whatever to any particular context of utterance. Consider the slogan "do it *now*" or "never put off till *tomorrow* what you can do *today.*" In this use "now," "today," "tomorrow" do not refer uniquely, but have a force in some (but not all) ways like that of a variable, and might be expanded into "now, to whatever moment 'now' may refer," or "today, whatever day 'today' may refer to." Another example: "the future is quite uncertain": as it stands, and without a context, this sentence is ambiguous, and might be used to make two quite different statements, or even two different kinds of statement; "the future" might be used in the uniquely referring way, so that we require to know the context of utterance in order to know what particular stretch of history is being referred to and described as uncertain; or "the future" might be used in the purely generalized way—"the future, at whatever point in history, is always uncertain." This familiar generalized, or quasi-variable, use is transferred to philosophy when we talk of "statements about *the past,*" "statements about the *other* side of the moon," and "statements about *other* minds." Confusion between the two kinds of use arises when a transition is made within a single argument from the generalized to the uniquely referring use, or vice versa, without this transition being noticed; and just this is what generally happens in arguments about our knowledge of "other minds" and in formulations of the so-called *ego*centric predicament. The solipsistic doubter will probably not put his question in the explicitly generalized form, but will ask: "How can *I* ever justify my inferences about what is going on in *your* mind, since *I* can have no independent

means of checking *my* inferences about *your* feelings?" There
may be a muddle in this: Does the "I" here mean "I, Hampshire"? Is it a lament about my, Hampshire's, peculiar isolation
and the peculiar inscrutability of you, Smith? Or does the "I"
mean "whoever 'I' refers to" and the "you" "you, whoever 'you'
may be"? If the latter is intended, and the pronoun is being
used in the generalized way, the question becomes: "How
can any one of us ever justify any inference to the feelings
of someone other than himself, since no one of us, whoever he
may be, has any means of checking any inference to the feelings of anyone other than himself?" And to this generalized
form of the question the commonsense answer again suggests
itself: each and every one of us, whoever he may be, has the
means of independently checking the reliability of the methods
of inference which he uses, although, naturally, on those occasions when he needs to use any particular method of inference,
he cannot be independently checking the inference on the
same occasion. When I, Hampshire, check in my own experience the reliability of the various particular methods of inference which I use when talking about the feelings of others, the
statements which I make at the conclusion of these checks are
*ex hypothesi* not themselves the conclusions of an inference;
but they are none the less efficient as checks to my methods
of inference. The solipsistic problem, cleared of these confusions, can now be restated: whenever anyone uses the sentence
"I feel giddy," one person and one person only is in a position
to know directly, and without need of inference, whether the
statement conveyed is true; whenever anyone says "you feel
giddy," or "he feels giddy," or "Smith feels giddy," one person
and one person only is in a position to know without need of
inference whether the statement is true; whenever anyone says
"we both feel giddy" or "they feel giddy," no one can ever
know directly, and without need of inference, whether the
conjoint statements conveyed are true. So the solipsist may correctly say that it is a distinguishing characteristic of statements
about feelings, as opposed to statements about physical things,

that at most one person can ever properly claim to know directly, and without needing to give evidence or justification, whether such statements are true. But the solipsist originally wanted to separate, within the class of statement about minds, a class of statements about *other* minds, as being dubious and problematical, from autobiographical statements, which were held to be privileged and not dubious. It is this distinction which is untenable.

Suppose that, in talking about our feelings, we each solipsistically confined ourselves to statements which we may properly claim to know to be true directly and without appeal to evidence or to methods of inference; I, Hampshire, would be allowed to say "I feel giddy," and you, Smith, would be allowed to say "I feel giddy"; but, since all uses of other cases of the verb require problematical inference, we would never be allowed to assent to or dissent from each other's statements, or to place ourselves in the position of an audience discussing them. Under such conditions the pronouns and cases of the verb would have no further function, and all argument and the detection of lies would be excluded: our psychological language would simply serve to convey a set of undiscussable announcements. Communication in the ordinary sense upon such topics would have ceased; for communication essentially involves the use of sentences to convey statements by an author to an actual or potential audience, in such a way that all users of the language, in denying and confirming, may change from the position of audience to author in respect of any statement made. To compare the use of personal pronouns with the uses of tenses again: because those statements which refer to events long prior or subsequent to the moment of utterance are *pro tanto* relatively uncertain at the time they are made, it might be suggested that only statements in the present tense should be accepted as completely reliable. But unless we recognize the sense of "same statement" as something to be reaffirmed in different contexts, we remove the last possibility of correcting and denying statements, and with this we remove the possibility of all argument about them and testing of them, and also the possibility of expressing belief or disbelief; we therefore remove the essential conditions or point of statement-making; and this we would have done by failing to recognize the function of those devices which relate the same statement to the changing circumstances of its assertion. The formula often used, "I am in a position to judge of the truth of statements about my own feeling, but not about the feeling of others," has only succeeded in misleading, because of the two ways in which the expression "I" and "other" may be used, and the often unnoticed shift from one use to the other; it is this shift which suggests a solipsistic conclusion—e.g., that one mind only can be known with certainty to exist and one set of feelings and sensations known with certainty to have occurred. But of course no such conclusion about *one* mind follows from the argument when correctly stated. The proper truism is "No one of us, whoever he may be, is in need of inference to assure himself of the truth of statements about his own feelings, but he can never assure himself directly, and without needing to appeal to evidence, of the truth of statements about the feelings of others"; stated in this form, with a quasi-variable expression as the subject term, the truism cannot serve as a premise to any *solipsistic* conclusion.

5. The peculiarity of the word "know" and of its cognates —that the conditions of their proper use in combination with any type of statement vary with the indicated context of utterance—is not confined to discourse about minds and feelings; it applies over the whole range of application of words like "know," "certain," "verify," with whatever kind of statement they are combined. Whatever may be the topic under discussion, whether a claim to knowledge or certainty is or is not in place, must always depend upon who makes the claim, when, and under what conditions; it can never be solely a matter of the form of the statement itself or of its topic. Any empirical statement whatever is a matter of uncertain inference under some conditions of its use or consideration. There is no mystery

in the fact that a statement which may be a matter of direct and certain knowledge for one person will always be a matter of uncertain inference for another, any more than there is mystery in the fact that the same statement which may be known with certainty to be true at one time must be a matter of uncertain inference at other times. Philosophers (Plato, Descartes, Russell) have invented the mystery by writing as if being known to be true and being uncertain were intrinsic properties of statements, properties somehow adhering to them independently of the particular circumstances in which they were made or considered. It is proper and necessary that formal logicians, who study patterns of transformations of sentence-forms, should disregard those features of statements which relate them to a context of utterance; but philosophers' questions about use and meaning hinge on the different contexts in which words like "know" and "certain" may occur in combination with sentences of different forms and different topics.

6. *Conclusion.* "Past," "Present," "Other" are not class terms but contextual terms, and there can be no class of events which are past events, and no class of minds which are other minds, and no class of statements which are statements about either of these. "Statements about other minds" is either an incomplete expression, requiring knowledge of the particular circumstance of its use in order that it should be intelligible—e.g., "minds other than mine, Hampshire's"; or the contextual expression may be used in the generalized sense and mean "statements about minds other than the author's, whoever the author may be"; if the latter is intended, then in raising the problem of other minds we are inquiring into the analogy which enables anyone to compare the situation in which he knows a statement about feelings to be true, independently of inference, with the situation in which he does not; and it is to this comparison that we refer when we talk of checking the reliability of any method of factual inference.

# INDUCTION AND OTHER MINDS

### ALVIN PLANTINGA

## [A]

I WISH TO CONSIDER a line of objection to the traditional Analogical Argument for other minds. Perhaps we may introduce it by considering A. J. Ayer's statement of that argument: "On the basis of my own experience I form a general hypothesis to the effect that certain physical phenomena are accompanied by certain feelings. When I observe that some other person is in the appropriate physical state, I am thereby enabled to infer that he is having these feelings; feelings which are similar to those that in similar circumstances I have myself." [1] Noting that this formulation seems open to the "one case alone" objection, Ayer suggests that

> the objection that one is generalizing from a single instance can perhaps be countered by maintaining that it is not a matter of extending to all other persons a conclusion which has been found to hold for only one, but rather of proceeding from the fact that certain properties have been found to be conjoined in various circumstances. . . . So the question that I put is not:

Reprinted by permission of the author and the editor, from *The Review of Metaphysics*, XIX (March, 1966), 441–461.

[1] *The Problem of Knowledge* (Harmondsworth, 1956), p. 249.

Am I justified in assuming that what I have found to be true only of myself is also true of others? but: Having found that in various circumstances the possession of certain properties is united with the possession of a certain feeling, does this union continue to obtain when the circumstances are still further varied? The basis of the argument is broadened by absorbing the difference of persons into the difference of the situations in which the psychophysical connections are supposed to hold.[2]

This version of the Analogical Argument may bear fuller statement. Initially it is pointed out that while a person can observe another's behavior and circumstances, he cannot perceive another's mental states. "The thoughts and passions of the mind are invisible," says Thomas Reid; [3] "intangible, odorless, and inaudible," we might add, "and they can't be tasted either." Hence we cannot come to know that another is in pain in the way in which we can learn that he has red hair; unlike his hair, his pain cannot be perceived. And, on the other hand, although some propositions ascribing pain to a person are incorrigible for *him,* no such proposition is incorrigible for anyone else. We cannot observe the thoughts and feelings of another; so we cannot *determine by observation* that another is in pain.

But here a preliminary difficulty must be dealt with: can't we sometimes *see that* a man is in pain? Can't we sometimes see that someone is thinking, depressed, or exuberant? And if *anything* would be "determining by observation" that another is in pain, surely *seeing that* he is would be: so why is a tenuous analogical inference necessary?

The Analogical Position must concede that there is an ordinary use of "see that" in which one can see that someone else is in pain. In that same use, one can see that a child has measles, that a pipe will give a sweet smoke, and that electrons of a certain sort are sporting in the cloud chamber. One can even see (if one reads the newspapers) that John Buchanan of the

[2] *Ibid.,* pp. 250–251.
[3] Reid, *Works,* p. 450.

House Un-American Activities Committee referred (no doubt mistakenly) to the Imperial Wizard of the Ku Klux Klan as the "Inferior Lizard." In the same use of the term the theist, impressed by the harmony and beauty of the universe or the profundity of the Scriptures, may justifiably claim to see that God exists.

And so of course the Analogical Arguer's use of "determine by observation" will have to be a technical use. How is it to be explained? Perhaps he can't explain it fully; perhaps he must give examples and hope for the best. One can determine by observation that Johnny's face is flushed and covered with red spots; one cannot determine by observation, in this special sense, that his blood contains measle germs. One can determine by observation that today's newspaper contains the sentence "Mr. Buchanan referred to the Imperial Wizard as the 'Inferior Lizard'"; but if one is not present at the hearings one cannot determine by observation that Mr. Buchanan thus misspoke himself. Furthermore, in the technical (but not the ordinary) use of the term, the sentence "S determines by observation that S' is in pain only if S is the same person as S'" expresses a necessary truth, as does the sentence "S determines by observation that a bodily area contains a pain only if he feels a pain in that area."

Now suppose we use "determines$_1$" for the narrower sense and "determines$_2$" for the broad. Then, the Analogical Arguer continues, a man can determine$_2$ that Mr. Buchanan referred to the Wizard as a lizard only if he determines$_1$ the truth of some *other* proposition, and knows or believes a proposition connecting what he determines$_1$ with the proposition about Mr. Buchanan and the Wizard. In the same way I can determine$_2$ that Jones is in pain only if I know or believe some proposition connecting what I determine$_1$ with his being in pain; and it is this knowledge that, according to the Analogical Position, I can get only via an Analogical Argument.

Whether this response to the objection is altogether satisfactory is not my concern here; let us suppose for the sake of

25

argument that it is. According to the Analogical Position, there-fore, I cannot determine₁ by observation that some other per-son is in pain or that some person is feeling pain in a bodily area in which I feel nothing. Nevertheless I have or can easily acquire evidence for such propositions. Let us say that S's *total evidence* is the set of propositions such that p is a member of it if and only if (1) p is either necessarily true or solely about S's mental states or solely about physical objects, or a conse-quence of such propositions [4] and (2) S knows p to be true. According to the Analogical Position, my total evidence yields an argument for each of the above conclusions. For

(1) Every case of pain behavior such that I have determined by observation whether or not it was accompanied by pain in the body displaying the behavior in question *was* accompanied by pain in that body.[5]

Applying the so-called "straight rule" of induction, I conclude that:

(2) Probably every case of pain behavior is accompanied by pain in the body displaying it.

But then on a certain occasion I observe that

(3) B over there (a body other than my own) is displaying pain behavior.

From (2) it follows that B is pained; since I don't feel a pain there, I conclude that

(4) Some other sentient creature has a pain.

But here an objection arises. Consider how I establish (4): I observe that B is displaying pain behavior, and no matter how

---

[4] Where a necessary (but not sufficient) condition of a proposition's being solely about my own mind or physical objects is that it not entail the existence of mental states that are not mine.

[5] Where the term "pain behavior" is simply a label for a recognizable pat-tern of behavior (and hence from the fact that a man displays pain behavior it does not follow that he is in pain).

intensely I concentrate, no matter how carefully I canvass my feelings, my attempt to feel a pain in *B* is futile. I feel no pain there. But does not this state of affairs provide me with a *disconfirming instance* of (2)? Should I not reject the suggestion that *B* contains a pain in favor of the conclusion that (2) is false? Consider the following analogy. Justice Douglas is walking through Racehorse Canyon, idly inspecting his surroundings. It occurs to him suddenly that every maple in the Canyon of which he has determined by observation whether it has leaves, has indeed had leaves. (Peculiar things occur to Justice Douglas.) So, he concludes, probably all the maples in Racehorse Canyon have leaves. Walking a bit further, he encounters another maple. Carefully inspecting this one, he fails to see any sign of leaves. He concludes that the maple has leaves he cannot see.

This procedure on Justice Douglas' part is surely perverse and absurd. What he should have concluded is not that there are leaves he cannot observe but that some of the maples in Racehorse Canyon lack leaves. And, by analogy, should not I take my failure to observe pain in *B* to provide me with a *counter instance* to the generalization that every case of pain behavior is accompanied by pain in the body displaying it?

One who accepts the Analogical Position, of course, will be quick to reject this suggestion. And perhaps his answer could proceed along the following lines. There is a difference, in general, between failing to observe the presence of *A*'s and observing the absence of *A*'s (observing that no *A*'s are present).[6] A man may fail to see the mountain goats on a distant crag without thereby seeing that no mountain goats are there. But just as there are circumstances in which killing someone constitutes murdering him, so there are circumstances in which failing to perceive a thing constitutes perceiving its absence. If, for example, a person with good eyesight is looking at a maple 10 feet away to see if it has leaves (and the light is ample, his view of the tree is unobstructed, etc.), but he does

[6] I owe this way of putting the distinction to Professor Robert C. Sleigh, Jr.

not see any leaves, then in failing to see leaves he sees that the tree has no leaves. We might call any set of conditions in which failing to observe leaves on a tree constitutes observing that it has no leaves, an *optimal* set of conditions for observing the presence or absence of leaves. And though it might be a bit difficult, perhaps, to specify the members of such an optimal set, there is no doubt that we are sometimes in circumstances of just that sort. Now if a man justifiably believes that he is in an optimal set of conditions for observing whether or not a tree has leaves, and fails to observe that it does, then he can justifiably believe that he is observing the absence of leaves there; perhaps, indeed, he is *rationally obliged,* in these circumstances, to take it that there are no leaves on the tree.

On the other hand, of course, if he knew that he was *not* in a position to observe whether leaves were present or absent, then his failure to observe leaves could scarcely oblige him to take it that he has a counter instance to the generalization in question. More generally, under what conditions is a man obliged to take his observing an *A* and failing to observe that it is *B* as providing him with a counter instance to *All A's are B?* Consider the following three conditions:

(5) There are no possible circumstances in which failing to observe that an *A* is *B* constitutes observing that it is not *B.*

(6) No one can ever be in a position to determine by observation that an *A* is not *B.*

(7) It is not possible to determine by observation that an *A* is not *B.*

(6) and (7), I believe, entail each other and each entails (5). I am also inclined to think that (5) entails (6) and (7) on the grounds that the proposition *If it is possible to determine by observation that an* A *is not* B, *then there are possible circumstances in which failing to observe that an* A *is* B *constitutes observing that it is not* B appears to be necessarily true.

28

These three conditions hold with respect to determining by observation whether or not a given bodily area is pained. There are no circumstances in which failing to feel pain in a body other than my own, for example, constitutes determining by observation that it is free from pain; I cannot observe the absence of pain in a body other than mine. But of course the same really holds for my own body as well; as Wittgenstein says, it is logically possible that someone else feel a pain in my body; hence I cannot determine by observation that my body is free from pain (although of course I can tell that *I* do not feel a pain there). Now a man who *knows* that one cannot tell by observation that a given bodily area contains no pain is not obliged to conclude that he has a counter instance to (2). So presumably

(8) A person S is obliged to take his observing that something is A and failing to observe that it is B as providing him with a counter instance to *All A's are B* only if (a) he does not know that it is impossible to determine by observation that an A is not B, and (b) he does not know that there are no circumstances in which failing to observe that an A is B constitutes observing that it is not B, and (c) he does not know that he cannot be in a position to determine by observation that an A is not B.

Since, of course, I might very well know any or all of these three things, I am not obliged, in discovering that (3) is true, to take it that I have a counter instance to (2); and hence this objection to the Analogical Position fails.

The fact that one cannot observe the absence of pain delivers the Analogical Position from the above objection; that fact, nevertheless, is the rock upon which it founders. To see this we must characterize more fully the sort of argument which, in the Analogical Position, is available to each of us. Let us say that *a simple inductive argument for S* is an argument of the following form:

Every $A$ such that $S$ has determined by observation whether or not $A$ is $B$ is such that $S$ has determined by observation that $A$ is $B$.[7] Therefore, probably every $A$ is a $B$.

And let us say that *a direct inductive argument for S* is an ordered pair of arguments of which the first member is a simple inductive argument $a$ for $S$, and the second a valid deductive argument one premise of which is the conclusion of $a$, the other premises being drawn from $S$'s total evidence.

The contention of the Analogical Position, then, is that for any person $S$ (or at least for most persons) there is a direct inductive argument for $S$, for such conclusions as that at a given time $t$ someone other than $S$ is in pain. But this is not all that the Analogical Position holds. For it is of course possible that there be for a person $S$ a direct argument for $p$ although $p$ is improbable on $S$'s total evidence. What the Analogical Position must hold here is that for any person $S$ there are direct arguments for the propositions in question and no comparable evidence against them: they must be *more probable than not* on his total evidence.

Finally, according to the Analogical Position, the bulk of my common sense beliefs [8] about minds and mental states must be more probable than not on my total evidence. It is not sufficient that my total evidence confirm the proposition that there are other sentient beings; it must also confirm, in one way or another, the whole range of common sense belief about the behavioral accompaniments or aspects of anger, joy, depression, pain, and our beliefs about the connections between body and mind generally. It need be no part of the Analogical Position to maintain that for *each* of these propositions there is, for me, a direct argument. For some of them, perhaps, my

---

[7] This account would be complicated but not essentially modified if it were so generalized as to take account of the sort of argument where, of his sample of $A$'s, $S$ determines by observation that m/n of them are $B$ and concludes that probably m/n $A$'s are $B$.

[8] The term "belief" is here so used that "Jones believes $p$" is not inconsistent with (and indeed is entailed by) "Jones knows $p$."

only evidence is the fact that they are probable with respect to *other* propositions for which I do have direct arguments. But each (or most) of us must have a basic set $K$ of such propositions for each member of which he has a direct argument; and perhaps the remainder of his relevant common sense beliefs can be shown to be confirmed by the conjunction of the members of $K$. Furthermore, then, not only must each member of $K$ be more probable than not on my total evidence; their *conjunction* must be. This, of course, is a much stronger claim; it is possible that $p_1 \ldots p_n$ are individually more probable than not on $q$ while their conjunction is not.[9] And among the members of $K$ we should certainly find such propositions as the following:

(a) I am not the only being that feels pain.
(b) There are some pains that I do not feel.
(c) Sometimes certain areas of my body are free from pain.
(d) There are some pains that are not in my body.
(e) There are some cases of pain that are not accompanied by pain behavior on the part of my body.
(f) I am the only person who feels pain in my body.
(g) Sometimes someone feels pain when I do not.

(a)–(g), of course, are stated for *me*; but there is for any person an analogue, in an obvious sense, of each of those propositions. Now, perhaps, we can summarily restate the Analogical Position as follows:

(9) For any (or almost any) person S there is a set of propositions $K$ such that the appropriate analogues of (a)-(g) are members of $K$; and S's total evidence *directly supports* each member of $K$ (i.e., for any member $m$ of $K$ there is a direct argument for S supporting $m$ but no direct argument for S against $m$); and the conjunction of the members of $K$ is more probable than not on S's total evidence.

[9] Let $q$ be *a fair die is about to be thrown;* let $p_1$ through $p_5$ be, respectively, *face one will not come up, face two will not come up, face three will not come up, face four will not come up,* and *face five will not come up.* Each of $p_1$ through $p_5$ is then more probable than not on $q$; but their conjunction is not.

So stated, this position is false. The conjunction of (a)–(g) is not more probable than not on the sort of evidence to which the Analogical Position directs our attention; nor (with one exception) does the Analogical Position give us any reason for supposing that (a)–(g) are individually more probable than not on that evidence.

## B

Suppose we begin with propositions (a) and (b). Recall that my argument for (a) involves a simple inductive argument from

(1) Every body which is displaying pain behavior at a time $t$, and is such that I have determined by observation whether or not a pain was occurring in it at $t$, is such that a pain *was* occurring in it at $t$,

to

(2) Probably every body which is displaying pain behavior at a time $t$ contains a pain at that time.

But

(3) $B$ over there (a body other than mine) is displaying pain behavior;

hence

(10) Probably $B$ contains a pain.

And since I feel no pain in $B$, I conclude that

(b) I do not feel every pain.

Of course if $B$ contains a pain, then some sentient creature or other is feeling a pain in $B$; hence

(a) I am not the only being that feels pain.

Such is my evidence, on the Analogical Position, for (a) and (b). There is a peculiarity about the inference of (2) from (1), however, that ought not to pass unmentioned. As we have

32

noted, I determine by observation (in the Analogical Arguer's technical sense) that a given body or bodily area contains a pain just in case I feel a pain there. Further, I cannot determine by observation that a bodily area does *not* contain a pain— not even if the area in question is part of my own body. The best I can do along these lines is to determine that *I* don't feel a pain there; but of course it does not follow that *no one* does. So, for any bodily area, I determine by observation whether or not that area is pained *only if* what I determine is that it *is* pained. And consequently no counter instance to (2) (the argument's conclusion) can possibly turn up in my sample. There are other arguments of this same sort and most of them deserve to be regarded with grave suspicion. Consider, for example, the inductive argument for epistemological idealism:

(11) Every physical object of which it has been determined whether or not it has ever been conceived (i.e., perceived or thought of) *has* been conceived.

Therefore,

(12) Probably every physical object is conceived; so there are no unconceived physical objects.

Now it might be said that an alleged inductive argument of this sort clearly proves nothing at all. For if there were any counter instances to the conclusion, it would be logically impossible for one of them ever to turn up in the sample; and hence we know, in any instance of this sort, that there is no reason to suppose that our sample is a random or fair one. Suppose we are drawing colored marbles from an inexhaustible urn and know that Descartes' evil genius is so guiding our hands that we draw only red ones; ought we then to take the fact that all the marbles we have so far drawn have been red as evidence for the view that all the marbles in the urn are red? If it is impossible for a counter instance to the conclusion of a simple inductive argument to turn up in its sample (where the conclusion is not itself necessarily true), then the argument is un-

33

acceptable. Perhaps we do well, therefore, to accept some such principle as the following:

> *A* A simple inductive argument is acceptable only if it is logically possible that its sample class contain a counter instance to its conclusion.

Now *A* appears to be inadequate [10] on the grounds that it fails to eliminate certain arguments that such a principle ought to eliminate. Consider, for example, the following argument for the conclusion that I am not the only human person. Let us say that *x* is a *crowman* just in case *x* is either a crow or a human body and that a thing is *minded* if it is the (human) body of a human person. Then

> (13) Every crowman such that I have determined by observation whether or not it was either black or minded, *was* either black or minded.

So probably

> (14) Every crowman is either black or minded.

But

> (15) *B* over there (a human body other than my own) is a crowman and is not black.

Hence *B* is probably minded; hence there is at least one other human person.

This argument will not meet with instant approval. And yet its premise will be true for any of us. For any crow in my sample will have the sample property (i.e., the property of being black or minded); my own body will be in my sample and will have the sample property; and of no human body will I be able to determine by observation that it lacks the sample property. Furthermore, the inference of (14) from (13) does not violate *A*; clearly it is *possible* (though it will not happen) that my sample class contain a counter instance (a white crow, for example) to (14).

[10] As I was reminded by Lawrence Powers.

An interesting peculiarity of this argument is that it will not serve to establish that *Negroes* are minded or are human persons; the analogue of (15) will not be true for a Negro. Emboldened by this unexpected turn of events, a Southern white segregationist (let us call him Jim Clarke) might go on to insist that for each of us Whites, there is an argument of the following kind for the conclusion that no Negroes have minds:

Where $x$ is a *swaneg* if $x$ is either a Negro or a swan,

(16) Every swaneg such that I have determined by observation whether or not it was either white or nonminded *was* either white or nonminded.

So probably

(17) Every swaneg is white or nonminded.

But

(18) S over there (a Negro) is a swaneg and S is not white.

So probably

(19) S is nonminded.

Jim Clarke's argument clearly has a true premise. Furthermore, it does not run afoul of A. But Jim Clarke probably fails to anticipate the reply that we might call "the Black Muslim Retort"; any Negro can argue as follows:

Where $x$ is a *croite* just in case $x$ is either a crow or a white human body,

(20) Every croite such that I have determined by observation whether or not it was either black or nonminded, *was* black or nonminded.

So probably

(21) Every croite is either black or nonminded.

But

(22) Jim Clarke over there is a croite and Jim Clarke is not black.

So probably

(23) Jim Clarke is nonminded.

None of these arguments violate *A*; and this is best construed as a deficiency of *A*. Perhaps, therefore, we can restate *A*. Let us suppose for the moment that we know what it is for a property to have a disjunct or conjunct: the property of *being black or minded,* for example, has as a disjunct the property of *being black.* And let us say that a property *P is a part of* a property *P'* just in case *P* is the same property as *P'* or *P* is a disjunct, conjunct, antecedent, or consequent of *P'* or of a part of *P'*. Then

> *A'* Where $\alpha$, $\beta$, is an inductive argument for *S*, $\beta$ is of the form *All A's have B,* and where *C* is any part of *B*, $\alpha$, $\beta$ is acceptable for *S* only if the propositions *S has examined an A and determined by observation that it lacks C* and *S has examined an A and determined by observation that it has C* are both logically possible.

I am not certain that *A'* rules out all of the sorts of arguments it is designed to. With sufficient patience and ingenuity we could perhaps construct an argument that does not violate *A'* but is nonetheless preposterous in pretty much the same way as the above arguments. But at any rate *A'* seems to be *true.* And if it is, the argument from (1) to (2) must be rejected, so that we are left without a direct argument for (a) or (b).

The following (merely suggestive) argument indicates that *any* direct argument for (a) will run afoul of *A'*. To get a direct argument for (a) we must first, presumably, get a direct argument for (b) (there are some pains I do not feel). (b) will presumably follow from some proposition of the form

(24) Every case of $\phi$ is accompanied by pain meeting condition $\psi$,

together with a premise asserting that I have observed a case of $\phi$ but feel no pain meeting condition $\psi$. The proposition (call it 24′) of the form exhibited by (24) will not, of course, be necessarily true; it will require inductive support. But any simple inductive argument for (24′) will run afoul of A′, since its premise will be of the form

(25) Every case of $\phi$ such that I have determined by observation whether or not it was accompanied by pain meeting condition $\psi$ *was* so accompanied.

(24′), of course, need not be the conclusion of a simple inductive argument; perhaps it follows from propositions of the forms

(26) Every case of $\phi$ is a case of $\beta$

and

(27) Every case of $\beta$ is accompanied by pain meeting condition $\psi$.

But then obviously the same problem will arise with the proposition of the form depicted in (27) (which is of course the same form as depicted in [13]). It looks as if any direct argument from my total evidence for (a) will involve a simple inductive argument for a proposition like (24′); but in that case we will find that no such direct argument for (a) is palatable if we accept A′. The fact that one can't observe the absence of pain appeared earlier to deliver the Analogical Position from disaster; here it returns to wreak vengeance upon it.

But perhaps we should ask at this juncture whether the argument I gave above for A′ is conclusive. (It *does* seem a bit harsh to insist that my observing that *some* cases of pain behavior are accompanied by pain gives me no reason at all for supposing that all such cases are so accompanied.) I think the argument is indeed conclusive; but on the other side it might be urged that we never have good reason to suppose that the sample of an inductive argument is a fair sample. This last is a large and complex question. Fortunately we need not enter it at present. For we cannot succor the Analogical Position by rejecting A′; if we reject A′ (and adopt no similar principle) we then open the gates to direct argument from my total evidence *against* (a) and (b):

(28) Every pain which is such that I have determined by observation whether or not it was felt by me, was felt by me.

So probably

(29) Every pain is felt by me

which is the denial of (b), and of an essential premise in our argument for (a). This, no doubt, is a preposterous argument. And yet its peculiarity consists just in the fact that it violates A'; if we reject A' we must accept this argument as of equal weight with the argument *for* (b). But then so far as direct arguments are concerned, the *denials* of (a) and (b) are as probable on my total evidence as (a) and (b) themselves, in which case my total evidence does not directly support the latter. Whether or not A' is to be accepted, therefore, my total evidence does not support (a) and (b).

## C

Next, let's consider

(c) Sometimes certain areas of my body are free from pain.

Each of us takes a proposition like (c) to be evidently and obviously true. What sort of evidence, according to the Analogical Position, do I have for (c)? I can't, of course, *observe* the absence of pain in my body any more than I can observe its absence in some other body; it is logically possible that when I feel no pain in my arm, someone else does.

However, it does not follow from this (contrary to what one might be tempted to suppose) that I can never, on the Analogical Position, get evidence for the proposition that a certain area of my body is at a certain time free from pain. For evidence of the following sort is available to me:

(30) Every pain which is such that I have determined by observation whether or not it was accompanied by pain behavior on the part of the body in which it was located, has been so accompanied.

So probably

(31) Every pain is accompanied by pain behavior on the part of the body in which it is located.

(And of course this inference does not violate $A'$.) But

(32) At present my body is not displaying pain behavior.

Hence probably

(33) No area of my body is presently pained.

From which, of course, (c) follows. Accordingly my total evidence provides me with a direct argument for (c). We might be tempted to think that it also provides me with a direct argument against (c). Consider those ordered pairs $(a, t)$ whose first members are areas of my body and whose second members are times:

(34) Every ordered pair $(a, t)$ which is such that I have determined by observation whether or not $a$ was pained at $t$, has been such that $a$ *was* pained at $t$.

So probably

(35) Every ordered pair $(a, t)$ is such that $a$ is pained at $t$.

But then

(36) Probably every area of my body always contains a pain.

But the inference of (35) from (34) runs afoul of $A'$, along with, apparently, any other direct argument from my total evidence against (c). If we accept $A'$, therefore, we get a direct argument for (c) but none against it; hence on $A'$ the Analogical Position with respect to (c) appears to be vindicated.

39

We might note parenthetically that if $A'$ is to be rejected, my total evidence provides me with direct arguments for propositions even more preposterous than (36); if we let $a$ range over human bodies generally, the analogue of (34) will remain true and we get the conclusion that probably every area of every human body is always pained. If we let $a$ range over areas of physical objects generally the analogue of (34) still remains true and we get the outrageous result that probably every area of every physical object is always pained. Leibniz and Whitehead apparently overlooked this fertile source of evidence for certain of their conclusions.

## D

(d) There are some pains that are not in my body

and

(e) There are some cases of pain that are not accompanied by pain behavior on the part of my body

may be considered together. What presents itself as the direct argument for (d) is the following:

(1) Every body which is displaying pain behavior at a time $t$ and is such that I have determined by observation whether or not a pain was occurring in it at $t$, is such that a pain *was* occurring in it at $t$.

Hence

(2) Probably every body is displaying pain behavior at a time $t$ contains a pain at that time.

But

(3) $B$ over there (a body other than mine) is displaying pain behavior;

hence

(10) Probably $B$ has a pain.

40

Hence

(d) There are some pains that are not in my body.

The argument for (e) shares steps (1), (2), (3), and (10) with the above argument. If in addition

(37) My body is not now displaying pain behavior

is part of my total evidence, (e) follows.

The inference from (1) to (2), again, is ruled out by $A'$. And, as in the case of (a) and (b), if we accept $A'$ we appear to have no direct argument at all for either (d) or (e). On the other hand, my total evidence appears to provide me with direct arguments *against* both (d) and (e):

(38) Every pain which is such that I have determined by observation whether or not it was in my body, *was* in my body.

Hence probably,

(39) All pains are in my body.

This argument does not violate $A'$. But is it an acceptable inductive argument? It might be objected that it is *causally impossible* for a person to feel pain anywhere but in his own body, and that, where it is impossible to observe an $A$ which is $B$ (although possibly some $A$'s are $B$), it is illegitimate to conclude that no $A$'s are $B$ from a premise reporting that no observed $A$'s are $B$. Now if a man *knows* that it is impossible to observe an $A$ which is $B$, then indeed he cannot reasonably conclude that no $A$'s are $B$ from the fact that every $A$ which is such that he has determined by observation whether or not it is $B$, has turned out not to be $B$. But things are quite different if he does not know this: ignorant of the fact that one cannot see mountain goats on a glacier at 800 yards, a tenderfoot might sensibly conclude, after futilely inspecting Kulshun Glacier from that distance several weeks running, that no mountain goats frequent it. And, of course, as an Analogical Arguer I don't initially know that one can feel pain only in his own body; it is just this sort of belief that the Analogical Argument is supposed to ground and justify. This argument, therefore, is apparently successful.

A similar direct argument holds against (e). Every case of pain which is such that I have determined by observation whether or not it was accompanied by pain behavior on the part of my body, *was* so accompanied; probably, therefore, every case of pain is accompanied by pain behavior on the part of my body, in which case (e) is false.

If we accept A', therefore, we get direct arguments against (d) and (e) but no direct arguments for them. If we reject A', of course, we get direct arguments both for and against them; hence in neither case does my total evidence directly support either (d) or (e).

E

This brings us to

(f) I am the only person who feels pain in my body

and (g):

(g) Sometimes someone feels pain when I do not.

Does my total evidence provide me with a direct argument for (f)? Apparently not.

(40) Every pain in my body which is such that I have determined by observation whether or not it is felt by me, has been felt by me

presents itself as the relevant premise; but of course the argument from (40) to (f) flatly conflicts with A'. Nor, on the other hand, does my total evidence seem to provide me with a direct argument against (f). To get such an argument we should need a direct argument for

(41) Sometimes my body contains a pain I do not feel.

And in order to do that we should need to employ some such premise as

42

(34) Every ordered pair $(a, t)$ such that I have determined by observation whether $a$ was pained at $t$ is such that $a$ was pained at $t$.

But as we have already seen any simple argument with (34) as its premise will violate $A$.

Now suppose (as seems to be the case) that my total evidence yields no direct argument for (f) but does yield a direct argument for $p$ and for $q$, where $p$ and $q$ are logically independent of each other, of (f), and of my total evidence; and where the conjunction of $p$ with $q$ entails (f). (In such a case, let us say that my total evidence provides an *indirect* argument for [f].) Would it then follow that my total evidence supports (f)? No. It is of course true that if $p$ is more probable than not on $q$, and $p$ entails $r$, then $r$ is more probable than not on $q$. But from the fact that $p$ is more probable than not on $q$, and $r$ is more probable than not on $q$, it does not follow that $p$ and $r$ are more probable than not on $q$. And of course where $p$ and $q$ are logically independent and $q$ supports $p$ and $q$ supports $r$, $q$ supports the conjunction of $p$ with $r$ to a lesser degree than it supports either $p$ or $r$. So even if my total evidence yielded an indirect argument for (f), it would not follow that my total evidence supports (f). But the fact is that we seem to be unable to find even an indirect argument from my total evidence. That evidence, as we have seen, yields a direct argument for

(42) Whenever my body is pained, it displays pain behavior

and for

(43) Whenever my body displays pain behavior, I feel pain.

But (42) and (43) do not entail that I feel every pain in my body or that I alone feel pain in my body; they entail only that whenever *anyone* feels pain there, I do. We seem, therefore, to be able to find neither a direct nor an indirect argument for (f) if we accept $A'$; if we reject $A'$, of course, we will find direct arguments both for and against (f).

(g) Sometimes someone feels pain when I do not

43

resembles (f) in that there seems to be no direct argument from my total evidence either for or against it. It differs from (f) in that there seems to be an indirect argument *against* it. My total evidence directly supports

(44) Every case of pain is accompanied by pain behavior on the part of my body.

It also yields an argument for

(45) Whenever my body displays pain behavior, I feel pain.

But (44) and (45) entail

(46) Whenever any sentient being feels pain, I feel pain,

which is the denial of (g).

The upshot of the above is clear. If we reject A', we find that a person's total evidence provides direct arguments both for and against each of those common sense beliefs which, of the Analogical Position, it is alleged to support. But if we accept A' (as I believe we should) we still find that a man's total evidence does not support the conjunction of those common sense beliefs. It does not even support the conjunction of the members of K. Indeed, it does not so much as support the members of K individually; (c) alone appears more probable than not on my total evidence while (d), (e), and perhaps (f) appear to be improbable on it. What the Analogical Arguer should conclude is that every pain occurs in his own body and is accompanied by pain behavior on the part of his body (so couldn't he perform a splendid humanitarian service by *destroying* that wretched body?).

The conclusion to be drawn, I believe, is that the Analogical Position is untenable.[11]

[11] I wish to record my gratitude to Hector Castañeda, Edmund Gettier, Keith Lehrer, and Robert C. Sleigh, Jr., for stimulating discussion and acute criticism. I am especially indebted to Sleigh and Gettier, with whom I have discussed the topics of this paper often, at great length, and over a period of several years. The ideas in the paper grew out of these discussions and are theirs as much as mine. (So of course they must share responsibility for all of my errors.)

# INDUCTION AND OTHER MINDS

THE ANSWER most frequently given by philosophers to the questions how and whether we know that there are other minds is that we do know that there are other minds and that we know this by analogy. In the present paper I shall argue that we can justify belief in other minds on the basis of one version of the Argument from Analogy.[1] To some it may seem that I am flogging a dead horse, since there has been so much criticism of the Argument from Analogy in recent years on the part of philosophers influenced by Wittgenstein. However in his book, *God and Other Minds* (. . . published by Cornell University Press), Prof. Alvin Plantinga has considered and (to my mind) successfully undermined the main sorts of Wittgensteinian objections to the Analogical Argument for other minds. On the other hand, it will seem to some that the

Reprinted by permission of the author and the editor, from *The Review of Metaphysics*, XX (1966), 341–360. The debate between Plantinga and Slote continues. Plantinga's reply to Slote's critique appears in "Induction and Others Minds II," *The Review of Metaphysics*, XII (1968), 524–533. Slote's reply to this response is found in his book, *Reason and Scepticism* (London: Allen and Unwin, 1970).

[1] I am *not* claiming as a fact about human experience that we first come to believe or to be justified in believing in other persons via this argument.

Argument from Analogy needs no bolstering. But in his article, "Induction and Other Minds," recently published in this *Review* (March, 1966), Prof. Plantinga has pointed up some very strong objections to the Argument from Analogy. The major burden of the present paper will be to answer those objections and provide a satisfactory version of the Argument from Analogy.

## I

In "Induction and Other Minds," Plantinga casts the Argument from Analogy in the form of an inductive argument in the following way:

(1) Every case of pain behavior such that I have determined by observation whether or not it was accompanied by pain in the body displaying the behavior in question *was* accompanied by pain in that body.

Applying the so-called "straight rule" of induction, I conclude that:

(2) Probably every case of pain behavior is accompanied by pain in the body displaying it.

But then on certain occasion I observe that

(3) B over there (a body other than my own) is displaying pain behavior.

From (2) it follows that B is [probably] pained; since I don't feel a pain there, I conclude that

(4) [Probably] some other sentient creature has a pain.[2]

Plantinga proceeds to make some telling criticisms of this argument. He points up an oddity in the inference from (1) to (2), namely, that it is logically impossible for a counter-example to (2) to turn in the sample (described in [1]) that serves

---

[2] "Induction and Other Minds," *The Review of Metaphysics*, XIX (March, 1966), 443f. According to Plantinga, one cannot determine by observation that another is, or is not, in pain, because one cannot see, touch, feel, etc., another's pain. And there is some sense (perhaps a technical sense) of "observation" in which this would seem to be so. By "pain behavior" Plantinga means a "recognizable pattern of behavior" from whose existence it does not follow that anyone is in pain.

as the basis for the inductive inference to (2). For if, as Plantinga believes, and I am inclined to believe, it is logically possible for someone else to feel pain in my body, then even though I can determine by observation that *I* do not feel pain in a certain body, I cannot determine by observation that no one feels pain in that body. Even in cases where my own body is pain behaving and I feel no pain anywhere in my body, someone else may be feeling pain in my body. Thus it is logically impossible for me to determine by observation that a case of pain behavior is not accompanied by pain in the body displaying the pain behavior. Plantinga points out that other, highly suspicious arguments resemble the above version of the Analogical Argument, and suggests the following Principle A to rule out such fallacious inductive arguments: "An . . . inductive argument [for some contingent conclusion] is acceptable only if it is logically possible that its sample class contain a counter instance to its conclusion." [3]

This principle recommends itself as valid, just because if one is sampling f's and finds them all to be g, but also knows that because of one's method of sampling all the f's in one's sample will have to be g's no matter what percentage of the whole class of f's is g, one knows that one's sample is not a fair one. And inductive arguments based on samples known to be unfair or biased are clearly unacceptable.

Plantinga then considers another inductive argument for other minds that does not run afoul of A. He defines a *crowman* as something that is either a crow or a human body. And he defines being *minded* as being the human body of a (human) person with a mind. He then argues:

(13) Every crowman such that I have determined by observation whether or not it was either black or minded, *was* either black or minded.

So probably

(14) Every crowman is either black or minded.

[3] *Ibid.*, p. 450.

But

(15) B over there (a human body other than my own) is a crowman and is not black.

Hence B is probably minded; hence there is [probably] at least one other human person.[4]

According to Plantinga the premise (13) of this argument is true for each of us, and the argument to (14) does not violate Principle A, since it is clearly possible for a counter-example to (14) to turn up in our sample, e.g., a white crow. However, Plantinga also points out that arguments of this form can be given to prove that certain human bodies do *not* possess minds. He defines a *croite* as something that is either a crow or a white human body, and points out that any Negro can argue as follows:

(20) Every croite such that I have determined by observation whether or not it was either black or nonminded, *was* black or nonminded.

So probably

(21) Every croite is either black or nonminded.

But

(22) Jim Clarke over there is a croite and Jim Clarke is not black.

So probably

(23) Jim Clarke is nonminded.[5]

A similar argument in terms of *swanegs* (things that are either Negroid bodies or swans) can be given by any white man to prove the nonexistence of Negroes (with minds).[6] Now none of these arguments seems to be an acceptable inductive argument, but none is ruled out by Principle A. So

---

[4] *Ibid.*, p. 451.
[5] *Ibid.*, p. 452.
[6] *Ibid.*, p. 451f.

Plantinga suggests a Principle A′ that he claims will rule out these and other such arguments as unacceptable. He first defines the notion of a property's being *part of* another property. P is part of P′ just in case P is the same property as P′ or is a disjunct or conjunct or antecedent or consequent of P′ or of a part of P′. And he assumes that being black is a disjunct of being black or nonminded, but not, presumably, of, e.g., being darkly colored. He then states A′ as: "Where $\alpha$, $\beta$ is an inductive argument for [person] S, $\beta$ is of the form *All A's have B*, and C is any part of B, $\alpha$, $\beta$ is acceptable for S only if the propositions S *has examined an A and determined by observation that it lacks C and S has examined an A and determined by observation that it has C* are both logically possible." [7]

This principle has some initial plausibility and Plantinga accepts it as valid and as capable of ruling out the crowman, croite, and swaneg arguments. It certainly does seem that these arguments fall afoul of A′; but even more significantly, from the point of view of the present paper, *if* A′ is *valid*, it will be impossible to put forward an acceptable, valid Analogical Argument for the existence of other minds. For as Plantinga points out,[8] any analogical-inductive argument for other minds will involve some sort of generalization about some psychological characteristic, and it would seem to be logically impossible to discover the absence of such a characteristic by observation.

It is by no means clear, however, that A′ is valid. For if one makes certain plausible assumptions, it turns out that this principle rules out as unacceptable every possible inductive argument—not just the crowman, croite, and swaneg arguments—and thus cannot be a valid principle, if any inductive argument is ever acceptable. For consider any property f-ness about the presence of which one wishes to make an inductive generalization. One's conclusion will be of the form *all g's are f*. Take the property of being either observed and f or unobserved and f. One of its parts is the property of being unobserved.

[7] *Ibid.*, p. 452f.
[8] *Ibid.*, p. 453f.

The question then arises whether the property of being either observed and f or unobserved and f is the same property as the property of being f. Clearly the properties are logically, analytically, even truth-functionally equivalent. And surely it would be to multiply entities in a needless way to say that they were not the same property. But if one assumes, as seems reasonable, that they are, then the property of being unobserved is part of the property of f-ness, through being part of a property, the property of being observed and f or unobserved and f, that is in turn identical with, and thus by definition part of, the property of f-ness. Now one cannot (logically) determine by observation that something is unobserved, so any inductive argument with a conclusion of the form *all g's are f* will be unacceptable according to Principle A', since some part of f-ness will be such that it is logically impossible for anyone to determine by observation that a g has that part. It would seem, then, that A' is too strong.

Even if the properties of f-ness and of being either observed and f or unobserved and f are *not* identical, A' can be shown to rule out as unacceptable certain inductive arguments that are as unimpeachable as any inductive arguments are likely to be, and is thus clearly too strong. For consider an inductive argument from the premise "All the men in the regiment whose last names begin with a vowel are bachelors" to the conclusion "All the men in the regiment are (probably) bachelors." If we but assume that the property of being a bachelor is identical with the property of being an unmarried man, such an argument will be ruled out by A'. For being a man will then be part of being a bachelor; and it is not logically possible that one have examined a man in the regiment and determined by observation that he is *not* a man. So there is a part of the property being generalized in the above argument that fails to satisfy the conditions set in A'. Indeed, a large number of inductive arguments, all of which seem just as acceptable as the above, are ruled out by A'. Any inductive argument to a conclusion of the form *all A's are F*, where "F" designates the same property as "A and B," for some predicate "B," will be ruled out by A′. It would seem then that if enumerative, inductive generalization is valid, A′ is too strong.

But this is not all that can be said against A′. For A′ rules out still other seemingly acceptable inductive arguments. Let us imagine, for example, that whenever I test a subject S by prodding him with a pin, he neither winces nor gives any other sign of pain. I argue from the fact that every case in which I have stuck or prodded him with a pin has been a case in which he has felt no pain to the conclusion that every case in which he is stuck by a pin is a case in which he does not feel pain. I conclude, that is, that he is one of those rare people who do not feel pain from pins. Now for the purposes of this inductive argument, I have assumed in a common-sense way that I can verify whether someone else is in pain from his behavior. And from the assumption that, in certain situations, S was not in pain, I have gone on to the conclusion that S never feels pain in such situations. But A′ rules out arguments of this sort, just because one cannot (logically) determine by observation of a case in which someone else is stuck with a pin that it is a case in which that other person does not feel pain. In fact, A′ rules out all inductive arguments about other persons that involve generalizations about their psychological characteristics (e.g., Aunt Mary is always depressed in the morning) based on assumptions about their psychological reactions on some occasions.

Now if such arguments are unacceptable, it can only be because they are based on faulty inductive inferences or on unreasonable (unjustified) premises. But surely the inferences on which psychological generalizations are based are in no great way different from acceptable inductive inferences in other areas. How many of us do not, at one time or another, make such generalizations and treat them as being perfectly in order? And although the premises of these arguments cannot be assumed by anyone attempting to prove the existence of other minds, they are, nonetheless, premises of a kind everyone, at one time or another, feels justified in believing. To claim that the premises of such arguments are unjustified or not reasonably believed would be to deny the common-sense belief that some of our beliefs about the states of mind of others are justified. And surely no one, not even someone considering the merits of the Analogical Argument, has any right or reason to assume that such beliefs are never justified, or, thus, to assume that the premises of the arguments we are considering must always be unjustified. Since, as we have seen, there seems to be no reason to condemn the inferences of these arguments either, one has no reason to assume that all inductive arguments for psychological generalizations are unacceptable, nor to believe in the validity of A′, which condemns all such arguments as unacceptable.

## II

But if we reject A′, we are clearly left with important problems. For we have as yet no other means for showing the unacceptability of the clearly fallacious crowman, croite, and swaneg arguments. And if we cannot show what is wrong with these arguments, we will be left with one argument (the crowman argument) for the existence of other minds and two arguments (the croite and swaneg arguments) against the existence of other minds, and we will have found no satisfying, unequivocal way of showing the reasonableness of belief in other minds. It will be our task in this section to discover principles that rule out the crowman, croite, and swaneg arguments without precluding the possibility of producing a valid Analogical Argument for other minds.

Consider a Negro who uses the croite argument. Realizing that he is and always has been a Negro, he sees that it is impossible that any of the croites such that he has determined by observation whether or not they were black or nonminded be minded. For he cannot have determined by observation that some white human body was minded or that some crow was minded, in Plantinga's sense of "minded." So he cannot have determined by observation of any croite that it was neither black nor nonminded. So he knows, without making any assumptions about other minds and independently of any sampling of croites, that all croites such that he has determined by observation whether or not they are black or nonminded are black or nonminded, or at least were when he examined them. And so he knows that all croites such that he has determined by observation whether they are black or nonminded are black or nonminded, *even if* most croites are *not* black or nonminded. (Indeed we normally assume that a large number of croites are white and minded, i.e., white men.) Now if we base an inductive argument for the conclusion that all x's are f on the premise that all z x's are f, and know independently of any sampling that all z x's will be f even if most x's are not f, then we know that our argument is based on an unfair, or biased, sample. Thus the croite argument is clearly based on an unfair sample of croites; and this is true, even though it is *logically* possible for a counter-example to the conclusion of the croite argument to have turned up in the sample, so that that argument does *not* fall afoul of A. (It is logically possible that the Negro using the croite argument should have acquired a white skin at some time before using the argument, and so logically possible that he should have determined by observation of some croite (namely, his own body) that it was neither black nor nonminded.)

I propose the following Principle K, therefore, to eliminate the croite (and also the swaneg) argument:

> An inductive argument to the conclusion that all x's are f based on the premise that all z x's are f is not acceptable if one knows independently of one's actual sampling of x's that all z x's will be f *even if* most x's are *not* f.

Principle K seems reasonable because any argument contravening it will be based on a biased or unfair sample. And K is clearly accepted in other areas of inductive reasoning. If I have a large sieve and can only see what comes through it and know that the holes in the sieve are very small, I cannot argue from the fact that all the stones that have come through the sieve have been small to the conclusion that all the stones (that have been) in it are small, since I know without having to watch what comes out of the sieve that even if most of the stones (that have been) in the sieve are large, only small stones will come through it.

Principle K cannot, however, eliminate the crowman argument, just because we cannot know before sampling crowmen that every crowman such that we shall determine by observation whether or not it is black or minded will be black or minded. For at that time we know nothing to preclude the possibility that many crowmen that are crows will be determined by our observation to be white and nonminded. Only investigation of crows (or of like creatures) gives us reason to think that all crows are black. However, the following Principle S presents itself as the beginning of a valid means of excluding the crowman argument:

An inductive argument to the conclusion that all x's are f is not acceptable if we know that the x's divide into two groups (the y x's and the non-y x's) such that the non-y x's are known to be very different (in their nature or behavior) from the y x's and we know that there are non-y x's, but that our sample of x's that are f includes only y x's.

Such arguments are not acceptable, it should be clear, because they involve unfair or biased samples. If all old men have the gout, it is unreasonable to argue that all people, young or old, have the gout, if one has not examined any young people to determine whether they have the gout, and knows that in many other respects young people differ greatly from old men. Now in the case of the crowman argument, our sample property of being black or minded has been observed to exist in many, indeed all, of the crow crowmen in our sample of crowmen, but has been observed to exist in only one noncrow crowman (the body of the person putting forward the argument); and we also know independently of any assumptions about other minds that human bodies exist and are very different in structure and behavior from crows. Now as far as the crowman argument is concerned, it is not the case that we have sampled y x's but not non-y x's, for anyone putting forward the crowman argument has in his sample one noncrow crowman, namely, himself. But perhaps the crowman argument can be ruled out by the following Principle U:

> An inductive argument to the conclusion that all x's are f is not fully acceptable (is doubtful as an argument) if the x's are known to divide into two groups (the y x's and the non-y x's) such that the non-y x's are known to be very different (in their nature or behavior) from the y x's and we know that there are many non-y x's and that our sample of x's contains almost no non y x's.

Principle U rules out the crowman argument as not being fully acceptable as an inductive argument, because we have only one noncrow crowman in our sample of crowmen and know that the other sampled crowmen (crows) are so different from our sampled noncrow crowman or any other noncrow crowman. Thus we have developed principles that seem to be both valid and capable of ruling out the crowman, croite, and swaneg arguments.

Plantinga puts forward one further argument whose unacceptability must be accounted for if we wish to reinstate the Argument from Analogy as an unequivocal means for proving the reasonableness of belief in other minds. This argument runs:

> (28) Every pain which is such that I have determined by observation whether or not it was felt by me, was felt by me.

So probably

> (29) Every pain is felt by me.[9]

It should be clear why this argument presents a challenge to any attempt to prove (the reasonableness of belief in) the

---

[9] *Ibid.*, p. 454.

existence of other people's pains, and how a similar argument could be constructed to challenge any inductive argument for the existence of any mental state other than our own. This argument contravenes Plantinga's Principle A', of course, but we have seen strong grounds for renouncing that principle. Plantinga claims that without A' we have no way of getting rid of this argument.[10] But in fact it turns out that the argument also runs afoul of Plantinga's earlier Principle A, which I am prepared to accept as valid. It is logically impossible for me to determine by observation that a pain is not felt by me, just because it is logically impossible for me to determine by observation that someone else is in pain. And thus it is logically impossible to find a counter-example to the conclusion of the argument from (28) to (29) in the sample on which the argument is based. There is no problem, then, in showing the unacceptability of that argument.

## III

We have shown the unacceptability of certain inductive arguments put forward by Prof. Plantinga to challenge the possibility of a valid analogical-inductive argument for the existence of other minds. It is now time actually to provide such an argument.

We cannot argue for other minds on the basis of the analogical-inductive argument from (1) to (4) given above, for that argument offends against A, as we have already seen. But consider the following analogical-inductive argument for other minds, based solely on assumptions about one's own mental states and about material objects, that diverges from the argument from (1) to (4) in its method of specifying the sample on which it is based:

(a) Every case of (full-blown) pain behavior on the part of my (human) body (that I can remember) has been accompanied by pain or the pretense of pain (namely, on my part).

[10] *Ibid.*

So

(b) (It is reasonable for me to believe that) every case of (full-blown) pain behavior (on the part of any human body) is accompanied by pain or the pretense of pain.

But

(c) That (human) body over there is displaying (full-blown) pain behavior.

So

(d) (It is reasonable for me to believe that) someone is feeling pain, or else pretending to be in pain.

But

(e) I am not feeling pain, nor pretending to be in pain.

So

(f) (It is reasonable for me to believe that) someone else (or something else) is either feeling pain or pretending to be in pain, and therefore there is at least one other mind.

This argument does not offend against Principle A, because it is logically possible for a case of pain behavior on the part of my body not to be accompanied by pain or the pretense of pain—although I could never determine by observation that this was so. But the above analogical argument and any similar argument for the existence of other minds are open to at least one traditional objection, the objection, namely, that they are arguments "from one case alone." In the above argument one is generalizing from a correlation of pain behavior with pain or pretense of pain that exists in one's own case to such a correlation in the case of other bodies. It should be clear, however, that there is ambiguity here in the notion of one case, for the argument from (a) to (b) above refers to many cases of pain behavior, not just one. That argument is based on one case alone only in the sense that those cases of pain behavior mentioned in (a) are all cases of the behavior of one and the same body or person. But even if there is a definite sense in which the basic premise (a) of the above argument is based on many cases, and not just one, a problem still arises from the fact that the cases described in (a) involve only the single body of a single person, the problem, namely, of how one knows that what is true of oneself in many cases will be true in general of others. This problem is basically just the problem of how one can know that cases of one's own body's pain behavior are a fair or unbiased sample of all cases of pain behavior, as far as the property of being accompanied by pain or the pretense of pain is concerned. And one cannot get around this problem, as has been suggested by A. J. Ayer,[11] by absorbing the difference between oneself and others into differences between one's own situation and characteristics and those of others. For if one is unique, i.e., if one has a scar or fingerprint or general look h that no one else has, one still is left with the problem of knowing that cases of pain behavior involving a body with h are a fair sample of all cases of pain behavior. And how can one ever know that having h does not make a difference with respect to the property of being accompanied by pain or pretense of pain in such a way that pain behavior of a body with h *is* thus accompanied, while pain behavior of a body lacking h is *not?*

My answer to those problems—and it is by no means an unfamiliar answer to these *problems*—is that it is not necessary to have definite *knowledge* that one's sample of x's that are f is a fair or representative or unbiased sample of all x's as far as f-ness is concerned, in order to be justified in believing that all x's are f. In order for it to be reasonable to believe in such generalizations it is usually only necessary that one have found, after thorough, careful, and rational scrutiny of the relevant empirical information available to one, no reason to believe that one's sample is biased, unfair, or unrepresentative. I wish to suggest, therefore, that the following *Strong Principle of*

[11] *The Problem of Knowledge* (Harmondsworth, 1956), p. 250f.

58

*Induction* is a valid one, one in accordance with which it is reasonable to make inductive inferences:

> If all the x's one has sampled have been found to be f (and one has sampled numerous x's), and if one has after careful, rational, thorough examination of one's evidence discovered no reason to think that one's sample is unfair or biased, then it is reasonable to believe that all x's are f.

If this principle is valid, then our above argument for other minds will give us a basis for reasonable belief in other minds, if we but supplement it with what seems to be a perfectly reasonable assumption, (a)', to the effect that I have, after careful, thorough, and rational examination of the relevant evidence (empirical information) available to me, discovered no reason for believing that cases of my own pain behavior are a biased or unfair sample of all cases of pain behavior on the part of human bodies, as far as the property of being accompanied by pain or the pretense of pain is concerned.[12] But why believe in the validity of this Strong Principle? The answer I propose to this question is that if inductive generalization, enumerative induction, represents a valid form of inference at all, this principle will be valid too, because it is fundamentally presupposed in such inferences. For typically when we generalize from what is true of observed x's to what is true of the whole class of x's, we do not *know* that the observed and unobserved x's resemble each other in the appropriate respect, do not *know* that our sample is unbiased and fair. Usually we have at best only the knowledge that we have not, even after much careful scrutiny, been able to find any reason to believe

[12] Actually we need only assume a somewhat weaker version of this Strong Principle to make the argument for the reasonableness of belief in other minds go through. We need only assume that: If all the x's one has sampled . . . then it is reasonable to believe of any given x that it is f. We can then argue from (a) and (a)' to a weakened version of (b), (b)', which states that it is reasonable for me to believe of any given case of pain behavior that it is accompanied by pain or pretense of pain; and from (b)' to (f).

in such bias. If, for example, I discover an urn in the desert and the first twenty things I pull out of it at random are red balls and I conclude that there are (probably) nothing but red balls in the urn, my basis for this claim is no more than the fact that all the things I have taken out of the urn so far are red balls plus the fact that I can discover no reason to think my sample of the contents of the urn is biased or unfair. I have no mysterious knowledge of the unobserved contents of the urn obtained through any special or occult psychic power. So if this sort of enumerative induction is valid, either our Strong Principle or something closely resembling it must also be valid.

There are many sorts of common-sense beliefs that can be justified in terms of our Strong Principle of Induction. This principle can, for example, be used in arguing inductively from past to future, from the fact that all past men have been mortal to the conclusion that all future men will be mortal. For there is no reason to think that past men are a biased or unfair sample of future men, as far as mortality is concerned. It is interesting that the Strong Principle can be used not only to answer the problem of the reasonableness of belief in other minds, but also to solve the age-old problem of the reasonableness of belief in the continued existence and lawlike behavior of objects when they are no longer being perceived. In his famous "Refutation of Realism," [13] Prof. Stace has argued that no deductive or inductive argument can show the reasonableness of the view that objects continue to exist and operate in the same way when not observed as when they are observed, a view that he considers to be a major, if not the major, tenet of Epistemological Realism. And so Stace concludes that even if Realism is true, we have no reason to believe it to be so. According to Stace, no inductive argument for (the reasonableness of belief in) the existence of unperceived physical objects is possible, because we cannot argue, for example, from the fact that all fires we have observed have kept burning when

[13] "The Refutation of Realism," *Mind*, XLIII (1934), 145–155.

no longer observed, to the conclusion that all fires do, without begging the question at issue. For the premise of the induction assumes knowledge of objects when they are not being observed, assumes that objects sometimes do behave the same way when unobserved as when observed. And this is, of course, just what has to be proved. So this sort of inductive argument cannot be used to show the reasonableness of Realism as Stace conceives it. It is surprising, however, that Stace did not see the possibility of another sort of inductive argument, based solely on premises about the nature of objects when observed, for the reasonableness of belief in Realism. Indeed, in a reply to Stace's article, R. E. Stedman and H. B. Acton suggest that very possibility, but then do nothing themselves about providing such an argument.[14] But consider the following argument, based on an inductive inference that accords with the Strong Principle of Induction:

(g) All roaring fires watched till they burned out have obeyed certain laws, and have continued to burn for a long time unless they were directly interfered with by some physical thing.

(h) I have, after careful, rational, and thorough examination of the relevant empirical evidence available to me, discovered no reason to believe that roaring fires that have been watched till they burned out constitute an unfair or biased sample of all roaring fires, as far as obeying certain laws and continuing to burn unless interfered with are concerned.

So

(i) (It is reasonable for me to think that) all roaring fires obey certain laws, etc.

But

(j) I just stopped watching and left a roaring fire, and have seen nothing interfere with it.

14 "Mr. Stace's 'Refutation of Realism,'" *Mind*, XLIII (1934), 349–353.

So

(k) (It is reasonable for me to think that) the fire I just left is obeying certain laws and continued to burn and will continue to burn for a long time after the time when I left it, unless some physical thing directly interferes or has interfered with it after that time.

So

(l) (It is reasonable for me to think that) at least one thing is obeying or has obeyed certain laws, even though it is (was) not being observed.

And

(m) (It is reasonable for me to think that) either the fire I left continued to burn thereafter or some physical thing that I didn't see interfered with its burning.

So

(n) (It is reasonable for me to think that) some physical thing or other has existed unobserved.[15]

This argument shows the reasonableness of Realism, as Prof. Stace and others have construed it. And of course similar arguments could be employed to show the reasonableness of belief in the existence of just about any of the objects in whose unobserved existence we all believe.

The fact that the Strong Principle of Induction is involved in inductive reasoning in many areas gives that principle much plausibility in general and helps to justify its use in an argument like the one given above for the existence of other minds. Of course, there are some philosophers who might reject the Strong Principle, or even the weaker version of that principle, because they reject enumerative induction. In a recent article, for example,[16] Prof. G. Harman has argued that enumerative

---

[15] Like the argument above for other minds, this argument could be altered in such a way as to make use only of the weaker version of the Strong Principle of Induction as its principle of inference.

[16] "The Inference to the Best Explanation," *Philosophical Review,* LXXIV (1965), 88–95.

induction is valid only as a part of hypothetico-deductive method, of abduction; according to Harman, enumerative induction is not in its own right a warranted form of inference, so that when inductive generalization is in order, it is only because there are other standards of scientific acceptability in terms of which the generalization can be justified. Similarly, when inference to what the next x will be like on the basis of the nature of previously examined x's is in order, it is only because that inference can be justified via some other standards of the acceptability of hypotheses. Now perhaps in the actual doing of science enumerative induction is rarely, if ever, used to justify conclusions, but even if this is so, it must be remembered that the enterprise of science typically presupposes a number of beliefs (belief in an external world, in the existence of other minds, in the existence of unobserved objects) that are clearly not "self-evident" and, thus, that must be justifiable in terms of some scientific or other standards of the acceptability of beliefs, if one is to have good reason to believe them. And if one asks what justifies our belief in other minds and in unobserved objects, one clearly *possible* answer is that they can be justified as we have done above via the Strong Principle of Induction, or its weaker version.[17] Now surely we want to hold that belief in other minds and in unobserved objects is or can be justified; and so the question arises whether anyone has ever pointed out any scientific or other principles of the rational acceptability of beliefs other than some form of principle of induction or some principle(s) whose validity clearly entails the validity of enumerative induction, in terms of which belief in other minds and in unobserved objects can be justified. Harman suggests that our belief in other minds, for example, can be justified, without recourse to inductive principles, by showing that that belief provides the best explanation of the behavior of human bodies other than our own. And he also

---

[17] Harman (*op. cit.*, p. 90) denies the possibility of giving an enumerative inductive argument for other minds; inasmuch as the present paper succeeds, this part of his reason for rejecting enumerative induction is vitiated.

indicates that he thinks that it is in terms of such standards of the acceptability of hypotheses as *simplicity* and *plausibility* that the hypothesis of other minds can be shown to be the best explanation of the behavior of bodies other than our own.[18] Similarly, P. Ziff has suggested that our belief in other minds can be justified as the most complete, simple, and coherent explanation of certain facts about bodies other than our own.[19] But in a reply to Ziff's paper,[20] Prof. Plantinga has cogently argued that it is far from clear that Ziff, or anyone else, has provided adequate reasons for believing that the hypothesis of other minds is a simpler, more complete, or more coherent explanation of the behavior of bodies other than our own than, e.g., the skeptical hypothesis of a demon who for certain motives and by certain means causes other human bodies to behave in such a way as to make them *appear* to have minds. Thus as far as I can see, there is no reason to think that belief in other minds or in unobserved objects can be justified on anything but an (enumerative) inductive basis, i.e., via something like the Strong Principle of Induction or the weaker version of that principle. So if we assume that such beliefs are justified, we have every reason to accept the validity of the inductive principles put forward here, at least until someone shows us a more plausible basis for the reasonableness of belief in other minds or unobserved objects and/or makes a better case than any I have yet seen for the unreasonableness of inferences by enumerative induction (by our Strong Principle or by the weaker version of that principle) that are not backed up by other, independent principles of scientific acceptability.

As I said earlier, in order to have a complete argument for other minds, the argument from (a) to (f) above must be supplemented by a premise (a)' to the effect that one has, after careful, etc. examination of the relevant available evidence,

---

[18] Harman, *op. cit.*, p. 91.

[19] "The Simplicity of Other Minds," *Journal of Philosophy*, LXII (1965), *passim*.

[20] "Comments," *Journal of Philosophy*, LXII (1965), 585f.

found no reason to think that cases of pain behavior on the part of one's body are an unfair sample of the class of all cases of pain behavior on the part of any human body. Then the argument to (b) and thence to (f) will go through making implicit use of the Strong Principle of Induction. Clearly we are usually justified in normal circumstances in which we are viewing pain behavior on the part of a human body other than our own in believing (a)'. But note that if the croite argument were a good one, a Negro could use it to show that every croite was black or nonminded and so that every white croite, every white human body—even those displaying pain behavior—was probably nonminded. And this would imply that we did have a reason to think our own cases of pain behavior were a biased or unfair sample of all cases of pain behavior as far as being accompanied by pain or the pretense of pain was concerned, in which case (a)' would be false and our argument for other minds would not go through. Fortunately, our Principle K rules out the croite (and swaneg) argument so that one cannot use it to show that we have a reason to think the sample described in (a) is biased, or thus to vitiate our argument for other minds. It is also worth pointing out that arguments that offend against A, K, S, or U will *not* be arguments whose validity is guaranteed by the validity of the Strong Principle of Induction. For example, arguments that fall afoul of A are arguments such that it is logically impossible for a counter-example to their conclusions to exist in the samples on which they (the arguments) are based. But such arguments will clearly be based on biased or unfair samples, and their validity will not be guaranteed by our Strong Principle of Induction (or the weaker version of that principle), which only certifies arguments based on samples we have no reason to think biased or unfair.[21] And we have argued in various places above that all

---

[21] One problem with the Strong Principle that has not been mentioned so far is one raised by Goodman's New Riddle of Induction. For I have not in the present paper shown that inductive arguments involving such nonprojectible predicates as "grue" are *not* sanctioned by that principle. And surely

arguments offending against K, S, or U will be based on biased or unfair samples; and so they will also not be sanctioned by the Strong Principle of Induction (or its weaker version). Thus we have found a way around Plantinga's objections to the Argument from Analogy and have devised principles on the basis of which we can give valid arguments both for the existence of other minds and for the existence of unobserved objects.*

such arguments should not be sanctioned by any valid principle of inductive inference. However, in an article on Goodman's Riddle that I hope to be publishing shortly, I have put forward reasons to think a) that arguments based on such predicates as "grue" are based on biased samples and are thus not sanctioned by any version of our Strong Principle and, thus, b) that inductive arguments involving such predicates as "grue" pose no threat to the validity of inductive arguments involving such projectible predicates as "green" that are made in accordance with our Strong Principle of Induction.

* I should like to record my indebtedness to Prof. Sidney Morgenbesser for many fruitful discussions of the ideas of this paper.

# II

*Behaviorism*

# PSYCHOLOGY IN PHYSICAL LANGUAGE

RUDOLF CARNAP

## 1. Introduction. Physical Language and Protocol Language

In what follows, we intend to explain and to establish the thesis that *every sentence of psychology may be formulated in physical language*. To express this in the material mode of speech: *all sentences of psychology describe physical occurrences, namely, the physical behavior of humans and other animals.* This is a sub-thesis of the general thesis of *physicalism* to the effect that *physical language is a universal language*, that is, a language into which every sentence may be translated. The general thesis has been discussed in an earlier article,[1] whose position shall here serve as our point of departure. Let us first briefly review some of the conclusions of the earlier study.

In meta-linguistic discussion we distinguish the customary *material mode of speech* (e.g., "The sentences of this language speak of this and that object.") from the more correct *formal mode of speech* (e.g., "The sentences of this language contain

Reprinted by permission of The Free Press, from A. J. Ayer, ed., *Logical Positivism.* Copyright 1959.

[1] Carnap, "Die physikalische Sprache als Universalsprache der Wissenschaft," *Erkenntnis,* II (1931), 432–465. [The English translation of this article by Max Black was published as a monograph under the title *The Unity of Science* (London: Kegan Paul, 1934).]

this and that word and are constructed in this and that manner."). In using the material mode of speech we run the risk of introducing confusions and pseudo-problems. If, because of its being more easily understood, we occasionally do use it in what follows, we do so only as a paraphrase of the formal mode of speech.

Of first importance for epistemological analyses are the *protocol language,* in which the primitive protocol sentences (in the material mode of speech: the sentences about the immediately given) of a particular person are formulated, and the *system language,* in which the sentences of the system of science are formulated. A person S *tests* (verifies) a system sentence by deducing from it sentences of his own protocol language, and comparing these sentences with those of his actual protocol. The possibility of such a deduction of protocol sentences constitutes the *content* of a sentence. If a sentence permits no such deductions, it has no content, and is meaningless. If the same sentences may be deduced from two sentences, the latter two sentences have the same content. They say the same thing, and may be translated into one another.

To every sentence of the system language there corresponds some sentence of the physical language such that the two sentences are inter-translatable. It is the purpose of this article to show that this is the case for the sentences of psychology. Moreover, every sentence of the protocol language of some specific person is inter-translatable with some sentence of physical language, namely, with a sentence about the physical state of the person in question. The various protocol languages thus become sub-languages of the physical language. The *physical language is universal and inter-subjective.* This is the thesis of physicalism.

If the physical language, on the grounds of its universality, were adopted as the system language of science, all science would become physics. Metaphysics would be discarded as meaningless. The various domains of science would become parts of unified science. In the material mode of speech there would, basically, be only one kind of object—physical occurrences, in whose realm law would be all-encompassing.

Physicalism ought not to be understood as requiring psychology to concern itself only with physically describable situations. The thesis, rather, is that psychology may deal with whatever it pleases, it may formulate its sentences as it pleases —these sentences will, in every case, be translatable into physical language.

We say of a sentence P that it is *translatable* (more precisely, that it is reciprocally translatable) into a sentence Q if there are rules, independent of space and time, in accordance with which Q may be deduced from P and P from Q; to use the material mode of speech, P and Q describe the same state of affairs; epistemologically speaking, every protocol sentence which confirms P also confirms Q and *vice versa*. The definition of an expression "a" by means of expressions "b," "c," . . . , represents a translation-rule with the help of which any sentence in which "a" occurs may be translated into a sentence in which "a" does not occur, but "b," "c," . . . , do, and *vice versa*. The translatability of all the sentences of language $L_1$ into a (completely or partially) different language $L_2$ is assured if, for every expression of $L_1$, a definition is presented which directly or indirectly (i.e., with the help of other definitions) derives that expression from expressions of $L_2$. Our thesis thus states that a definition may be constructed for every psychological concept (i.e., expression) which directly or indirectly derives that concept from physical concepts. We are not demanding that psychology formulate each of its sentences in physical terminology. For its own purposes psychology may, as heretofore, utilize its own terminology. All that we are demanding is the production of the definitions through which psychological language is linked with physical language. We maintain that these definitions can be produced, since, implicitly, they already underlie psychological practice.

If our thesis is correct, the generalized sentences of psychology, the *laws* of psychology, are also translatable into the physical language. They are thus physical laws. Whether or not these physical laws are deducible from those holding in inorganic physics, remains, however, an open question. This question of the deducibility of the laws is completely independent of the question of the definability of concepts. We have already considered this matter in our discussion of biology.[2] As soon as one realizes that the sentences of psychology belong to the physical language, and also overcomes the emotional obstacles to the acceptance of this provable thesis, one will, indeed, incline to the conjecture, which cannot as yet be proved, that the laws of psychology are special cases of physical laws holding in inorganic physics as well. But we are not concerned with this conjecture here.

Let us permit ourselves a brief remark—apart from our principal point—concerning the emotional resistance to the thesis of physicalism. Such resistance is always exerted against any thesis when an Idol is being dethroned by it, when we are asked to discard an idea with which dignity and grandeur are associated. As a result of Copernicus' work, man lost the distinction of a central position in the universe; as a result of Darwin's, he was deprived of the dignity of a special supra-animal existence; as a result of Marx's, the factors by means of which history can be causally explained were degraded from the realm of ideas to that of material events; as a result of Nietzsche's, the origins of morals were stripped of their halo; as a result of Freud's, the factors by means of which the ideas and actions of men can be causally explained were located in the darkest depths, in man's nether regions. The extent to which the sober, objective examination of these theories was obstructed by emotional opposition is well known. Now it is proposed that psychology, which has hitherto been robed in majesty as the theory of spiritual events, be degraded to the status of a part of physics. Doubtless, many will consider this an offensive presumption. Perhaps we may therefore ex-

[2] "Die physikalische Sprache," pp. 449ff. (*The Unity of Science*, pp. 68ff.).

press the request that the reader make a special effort in this case to retain the objectivity and openness of mind always requisite to the testing of a scientific thesis.

## *2. The Forms of Psychological Sentences*

The distinction between singular and general sentences is as important in psychology as in other sciences. A *singular psychological sentence*, e.g., "Mr. A was angry at noon yesterday" (an analogue of the physical sentence "Yesterday at noon the temperature of the air in Vienna was 28 degrees centigrade"), is concerned with a particular person at a particular time. *General psychological sentences* have various forms, of which the following two are perhaps the most important. A sentence may describe a specific quality of a specific kind of event, e.g., "An experience of surprise always (or: always for Mr. A, or: always for people of such and such a society) has such and such a structure." A physical analogy would be: "Chalk (or: chalk of such and such a sort) always is white." The second important form is that of universal-conditional statements concerning sequences of events, that is, of causal laws. For instance, "When, under such and such circumstances, images of such and such a sort occur to a person (or: to Mr. A, or: to anyone of such and such a society), an emotion of such and such a sort always (or: frequently, or: sometimes) is aroused." A physical analogy would be: "When a solid body is heated, it usually expands."

Research is primarily directed to the discovery of general sentences. These cannot, however, be established except by means of the so-called method of induction from the available singular sentences, i.e., by means of the construction of hypotheses.

*Phenomenology* claims to be able to establish universal synthetic sentences which have not been obtained through induction. These sentences about psychological qualities are, allegedly, known either *a priori* or on the basis of some single illustrative case. In our view, knowledge cannot be gained by such means. We need not, however, enter upon a discussion of this issue here, since even on the view of phenomenology itself, these sentences do not belong to the domain of psychology.

In physics it sometimes seems to be the case that a general law is established on the basis of some single event. For instance, if a physicist can determine a certain physical constant, say, the heat-conductivity of a sample of some pure metal, in a single experiment, he will be convinced that, on other occasions, not only the sample examined but any similar sample of the same substance will, very probably, be characterizable by the same constant. But here too induction is applied. As a result of many previous observations the physicist is in possession of a universal sentence of a higher order which enables him in this case to follow an abbreviated method. This higher-order sentence reads roughly: "All (or: the following) physical constants of metals vary only slightly in time and from sample to sample."

The situation is analogous for certain conclusions drawn in psychology. If a psychologist has, as a result of some single experiment, determined that the simultaneous sounding of two specific notes is experienced as a dissonance by some specific person A, he infers (under favorable circumstances) the truth of the general sentence which states that the same experiment with A will, at other times, have the same result. Indeed, he will even venture—and rightly—to extend this result, with some probability, to pairs of tones with the same acoustic interval if the pitch is not too different from that of the first experiment. Here too the inference from a singular sentence to a general one is only apparent. Actually, a sentence inductively obtained from many observations is brought into service here, a sentence which, roughly, reads: "The reaction of any specific person as to the consonance or dissonance of a chord varies only very slightly with time, and only slightly on a not too large transposition of the chord." It thus remains the case that every general sentence is inductively established on the basis of a number of singular ones.

Finally, we must consider sentences about psycho-physical interrelations, such as for instance, the connection between physical stimulus and perception. These are likewise arrived at through induction, in this case through induction in part from physical and in part from psychological singular sentences. The most important sentences of gestalt psychology belong also to this kind.

General sentences have the character of hypotheses in relation to concrete sentences; that is, the testing of a general sentence consists in testing the concrete sentences which are deducible from it. A general sentence has content insofar and only insofar as the concrete sentences deducible from it have content. Logical analysis must therefore primarily be directed towards the examination of the latter sort of sentences.

If A utters a singular psychological sentence such as "Yesterday morning B was happy," the epistemological situation differs according as A and B are or are not the same person. Consequently, we distinguish between sentences about *other minds* and sentences about *one's own mind*. As we shall presently see, this distinction cannot be made among the sentences of inter-subjective science. For the epistemological analysis of subjective, singular sentences it is, however, indispensable.

### 3. *Sentences about Other Minds*

The epistemological character of a singular sentence about other minds will now be clarified by means of an analogy with a sentence about a physical property, defined as a disposition to behave (or respond) in a specific manner under specific circumstances (or stimuli). To take an example: a substance is called "plastic" if, under the influence of deforming stresses of a specific sort and a specific magnitude, it undergoes a permanent change of shape, but remains intact.

We shall try to carry out this analogy by juxtaposing two

examples. We shall be concerned with the epistemological situation of the example taken from psychology; the parallel example about the physical property is intended only to facilitate our understanding of the psychological sentence, and not to serve as a specimen of an argument from analogy. (For the sake of convenience, where the text would have been the same in both columns, it is written only once.)

| A sentence about a property of a physical substance. | A sentence about a condition of some other mind. |
|---|---|
| Example: I assert the sentence $P_1$: "This wooden support is very firm." | Example: I assert the sentence $P_1$: "Mr. A is now excited." |

There are two different ways in which sentence $P_1$ may be derived. We shall designate them as the "rational" and the "intuitive" methods. The *rational* method consists of inferring $P_1$ from some protocol sentence $p_1$ (or from several like it), more specifically, from a perception-sentence

| about the shape and color of the wooden support. | about the behavior of A, e.g., about his facial expressions, his gestures, etc., or about physical effects of A's behavior, e.g., about characteristics of his handwriting. |
|---|---|

In order to justify the conclusion, a major premise O is still required, namely, the general sentence which asserts that

| when I perceived a wooden support to be of this color and form, it (usually) turns out to be firm. (A sentence about the perceptual signs of firmness.) | when I perceive a person to have this facial expression and handwriting he (usually) turns out to be excited. (A sentence about the expressional or graphological signs of excitement.) |
|---|---|

The content of $P_1$ does not coincide with that of $p_1$, but goes beyond it. This is evident from the fact that to infer $P_1$ from $p_1$ O is required. The cited relationship between $P_1$ and $p_1$ may also be seen in the fact that under certain circumstances, the inference from $p_1$ to $P_1$ may go astray. It may happen that, though $p_1$ occurs in a protocol, I am obliged, on the grounds of further protocols, to retract the established system sentence $P_1$. I would then say something like, "I made a mistake. The test has shown

| | |
|---|---|
| that the support was not firm, even though it had such and such a form and color." | that A was not excited, even though his face had such and such an expression." |

In practical matters the *intuitive* method is applied more frequently than this rational one, which presupposes theoretical knowledge and requires reflection. In accordance with the intuitive method, $P_1$ is obtained without the mediation of any other sentence from the identically sounding protocol sentence $p_2$.

| | |
|---|---|
| "The support is firm." | "A is excited." |

Consequently, one speaks in this case of *immediate perceptions*

| | |
|---|---|
| of properties of substances, e.g., of the firmness of supports. | of other minds, e.g., of the excitement of A. |

But in this case too the protocol sentence $p_2$ and the system sentence $P_1$ have different contents. The difference is generally not noted because, on the ordinary formulation, both sentences sound alike. Here too we can best clarify the difference by considering the possibility of error. It may happen that, though $p_2$ occurs in my protocol, I am obliged, on the basis of further protocols, to retract the established system sentence $P_1$. I would then say "I made a mistake. Further tests have shown

| | |
|---|---|
| that the support was not firm, although I had the intuitive impression that it was." | that A was not excited, although I had the intuitive impression that he was." |

[The difference between $p_2$ and $P_1$ is the same as that between the identically sounding sentences p and $P_1$: "A red marble is lying on this table," of an earlier example.[3] The argument of

[3] See *Erkenntnis*, II, 460 (*The Unity of Science*, p. 92).

that article shows that the inference of $P_1$ from $p_2$, if it is to be rigorous, also requires a major premise of general form, and that it is not in the least simple. Insofar as ordinary usage, for convenience's sake, assigns to both sentences the same sequence of words, the inference is, in practice, simplified to the point of triviality.]

Our problem now is: *what does sentence $P_1$ mean?* Such a question can only be answered by the presentation of a sentence (or of several sentences) which has (or which conjointly have) the same content as $P_1$. The viewpoint which will here be defended is that $P_1$ has the same content as a sentence $P_2$ which asserts the existence of a physical structure characterized by the disposition to react in a specific manner to specific physical stimuli. In our example, $P_2$ asserts the existence of that physical structure (micro-structure)

of the wooden support that is characterized by the fact that, under a slight load, the support undergoes no noticeable distortion, and, under heavier loads, is bent in such and such a manner, but does not break.

of Mr. A's body (especially of his central nervous system) that is characterized by a high pulse and rate of breathing, which, on the application of certain stimuli, may even be made higher, by vehement and factually unsatisfactory answers to questions, by the occurrence of agitated movements on the application of certain stimuli, etc.

On my view, there is here again a thoroughgoing analogy between the examples from physics and from psychology. If, however, we were to question the experts concerning the examples from their respective fields, the majority of them nowadays would give us thoroughly nonanalogous answers. The identity of the content of $P_2$

and of the content of the physical sentence $P_1$ would be agreed to as a matter of course by all

and of the content of the psychological sentence $P_1$ would be denied by almost all psycholo-

physicists.

The contrary view which is most frequently advocated by psychologists is that "A sentence of the form of $P_1$ asserts the existence of a state of affairs not identical with the corresponding physical structure, but rather, only accompanied by it, or expressed by it. In our example:

$P_1$ states that the support not only has the physical structure described by $P_2$, but that, besides, there exists in it a certain force, namely its *firmness.*

This firmness is not identical with the physical structure, but stands in some parallel relation to it in such a manner that the firmness exists when and only when a physical structure of the characterized sort exists.

Because of this parallelism one may consider the described reaction to certain stimuli—which is causally dependent upon that structure—to be an *expression* of firmness.

Firmness is thus an occult property, an obscure power which stands behind physical structure, appears in it, but itself remains unknowable."

$P_1$ states that Mr. A not only has a body whose physical structure (at the time in question) is described by $P_2$, but that—since he is a *psycho-physical being*—he has, besides, a consciousness, a certain power or entity, in which that excitement is to be found.

This excitement cannot, consequently, be identical with the cited structure of the body, but stands in some parallel relation (or in some relation of interaction) to it in such a manner that the excitement exists when and only when (or at least, frequently when) a physical, bodily structure of the characterized sort exists.

Because of this parallelism one may consider the described reaction to certain stimuli to be an *expression* of excitement.

Excitement, or the consciousness of which it is an attribute, is thus an occult property, an obscure power which stands behind physical structure, appears in it, but itself remains unknowable."

This view falls into the error of a hypostatization as a result of which a remarkable duplication occurs: besides or behind a state of affairs whose existence is empirically determinable, another, *parallel* entity is assumed, whose existence is not determinable. (Note that we are here concerned with a sentence about other minds.) But—one may now object—is there not really at least one possibility of testing this claim, namely, by means of the protocol sentence $p_2$ about the intuitive impression of

the firmness of the support?      the excitement of A?

The objector will point out that this sentence, after all, occurs in the protocol along with the perception sentence $p_1$. May not then a system sentence whose content goes beyond that of $P_2$ be founded on $p_2$? This may be answered as follows. A sentence says no more than what is testable about it. If, now, the testing of $P_1$ consisted in the deduction of the protocol sentence $p_2$, these two sentences would have the same content. But we have already seen that this is impossible.

There is no other possibility of testing $P_1$ except by means of protocol sentences like $p_1$ or like $p_2$. If, now, the content of $P_1$ goes beyond that of $P_2$, the component not shared by the two sentences is not testable, and is therefore meaningless. If one rejects the interpretation of $P_1$ in terms of $P_2$, $P_1$ becomes a metaphysical pseudo-sentence.

The various sciences today have reached very different stages in the process of their decontamination from metaphysics. Chiefly because of the efforts of Mach, Poincaré, and Einstein, physics is, by and large, practically free of metaphysics. In psychology, on the other hand, the work of arriving at a science which is to be free of metaphysics has hardly begun. The difference between the two sciences is most clearly seen in the different attitudes taken by experts in the two fields towards the position which we rejected as metaphysical and meaningless. In the case of the example from physics, most physicists would reject the position as anthropomorphic, or mythological, or metaphysical. They thereby reveal their anti-metaphysical orientation, which corresponds to our own. On the other hand, in the case of the example from psychology (though, perhaps, not when it is so crudely formulated), most psychologists would today consider the view we have been criticizing to be self-evident on intuitive grounds. In this one can see the metaphysical orientation of psychologists, to which ours is opposed.

### 4. Rejoinder to Four Typical Criticisms

Generalizing the conclusion of the argument which, with reference to a special case, we have been pursuing above, we arrive at the thesis that *a singular sentence about other minds always has the same content as some specific physical sentence.* Phrasing the same thesis in the material mode of speech, a sentence about other minds states that the body of the person in question is in a physical state of a certain sort. Let us now discuss several objections against this thesis of physicalism.

A. *Objection on the ground of the undeveloped state of physiology.* "Our current knowledge of physiology—especially our knowledge of the physiology of the central nervous system—is not yet sufficiently advanced to enable us to know to what class of physical conditions something like excitement corresponds. Consequently, when today we use the sentence 'A is excited,' we cannot mean by it the corresponding physical state of affairs."

*Rebuttal.* Sentence $P_1$, "A is excited," cannot, indeed, today be translated into a physical sentence $P_3$ of the form "such and such a physico-chemical process is now taking place in A's body" (expressed by a specification of physical state-coordinates and by chemical formulae). Our current knowledge of physiology is not adequate for this purpose. Even today, however, $P_1$ may be translated into another sentence about the physical condition of A's body, namely, into the sentence $P_2$, to which we have already referred. This takes the form "A's body is now in a state which is characterized by the fact that

81

when I perceive A's body the protocol sentence $p_1$ (stating my perception of A's behavior) and (or) the protocol sentence $p_2$ (stating my intuitive impression of A's excitement) or other, analogous, protocol sentences of such and such a sort are produced." Just as, in our example from physics, sentence $P_1$, "The wooden support is firm," refers to the physical structure of the wooden support—and this even though the person using the sentence may sometimes not be capable of characterizing this physical structure by specifying the distribution of the values of the physical state-coordinates—so also does the psychological sentence $P_1$, "A is excited," refer to the physical structure of A's body—though this structure can only be characterized by potential perceptions, impressions, dispositions to react in a specific manner, etc., and not by any specification of state-coordinates. Our ignorance of physiology can therefore affect only the mode of our characterization of the physical state of affairs in question. It in no way touches upon the principal point: that sentence $P_1$ refers to a physical state of affairs.

B. *Objection on the ground of analogy.* "When I myself am angry, I not only act out the behavior-pattern of an angry man, I experience a special *feeling* of anger. If, consequently, I observe someone else acting out the same behavior-pattern I may, on grounds of analogy, conclude (if not with certainty, at least with probability) that he too, besides acting as he does, now has a *feeling* of anger (which is not meant as a physical state of affairs)."

*Rebuttal.* Though arguments from analogy are not certain, as probability arguments they are undoubtedly admissible. By way of an example let us consider an everyday argument from analogy. I see a box of a certain shape, size, and color. I discover that it contains matches. I find another box of a similar appearance, and now, by analogy, draw the probability inference that it too contains matches. Our critic believes that the argument from analogy he presents is of the same logical form as the argument just presented. If this were the case, his conclusion would certainly be sound. But this is not the case. In our critic's argument, the conclusion is *meaningless*—a mere pseudo-sentence. For, being a sentence about other minds, not to be physically interpreted, it is in principle not testable. This was the result of our previous considerations; objection D will offer us an opportunity for discussing it again. In the nontestability of our critic's conclusion rests also the difference between his arguments and the example just cited. That the second box also contains matches may in principle be tested and confirmed by observation sentences of one's protocol. The two analogous sentences, "The first box contains matches" and "The second box contains matches" are both logically and epistemologically of the same sort. This is why the analogy holds here. The case is different with "I am angry" and "That person is angry." We consider the former of these two sentences to be meaningful and the latter (if its physical interpretation is rejected) to be meaningless. Our critic, who considers the latter as well as the former sentence to be meaningful, will believe that the person who asserts the sentence finds it testable, only in a manner altogether different from that in which the former is testable. Thus both of us agree that the latter sentence is epistemologically different from the former. The use of the same grammatical structure in these two sentences is logically illegitimate. It misleads us into believing that the two sentences are of the same logical form, and that one may be used as an analogue of the other.

If the conclusion is acknowledged to be meaningless, it remains to be explained how this pseudo-sentence was introduced into the argument. The logical analysis of concept formation and of sentences in science and (especially) in philosophy very frequently discloses pseudo-sentences. However, a pseudo-sentence rarely turns up as the conclusion of an argument from analogy with meaningful premises. This may readily be accounted for. An argument from analogy has (in a simple case) the following form. Premises: If A has the property E, it always also has the property F; A' resembles A in many respects; A′ has the property E. We conclude (with probability): A′ also has the property F. Now, according to semantics, if "A" and "B" are object-names, "E" and "F" property-names, and "E(A)" means that A has the property E, then a) if "E(A)" and "E(B)" are meaningful (i.e., either true or false), "A" and "B" belong to the same semantic type; b) if two names, "A" and "B," belong to the same semantic type, and "F(A)" is meaningful, then "F(B)" is also meaningful. In the case under discussion here "E(A)" and "E(A′)" are meaningful, and consequently—in accordance with b)—"F(A′)," the conclusion of the argument from analogy, is also meaningful. Thus if the premises of an argument from analogy are meaningful and yet the conclusion is meaningless, the formulation of the premises must be in some way logically objectionable. And this is indeed the case with the argument from analogy presented by our critic. The predicative expression "I am angry" does not adequately represent the state of affairs which is meant. It asserts that a certain property belongs to a certain entity. All that exists, however, is an experienced feeling of anger. This should have been formulated as, roughly, "now anger." On this correct formulation the possibility of an argument from analogy disappears. For now the premises read: when I (i.e., my body) display angry behavior, anger occurs; the body of another person resembles mine in many respects; the body of the other person is now displaying angry behavior. The original conclusion can now no longer be drawn, since the sentence "Anger occurs" contains no "I" which may be replaced by "the other person." If one wanted to draw the appropriate conclusion, in which no substitution is made but the form of the premises simply retained, one would arrive at the meaningful but plainly false conclusion, "Anger occurs"—which states what would be expressed in ordinary language by "I am now angry."

C. *Objection on the ground of mental telepathy.* "The telepathic transmission of the contents of consciousness (ideas, emotions, thoughts) occurs without any determinable physical mediation. Here we have an instance of the knowledge of other minds which involves no perception of other people's bodies. Let us consider an example. I wake up suddenly one night, have a distinct sensation of fear, and know that my friend is now experiencing fear; later, I discover that at that very moment my friend was in danger of death. In this case, my knowledge of my friend's fear cannot refer to any state of his body, for I know nothing of that; my knowledge concerns itself immediately with my friend's sensation of fear."

*Rebuttal.* Psychologists are not yet unanimously decided on the degree to which they ought properly to credit the occurrence of cases of telepathy. This is an empirical problem which it is not our business to solve here. Let us concede the point to our critic, and assume that the occurrence of cases of telepathic transmission has been confirmed. We shall show that, even so, our earlier contentions are not affected in the least. The question before us is: what does sentence $P_1$, "My friend now experiences fear," mean, if I take $P_1$ to be a statement of telepathically derived cognition? We maintain that the meaning of $P_1$ is precisely the same as it would be if we used it on the grounds of some normally (rationally or intuitively) derived cognition. The occurrence of telepathy in no way alters the meaning of $P_1$.

Let us consider a precisely analogous situation involving the cognition of some physical event. I suddenly have the impression that a picture has fallen from the wall at my house, and this when neither I nor anyone else can in any normal way perceive that this has happened. Later, I discover that the picture has, indeed, fallen from the wall. I now express this cognition which I have obtained by clairvoyance in sentence Q, "The picture has now fallen from the wall." What is the meaning of this sentence? The meaning of Q here is clearly the same as it would be if I used it on the ground of some normally derived cognition, that is, on the ground of some cognition by direct perception of the event in question. For in both cases Q asserts that a physical event of a certain sort, a specific displacement of a specific body, has taken place.

The case is the same with telepathic cognition. We have already considered the case in which the state of some other mind is intuitively grasped, though by means of a perception of the other person's body. If a telepathic cognition of the state of some other mind occurs, it too is based on an intuitive impression, this time without a simultaneous perception. That which is cognized, however, is the same in both cases. Earlier, we remarked that $P_1$ does not have the same content as the protocol sentence $p_2$ about the (normally) intuitive impression, and that $p_2$ cannot support a sentence about something beside or behind the physical condition of the other person's body. Our remarks hold equally for telepathically intuitive impressions.

D. *Objection on the ground of statements by others.* "We are, to begin with, agreed that A is in a certain physical state which is manifested by behavior of a certain sort and produces in me, apart from sense-perceptions, an intuitive impression of A's anger. Beyond this, however, I can find out that A really does experience anger by questioning him. He himself will testify that he experienced anger. Knowing him to be a truthful person and a good observer, why should I not consider his statement to be true—or at least probably true?"

*Rebuttal.* Before I can decide whether I should accept A's statement as true, or false, or probably true—before, indeed, I can consider this question at all—I must first of all understand the statement. It must have meaning for me. And this is the case only if I can test it, if, that is, sentences of my protocol are deducible from it. If the expression is interpreted physically, it is testable by means of protocol sentences such as my $p_1$ and $p_2$, that is, by sentences about specific perceptions and intuitive expressions. Since, however, our critic rejects the physical interpretation of the expression, it is in principle impossible for me to test it. Thus it is meaningless for me, and the question whether I should consider it to be true, or false, or probable, cannot even be posed.

Should unusual, brilliant patterns suddenly appear in the sky—even if they took the form of letters which seemed to compose a sentence—science could not comprehend them except by first conceiving them, describing them, and explaining them (i.e., subsuming them under general causal-sentences) as physical facts. The question whether such an arrangement of symbols constitutes a meaningful sentence must be decided without taking into consideration whether or not it appears in the sky. If this symbol-arrangement is not a meaningful sentence at other times, it cannot become one no matter how effulgent an appearance it makes in the sky. Whether a sentence is true or false is determined by empirical contingencies; but whether a sentence is or is not meaningful is determined solely by the syntax of language.

It is no different in the case of those acoustic phenomena that issue from the mouths of certain vertebrates. They are first of all facts, physical occurrences, and specifically, sound waves of a certain sort. We can, further, also interpret them as symbols. But whether or not such an arrangement of symbols is meaningful cannot depend on its occurrence as an acoustic phenomenon. If the sentence "A was angry yesterday at noon" has no meaning for me—as would be the case if (insofar as our critic rejects its physical meaning) I could not test it—it will not be rendered meaningful by the fact that a sound having the structure of this sentence came from A's own mouth.

But—it will be asked—do we not need the statements of our fellowmen for the elaboration of inter-subjective science? Would not physics, geography, and history become very meager studies if I had to restrict myself in them to occurrences which I myself had directly observed? There is no denying that they would. But there is a basic difference between a statement by A about the geography of China or about some historical event in the past on the one hand, and, on the other, a statement by A about the anger he felt yesterday. I can, in principle, test the statements of the first sort by means of perception sentences of my own protocol, sentences about my own perceptions of China, or of some map, or of historical documents. It is, however, in principle impossible for me to test the statement about anger if our critic asks me to reject the physical meaning of the sentence. If I have often had occasion to note that the geographical or historical reports that A makes can be confirmed by me, then, on the basis of an inductive probability inference, I consider myself justified in using his other statements—insofar as they are meaningful to me—in the elaboration of my scientific knowledge. It is in this way that inter-subjective science is developed. A sentence, however, which is not testable and hence not meaningful prior to its statement by A is not any the more meaningful after such a statement. If, in accordance with our position, I construe A's statement about yesterday's anger as a statement about the physical condition of A's body yesterday, this statement *may* be used for the development of inter-subjective science. For we use A's sentence as evidence (just to the extent to which we have found A to be trustworthy) in support of the attribution of a corresponding physical structure to the corresponding spatio-temporal region of our physical world. Neither do the consequences which we draw from this attribution generically differ from those that are obtained from any other physical statement. We build our expectations of future perceptions on it—in this case with respect to A's behavior, as in other cases with respect to the behavior of other physical systems.

The assertions of our fellow men contribute a great deal to extending the range of our knowledge. But they cannot bring us anything *basically* new, that is, anything which cannot also be learned in some other way. For the assertions of our fellow men are, at bottom, no different from other physical events. Physical events are different from one another as regards the extent to which they may be used as signs of other physical events. Those physical events which we call "assertions of our fellow man" rank particularly high on this scale. It is for this reason that science, quite rightly, treats these events with special consideration. However, between the contribution of these assertions to our scientific knowledge and the contributions of a barometer there is, basically, at most a difference of degree.

## 5. Behaviorism and "Intuitive" Psychology

The position we are advocating here coincides in its broad outlines with the psychological movement known as "behaviorism"—when, that is, its epistemological principles rather than its special methods are considered. We have not linked our exposition with a statement of behaviorism since our only concern is with epistemological foundations while behaviorism is above all else interested in a specific method of research and in specific concept formations.

The advocates of behaviorism were led to their position through their concern with animal psychology. In this domain, when the material given to observation does not include statements but only inarticulate behavior, it is most easy to arrive at the correct method of approach. This approach leads one to the correct interpretation of the statements of human experimental subjects, for it suggests that these statements are to be conceived as acts of verbalizing behavior, basically no different from other behavior.

Behaviorism is confronted with views, more influential in Germany than in the United States, which uphold the thesis that psychology's concern is not with behavior in its physical aspect, but rather, with *meaningful behavior*. For the comprehension of meaningful behavior the special method known as "intuitive understanding" ("Verstehen") is said to be required. Physics allegedly knows nothing of this method. Neither meaningful behavior considered collectively nor the individual instances of such behavior which psychology investigates can possibly—so it is maintained—be characterized in terms of physical concepts.

In intuitive psychology this view is generally linked with the view that beside physical behavior there is yet another, psychical event, which constitutes the true subject-matter of psychology, and to which intuitive understanding leads. We do not want to consider this idea any further here, since we have already thoroughly examined it.

But even after one puts this idea aside, intuitive psychology poses the following objection to physicalism.

*Objection based on the occurrence of "meaningful behavior."* "When psychology considers the behavior of living creatures (we disregard here the question whether it deals only with such behavior), it is interested in it as meaningful behavior. This aspect of behavior cannot, however, be grasped in terms of physical concepts, but only by means of the method of intuitive understanding. And this is why psychological sentences cannot be translated into physical sentences."

*Rebuttal.* Let us recall a previous example of the *physicalization* of an intuitive impression, i.e., of a qualitative designation in the protocol language.[4] We there showed that it is possible by investigating optical state-coordinates, to determine the entirety of those physical conditions which correspond to "green of this specific sort" and to subsume them under laws. The same is the case here. It simply depends on the physical nature of an act—say, of an arm-movement—whether I can intuitively understand it—as, say, a beckoning motion—or not. Consequently, physicalization is possible here too. The class of arm-movements to which the protocol-designation "beckoning motion" corresponds can be determined, and then described in terms of physical concepts. But perhaps doubts may be raised as to whether the classification of arm-movements as intelligible or unintelligible, and, further, the classification of intelligible arm-movements as beckoning motions or others really depends, as our thesis claims, solely on the physical constitution of the arms, the rest of the body, and the environment. Such doubts are readily removed if, for instance, one thinks of films. We understand the *meaning* of the action on the movie screen.

[4] *Erkenntnis*, II, 444ff. (*The Unity of Science*, pp. 58ff.).

And our understanding would doubtless be the same if, instead of the film presented, another which resembled it in every physical particular were shown. Thus one can see that both our understanding of meaning and the particular forms it takes are, in effect, completely determined by the physical processes impinging on our sense-organs (in the film example, those impinging on our optic and auditory sense-organs).

The problem of physicalization in this area, that is, the problem of the characterization of *understandable* behavior as such and of the various kinds of such behavior by means of concepts of systematized physics, is not as yet solved. But does not then our basic thesis rest on air? It states that all psychological sentences can be translated into physical sentences. One may well ask to what extent such a translation is possible, given the present state of our knowledge. Even today every sentence of psychology *can* be translated into a sentence which refers to the physical behavior of living creatures. In such a physical characterization terms do indeed occur which have not yet been physicalized, i.e., reduced to the concepts of physical science. Nevertheless, the concepts used *are* physical concepts, though of a primitive sort—just as "warm" and "green" (applied to bodies) were physical concepts before one could express them in terms of physical state-coordinates (temperature and electro-magnetic field, respectively).

We should like, again, to make the matter clear by using a *physical example*. Let us suppose that we have found a substance whose electrical conductivity is noticeably raised when it is irradiated by various types of electro-magnetic radiation. We do not yet, however, know the internal structure of this substance and so cannot yet explain its behavior. We want to call such a substance a "detector" for radiation of the sort involved. Let us suppose, further, that we have not yet systematically determined to what sorts of radiation the detector reacts. We now discover that the sorts of radiation to which it responds share still another characteristic, say, that they accelerate specific chemical reactions. Now suppose that we are interested in the photo-chemical effects of various sorts of radiation, but that the determination of these effects, in the case of a specific sort of radiation, is difficult and time-consuming, while the determination of the detector's reaction to it is easy and quickly accomplished; then we shall find it useful to adopt the detector as a test-instrument. With its aid we can determine for any particular sort of radiation whether or not it is likely to have the desired photo-chemical effect. This practical application will not be impeded by our ignorance of the detector's micro-structure and our inability to explain its reaction in physical terms. In spite of our ignorance, we can certainly say that the detector isolates a certain physically specified class of rays. The objection that this is not a physical class since we cannot characterize it by a specification of optical state-coordinates but only by the behavior of the detector will not stand. For to begin with, we know that if we carried out a careful empirical investigation of the electro-magnetic spectrum, we could identify the class of rays to which the detector responds. On the basis of this identification we could then physicalize the characterization of the rays in terms of detector-reactions, by substituting for it a characterization in terms of systematic physical concepts. But even our present way of characterizing the radiation in terms of the detector-test is a physical characterization, though an indirect one. It is distinguished from the direct characterization which is our goal only through being more circumstantial. There is no difference of kind between the two characterizations, only one of degree, though the difference of degree is indeed sufficiently great to give us a motive for pursuing the empirical investigations which might bring the direct physical characterization within our grasp.

Whether *the detector is organic or inorganic* is irrelevant to the epistemological issue involved. The function of the detector is basically the same whether we are dealing with a physical detector of specific sorts of radiation or with a tree-frog as a detector of certain meteorological states of affairs or (if one may believe the newspapers) with a sniffing dog as a detector of certain human diseases. People take a practical interest in meteorological forecasts. Where barometers are not available they may, consequently, use a tree-frog for the same purpose. But let us be clear about the fact that this method does not determine the state of the tree-frog's soul, but a physically specified weather condition, even if one cannot describe this condition in terms of the concepts of systematized physics. People, likewise, have a practical interest in medical diagnoses. When the directly determinable symptoms do not suffice, they may, consequently, enlist a dog's delicate sense of smell for the purpose. It is clear to the doctor that, in doing so, he is not determining the state of the dog's soul, but a physically specified condition of his patient's body. The doctor may not be able, given the present state of physiological knowledge, to characterize the diseased condition in question in terms of the concepts of systematic physics. Nonetheless, he knows that his diagnosis—whether it is based on the symptoms he himself has directly observed or on the reactions of the diagnostic dog— determines nothing and can determine nothing but the physical condition of his patient. Even apart from this, the physiologist acknowledges the need for physicalization. This would here consist in describing the bodily condition in question, i.e., defining the disease involved in purely physiological terms (thus eliminating any mention of the dog's reaction). A further task would be to trace these back to chemical terms, and these, in turn, to physical ones.

The case with *intuitive psychology* is precisely analogous. The situation here happens to be complicated for epistemological analysis (though for psychological practice it is simplified) by the fact that in the examination of an experimental subject the intuitive psychologist is both the observer and detector. The doctor here is his own diagnostic dog; which, indeed, is also often the case in medical diagnoses—in their intuitive phases. The psychologist calls the behavior of the experimental subject "understandable" or, in a special case, for instance, "a nod of affirmation," when his detector responds to it, or—in our special case—when it results in his protocols registering "A nods affirmatively." Science is not a system of experiences, but of sentences; it does not include the psychologist's experience of understanding, but rather, his protocol sentence. The utterance of the psychologist's protocol sentence is a reaction whose epistemological function is analogous to the tree-frog's climbing and to the barking of the diagnostic dog. To be sure, the psychologist far surpasses these animals in the variety of his reactions. As a result, he is certainly very valuable to the pursuit of science. But this constitutes only a difference of degree, not a difference of kind.

In the light of these considerations, two demands are to be made of the psychologist. First, we shall expect him (as we expect the doctor) to be clear about the fact that, in spite of his complicated diagnostic reaction, he establishes nothing but the existence of some specific physical condition of the experimental subject, though a condition which can be characterized only indirectly—by his own diagnostic reaction. Secondly, he must acknowledge (as the physiologist does) that it is a task of scientific research to find a way of physicalizing the indirect characterization. Psychology must determine what are the physical conditions to which people's detector-reactions correspond. When this is carried out for every reaction of this sort, i.e., for every result of intuitive understanding, psychological concept formation can be physicalized. The indirect definitions based on detector-reactions will be replaced by direct definitions in terms of the concepts of systematized physics. Psychology, like the other sciences, must and will reach the level of development at which it can replace the tree-frog by the barometer. But even in the tree-frog stage psychology already uses physical language, though of a primitive sort.

### 6. Physicalization in Graphology

The purpose of this section is not to justify physicalism, but only to show how psychological concepts can in fact be physicalized. To this end we shall examine a branch of psychology in which physicalization has already been undertaken with some success. In doing so we may perhaps also meet the criticism which is occasionally voiced, that the achievement of physicalization, assuming it were possible, would in any case be fruitless and uninteresting. It is held that given sufficient information concerning the social group and the circumstances of the people involved, one might perhaps be able to specify arm-movements which are interpreted as beckoning motions in such a way that they would be characterizable in terms of kinematic (i.e., spatio-temporal) concepts. But it is alleged that this procedure would not provide us with any further insight into anything of interest, least of all into the connections of these with other events.

Remarkably enough, physicalization can show significant success in a branch of psychology which until comparatively recent times was pursued in a purely intuitive (or at most a pseudo-rational) manner and with wholly inadequate empirical data, so that it then had no claim to scientific status. This is graphology. Theoretical graphology—we shall concern ourselves here with no other sort—investigates the law-like relationships which hold between the formal properties of a person's handwriting and those of his psychological properties that are commonly called his "character."

We must first of all explain what is meant by *character* in physical psychology. Every psychological property is marked out as a disposition to behave in a certain way. By "actual property" we shall understand a property which is defined by characteristics that can be directly observed: by "disposition" (or "dispositional concept") we shall understand a property which is defined by means of an implication (a conditional relationship, an if-then sentence). Examples of familiar dispositional concepts of physics may serve to illustrate this distinction, and will, at the same time, illustrate the distinction between occurrent and continuant properties, a distinction which is important in psychology. An example of a physical *occurrent prop-*

95

*erty* is a specific degree of temperature. We define "Body K has temperature T" to mean "When a sufficiently small quantity of mercury is brought into contact with K, then . . ." When defined in this way, the concept of temperature is a dispositional concept. Now that physics has disclosed the micro-structure of matter and determined the laws of molecular motion, a different definition of temperature is used: temperature is the mean kinetic energy of molecules. Here, then, temperature is no longer a dispositional concept, but an actual property. The *occurrent properties of psychology* are logically analogous to the familiar dispositional concepts of physics. Indeed, on our view, they are themselves nothing else than physical concepts. Example: "Person X is excited" means "If, now, stimuli of such and such a sort were applied, X would react in such and such a manner" (both stimuli and reactions being physical events). Here too the aim of science is to change the form of the definition; more accurate insight into the micro-structure of the human body should enable us to replace dispositional concepts by actual properties. That this is not a utopian aim is shown by the fact that even at the present time, a more accurate knowledge of physiological macro-events has yielded us a set of actual characteristics of occurrent states (e.g., for feelings of various sorts: frequency and intensity of pulse and respiration, glandular secretion, innervation of visceral muscles, etc.). Such a change of definitions is markedly more difficult when the states which have to be delimited are not emotional, for it then presupposes a knowledge of the micro-structure of the central nervous system which far surpasses the knowledge currently available.

Physical constants, e.g., heat-conductivity, coefficient of refraction, etc., might be taken as examples of physical *continuant properties*. These too were originally defined as dispositional concepts, e.g., "A substance has a coefficient of refraction n" means "If a ray of light enters the substance, then . . ." Here again the aim of transforming the definition has already been achieved for some concepts, and is being pursued in the

96

case of the remainder. The reference to dispositions gives way to an actual designation of the composition (in terms of atoms and electrons) of the substance in question. The *psychological continuant properties* or "character properties" (the word "character" is here being used in a broad, neutral sense—to mean more than volitional or attitudinal properties) can, at present, be defined only in the form of dispositional concepts. Example: "X is more impressionable than Y" means "If both X and Y have the same experience under the same circumstances, more intense feelings are experienced by X than by Y." In these definitions, both in the characterization of the stimuli (the statement of the circumstances) and in that of the reaction, there are names which still designate psychological occurrent properties, for which the problem of physicalization has not yet been solved. To physicalize the designations of continuant properties will be possible only when the designations of occurrent properties have been dealt with. So long as these are not completely physicalized, the physicalization of continuant properties and, as a result, that of characterology as a whole, must remain in a scientifically incomplete state, and this no matter how rich our stock of intuitive knowledge may be.

There is no sharp division between occurrent and continuant designations. Nonetheless, the difference of degree is large enough to justify their being differently labelled and differently treated, and, consequently, large enough to justify the separaration of characterology from psychology as a whole (considered as the theory of behavior). Graphology sets itself the task of finding in the features of a person's handwriting indications of his character and, to some extent, of his occurrent properties. The practicing graphologist does not intend the rational method to replace intuition, but only to support or to correct it. It has, however, become clear that the pursuit of the task of physicalization will serve even this purpose. Along these lines graphology has already, of late, made some significant discoveries.

Since the problem of graphology is to discover the corre-

spondences holding between the properties of a person's handwriting and those of his character, we may here divide the
problem of physicalization into three parts. The physicalization
of the properties of handwriting constitutes the *first part of the
problem*. A certain script gives me, for instance, an intuitive
impression of something full and juicy. In saying so, I do not
primarily refer to characteristics of the writer, but to characteristics of his script. The problem now is to replace intuitively
identified script-properties of this sort by properties of the
script's shape, i.e., by properties which may be defined with
the aid of geometrical concepts. That this problem can be
solved is clear. We need only thoroughly investigate the system
of forms which letters, words, and lines of script might possibly
take in order to determine which of these forms make the intuitive impression in question on us. So, for instance, we might
find that a script appears full or two-dimensional (as opposed
to thin or linear) if rounded connections are more frequent
than angles, the loops broader than normal, the strokes thicker,
etc. This task of the physicalization of the properties of handwriting has in many cases been accomplished to a large extent.[5] We are not objecting to the retention of the intuitively
derived descriptions (in terms, for instance, of "full," "delicate," "dynamic," etc.). Our requirement will be adequately
met as soon as a definition in exclusively geometric terms is
provided for each such description. This problem is precisely
analogous to the problem, to which we have frequently referred, of identifying in quantitative terms those physical conditions which correspond to a qualitative designation—such as
"green of such and such a sort"—in the protocol language.

The *second part of the problem* consists of the physicalization of the character properties referred to in graphological
analyses. The traditional concepts of characterology—whose
meaning is as a rule not clearly defined, but left to be expressed
in our everyday vocabulary or by means of metaphorical lan-

[5] *Cf.* L. Klages, *Handschrift und Character* (Leipzig, 1920). Several of our
examples are taken from this book or suggested by it.

guage—have to be systematized and given physicalistic (behavioristic) definitions. We have already seen that such a definition refers to a disposition to behave in a certain way, and further, that the task of the construction of such definitions is difficult and presupposes the physicalization of psychological occurrent properties.

We can see that in both parts of the problem the task is one of replacing primitive, intuitive concept formations by systematic ones, of replacing the observer with a tree-frog by the observer with a barometer (in graphology, as in intuitive medical diagnoses, the observer and the tree-frog coincide).

In addition to these questions there is a *third aspect of the problem* to be considered: the basic empirical task of graphology. This consists of the search for the correlations which hold between the properties of handwriting and those of character. Here too a systematization, though of a different sort, takes place. The correspondence of a specific property of handwriting to a specific property of character may, at first, be recognized intuitively—for instance, as a result of an empathetic reflection on the arm-movements which produced the script in question. The problem of systematization here is to determine the degree of correlation of the two properties by a statistical investigation of many instances of script of the type in question and the characters of the corresponding writers.

Our position now is that the further development and clarification of the concepts of psychology as a whole must take the direction we have illustrated in our examination of graphology, the direction, that is, of physicalization. But, as we have already emphasized several times, psychology is a physical science even prior to such a clarification of its concepts—a physical science whose assignment it is to describe systematically the (physical) behavior of living creatures, especially that of human beings, and to develop laws under which this behavior may be subsumed. These laws are of quite diverse sorts. A hand-movement, for instance, may be examined from various aspects: first, semiotically, as a more or less conventional sign for some designated state of affairs; secondly, mimically, as an expression of the contemporaneous psychological state—the occurrent properties of the person in question; thirdly, physiognomically, as an expression of the continuant properties— the character of the person in question. In order to investigate, say, the hand-movements of people (of certain groups) in their mimical and physiognomic aspects one might perhaps take motion pictures of them, and, from these, derive kinematic diagrams of the sort which engineers construct for machine parts. In this manner the shared kinematic (i.e., spatio-temporal) characteristics of the hand-movements with whose perception certain intuitive protocol designations tend to be associated (e.g., "This hand-movement looks rushed," ". . . grandiose," etc.) would have to be determined. It will now be clear why precisely graphology—the characterological investigation of writing movements, a very special sort of hand-movement, identifiable in terms of their specific purpose—should be the only study of this sort which can as yet show any results. The reason is that writing movements themselves produce something resembling kinematic diagrams, namely, the letters on the paper. To be sure, only the track of the movements is drawn. The passage of time is not recorded—the graphologist can subsequently only infer this, imperfectly, from indirect signs. More accurate results would be demonstrable if the complete three-dimensional spatio-temporal diagram, not only its projection on the writing plane, were available. But even the conclusions to which graphology currently subscribes allay whatever misgivings there might have been that investigations directed at the physicalization of psychological concepts would prove to be uninteresting. It may not even be too rash a conjecture that interesting parallels may be found to hold between the conclusions of characterological investigations of both the involuntary and the voluntary motions of the various parts of the human body on the one hand, and on the other hand, the conclusions of graphology which are already available to us. If specific properties of a person's character express themselves both in a specific form of handwriting and in a specific form of arm motion, a specific form of leg motion, specific facial features, etc., might not these various forms resemble one another? Perhaps, after having first given fruitful suggestions for the investigation of other sorts of bodily movements, graphology may, in turn, be stimulated by the results to examine script properties it had previously overlooked. These, of course, are mere conjectures; whether or not they are justifiable cannot affect the tenability of our thesis, which maintains the possibility of translating all psychological sentences into physical language. This translatability holds regardless of whether or not the concepts of psychology are physicalized. Physicalization is simply a higher-level, more rigorously systematized scientific form of concept formation. Its accomplishment is a practical problem which concerns the psychologist rather than the epistemologist.

### 7. Sentences about One's Own Mind; "Introspective Psychology"

Our argument has shown that a sentence about other minds refers to physical processes in the body of the person in question. On any other interpretation the sentence becomes untestable in principle, and thus meaningless. The situation is the same with sentences about one's own mind, though here the emotional obstacles to a physical interpretation are considerably greater. The relationship of a sentence about one's own mind to one about someone else's may most readily be seen with respect to a sentence about some *past state* of one's own mind, e.g., $P_1$: "I was excited yesterday." The testing of this sentence involves either a *rational* inference from protocol sentences of the form of $p_1$—which refer to presently perceived script, photographs, films, etc. originating with me yesterday; or it involves an *intuitive* method, e.g., utilizing the protocol sentence $p_2$, "I recall having been excited yesterday." The content of $P_1$ exceeds both that of the protocol sentence $p_1$ and that of the protocol sentence $p_2$, as is most clearly indicated by the possibility of error and disavowal where $P_1$ is concerned. $P_1$ can only be progressively better confirmed by sets of protocol sentences of the form of $p_1$ and $p_2$. The very same protocol sentences, however, also confirm the physical sentence $P_2$: "My body was yesterday in that physical condition which one tends to call 'excitement.'" $P_1$ has, consequently, the same content as the physical sentence $P_2$.

In the case of a sentence about the *present state* of one's own mind, e.g., $P_1$: "I now am excited," one must clearly distinguish between the system sentence $P_1$ and the protocol sentence $p_2$, which, likewise, may read "I now am excited." The difference rests in the fact that the system sentence $P_1$ may, under certain circumstances, be disavowed, whereas a protocol sentence, being an epistemological point of departure, cannot be rejected. The protocol sentences $p_1$ which rationally support $P_1$ have here some such form as "I feel my hands trembling," "I see my hands trembling," "I hear my voice quavering," etc. Here too the content of $P_1$ exceeds that of both $p_1$ and $p_2$, in that it subsumes all the possible sentences of this sort. $P_1$ has the same content as the physical sentence $P_2$, "My body is now in that condition which, both under my own observation and that of others, exhibits such and such characteristics of excitement," the characteristics in question being those which are mentioned both in my own protocol sentences of the sort of $p_1$ and $p_2$ and in other people's protocol sentences of corresponding sorts (discussed above in our example of sentences about other minds).

The table below shows the analogous application of the physicalist thesis to the three cases we have discussed by exhibiting the parallelism of sentences about other minds, sentences about some past condition of one's own mind, and sentences about the present condition of one's own mind, with the physical sentence about the wooden support.

*Objection from introspective psychology.* "When the psychologist is not investigating other experimental subjects, but pursues self-observation, or 'introspection,' instead, he grasps, in a direct manner, something nonphysical—and this is the proper subject-matter of psychology."

*Rebuttal.* We must distinguish between a question of the justification of the use of some prevalent practical method of inquiry and a question of the justification of some prevalent interpretation of the results of that method. *Every* method of inquiry is justified; disputes can arise only over the question of the purpose and fruitfulness of a given method, which is a question our problem does not involve. We may apply any method we choose; we cannot, however, interpret the obtained sentences as we choose. The meaning of a sentence, no matter how obtained, can unequivocally be determined by a logical analysis of the way in which it is derived and tested. A psychologist who adopts the method of what is called "introspection" does not thereby expose himself to criticism. Such a psychologist admits sentences of the form "I have experienced such and such events of consciousness" into his experiment-protocol and then arrives at general conclusions of his own by means of inductive generalization, the construction of hypotheses, and, finally, a comparison of his hypotheses with the conclusions of other persons. But again we must conclude, both on logical and epistemological grounds, that the singular as well as the general sentences must be interpreted physically. Let us say that psychologist A writes sentence $p_2$: "(I am) now excited" into his protocol. An earlier investigation [6] has shown that the view which holds that protocol sentences cannot be physically interpreted, that, on the contrary, they refer to something nonphysical (something "psychical," some "experience-content," some "datum of consciousness," etc.) leads directly to the consequence that every protocol sentence is meaningful only to its author. If A's protocol sentence $p_2$ were not subject to a physical interpretation, it could not be tested by B, and would, thus, be meaningless to B. On the previous occasion in question we showed, further, that the nonphysical interpretation leads one into insoluble contra-

[6] *Erkenntnis*, II, 454 (*The Unity of Science*, pp. 78–79).

dictions. Finally, we found that every protocol sentence has the same content as some physical sentence,[7] and that this physical translation does not presuppose an accurate knowledge of the physiology of the central nervous system, but is feasible even at present. Sentences about one's own mind—whether one takes these to be inter-subjective system sentences or so-called introspective protocol sentences—are thus in every case translatable into sentences of the physical language.

One may perhaps object that there is, after all, a difference between an experience and an utterance about it, and that not every experience has to be expressed in a protocol sentence. The difference referred to certainly exists, though we would formulate it differently. Sentences $P_1$: "A now sees red," and $P_2$: "A now says 'I see red,'" do not have exactly the same content. Nor does $P_1$ justify the inference of $P_2$; only the conditional sentence "If this and that occurs, then $P_2$" may be inferred. For $P_1$ ascribes a physical state to A of such a kind that, under certain circumstances, it leads to the event of speaking the sentence referred to in $P_2$.

If we consider the method in accordance with which the conclusions of so-called introspection are generally integrated with the body of scientific knowledge, we shall note that these conclusions are, indeed, physically evaluated. It so happens that the physicalism adopted in practice is generally not acknowledged in theory. Psychologist A announces his experimental results; reader B reads in them, among others, the sentence "A was excited" (for the sake of clarity we write "A" instead of the word "I" which B in reading must replace by "A"). For B, this is a sentence about someone else's mind; nothing of its claim can be verified except that A's body *was* in such and such a physical condition at the time referred to. (We argued this point in our analysis of sentence $P_1$ about someone else's mind.) B himself could not, indeed, have observed this condition, but he can now indirectly infer its having existed. For, to begin with, he sees the sentence in question in a book

[7] *Ibid.*, pp. 457ff. (*The Unity of Science*, pp. 84ff.).

| | 1. Sentence about the Wooden Support (As an Analogy) | 2. Sentence about the State of Someone Else's Mind | 3. Sentence about the State of One's Own Mind at Some Time in the Past | 4. Sentence about the Present State of One's Own Mind |
|---|---|---|---|---|
| *System sentence* $P_1$: a) *rationally* derived from protocol sentence $p_1$: | "The support is firm" | "A is excited" | "I was excited yesterday" | "I am now excited" |
| or b) *intuitively* derived from protocol sentence $p_2$: | "The support has such and such a color and shape" | "A has such and such an expression" | "These letters (written by me yesterday) have such and such a shape" | "My hands are now trembling" |
| $P_1$ has the same content as the *physical sentence* $P_2$: | "The support looks firm" | "A is excited (A looks excited)" | "Now a recollection of excitement" | "Now excited" |
| | "The support is physically firm" | "A's body is physically excited" | "My body was physically excited yesterday." | "My body is now physically excited" |
| The physical term: is hereby defined as a disposition to react under certain circumstances in a specified way: | "physically firm" | "physically excited" | | |
| | "Under such and such a load, such and such a distortion occurs; under such and such a load, breakage occurs" | "Under such and such circumstances, such and such gestures, expressions, actions, and words occur." | | |

on whose title-page A is identified as the author. Now, on the basis of a general sentence for which he has already obtained indirect evidence, B infers (with some degree of probability) that A wrote the sentences printed in this book; from this, in its turn, on the basis of a general sentence, with regard to A's reliability, for which he again has good inductive evidence, B infers that, had he observed A's body at the relevant time he would (probably) have been able to confirm the existence of the state of (physical) excitement. Since this confirmation can refer only to some physical state of A's body, the sentence in question can have only a physical meaning for B.

Generally speaking, a psychologist's spoken, written, or printed protocol sentences, when they are based on so-called introspection, are to be interpreted by the reader, and so figure in inter-subjective science, *not chiefly as scientific sentences, but as scientific facts.* The epistemological confusion of contemporary psychology stems, to a large extent, from this confusion of facts in the form of sentences with the sentences themselves considered as parts of science. (Our example of the patterns in the sky is relevant here.) The introspective statements of a psychologist are not, in principle, to be interpreted any differently from the statements of his experimental subjects, which he happens to be reporting. The only distinction the psychologist enjoys is that, when the circumstances justify it, one may accept his statement as those of an exceptionally reliable and well-trained experimental subject. Further, the statements of an experimental subject are not, in principle, to be interpreted differently from his other voluntary or involuntary movements—though his speech movements may, under favorable circumstances, be regarded as especially informative. Again, the movements of the speech organs and of the other parts of the body of an experimental subject are not, in principle, to be interpreted differently from the movements of any other animal—though the former may, under favorable circumstances, be more valuable in the construction of general sentences. The movements of an animal are not, again, in principle, to be interpreted any differently from those of a volt-meter—though under favorable circumstances, animal movements may serve scientific purposes in more ways than do the movements of a volt-meter. Finally, the movements of a volt-meter are not, in principle, to be interpreted differently from the movements of a raindrop—though the former offer more opportunities for drawing inferences to other occurrences than do the latter. In all these cases, the issue is basically the same: from a specific physical sentence, other sentences are inferred by a causal argument, i.e., with the help of general physical formulae—the so-called natural laws. The examples cited differ only in the degree of fruitfulness of their premises. Volt-meter readings will, perhaps, justify the inference of a greater number of scientifically important sentences than the behavior of some specific raindrop will; speech movements will, in a certain respect, justify more such inferences than other human bodily movements will. Now, in the case with which we are concerned here, the inference from the sign to the state of affairs signified has a quite remarkable form. In using someone's introspective statement about the state of his own mind (e.g., A's statement: "A is excited"), the statement, taken as an acoustic event, is the sign; under favorable conditions, which are frequently satisfied in scientific contexts, the state of affairs referred to is such that it can be described by a sentence ("A is excited") of the very same form as the acoustic event which functions as a sign of it. [The requisite conditions are that the person in question be considered reliable and qualified to make psychological reports, and further that the language of these reports be the same as that of the scientific system.] This identity of the form of the acoustic fact and the scientific sentence which is to be inferred from it explains why the two are so easily and so obstinately confused. The disastrous muddle into which this confusion leads us is cleared up as soon as we realize that here, as in the other cases cited, it is only a question of drawing an inference from a sign to that which it indicates.

It becomes all the more clear that so-called introspective

statements cannot be given a nonphysical interpretation when we consider how their use is learned. A tired child says "Now I am happy to be in bed." If we investigated how the child learned to talk about the states of his own mind, we would discover that, under similar circumstances, his mother had said to him, "Now you are happy to be in bed." Thus we see that A learns to use the protocol sentence $p_2$ from B—who, however, interprets this series of words as constituting the system sentence $P_2$, a sentence, for B, about someone else's mind. Learning to talk consists of B's inducing a certain habit in A, a habit of "verbalizing" (as the behaviorists put it) in a specific manner in specific circumstances. And, indeed one tends so to direct this habit that the series of words produced by the speech movements of the child A coincides with the sentence of the inter-subjective physical language which not only describes the appropriate state of A, but—and this is the essential point—describes A's state *as B perceives it,* that is, the physical state of A's body. The example of the child shows this especially clearly. The sentence "You are happy," spoken by the mother, is a sentence about someone else's mind, and thus, according to our earlier analysis, can designate nothing but some physical state of affairs. The child is thus induced to develop the habit of responding to specific circumstances by uttering a sentence which expresses a physical state observed by some other person (or inferred by some other person from observed signs). If the child utters the same sounds again on some other occasion, no more can be inferred than that the child's body is again in that physical state.

### 8. Summary

So-called psychological sentences—whether they are concrete sentences about other minds, or about some past condition of one's own mind, or about the present condition of one's own mind, or, finally, general sentences—are always translatable into physical language. Specifically, every psychological sentence refers to physical occurrences in the body of the person (or persons) in question. On these grounds, psychology is a part of the domain of unified science based on physics. By "physics" we wish to mean, not the system of currently known physical laws, but rather the science characterized by a mode of concept formation which traces every concept back to state-coordinates, that is, to systematic assignments of numbers to space-time points. Understanding "physics" in this way, we can rephrase our thesis—a particular thesis of physicalism—as follows: *psychology is a branch of physics.*

## Remarks by the Author (1957)

While I would still maintain the essential content of the main thesis of this article, I would today modify some special points. Perhaps the most important of them is the following. In the article I regarded a psychological term, say "excited," as designating a state characterized by the disposition to react to certain stimuli with overt behavior of certain kinds. This may be admissible for the psychological concepts of everyday language. But at least for those of scientific psychology, as also of other fields of science, it seems to me more in line with the actual procedure of scientists, to introduce them not as disposition concepts, but rather as theoretical concepts (sometimes called "hypothetical constructs"). This means that they are introduced as primitives by the postulates of a theory, and are connected with the terms of the observation language, which designate observable properties, by so-called rules of correspondence. This method is explained and discussed in detail in my article "The Methodological Character of Theoretical Concepts," in H. Feigl and M. Scriven, eds., *Minnesota Studies in the Philosophy of Science,* vol. I.

The main thesis of physicalism remains the same as before. It says that psychological statements, both those of everyday life and of scientific psychology, say something about the physical state of the person in question. It is different from the corresponding statements in terms of micro-physiology or micro-physics (which at the present stage of scientific development are not yet known, comp. § 4A above) by using the conceptual framework of psychology instead of those of the two other fields. To find the specific features of the correspondence will be an empirical task (comp. § 6, the third part of the procedure of physicalization). Once known, the correspondence can be expressed by empirical laws or, according to our present view, by theoretical postulates. Our present conception of physicalism, the arguments for it, and the development which led to it, are represented in the following two articles by Herbert Feigl: (1) "Physicalism, Unity of Science and the Foundations of Psychology," in P. A. Schilpp, ed., *The Philosophy of Rudolf Carnap* (Library of Living Philosophers); see also my reply to Feigl in the same volume; (2) "The 'Mental' and the 'Physical,'" in vol. II of *Minnesota Studies in the Philosophy of Science.*

# ABOUT BEHAVIORISM

## PAUL ZIFF

"One behaviorist meeting another on the street said 'You feel fine! How do I feel?'" This bad joke embodies two bad arguments against behaviorism. I want to explain why they are bad arguments.

1. I say "I am angry." My statement is true if and only if a certain organism is behaving in certain ways. If I say "George is angry," my statement is true if and only if a certain organism, viz. George, is behaving in certain ways. The only way I can tell whether or not George is angry is by observing George's behavior, verbal or otherwise. (There is nothing else to tell.) But I do not find out whether or not I am angry by observing my own behavior because I do not find out whether or not I am angry. (That I sometimes suddenly realize that I am or that I have become angry is essentially irrelevant here.) To talk of my finding out whether or not I am angry is generally odd: it would not be odd only in peculiar cases.

2. The first bad argument is not particularly interesting. It is this: if my being angry were a matter of my behaving in certain ways, then I should be able to find out whether or not

Reprinted by permission of the editor, from *Analysis*, XVIII (1957–58), 132–136.

I am angry for I can find out whether or not I am behaving in certain ways. Since it is generally odd to speak of my finding out whether or not I am angry, my being angry cannot be a matter of my behaving in certain ways. (Thus: "How do I feel?")

The mistake here is in the assumption that I can find out whether or not I am behaving in the relevant ways. A behaviorist maintains that to be angry is to behave in certain ways. I shall accordingly speak of "anger behavior" and of "anger behaving."

It is generally odd to speak of my finding out whether or not I am angry: it is neither more nor less odd to speak of my finding out whether or not I am anger behaving.

3. It is not always odd to speak of my finding out whether or not I am behaving in a certain way. Suppose I have my hands behind my back, my fingers intermeshed. I am asked to move the third finger of my left hand. I may not know whether or not I am in fact moving that finger. I may have to look in a mirror to find out. So it is not in every case odd to speak of my finding out whether or not I am behaving in a certain way. It does not follow that it is not sometimes odd.

I am at this moment talking, hence behaving in a certain way. It would be odd to speak of my finding out whether or not I am talking at this moment. No doubt one can think up cases in which it would not be odd to speak of my finding out whether or not I am talking. That is irrelevant. I am not talking about those cases: I am talking about this case, here and now, and here and now I cannot doubt that I am talking. (More can be said about this point, but I shall not try to say it here.)

It would generally be odd to speak of my finding out whether or not I am anger behaving, e.g., gnashing my teeth.

4. The second bad argument is more serious. It is this: if my being angry were a matter of my behaving in certain ways, then you should be able to find out whether or not I am angry for you can find out whether or not I am behaving in certain

ways. But sometimes you cannot find out whether or not I am angry. Since you can, in principle at least, always find out whether or not I am behaving in certain ways, my being angry cannot be a matter of my behaving in certain ways. (Thus: "You feel fine!")

The mistake here is in the assumption that there is a difference between your finding out whether or not I am anger behaving and your finding out whether or not I am angry. There is no difference.

5. You cannot in fact always find out whether or not I am angry. I may be artful at concealing my anger and I may refuse to tell you. Neither can you in fact always find out whether or not I am behaving in certain ways. You cannot in fact find out whether or not I am flexing my abdominal muscles. I will not tell you and no one else can.

So what you can or cannot in fact find out is beside the point. What is not beside the point?

6. "You can in principle if not in fact always find out whether or not I am behaving in certain ways. But you cannot even in principle always find out whether or not I am angry." This contention will not bear scrutiny.

(I will not cavil over the locution "you can in principle find out." I consider it an instrument of obfuscation. Even so, I shall let it pass: I believe I can more or less grasp what is intended.)

You can in principle always find out whether or not I am angry because I can tell you. Hence you need attend only to my verbal behavior. (I assume that it would generally be odd to speak of my being mistaken about whether or not I am angry.) To suppose that you cannot in principle find out whether or not I am angry would be to suppose that I cannot in principle tell you whether or not I am angry. I find such a supposition unintelligible.

7. The preceding contention can be reformulated as follows: "You can in principle if not in fact always find out whether or not I am behaving in certain ways. In some cases at

113

least, being angry does not involve verbal behavior. Let us restrict our attention to such cases. Then apart from my subsequent verbal behavior, you cannot even in principle always find out whether or not I am angry."

As I said before, I more or less grasp what is intended by the locution "you can in principle find out": I would not pretend I have a firm grasp. (One cannot have a firm grip on a jellyfish.) In so far as I can grasp what is intended, I am inclined to agree that apart from my subsequent verbal behavior you cannot even in principle always find out whether or not I am angry. But I deny that apart from my subsequent verbal behavior you can in principle always find out whether or not I am anger behaving.

8. Let us suppose that in a certain case my anger behavior consists, amongst other things, in my gnashing my teeth. If we are to suppose that apart from my subsequent verbal behavior you can in principle always find out whether or not I am anger behaving, then we must suppose that apart from my subsequent verbal behavior you can in principle always find out whether or not I am gnashing my teeth.

There is a difference between my gnashing my teeth and the gnashing of my teeth. It is conceivable that by supplying the appropriate stimuli directly to the appropriate muscles one could effect the gnashing of my teeth. In the kind of case I envisage, I could not truly say "I was gnashing my teeth" though I could truly say "My teeth were gnashing" and perhaps add "It felt queer."

I would not deny that apart from my subsequent verbal behavior you can in principle always find out whether or not my teeth are gnashing. But I deny that apart from my subsequent verbal behavior you can in principle always find out whether or not I am gnashing my teeth.

9. Can a behaviorist make a distinction between my gnashing my teeth and the gnashing of my teeth? I see no reason why not.

It is true that my teeth are gnashing if and only if it is true that certain teeth and jaws are moving in certain ways. But it is true that I am gnashing my teeth if and only if it is true that a certain organism is behaving in certain ways. If a certain organism is behaving in certain ways, then it may be the case that certain teeth and jaws are moving in certain ways. But the converse need not hold: it does not follow that if certain teeth and jaws are moving in certain ways, then a certain organism is behaving in certain ways.

10. There is a difference between someone gnashing his teeth and the gnashing of someone's teeth. But the difference is not a difference in behavior: only the former is an instance of behavior; the latter may be a component of behavior.

If George is gnashing his teeth, then George's teeth are gnashing. But whether or not a case in which his teeth are gnashing can rightly be characterized as a case in which he is gnashing his teeth depends (not on whether or not the gnashing of his teeth is accompanied by "a movement of the soul" but simply) on contextual and relational matters.

11. I said that whether or not a case in which George's teeth are gnashing can rightly be characterized as a case in which George is gnashing his teeth depends on contextual and relational matters. I am not saying "Whether or not a case in which my teeth are gnashing can rightly be characterized by me as a case in which I am gnashing my teeth depends on contextual and relational matters": that would be odd. It would indicate that I could in general answer the following generally odd question: "Given that your teeth are gnashing, what entitles you to say not merely that your teeth are gnashing but that you are gnashing your teeth, that you are doing it?" (I believe that Wittgenstein once said "The first mistake is to ask the question": the second is to answer it.)

What is in question here is what entitles you to say that I am gnashing my teeth and not merely that my teeth are gnashing. The question whether I am gnashing my teeth or whether my teeth are merely gnashing is a question for you, not for me. It would generally be odd for me to ask "Am I gnashing my teeth or are they merely gnashing?"

12. Whether or not a case in which my teeth are gnashing can rightly be characterized by you as a case in which I am gnashing my teeth depends on contextual and relational matters.

The teeth of a corpse may be gnashing but the corpse cannot (without oddity) be said to be gnashing its teeth. So I must be alive, I must behave in characteristic ways. What more is required? Primarily this: my subsequent behavior, both verbal and otherwise, must be consonant with the claim that I was in fact gnashing my teeth. This is not to say that if I assert "I was not gnashing my teeth," then I was not gnashing my teeth: I may be lying, or forgetful, or confused, etc. But my subsequent behavior, both verbal and otherwise, is clearly relevant.

Therefore I deny that apart from my subsequent verbal behavior you can in principle always find out whether or not I am gnashing my teeth. And in consequence I deny that there is a difference between finding out whether or not I am behaving in certain ways and finding out whether or not I am angry.

Philosophical behaviorism is not a metaphysical theory: it is the denial of a metaphysical theory. Consequently, it asserts nothing.

# III

*Identity*

# OTHER MINDS AND
# THE EGOCENTRIC PREDICAMENT

THE CONTINUING CONTROVERSIES concerning the problem of
other minds center about a perplexity which may be stated in
the following form: If we want to retain as cognitively significant the common beliefs in the occurrence of mental states in
other persons (and possibly also in some of the "higher" animals), then we must abandon the ("strong") verifiability criterion of factual meaningfulness. And, by simple contraposi-
tion, if we want to retain this restrictive empiricist criterion, we
cannot interpret statements about other minds in the literal
way intended by common sense, and obviously presupposed by
many moral maxims (e.g., those forbidding cruelty or those
enjoining sympathy and kindness). The conclusion to be drawn
seems all too obvious, but perhaps a more detailed discussion
will be helpful.

The philosophical trouble with inferring another person's
mental states consists in the impossibility of an independent,
direct check-up. There seems to be no criterion, in the sense of
necessary and sufficient conditions, which would enable one

Reprinted by permission of the author and editor, from *The Journal of Philosophy*, LVI (1959), 980–987.

person to convince himself conclusively of the actual occurrence of mental states on the part of the other person. The analogical argument concerning other minds thus differs fundamentally from the ordinary type of analogical inference. In the ordinary cases *direct* evidence can be obtained for the truth of the conclusion. If we reason, for example, from the many similarities between two human bodies and the presence of a brain in one of them, to the presence of a brain in the other, the conclusion by itself is clearly open to direct (surgical) examination. In any case, it is safe to say that the conclusion here may be verified with the same degree of certainty that attaches to the premises of the analogical argument. But if person A, on the basis of the regular concomitance of his own mental states with certain aspects of his behavior (or ultimately with his brain processes) infers similar mental states as concomitant with the other person's, i.e., B's, behavior (or brain processes), then he cannot by any known or even conceivable procedure convince himself of the truth of his conclusion—certainly not in the manner he can know the truth of the premises of his analogical argument.

An analysis of this peculiar situation should begin with a clarification of the meaning and the validity of the phrase "cannot" in the above statement. First of all, it should be noted that there are analogical inferences also concerning physical states in which a direct check of the conclusion is impossible, but which are generally regarded as legitimate. For example, the astrophysical inference as to the chemical constitution of the surface of Sirius is considered well established, though a direct test of the conclusion is not feasible. The analogical inference rests upon well established physical laws (e.g., concerning special lines and their lawful relation to chemical elements), and on this basis, together with the spectroscopic data obtained by telescopic observations of Sirius, the conclusion—e.g., that there is hydrogen, helium, etc., in the surface of that star—is rendered highly probable. It is probable only, and not completely certain, in that the underlying assumption of the universality of the spectroscopic laws involves the usual inductive risk. Other assumptions enter into this reasoning as well, e.g., the assumption that the observed spectrum is not due to material in interstellar space or in the earth's atmosphere, etc. But all of these assumptions are relatively independently certifiable. What is not *directly and independently* certifiable is the conclusion. Even if interstellar journeys became feasible, any conceivable physical and chemical testing instruments would long have evaporated before getting anywhere near the surface of Sirius. This sort of impossibility is hence more fundamental than the merely practical-technical impossibility of, e.g., determining the heights of the mountains on the far side of the moon. Once astronautics becomes a reality, this particular impossibility will be overcome.

Are these same distinctions applicable to the other-minds problem? In the contexts of everyday life as well as in (behavioral) clinical psychology, it is often *practically* impossible to be *sure* about ascriptions of mental states to others. There is no question, however, that we do utilize "criteria" of a sort when, e.g., we decide that our friend, although he smiled, and said he was pleased with a gift, was "really" annoyed. His subsequent behavior, his answers to searching questions (e.g., what he said to his wife about it, etc.) may furnish practically sufficient evidence. We do have "criteria" for discriminating between mere pretending and genuine feeling, but these criteria are never statable in the form of necessary and sufficient conditions. They must be regarded as probabilistic indicators very much in the manner in which symptoms in general medicine are regarded as probabilistic indicators of diseases.

But suppose, now, that in a future psychophysiology the total set of one-one correspondences between cerebral and mental states were thoroughly well established. Would not this be like the case of chemical elements and their respective spectra? In other words, given very sensitive and reliable instruments for the observation of the cerebral states of the other person, we could infer his mental states. Obviously any *direct* evidence for the correspondence laws could be obtained only in first-person experience—say by an autocerebroscope which would enable me to observe my own brainstates along with my introspected sensations, images, emotions, thoughts, etc.

What sort of impossibility prevents me from checking on the validity of the psychophysiological correspondence laws for another person? Answers to this question are notoriously diverse. Someone addicted to science fiction might maintain that direct inspection of another person's experience could be achieved by connecting his brain centers with mine. But the obvious objection to this is that it would still be *my* experience, and not really his, which I would introspectively report. Or, more plausibly, a new "joint" sort of experience might arise; yet this could not by any stretch of the imagination be regarded as a case of one mind inspecting another. The difficulty seems to be more fundamental than a mere technical impossibility. Is it then a *logical* impossibility, as in the case of a demand which can be disclosed as self-contradictory? I think not. An outright logical impossibility would be involved in a demand such as: "Please determine the weight of a stone which is spherical and not spherical at the same time." Quite generally, what is considered by some thinkers a logical impossibility often reveals itself on closer analysis as an incompatibility with certain tacit assumptions. These tacit assumptions seem so obvious that it requires an effort of the analytic imagination to recognize them as logically contingent. The "unbridgeable chasm" between two minds (as William James chose to describe it) is a matter of deep-rooted conviction, especially in Western philosophy and science. Certain panpsychistic oriental philosophies may deny this utter separation. Built right into the most fundamental conceptions of our (occidental) world view is the assumption of the strict disparity, the non-overlap, of the individual streams of experience. And this conviction is not metaphysical in the sense that we could not adduce empirical evidence for it (or so it seems): When my friend and I attend a musical show, and I close my eyes and stuff my ears with wax, something disappears from *my* experience but not from his; and vice versa, *mutatis mutandis.* But, of course, it may be said that in adducing whatever empirical evidence *I* can utilize, I merely beg the question at issue. I already assume that my friend "enjoys" (or "suffers") his own experiences, which are "private" to him. And when I say that I don't mean *absolute* privacy, but only the relative privacy which allows for inferences regarding his subjective experiences on the grounds of behavior symptoms, behavior tests, or neural processes, then I still beg the same question in that I assume the legitimacy of these inferences.

Various attempts to undercut the whole tormenting issue have been proposed. Philosophical analysts ("therapists") maintain that the agonizing perplexities can be avoided if we distinguish philosophical doubt from ordinary empirical doubt. We are warned that ordinary, meaningful, and possibly justifiable doubt must not be extended illegitimately. For then it becomes absolutely irresolvable doubt, and we get stuck with the problem. In other words, we are told that this mistake consists in artificially and arbitrarily lifting "private experience" out of the causal contexts in which it manifestly occurs; and that by thus radically severing the relations of private experience from its publicly ascertainable symptoms we bar ourselves even from (indirectly) *confirming* statements which are admittedly not open to direct verification. In common life and in science there are more or less reliable, though never absolutely conclusive procedures, for removing empirical doubt. But these procedures rely on the publicly observable facts of behavior or of physiology.

As a first step of clarification, the distinction between empirical and philosophical doubt is eminently helpful. "Is the patient really unconscious or does he merely pretend?" Questions of this sort may be answered with fairly high probability by the usual behavioral tests. But since these tests do not get directly at the subjective experience of the patient, we must conclude that this type of philosophical "therapy" comes down to one form or another of logical behaviorism. That is to say that the only criteria for, and hence the only meaning of, subjective or mentalistic terms is "physicalistic." The particular remedy proposed by Professor Malcom (and generally by the Neo-Wittgensteinians) consists in denying cognitive status to the "avowals" of one's own experience. While I do not for a moment deny the legitimacy or the desirability of causal explanations of my own verbal behavior, I find the remedy too drastic in that it makes nonsense out of what seems patently good sense to me, viz., the possibility of either truly or falsely reporting about my direct experience. The "therapeutic surgery" may succeed, but I fear the patient will be dead.

I am somewhat of a musical eidetic, and I can report about "hearing internally" passages of symphonies, with full orchestral tone colors, etc. Some visual eidetics are known to be able to count a crocodile's teeth right off their image of the beast— I am not particularly bothered by the linguistic differences between "avowals" of my own experience and my assertions about another person's experience. It is true, the question "How do you know you are experiencing a twinge of pain?" sounds queer in comparison with the much more plausible question, "How do you know *he* has a twinge of pain?"; but perhaps this simply boils down to the difference between direct and indirect verification.

Introspective statements formulated in phenomenal terms can be verified by direct confrontation with immediate experience. "I feel pleased" may be a true description of my present experience (and hence "I feel annoyed" a false description). There is indeed no other criterion but intuitive cogency for the correct recognition of one's own private states. But since errors (due to slips of the tongue, etc.) are even here possible, they must be corrigible in the light of other evidence (e.g., records of my behavior, testimony of others, etc.). Consultation of records, comparison with testimonies, etc., however, presuppose ultimately the sort of "self-evident" recognition of similarity between the qualities that I experience privately at different times. And since "privacy" is not conceived as "absolute," we assume, of course, empirical relations between the private data and the rest of the world. In the light of these relations, the intuition of similarity may be explained (more or less scientifically) by reference to the publicly certifiable regularities of remembrance, perception, etc. Since introspective statements about my own direct experience can be clearly true or false (false at least in the case of lying or mis-speaking), I cannot accept this latest version of a behavioristic rejection of the subjectively given.

I shall not waste time in criticizing the similarly abortive "solutions" proposed respectively by neutral monism, phenomenalism, subjective idealism, or solipsism. Neutral monism and phenomenalism are now fairly generally repudiated because these views do not even give a plausible reconstruction of our knowledge of physical objects. Subjective idealism, if not solipsistic, merely assumes but does not justify the existence of a plurality of minds. And solipsism (in addition to its inadequacy in regard to physical objects) introduces an utterly implausible asymmetry in regard to the "animation" of organisms.

A more hopeful approach seems suggested by an analysis of the role of egocentric particulars in our common language. The very language that we speak in common life, the language which is our medium of communication, operates according to rules in which the peculiar role of egocentric particulars is fully allowed for.[1] Very briefly, we can replace the egocentric particulars ("this," "now," "here," "I," "you," etc., as well as the closely related tensed verbs) by proper names, and by place and time coordinates in an objective description or history of the world. A fully explicit understanding of the rules of correspondence between "subjective" avowals and "objective" (in-

[1] For some helpful analyses of the role of egocentric particulars, cf.: H. Reichenbach, *Elements of Symbolic Logic* (New York, 1947); Y. Bar-Hillel, "Indexical Expressions," *Mind*, LXIII (1954), 359–379; A. Pap, "Other Minds and the Principle of Verifiability," *Rev. Int. de Phil.*, Nos. 17–18, Fasc. 3–4 (1951).

tersubjective) statements will go a long way toward dispelling the philosophical puzzles about other minds. Consider for example: if my doctor, getting ready to lance my abscess, tells me: "This will hurt," *I* can verify directly the truth of his prediction. My subsequent avowal, "This is very painful" or "I feel a sharp pain," corresponds to the objective statement which the doctor could have made: "H. F. at 10:30 A.M. experiences sharp pain." It is clear that the rules of our ordinary language are such that both the doctor and I talk *about* the *same* state of affairs, even if he can merely *confirm* what I can *verify*. And that this should be so is in turn explainable in objective language: The abscess is located on H. F.'s arm, and thus much more directly connected to H. F.'s nervous system than to that of the doctor, etc.

But the "tormenting" question might be raised again: how does the doctor know, that over and above all the behavioral symptoms, and possibly even in addition to all discoverable cerebral processes, there is a pain-experience in H. F.? It is at this point that a more detailed analysis of both the scientific methodology as well as of basic epistemology may provide a more satisfactory answer. It has become increasingly clear that the early ("radical") behavioristic identification of the meaning of subjective terms with behavioral terms (designating symptoms) will not do. Embarrassment is not identical with blushing; pain is not identical with cringing or writhing. In order to exorcise the "ghost in the machine" (i.e., to repudiate Cartesian dualism) we need not resort to such drastic measures. It is quite legitimate, although it requires a little care, to speak of "manifestations" and "symptoms," and of *central states* which are thus manifested or indicated. A peripheralistic behaviorism is to be rejected, because it does not render justice to the logical role of theoretical terms in psychology.[2] Quite

---

[2] Cf. the articles by R. Carnap, L. J. Cronbach, and P. E. Meehl, and W. Sellars, in vol. I of *Minnesota Studies in the Philosophy of Science* (Minneapolis, 1956), and my own essay on "The 'Mental' and the 'Physical'" in vol. II (1958).

generally our theories, whether in atomic physics or in psychophysiology, explicitly relate the postulated unobserved or unobservable events or processes to the observable facts. Theoretical postulates are never verifiable in complete isolation. We
always test a conjunction of several such postulates in the light
of their observable consequences. (I do not, however, hold a
radical "holism," such as that of Duhem or Quine. *Relatively*
independent testings of some postulates, and procedures of
"securing" them by successive confirmation, are common in
science.) In current behavior theory there is no detailed specification of the neurophysiological nature of central states. For
example, "memory traces" are postulated, but their specific
structure and neural basis are left indefinite. This is quite like
the early stages of the theory of electricity, in which a detailed
statement concerning the flow of electrons in conductors was
not as yet worked out. But suppose we had a workable theory
of memory traces in neurophysiology, just as we do have a
theory of electric currents in terms of the quantum dynamics
of the "electron gas." Such a theory would enable us to derive
certain aspects of the learning process; i.e., a number of empirical regularities of psychology would thus be explained by
neurophysiology. Any *good* theory furnishes us with a vocabulary of terms in which we can express not only laws but also
singular descriptive statements. "Mr. N. is now reminiscing
about his first love affair." This would be rendered in neurophysiological language. And if, according to our (admittedly
rather fantastically good and complete) neurophysiological
theory, all the associated verbal and other behavior of Mr. N.
is derivable from this description, what could be missing? The
traditional epistemologist would of course answer: a description of the "subjective experience." Is it, then, according to the
traditional outlook, that we have to acknowledge two steps of
inference—from peripheral behavior to central physiological
states, and from central physiological states to the subjective
experience? It may be urged that the latter inference is super-
fluous, since the "surplus" of the subjective experience would

not be a difference that makes a difference in scientific description, explanation, or prediction. "But it does make a difference for our practical attitudes and actions," we are told. "I have reason to abstain from cruelty only if in addition to the acceptance of certain moral rules I have good grounds for assuming that the other person's pain is similar to my own (which I know by acquaintance). And how could this similarity be known except on the grounds of analogy; and *this* analogical argument cannot be certified by behavioral or physiological evidence." Are we, then, back to our tormenting doubts? I think not. The arguments submitted thus far suggest that we may well *identify* the referent of subjective-acquaintance statements with the referent of certain central-state-descriptions.[3] The impossibility of a direct check-up on the truth of the analogical inference is part of the accepted theoretical scheme; and by way of what might be called "infra-scientific" theory, it is an essential part of the conceptual frame of common-sense knowledge. The "egocentric predicament," as R. B. Perry rightly pointed out a long time ago, is no barrier to knowledge. It is a natural (if you will, "physical") limitation only of *direct* verifiability. But once it is realized that almost all of our knowledge is capable of confirmation only (and not of direct verification), the torments of the other-minds problem should fade away. The situation here (as noted by Ayer, Pap, and others) is very much the same as in our inference of events in the past. If we are given to philosophical doubts, we may ("perversely") wonder whether the natural laws did not radically change from period to period in the past and that hence any inference on the basis of present evidence to past events may be hopelessly precarious. Or we may go further and deny (à la Philipp Gosse—but without his theological hypotheses) that there were any events before 4004 B.C. The first idea corresponds to the idea about the "inverted spectrum"

[3] I have defended this (empirical) identification against various *prima facie* plausible objections in "The 'Mental' and the 'Physical,'" *Minnesota Studies in the Philosophy of Science*, vol. II (Minneapolis, 1958).

(the systematic variations of direct qualia among different persons); the second corresponds to solipsism. Once the natural limitations of direct verifiability are recognized and incorporated into our conceptual frame, the wish for direct certification of other people's mental states, while psychologically understandable, must be acknowledged as chimerical—very much in the sense in which the idea of H. G. Wells' time machine is chimerical in that it is not merely a practical-technical but a fundamental natural-empirical impossibility.

It may be objected that, by admitting unverifiability for certain parts of our conceptual frame, we open the floodgates to limitless metaphysical (transempirical) speculations. This is not so, however. The cutting edge of the (liberalized) empiricist meaning criterion remains just as sharp. Theories which are protected against any and all sorts of confirmation or disconfirmation are indeed factually empty; for, by thus protecting them, we have deprived ourselves of the ability to give any *reasons* for or against them. But, I conclude, in the normal frame of confirmation there are eminently good reasons for the ascription of mental states to other persons, and on a decreasing scale of analogies also to animals.

A final question: do the criteria of confirmation presuppose synthetic *a priori* principles? Bertrand Russell (in *Human Knowledge*, New York, 1948) thought so. As I understand him, he felt that his realistic view of the physical world as well as of other minds required an important emendation of empiricism. This is a large topic in itself, and perhaps beyond the scope of the present issue. My own attitude in this matter, very briefly, is this: If there are synthetic *a priori* principles at the basis of cognition, they don't have the absolute validity that Kant ascribed to them. They might just as well be called "analytic *a posteriori*." The frame-presuppositions of knowledge consist in the formation and transformation rules of our language. These rules do not state anything specifically about the world, but they "reflect" (cf. Wittgenstein's *Tractatus*) certain very basic and pervasive features of the world. While questions concerning the conceptual frame of cognition cannot be decided in the same relatively straightforward manner as questions within, and presupposing that frame,[4] the adoption of the realistic frame can be pragmatically justified in a manner that includes empirical considerations though it is not fully demonstrable by them. The justification is in some, but by no means all, respects similar to the justification of scientific theories. We need theories in order to explain the facts of observation. Analogously, we need a frame allowing for (confirmable) unobservables and their relations to (verifiable) observables; we need the relative privacy of minds, of mental events, and the relations to publicly certifiable behavior in order to give an all-around coherent and synoptic account of reality-as-we-conceive-it and of the language that describes it. In the reconstruction and justification of this frame, principles of analogy are indispensable. I assume other centers of subjectivity similar to the one I know by acquaintance; and while this assumption is not directly verifiable, the total set of assumptions I make about the world (and myself as a small part of it) is confirmable and nonredundant.

[4] Cf. my essay: "De Principiis non disputandum . . . ?" in M. Black, ed., *Philosophical Analysis* (Ithaca, N.Y., 1950).

# IV

*Hypothesis*

# OUR EVIDENCE FOR
# THE EXISTENCE OF OTHER MINDS

H. H. PRICE

1. In ordinary life everyone assumes that he has a great deal of knowledge about other minds of persons. This assumption has naturally aroused the curiosity of philosophers; though perhaps they have not been as curious about it as they ought to have been, for they have devoted many volumes to our consciousness of the material world, but very few to our consciousness of one another. It was thought at one time that each of us derives his knowledge of other minds from the observation of other human organisms. I observe (it was said) that there are a number of bodies which resemble my own fairly closely in their shape, size, and manner of movement; I conclude by analogy that each of these bodies is animated by a mind more or less like myself. It was admitted that this argument was not demonstrative. At the best it would only provide evidence for the existence of other minds, not proof; and one's alleged knowledge of other minds would only be at the most well-grounded opinion. It was further admitted, by some philosophers, that our belief in the existence of other minds was probably not *reached* by an argument of this sort, indeed was not reached by an

Reprinted by permission of the editor, from *Philosophy*, XIII (1938), 425–456.

argument at all, but was an uncritical and unquestioning taking-for-granted, a mere piece of primitive credulity; but, it was claimed, the belief can only be justified by an argument of this sort.

This theory, which may be called the Analogical Theory, has come in for a good deal of criticism, and has now been generally abandoned. Perhaps it has sometimes been abandoned for the wrong reasons; for some of its critics (not all) seem to have overlooked the distinction between the genesis of a belief and its justification. However this may be, I shall not discuss the theory any further at present. My aim in this paper is to consider certain other theories which have been or might be suggested in its place, and to develop one of them at some length.

With the abandonment of the Analogical Theory a very different view, which I shall call the Intuitive Theory, came into favor. It was maintained that each of us has a direct and intuitive apprehension of other minds, just as he has of his own, or at least that he intuitively apprehends some other minds on some occasions, for instance in a conversation or a quarrel. It was said that there is social consciousness as well as self-consciousness, a direct awareness of the "thou" as well as a direct awareness of the "me." I wish to emphasize that this consciousness was held to be a form of knowing, not merely belief (however well-grounded), still less taking for granted. And I think it would have been said to be knowing by acquaintance— extrospective acquaintance as we might call it—though doubtless this acquaintance would make possible a certain amount of "knowledge about," just as when I am acquainted with a noise I may know about the noise that it is shrill or louder than some previous noise.

This view might be worked out in several different ways. Do I have extrospective acquaintance with foreign selves, or only with foreign psychical events, from which foreign selves can somehow be inferred? Or would it be said that foreign selves, and my own self too, are only logical constructions out of extrospectible or introspectible data? Again, is my extrospective acquaintance confined to human minds, or does it extend to sub-human and super-human ones, if such there be? It is certain that some who held this kind of theory thought that it did extend to super-human minds at any rate; for they thought that religious experience, or at any rate one of the types of experience covered by that label, was an extrospective acquaintance with the Divine Mind. And I suppose that some might claim an extrospective acquaintance with what we may call ex-human minds, minds which once animated human bodies, but now animate them no longer (and perhaps with ex-animal minds, if there are any?).

We should also have to ask just what the special circumstances are which make this extrospective acquaintance possible. For clearly it does not occur in all circumstances. Otherwise we shall never be deceived by waxworks; we could tell at a glance whether the man we see lying by the roadside is unconscious, or dead, or only shamming; and we should know at once whether the words we hear are uttered by a gramophone or by an animate and conscious human organism.

I do not propose to pursue these questions any further. I only mention them to suggest that the theory requires a more detailed and thorough working out than it has yet received. But perhaps it is well to add that it derives no support whatever from the phenomena of telepathy. No doubt there is strong empirical evidence for the occurrence of telepathy. But the telepathic relation appears to be causal, not cognitive; it is more like infection than like knowledge. An event $E_1$ in mind No. 1 causes an event $E_2$ in mind No. 2, without any discoverable physical intermediary. It may be that $E_2$ resembles $E_1$ fairly closely. For instance, $E_1$ might be the seeing of a certain scene accompanied by a feeling of horror, and $E_2$ might be the imaging of a visual image closely resembling that scene, accompanied by a similar feeling of horror. But $E_2$ is not a *knowing* of $E_1$; just as, when you have scarlet fever and I catch it from you, my fever is not a knowing of yours.

But some advocates of the Intuitive Theory proceeded to

take a further step, which we must now consider. We were told, and still are, that the problem before us was mis-stated. We started by assuming that every man has from the first a direct introspective awareness of himself, or of mental events in himself, and the problem was to justify his beliefs concerning other selves. The Analogical Theory said that they were justified by observation of other human bodies. The Intuitive Theory said that they were justified by occasional acts of extrospective acquaintance; or rather it said that some of them are not beliefs, but intuitive knowings, and that the rest (which *are* only beliefs) are justified by the evidence which these occasional extrospective knowings provide. But, it is now suggested, the problem has been stated the wrong way round; we are being puzzled at the wrong things. The really puzzling thing, it is suggested, is *self*-consciousness, not consciousness of other people. What comes first in the historical order is consciousness of one's neighbor, extrospective consciousness. Consciousness of oneself only comes later, after considerable mental development; in some cases perhaps, say in the idiot or the very primitive savage, it never comes at all. Nor is the order merely historical. It is epistemological too. When I do come to know my own mind, I only come to know it by contrast with my neighbors' minds which I have been knowing from the first.

It may, however, be objected that this is only true of attentive and discriminating self-consciousness. Might I not have been *aware* of myself from the first, even though it required time and pain before I attended to this internal datum and discriminated it from other objects of my awareness? To meet this difficulty, the theory is sometimes stated in a still more radical way. It is suggested that the primary thing both in the historical and the epistemological order is a consciousness whose object is not "you" nor "me," but "us." This primitive *we-consciousness* can be called neither introspective nor extrospective, but is that out of which both introspection and extrospection have developed. Each man as he grows up gradually learns to distinguish between different parts of this originally given we-object, and in particular to distinguish between "me," "you," and "the rest." But this achievement, it is suggested, is not an entirely stable one. In times of great emotional stress, as in a battle or a riot, it may break down. One then slips back into the primitive and undiscriminating we-consciousness, and is aware only that "we" are doing or feeling so and so. Such occasions are very rare in the life of the civilized man. But in the very primitive savage it may well be the other way round. Perhaps he only manages to distinguish between "me" and "you" once or twice in a lifetime.

We have now described several different forms of the Intuitive Theory. They differ as to the relation between introspective acquaintance and extrospective acquaintance, between self-consciousness and social consciousness. But they all have one very important contention in common. They all maintain that there is such an experience as extrospective acquaintance, a direct and intuitive knowing whose object is either another mind, or at any rate an event in or state of another mind. But *does* extrospective acquaintance ever occur? Am I ever acquainted with a feeling of anger or of fear which is not my own? I am sometimes acquainted with my own thinking-processes. Am I ever *acquainted* with thinking-processes which do not occur in myself and have nothing to do with me? It seems to me perfectly clear that the answer to these questions is, No. Of course I am constantly taking for granted the existence of all sorts of foreign emotions and foreign thinking-processes. I take their existence for granted without the least hesitation or doubt. But this is a very different thing indeed from knowing them by acquaintance. If anyone professes that he does sometimes have such extrospective acquaintance with his neighbor's mental processes, I do not see how to refute him. But I can easily conceive both of a strong motive, and of a plausible but inconclusive argument, which might lead him to claim that he had such acquaintance when in fact he had not.

First, the motive. As a distinguished philosopher has said, "we don't want inferred friends." But still, though one does not want them, one may have to put up with them for lack of anything better. Secondly, the argument. It may be urged that unless there is some extrospective acquaintance, the beliefs which each one of us holds concerning other minds could not have the high degree of probability which some of them obviously do have. For where else could the evidence come from which is to give them this high degree of probability? Mere observation of other human organisms, such as the Analogical Theory appeals to, provides but weak evidence, if it provides any at all. One might try to cut the knot by offering a Behavioristic analysis of statements about other minds, as Logical Positivism did in its wilder youth, on the ground that otherwise these statements would be unverifiable and so nonsensical. If my belief about another mind is really only a belief about the behavior of a certain human organism, then no doubt I can find abundant evidence to justify it. But then what about statements concerning my own mind? These can be verified or refuted by introspection; so they are *not* to be analyzed in a purely Behavioristic way. But this leaves us with an intolerable asymmetry between statements about myself and statements about my neighbor. It seems perfectly obvious that words like "hear," "see," "fear," "think," have exactly the same meaning when I apply them to my neighbor as when I apply them to myself. If "*I* see a cat" means simply "this retina here is being stimulated by light-rays and these muscles are adjusting themselves to respond to that stimulus" (e.g., by stroking the cat, or offering it a saucer of milk), well and good; then we may analyze "Smith sees a cat" in an analogous way. Only, what is sauce for Smith must be sauce for me as well. The Behavioristic analysis must apply to both statements alike, or else to neither. But as a matter of fact it seems to me clear that "*I* see a cat" cannot be analyzed in this way. However much truth we recognize in the detailed contentions of the Behaviorists—and for my part I am prepared to recognize a great deal—I do not understand how anyone can hold a purely Behavioristic theory about himself. Much of what we are pleased to call our thinking is doubtless nothing but talking or twitching of throat-muscles, and much of what looks like deliberate action may well be nothing but a complicated chain of conditioned reflexes. But unless I sometimes do think in the literal and non-Behavioristic sense, how could I discover that at other times my alleged thinking is only talking? How indeed could I *discover* anything at all, or even understand the statements which Behaviorists make to me?

For these reasons it is certainly plausible to argue that unless extrospective acquaintance sometimes occurs, one's beliefs about other minds could not have the high probability which some of them obviously do here. For if extrospective acquaintance be excluded, we must fall back on ordinary perceptual observation. And then it seems we must have recourse either to the Analogical Theory or to Behaviorism, and neither gives us what we want. But I think that this argument, though plausible, is not conclusive. For Behaviorism and the Analogical Theory are perhaps not the only alternatives available. There is at least one other which deserves to be considered, and I propose to devote the rest of this paper to the consideration of it.

2. The suggestion I wish to examine is that one's evidence for the existence of other minds is derived primarily from the understanding of language. I shall use the word "language" in a wide sense, to include not only speech and writing, but also signals such as waving a red flag, and gestures such as beckoning and pointing. One might say, the suggestion is that one's evidence for the existence of other minds comes from *communication*-situations. But this would be question-begging. For communication is by definition a relation between two or more minds. Thus if I have reason to believe that a communication is occurring, I must already have reason to believe that a mind other than my own exists. However, it would be true, according to the theory which I am about to consider, that the study of communication is of fundamental importance. For

according to it one's most important evidence for the existence of another mind is always also evidence for the occurrence of communication between that mind and oneself. Even so, the word "communication" has to be taken in a wide sense, as the word "language" has to be. Utterances which I am not intended to hear, and writings or signals which I am not intended to see, will have to be counted as communications, provided I do in fact observe and understand them. In other words, we shall have to allow that there is such a thing as involuntary communication.

Let us consider some instances. Suppose I hear a foreign body [1] utter the noises "Look! there is the bus." I understand these noises. That is to say, they have for me a *symbolic* character, and on hearing them I find myself entertaining a certain proposition, or if you like entertaining a certain thought. (It does not matter how they came to have this symbolic character for me. The point is that they do have it now, however they got it.) As yet I only *entertain* what they symbolize, with perhaps some slight inclination towards belief; for as yet I have no decisive ground for either belief or disbelief. However, I now proceed to look round; and sure enough there is the bus, which I had not seen before, and perhaps was not expecting yet. This simple occurrence, of hearing an utterance, understanding it, and then verifying it for oneself, provides some evidence that the foreign body which uttered the noises is animated by a mind like one's own. And at the same time it provides evidence that the mind in question is or recently has been in a determinate state. Either it has been itself observing the bus, or it has been observing some other physical object or event from which the advent of the bus could be inferred.

Now suppose that I frequently have experiences of this sort in connection with this particular foreign body. Suppose I am often in its neighborhood, and it repeatedly produces utter-

---

[1] I use a phrase "a foreign body" to mean "a body other than my own." As we shall see, it need not be a *human* body.

ances which I can understand, and which I then proceed to verify for myself. And suppose that this happens in many different kinds of situations. I think that my evidence for believing that this body is animated by a mind like my own would then become very strong. It is true that it will never amount to demonstration. But in the sphere of matters of fact it is a mistake to expect demonstration. We may expect it in the spheres of Pure Mathematics and Formal Logic, but not elsewhere. So much at least we may learn from Hume. If I have no direct extrospective acquaintance with other minds, the most that can be demanded is adequate *evidence* for their existence. If anyone demands *proof* of it, his demand is nonsensical, at least if the word "proof" is used in the strict sense which it bears in Pure Mathematics. It is not that the demand unfortunately cannot be fulfilled, owing to the limitations of human knowledge. It is that it cannot really be made at all. The words which purport to formulate it do not really formulate anything.

To return to our argument: the evidence will be strongest where the utterance I hear gives me new information; that is to say, where it symbolizes something which I do *not* already believe, but which I subsequently manage to verify for myself. For if I did already believe it at the time of hearing, I cannot exclude the possibility that it was my own believing which caused the foreign body to utter it. And this might happen even if my own believing were, as we say, "unconscious"; as when I have been believing for many hours that today is Saturday, though until this moment I have not thought about the matter. I know by experience that my believings can cause my own body to utter symbolic noises; and for all I can tell they may sometimes cause a foreign body to do the same. Indeed, there is some empirical evidence in favor of this suggestion. The utterances of an entranced medium at a spiritualistic séance do sometimes seem to be caused by the unspoken beliefs of the sitters. That one mind—my own—can animate two or more bodies at the same time is therefore not an absurd hypothesis, but only a queer one. It cannot be ruled out of court *a priori*, but must be refuted by specific empirical evidence.

It might, however, be suggested that we are demanding too much when we require that the foreign utterance should convey new information. Would it not be sufficient if the information, though not new, was, so to speak, *intrusive*—if it broke in upon my train of thought, and had no link, either logical or associative, with what I was thinking a moment before? Thus, suppose that while I am engaged in a mathematical calculation I suddenly hear a foreign body say "today is Saturday." I did in a sense believe this already. I have received no new information. Still, the utterance has no logical relevance to the propositions which were occupying my mind, and there was nothing in them to suggest it by association. Would not the hearing of this utterance provide me with evidence for the existence of another mind? I admit that it would, but I think the evidence would be weak. For I know by experience that my powers of concentration are exceedingly limited. Sentences proceeding from my own unconscious sometimes break in upon my train of thought in just this intrusive way. It is true that they usually present themselves to my mind in the form of verbal images. But occasionally they are actually uttered in audible whispers, and sometimes they are uttered aloud. How can I tell that these same unconscious processes in myself may not sometimes cause a foreign body to utter such intrusive noises? Their intrusive character is no bar to their unconscious origin. What we require is that they should symbolize something which I did not believe beforehand at all, even unconsciously. It is still better if they symbolize something which I *could* not have believed beforehand because I was not in a position to make the relevant perceptual observations. For instance, I hear a foreign body say "there is a black cloud on the horizon" at a time when my back is turned to the window, and then I turn round and see the cloud for myself. Or I am walking in pitch darkness in a strange house, and hear someone say "there are three steps in front of you," which I had no means of guessing beforehand; and I then verify the proposition for myself by falling down the steps.

3. It follows from what has been said that if there were a foreign body which never uttered anything but platitudes, I should be very doubtful whether it was independently animated, no matter how closely it resembled my own. In the instance given ("today is Saturday," when I already believe that today *is* Saturday) the platitude was a *singular* platitude, stating a particular matter of fact. But there are also *general* platitudes. Among these some are empirical, such as "there is always a sky above us," "all cats have whiskers"; while others are *a priori,* such as "2 + 2 = 4," or "it is either raining or not raining," and are true at all times and in all possible worlds. If there was a body which uttered only singular platitudes, I should be inclined to conclude (as we have said) that it was not independently animated; I should suspect that its noises were caused by my own believings, conscious and unconscious. If it uttered nothing but general platitudes, I might doubt whether it was animated at all. I should be inclined to think that it was a mere mechanism, a sort of talking penny-in-the-slot machine, especially if its repertoire of platitudes was limited; though it might occur to me to wonder whether any intelligent being had constructed it.

So far, then, it appears that if the noises uttered by a foreign body (or its visible gesticulations) are to provide adequately strong evidence for the existence of another mind, they must give me information. They must symbolize something which I did not know or believe beforehand, and which I then proceed to verify for myself. If these conditions are fulfilled, I have evidence of the occurrence of a foreign act of perceiving—an act of perceiving which did not form part of my own mental history. But it is not really necessary that the information conveyed should be a singular proposition, restricted to one single perceptible situation. It might be general, as if I hear a foreign body say "some cats have no tails," or "all gold dissolves in *aqua regia.*" Neither of these is restricted to one single perceptible object or situation. Still, they are both empirical, and there is a sense in which even the second can be empirically verified, or at any rate confirmed, by suitable observations and experiments. Clearly such utterances as these do give me evidence for the existence of another mind, but not in the way that the previous utterances did, such as "there is the bus," or "there is a black cloud on the horizon now." They do not show that a specific perceptual act falling outside my own mental history is now occurring, or has just occurred. In one way they show something less—merely that some perceivings of cats or of gold have occurred at some time or other. But in another way they show something more: namely, that a foreign act of *thinking* is occurring or has recently occurred, directed upon the *universals* "cat," "tail," "gold," and "aqua regia." (Or if it be objected that even perceiving involves some thinking, directed upon universals in abstraction from their instances.)

But further, the information I received need not be empirical at all. Suppose I hear a foreign body utter the noises "if 345 is added to 169, the result is 514." I understand these noises, but as yet I neither accept nor reject what they say. For I have never worked out that particular sum before, or if I have, I have forgotten the result. However, I now proceed to work it out, and sure enough the result *is* 514. This, too, gives me evidence of the existence of another mind. But this time I get evidence simply of a foreign act of thinking, and not of any foreign perceptual act at all.

Here, however, we encounter a difficulty. It may be objected that this argument for the existence of another mind is quite different from the one used hitherto, and even inconsistent with it. In the previous cases everything turned on the difference between utterances which give me information and utterances which do not. But a mathematical statement, it is often said, tells me nothing about the world. For it is true whatever state the world may be in. And the like holds of all other *a priori* statements. (Accordingly some philosophers have said that all *a priori* statements are *tautologies*.) If so, how can a mathematical statement be called informative? But if it is not informative, then according to our previous argument the hearing and understanding of it can give us no evidence for the existence of a foreign act of thinking. Indeed, we ourselves gave the utterance "2 + 2 = 4" as an instance of a platitude above.

To this I reply that there is a sense in which many mathematical and other *a priori* statements *are* informative. It is true that they do not give information about empirical matters of fact, in the way in which such statements as "it is now raining" do, or "some cats have no tails." But they do assert something. They assert certain *entailments* (or necessitations, if you will). And though any entailment, once you have seen it, may be called obvious or evident, it is not on that account necessarily a platitude. The term "platitude" is relative. That which is a platitude to you need not be a platitude to me; and that which is a platitude to me at one time of my life may have been non-platitudinous to me at another. A statement is only a platitude to me when its truth is *already* obvious to me, *before* I hear the statement. If the truth of it was not obvious beforehand, but only becomes so afterwards when I have attended to the meaning of the symbols and to their mode of combination, then it has certainly told me something new which I did not know before. At the time when I heard it, it was certainly not a platitude for me, though it will be one in future if my memory is good. Even "2 + 2 = 4," though it is a platitude to me now, perhaps was not always one. When I first heard it, perhaps it told me something new which I had not been able to work out for myself. As Mr. Russell says somewhere, even the Multiplication Table was probably exciting in the time of King Aahmes; for at that time it was not platitudinous to anybody.

It appears, then, that mathematical statements (and likewise other *a priori* statements) can very well be informative, in the sense that they can tell one something which one had not previously found out for oneself; though the something which they tell is an entailment, and not an empirical matter of fact. If it be said that such statements are tautologies, then we must insist that there are novel tautologies as well as stale ones; and the hearing and understanding of a novel one does give strong evidence for the existence of another mind, though the hearing of a stale one gives none or very little.

4. In the situations hitherto mentioned the noises which I hear and understand are uttered by a foreign organism which I observe. And the foreign organism is more or less similar to my own. But of course I need not actually observe it. It suffices if I hear an intelligible and informative utterance proceeding from a megaphone or a telephone, from the next room or from behind my back. It may, however, be thought that such a foreign organism must be in principle observable if I am to have evidence of the existence of another mind, and further that it must be more or less similar to my own organism. But I believe that both of these opinions are mistaken, as I shall now try to show by examples.

There is a passage in the Old Testament which reads, "Thou shalt hear a voice behind thee saying, 'This is the way, walk ye in it.'" Now suppose that something like this did actually occur. For instance, I am lost on a mountain-top, and I hear a voice saying that on the other side of such-and-such a rock there is a sheep-track which leads down the mountain. After the best search that I can make, I can find no organism from which the voice could have proceeded. However, I go to the rock in question, and I do find a sheep-track which leads me down safely into the valley. Is it not clear that I should then have good evidence of the existence of another kind? The fact that so far as I can discover there was no organism, human or other, from which the voice proceeded makes no difference, provided I hear the noises, understand them, and verify the information which they convey. Now suppose I go up the mountain many times, and each time I hear an intelligible set of noises, conveying information which is new to me and subsequently verified; but I never find an organism from which they could have proceeded, search as I may. I should then have reason for concluding that the place was "haunted" by an unembodied mind. Such things do not happen, no doubt. But still there is no contradiction whatever in supposing them. The point is that if they did happen they would provide perfectly good evidence for the existence of another mind. And this is sufficient to show that the presence of an observable organism is not essential; *a fortiori,* the presence of an observable organism more or less resembling my own is not essential.

Now suppose an even more extravagant case. The clouds might form themselves into Chinese ideographs before my eyes. I might be able to read Chinese, and I might find that these ideographs made up intelligible sentences, conveying new information which I could verify by subsequent observation. Or I might find that they stated a geometrical theorem which I could follow when it was put before me, but could not have discovered for myself. Here, again, I should have good ground for thinking that there was another mind communicating to me. But I could not form the remotest notion of what sort of organism it had; and so far as I could tell, it might have none at all.

In the two cases just considered no body was observed to produce the words, but at least the words themselves were perceived by hearing or sight. But even this is not essential. It might be enough if they presented themselves to me in the form of mental imagery, auditory or visual. Suppose that a sentence came into my mind in this way which conveyed information entirely new to me, information which I could not have inferred from anything I already knew or believed; suppose further that there was nothing in the preceding train of thought to suggest it by association. Then I should be inclined to think that this image-sentence was produced by some unconscious process in myself. The sentence might be "there is a wrecked motor car round the next corner." Suppose that on turning the corner I did find a wrecked motor car. I should be somewhat astonished, especially if the sentence had been a long and circumstantial one (mentioning, say, the color and make of the car, and the number of its number-plate), and was verified in all or most of its details. Still, I should stick to the hypothesis that it was produced by my own unconscious, and should attribute the verification to coincidence. But if such things happened to me several times, it would be reasonable to consider the hypothesis that there was another mind, or several, communicating to me telepathically. And if experiences of this sort went on happening, all giving me new information which was subsequently verified, the evidence might become very strong.

It appears then that I could conceivably get strong evidence of the existence of another mind even if there was no observable organism with which such a mind could be connected. This incidentally is a new and fatal argument against the old Analogical Theory which was referred to at the beginning of this paper. For that theory maintained that one's evidence of the existence of other minds could *only* come from observing foreign bodies which resemble one's own. It is also clear that even when I do observe a foreign body producing the relevant utterances, that body need not be in the least like my own. There is no logical absurdity in the hypothesis of a rational parrot or a rational caterpillar. And if there was such a creature, I could have as good evidence of its rationality as I have in the case of my human neighbors; better evidence indeed than I can have in the case of a human idiot. There is no *a priori* reason why even vegetable organisms should not give evidence of being animated by rational minds, though as it happens they never do. If the rustlings of the leaves of an oak formed intelligible words conveying new information to me, and if gorse-bushes made intelligible gestures, I should have evidence that the oak or the gorse-bush was animated by an intelligence like my own.

Here it may be well to consider the case of parrots more closely, for they appear to cause some difficulty to my thesis.

Parrots do make intelligible utterances. But we do not usually think that they are animated by minds like our own; and some even hold that they are not animated at all in the sense in which human bodies are, but are simply behaving organisms which respond in a complicated way to environmental stimuli. It is true that the utterances of parrots do not usually tell us anything new. But it is quite conceivable that they might. Suppose that I do hear a parrot make an utterance which gives me new information. This certainly gives me evidence for the existence of a mind *somewhere*, an intelligent mind like my own. But I should usually assume that the mind in question does not animate the parrot-organism itself. Why should I assume this? In default of further evidence, it would be quite unreasonable to do so. But, as it happens, I have learned from observation of other parrots that when they make intelligible noises they are not, so to speak, the original sources of these noises, but are merely repeating the utterances which some human body has made in their neighborhood. Thus, when I receive information from the utterances of *this* parrot, I have reason to think that the mind which is responsible for it does not animate the parrot-body itself, but does (or did) animate some human body in whose neighborhood the parrot has lived. The case is parallel to that of an echo. An echo coming from a wall might consist of intelligible noises, and they might give me new information. But I should not conclude that the wall was animated by an intelligent mind, because I know that walls do not spontaneously produce noises of that sort, but only *re*produce noises which are going on in the neighborhood. The parrot is merely a sort of delayed echo. The like holds for gramophones and telephones, and possibly also for human sleep-walkers.

It must, however, be noticed that my reasons for thinking that these things are *not* animated by intelligent minds are all, so to speak, extraneous reasons, drawn from observations falling outside the situation itself. Suppose one did not have this extraneous information: one might, for instance, be a savage who understood English but had had no previous experience of the behavior of these particular sorts of objects. It would then be perfectly reasonable to believe that parrots, gramophones, and telephones *are* animated by intelligent minds. For since the noises they utter are *ex hypothesi* intelligible and informative, there is evidence for the existence of an intelligent mind which produced those noises. And as one would then have no evidence for thinking that the production was indirect, it would be perfectly reasonable to conclude that the object from which the noises emanate was itself directly controlled by the mind in question. The conclusion, though reasonable, would of course be mistaken. But perhaps we ourselves are sometimes mistaken in just the same way. For all we can tell, some of the human talkers we meet with may be nothing but living gramophones controlled by minds not their own. Indeed, there is reason to think that something of this kind does happen temporarily in hypnosis.

We have seen that one's evidence of the existence of another mind comes from the receiving of *information* by means of intelligible symbols. In the cases hitherto considered the information turned out to be true, and I discovered this by testing it for myself. But it is not really necessary that it should be true, nor that I should test it. False information is just as good, so long as it *is* information. What is required is that the utterance should convey something which goes beyond what is already present to my mind, something which I did not consciously think of for myself, and which could not (so far as I can tell) have been presented to me by some process in my own unconscious. A piece of true information which I did not previously possess has this "going beyond" character. But a piece of outrageous fiction may also have it. Of course some fictions are as familiar to me as some truths. These stand on the same footing as platitudes, and the hearing or reading of them gives me no decisive evidence of the existence of another mind. But when I read a novel which I did not write, or hear for the first time a tall story which I did not invent, then I do have good evidence for the occurrence of mental acts not forming part of my own mental history. These foreign mental acts of which I get evidence are primarily acts of thinking. But I can infer that the mind in which they occur must also have had perceptual experiences more or less like my own at some time or other. For one can only make up a fictitious narrative by conceiving of universals, and these must have been abstracted from perceived instances. Or if it be said that there are some universals which are not abstracted from perceived instances, but are known somehow else (innately perhaps?)—viz., such formal or categorical universals as "cause" and "substance"—we may reply that no narrative could consist wholly of these. If it is to be a narrative at all, it must also contain noncategorical universals, such as "cat," "green," "to the right of"; and these at any rate must have been abstracted from perceived instances.

5. I have now tried to show by a number of examples that it is the perceiving and understanding of noises and other symbols which gives one evidence for the existence of other minds. I think it is clear that the situations I have described do provide evidence for this conclusion. But exactly *how* they do so is not yet clear. Before we discuss this question, however, there are three preliminary points to be made.

First, it is necessary to insist that there is nothing recondite about this evidence for the existence of other minds. It is not the sort of evidence which only philosophers or scientists or other experts can discover. Perhaps I have spoken as if it were suddenly presented to the notice of an intelligent and reflective adult, who has reached years of discretion without ever finding any good reasons for believing in the existence of another mind, and now finds some for the first time. But of course this is not really the position. The evidence I have spoken of is available to anyone, however youthful and inexperienced, as soon as he has learned the use of language. All that is required is that he should be able to receive information by means of words or other symbols, and that he should be able to distinguish between observing something and being told about it. (Perhaps he is not *self*-conscious until he is able to draw this distinction. If so, we may agree with those who say that consciousness of self and consciousness of others come into being simultaneously, though not with their further contention that consciousness of others is a form of acquaintance or intuitive knowledge.) Thus by the time that he has reached years of discretion evidence of the sort described is exceedingly familiar to him, little though he may have reflected upon it.

The second point is more serious. It may be objected that one cannot learn to understand language unless one *already* believes (or knows?) that the noises one hears are produced by a mind other than oneself. For if not, how would it ever occur to one that those queer noises which one hears are symbols at all? Must one not assume from the start that these noises are *intended* to stand for something? Then, but not otherwise, one can proceed to discover what in particular they stand for.

To this I reply, at first it does not occur to one that the noises *are* symbols. One has to discover this for oneself. And one discovers it by learning to *use* them as symbols in one's own thinking. One begins by merely noticing a correlation between a certain type of object and a certain type of noise, as one might notice a correlation between any other two types of entities which are frequently combined, say, thunder and lightning. The correlation is at first far from complete, for one sometimes observes the object without hearing the noise. But gradually one comes to imitate the noise for oneself. And thus the correlation becomes more nearly complete; if no foreign body says "cat" when I see a cat, I shall say "cat" myself. Thus a strong association is set up in my mind between that type of noise and that type of object. The next step after this is certainly a mysterious one, the more so as it is perhaps not literally a "next" step, but merely the continuation and completion of something which has been going on from the start. But the mystery has nothing to do with awareness of other people's intentions. It has to do with what used to be called the abstraction of universals from particulars. We must suppose that all conscious beings have the power of recognizing that two or more particulars are similar to each other. No consciousness devoid of this power would be of the faintest use to its possessor; so it must be assumed that the lower animals, if they are conscious at all, can recognize at least some similarities, namely, those which are important for their biological welfare. But only some conscious beings can single out within the similar particulars that common factor in respect of which they are similar, and can conceive of it in abstraction; that is, at times when they are not actually perceiving or remembering any particular of the sort in question. This conceiving of universals in the absence of their instances is what we commonly call thinking. And it is for this that symbols are required; conversely, noises and the like only become symbols in so far as they are used as means to such conceiving. For example, I have seen many cats, and for some time I have found that the noise "cat" occurs when I see one (whether it is uttered by a foreign body or by myself, or by both). I must now attend to the common feature of all these objects, and learn to associate the noise with that. Then, when I hear the noise in future, whether uttered by myself or not, it will bring that common feature—that universal—before my mind, even if no cat is actually being perceived by me. When this happens, and not till then, the noise "cat" has become a symbol for me. The process is very puzzling, and I do not profess to have given anything like an adequate account of it. But whatever difficulties there may be about it, it does not seem to presuppose at any stage that one has a prior knowledge of other minds, or even a prior belief in their existence.

Thirdly, a word must be said about so-called Primitive Animism. According to some Anthropologists, primitive men take for granted that all bodies whatever (or at any rate all striking and noticeable ones) are animated by minds; and if this is so, it is plausible to suppose that civilized infants do the same. In that case, have we not stated our problem the wrong way round? The problem will really be "What leads us to believe that most of the bodies in the universe are *not* animated by minds?" rather than "What leads us to believe that certain one *are* so animated?"

This objection is difficult to discuss because the facts are in dispute. When people say that the savage or the infant is an animist, they seem to be attributing a kind of philosophical theory to him—a set of explicit and formulated beliefs about the universe. But this seems to be an over-rationalization. Beings so primitive and unreflective cannot be accused of subscribing to any kind of "-ism." It would be nearer the mark to say that the savage or the infant *acts as if* he thought that most of the bodies he meets with are animated. But I suspect that even this goes too far. All we can be reasonably sure of is that he acts as if he *did not distinguish* between the animate and the inanimate—he speaks angrily to the chair-leg against which he bumps, or tries a stone for murder [1]—whereas we ourselves treat the animate in one way and the inanimate in another. If so, the question is this: what evidence has one got that this nondistinguishing treatment, which is observed in savages and infants, is unreasonable; what reason is there for thinking that a human body differs in some very important way from a rock or a tree, or even from a cow? And the evidence is the sort of evidence already mentioned. Rocks and trees never utter noises which convey information to us, nor make informative gestures, and it is exceedingly doubtful whether cows ever do; but it is certain that human bodies do frequently utter informative noises and make informative gestures.

However, even if it is literally true that savages and infants hold explicit "animistic" beliefs, this need not worry us. It is just a curious psychological fact, if fact it be. It makes no difference to the logic of the matter. For the point is, what *reasons* has one got for believing the proposition that all bodies are animate? And the answer is that in the case of human bodies

[1] This is said to have happened in ancient Athens even in classical times.

one has strong reasons, whereas in the case of other bodies one has not. One could perfectly well discover this even though one did *not* start by believing the proposition to begin with, as the "Primitive Animist" is supposed to do. The initial believing, if indeed it occurs, is not a logical presupposition of the discovery. The evidence for a proposition is neither strengthened nor weakened by the fact that I believed the proposition before I began my inquiry.

6. We may now return to the main argument. We have described a number of situations in which the perceiving and understanding of symbols gives one evidence of the existence of another mind. But how exactly do they provide evidence for this conclusion? Let us confine ourselves for simplicity to the cases in which the evidence comes from the hearing of sounds. Two conditions, we have seen, must be fulfilled. The first, and most important, is that they must have a symbolic character. And they must be symbolic *for me.* It is obvious that the characteristic of being symbolic is a relational character. An entity S is only a symbol in so far as it stands for some object—whatever the right analysis of "standing for" may be. It is no less obvious, though sometimes forgotten, that the relation is not a simple two-term relation. It involves at least three terms: the entity S, the object O, and in addition a mind or minds. S symbolizes O *to someone.* The relation is more like "to the right of" than it is like "larger than." A is to the right of B from somewhere, from a certain limited set of places. From other places it is not to the right of B, but to the left of it, or in front of it or behind it.

But if the hearing or seeing of S, or its presentation to me in the form of an image, is to provide me with evidence of the existence of another mind, it is not sufficient that S should symbolize some object to someone. It must symbolize some object *to me.* I myself must understand it. Otherwise all I know about it is that it is a noise or black mark having such-and-such sensible qualities. It is true that if I heard sounds uttered in the Arabic language, which I do not understand, I could reasonably conclude to the existence of another mind. But only by analogy. The sounds have some similarity to others which *are* symbolic to me; I therefore assume that they, too, might come to be symbolic to me if I took the trouble.

Secondly, it is essential, I think, that the sounds should symbolize to me something *true or false*. They must propound *propositions* to me. It is not, however, necessary that they should have the grammatical form of a statement. A single word may propound a proposition. Thus the word "snake" may be equivalent to "there is a snake in the immediate neighborhood." Again, the phrase "the bus" may be equivalent to "the bus is now approaching." Must the proposition propounded be such that I can *test* it, whether in fact I do test it or not? It must certainly be such that I know what the world would be like if it were true. Otherwise I have not understood the symbols: for me they are not symbols at all. But it is not necessary that I should be able to discover by direct observation that the world is in fact like that, or is not. Otherwise I could not understand statements about the remote past, whereas actually I can understand them perfectly well.

The third condition is the one which we have already emphasized. The noises must not only be symbolic to me; they must give me information. The proposition which they propound must be new to me. That is, it must be new to me as a whole, though of course its constituents and their mode of combination must be familiar to me; otherwise I do not understand the utterance. If it is not new (i.e., new as a whole), the noises do still give evidence of the occurrence of a mental act other than the present act which understands them, and even of a mental act which is in a sense "foreign." But as we have seen, it might conceivably be an unconscious mental act of my own. And this greatly diminishes the evidential value of the utterance.

Now suppose these conditions are fulfilled. I hear noises which are symbolic to me; they propound to me something true or false; and what they propound is new to me. For instance, I hear the noises "here is a black cat" at a time when I do not myself see the cat and was not expecting it to appear. How exactly does this situation provide me with evidence of the existence of another mind? (It is well to insist once again that evidence, not proof, is all that can be demanded.)

It might be said: I have direct access to a number of cognitive acts by my own introspection. I find that these acts are usually accompanied by noises, audible or imaged. Moreover, I find by introspection that an act directed upon one sort of object, e.g., a cat, is usually accompanied by one sort of noise; and that an act directed upon another sort of object, e.g., blackness, is usually accompanied by another sort of noise. Thus there is a correspondence between the noises and the acts. Differences in the noises are accompanied by differences in the "direction" of the acts. When the object of the act is complex, I usually find a corresponding complexity in the noise. If $n_1$ usually accompanies an act directed upon $O_1$ and $n_2$ usually accompanies an act directed upon $O_2$, then I find that the complex noise $n_1n_2$ is usually accompanied by an act directed upon the complex object $O_1O_2$. And the structure of the complex noise (the way the constituent noises are arranged) varies with the structure of the object-complex upon which the accompanying act is directed. In this way, it may be said, I know from introspection that when the noise-complex "here is a black cat" occurs it is usually accompanied by a specific sort of cognitive act, namely, by the seeing and recognizing of a black cat. But this time it cannot have been a cognitive act of my own, for *I* was not seeing any black cat at the time when the noise-complex occurred. It must therefore have been a foreign cognitive act, an act extraneous to myself, and therefore presumably forming part of the history of some *other* mind.

However, such an account of the matter is not altogether satisfactory. The relation between the noises and the mental acts is really much more intimate than this. It is not a mere accompanying. If it were, the noises would not be functioning as *symbols*. When I am thinking I am always aware of symbols of some sort or another. But they do not just occur along with the thinking. The occurrence of them, whether in a sensible or an imaged form, is an integral part of the thinking itself. One might even define thinking as awareness by means of symbols. Perhaps, indeed, I can *perceive* without symbols. But in fact symbols usually are present to my mind in perceiving as well. And if they are present, again they do not merely accompany the perceiving. They enable me to analyze what I perceive, to recognize and classify the various factors in it, so that the perceiving turns into what philosophers call perceptual judgment, a piece of intelligent or thoughtful perceiving.

Thus the argument should be restated as follows: I know from introspection that noises of this sort frequently function as *instruments to* a certain sort of mental act (not merely accompany it). Therefore they are probably functioning as instruments to an act of that sort in the present case. But in the present case the act is not mine.

But there is still a further amendment to be made. There is a sense in which the noises *are* functioning as symbolic instruments to a mental act of my own. For after all, I do understand them. It is true that I am not seeing the black cat. But I do entertain the thought that a black cat is in the neighborhood. And I think this *by means of* the noises that I hear. But if the noises are in any case functioning as instruments to a mental act of my own, what need have I to suppose that there is also some other mental act—some foreign one—to which they are instrumental?

To clear up this point, we must distinguish two different ways in which symbols can be instrumental to cognitive acts. We must distinguish *spontaneous* thinking from *imposed* thinking. In the present case, my entertaining of the thought that there is a black cat in the room is *imposed* by the noises which I hear. What causes me to use these noises as symbols is the noises themselves, or rather my hearing of them. When I hear them, they arouse certain cognitive dispositions in me (dispositions arising from my learning of English, which are there whether I like it or not); and the result is that I am forced to use them for the entertaining of a certain determinate thought, one which but for them I should not on this occasion have entertained.

But how did these noises happen to present themselves to me? I did not originate them, either consciously, or—so far as I can discover—unconsciously either. And how did they happen to be arranged in just that way? They are so arranged that they make up a whole which is for me a single complex symbol, symbolizing something true or false about the world. That is how they manage to impose an act of thought upon me, which many of the noises I hear do not, striking and complicated though they be. How did this remarkable combination of events come about? How is it that each of the noises was for me a symbol, and how is it, moreover, that they were so combined as to make a single complex symbol, symbolizing something true or false? Well, I know from my own experience how it might have happened, because I know what happens in *spontaneous* thinking. In the spontaneous acts of thinking which introspection reveals to me, noises often function as symbolic instruments. And when they do, they are not usually found in isolation. They are ordered into complexes, each of which is symbolic as a whole and signifies something true or false. It would not be correct to say that I find two acts occurring at once: on the one hand, an act of spontaneous thinking, on the other an act of spontaneously producing symbols and ordering them into a symbol-complex which is true or false as a whole. What happens is that the producing of the significant symbol-complex occurs *in the process of performing* the spontaneous act of thinking. Sometimes this spontaneous act of thinking is concerned with something which I am perceiving. It is then a so-called perceptual judgment.

Thus I can now guess how the noises which I hear have come about, and how they have come to be such and so arranged that I am made to use them as instruments for an act of imposed thinking. For I know by introspection that just such noises, and just such an arrangement of them, are often produced in the course of acts of spontaneous thinking. This makes it likely that here, too, they were produced in the course of an act of spontaneous thinking. But in this case no spontaneous thinking of that particular sort was occurring in myself. Therefore in this case the spontaneous act of thinking must have been a *foreign* act, occurring in some other mind. If the noises are "here is a black cat," the act was probably a perceptual judgment, occasioned by the perceiving of a black cat. But if on investigating the matter for myself I find no black cat, the evidence for a foreign act of thinking still stands. (As we pointed out earlier, false information is just as evidential as true.) Only I shall then have to conclude that this act of thinking was not a perceptual judgment after all, but a piece of fiction-making or story-telling.

In this instance the noise-complex was already familiar to me as a whole. I have often seen black cats and said to myself "here is a black cat." But this is not always so. When I hear a complex noise and find myself using it as an instrument for an act of imposed thinking, it frequently happens that the complex as a whole is one which I am not familiar with. Thus the noise-complex, "the steward of Common-Room keeps a tame mongoose," may be one which I have never myself made use of in an act of spontaneous thinking. Still, if I hear it, it will impose an act of thinking on me; not less so if I am sure that what I am being made to think of is false. And it will accordingly provide me with evidence of a foreign act of spontaneous thinking. This is because I often have used the *constituents* of the noise-complex in the course of my own spontaneous thinkings, for instance the noises "mongoose" and "steward" and "Common-Room." Moreover, although this actual combination of noises is new to me, the *manner* of combination, the structure which the noise-complex has, is perfectly familiar. I have often used it myself in the course of my spontaneous thinkings.

Thus the noise-complex as a whole functions as a symbol for me, and imposes an act of thinking on me, even though I have never made use of it in any of my own spontaneous thinkings.

7. We must now raise certain general questions about this argument for the existence of other minds. Though very different in detail from the one used by the old Analogical Theory, it is clearly an argument from analogy. The form of the argument is: situations *a* and *b* resemble each other in respect of a characteristic $C_1$; situation *a* also has the characteristic $C_2$; therefore situation *b* probably has the characteristic $C_2$ likewise. The noises I am now aware of closely resemble certain ones which I have been aware of before (in technical phraseology, they are *tokens* of the same *type*), and the resemblance covers both their qualities and their manner of combination. Those which I was aware of before functioned as symbols in acts of spontaneous thinking. Therefore these present ones probably resemble them in that respect too; they too probably function as instruments to an act of spontaneous thinking, which in this case is not my own.

But the argument is not only analogical. The hypothesis which it seeks to establish may also be considered in another way. It provides a simple *explanation* of an otherwise mysterious set of occurrences. It explains the curious fact that certain noises not originated by me nevertheless have for me a symbolic character, and moreover are combined in complexes which are symbolic for me as wholes (i.e., propound propositions). Many varieties of sounds occur in the world, and of these only a relatively small proportion are symbolic for me. Those which are symbolic for me can occur in a variety of combinations, and the number of mathematically possible combinations of them is very large; of these combinations only a small proportion "make sense," that is, result in noise-complexes which are symbolic for me *as wholes*. But if there is another mind which uses the same symbols as I do and combines them according to the same principles, and if this mind has produced these noises in the course of an act of spontaneous thinking, then I can account for the occurrence of these noises, and for the fact that they are combined in one of these mathematically improbable combinations. When I say that these facts are "explained" or "accounted for" by our hypothesis, I mean that if the hypothesis is true these facts are instances of a rule which is already known to hold good in a large number of instances. The rule is, that symbolically functioning noises combined in symbolically functioning combinations are produced in the course of acts of spontaneous thinking; and the instances in which it is already known to hold good have been presented to me by introspection.

It may be objected by some that the hypothesis is worthless because it is *unverifiable*. Accordingly it may be said that it has no explanatory power at all, nor can any argument (analogical or other) do anything to increase its probability. For being unverifiable, it is nonsensical; that is, the words which purport to formulate it do not really formulate anything which could conceivably be true or even false.

Now it is true that the hypothesis of the existence of other minds is "unverifiable" in a very narrow sense of that word, namely, if verifying a proposition entails observing some event or situation which makes it true. I cannot *observe* another mind or its acts—unless extrospective acquaintance is possible, which there is no reason to believe it is. But the hypothesis is a perfectly conceivable one, in the sense that I know very well what the world would have to be like if the hypothesis were true—what sorts of entities there must be in it, and what sort of events must occur in them. I know from introspection what acts of thinking and perceiving are, and I know what it is for such acts to be combined into the unity of a single mind (however difficult it may be to give a satisfactory philosophical *theory* of such unity). Moreover, the hypothesis *is* verifiable in what is called the "weak" sense. I know what it would be like to find evidence to support it, because I have in fact found a great deal of evidence which does support it; and this evidence can be increased without assignable limit. It seems to me to be a mistake to demand that all the different types of hypothesis should be verifiable in the same manner. What is to be demanded is, first, that the hypothesis should be conceivable (otherwise certainly it is nonsense); and, secondly, that it should be verifiable or refutable in its own appropriate manner, in accordance with the methods suitable to that particular sort of subject-matter.

However, it is instructive to ask what one would be left with if one refused to entertain the hypothesis of the existence of other minds on the ground of its unverifiability. It would still remain the case that one thinks by means of symbols. Further, the distinction between spontaneous and imposed thinking would still hold good. Nor could one possibly deny that in imposed thinking one acquires information which one did not possess before. It is a rock-bottom fact, and one must accept it whatever philosophy one holds, that the thinking imposed by heard or seen symbols enlarges one's consciousness of the world far beyond the narrow limits to which one's own perception and one's own spontaneous thinking would confine it.[1] An extreme empiricist must accept this fact like anyone else. But the purity of his principles prevents him from attempting any explanation of it, since they force him to conclude that the hypothesis of other minds is nonsensical. So he must just be content to accept the fact itself. Or perhaps he may say: what I *mean* by asserting that there are other minds is simply this fact, that my own consciousness of the world is constantly being enlarged by the hearing of noises and the seeing of marks which are symbolic to me, and by the consequent acts of imposed thinking which go on in me; so that "you" is just a label

---

[1] Here we may note that even the most rigorous course of Cartesian doubt requires the use of symbols. One cannot doubt without symbols to bring before one's mind the proposition which is to be doubted. And philosophical doubt, which is concerned with complicated and highly abstract matters, is scarcely conceivable without the use of *verbal* symbols. We may conjecture that Descartes himself conducted his doubt in French, with some admixture of Latin.

for certain pieces of information which I get in this fashion, and "Jones" is a label for certain other pieces of information, and so on. In that case he, too, can admit that there are other minds. Indeed, he can say it is a certainty that there are, and not merely (as we have suggested) a hypothesis for which there is strong evidence. But obviously he is giving a very strange sense to the phrase "other minds," a sense utterly different from the one which he gives to the phrase "my own mind."

If I am right, there is no need to go to such lengths. One has evidence of the existence of other minds in the ordinary literal sense of the word "mind," the sense in which one applies the word to oneself. Nevertheless, the argument I have offered does have its skeptical side. Any mind whose existence is to be established by it must be subject to certain restrictive conditions, which follow from the nature of the argument itself. In the first place, it must use symbols which I can understand; and I shall only be able to do this if I am able to use them myself. It is true that I may be able to guess that certain noises or marks are symbolic even if I cannot myself understand them. But this, as we have seen, is because they have a fairly close resemblance to other noises or marks which I do understand. If I never understood *any* of the noises or marks which I hear or see, I should have no evidence for the existence of other minds. (Strictly speaking we ought to add "tactual data" as well. They, too, may be symbols for the person who feels them, as the case of Helen Keller shows.)

There is a second restriction of great importance: any mind whose existence is to be established by an argument must be aware of the same world as I am aware of. It must be such that the world which I am aware of is *public* to me and to it, *common* to both of us. This restriction really follows from the first. Unless the foreign symbols refer to objects which I too am aware of they will not be for me symbols at all. These public entities need not be sense-data. Sense-data might still be private, as many philosophers hold. It might even be, as some hold, that the sense-datum analysis of perception is mistaken from beginning to end, and that sensing is not a cognitive process at all, but is merely the being in a certain state ("seeing bluely," or the like). But still, if I am to have evidence of your existence, there must be publicity *somewhere*. Somehow or other we must both have access to one and the same world, if not by sensing, then by some other form of consciousness which sensing makes possible. Suppose this was not so. Suppose that there is another mind which is not aware of the same world which I am aware of, and suppose that it somehow produces noises which I hear or marks which I see. When it makes these noises, obviously I shall not have the faintest idea what it is talking about. How can I, since *ex hypothesi* the noises do not refer to any objects which I am aware of? But this is equivalent to saying that I have no reason whatever for thinking that it is *talking* at all. And so I shall have no reason whatever for believing that it exists, or even for suspecting that it does. The noises which I hear, even though in fact they state the profoundest truths, will be for me mere noises, like the soughing of the wind or the roaring of waves.

It appears, then, that any evidence which I can have of the existence of another mind must also be evidence that the other mind is aware of the same world as I am aware of myself. Philosophers have sometimes suggested that each mind perhaps lives in a private world of its own. Probably no one believes this. But some people have been worried by the suggestion. They have suspected that though incredible it could not be rationally refuted, and have had recourse to mysterious acts of faith to get them out of their difficulty. But the difficulty does not exist, for this speculation of philosophers is nothing but a baseless fancy. The theory is such that there could not conceivably be any evidence in favor of it. Any relevant evidence one can get is bound from the nature of the case to tell against it. Any evidence that I can get of your existence is bound also to be evidence that you do *not* live in a private world, but in the public world which is common to all intelligences, or at least to all those which can have any good reason to believe in one another's existence.

Another and less welcome restriction which our argument imposes concerns the minds of the lower animals. It is commonly held that the lower animals do not use symbols. Now this may be an over-statement. Possibly some of the higher vertebrates do use them on some occasions. It may be that some of their cries have a symbolic character (though they would be extremely vague and ambiguous symbols), and some of their bodily movements and postures may constitute a crude kind of gesture-language. If this is so, then our evidence for consciousness in them is the same in kind as our evidence for the consciousness of our human neighbors, though it is very much smaller in extent. But there is no reason to suppose that snails and oysters speak, even in the widest sense of the word "speak," or that anyone has ever received information from a caterpillar; not that there is any *a priori* reason why these things should not happen (cf. our remarks on parrots above), but so far as we know they do not. However, these are empirical questions of Natural History, which do not concern me. I only wish to insist that *if* the lower animals do not use symbols—symbols which we can understand and which convey information to us—then our evidence for the existence of animal minds is different in kind, and not merely in degree, from our evidence for the existence of human minds. It can only be evidence of a teleological sort, derived from observation of their bodily behavior. Much of the behavior of animal bodies has an apparently purposive character, and suggests that they are moved by wishes and are adapting means to preconceived ends. But it is not easy to say how strong this evidence is. How are we to distinguish between genuine purposiveness and mere *de facto* conduciveness to certain results, say to the survival of the animal or its species? The movements of the cat in the presence of a mouse are such as to increase the probability that the mouse will be caught. But is there more in the situation than this? Is it at all clear that the cat *wishes* to catch the mouse, and consciously controls its movements in accordance with this wish? Moreover, we find the same appearances of purposiveness in plants. We also find it in all sorts of biological phenomena which no one supposes to be under conscious control: in the anatomical structure of every type of organism, in the mutually coordinated growth of its parts, in the circulation of the blood, and in countless other cases. If once we start assuming that wherever there is purposiveness there is mind, we shall end with a most unplausible and extravagant form of Vitalism; every organism, even the humblest vegetable, will have to be endowed with an intelligence—an intelligence far exceeding our own in its scientific knowledge and its inventive capacity.

I shall not pursue these questions further. Perhaps the difficulties which I have mentioned can be met. I only wished to point out that when communication by means of symbols is lacking, the existence of foreign minds cannot be established in any simple or straightforward way; or if it can, it looks as if the word "mind" would have to be used in a sense somewhat different from that which it has when applied to beings who do communicate by means of symbols. (Cf. the difficulties which arise concerning "unconscious mind" in ourselves.) Thus, when Descartes maintained that human beings are conscious but the lower animals are not, this theory was by no means a foolish one, though it may be mistaken. Certainly there was no logical inconsistency in it. Our reasons for attributing consciousness to other human beings are radically different from our reasons (such as they are) for attributing it to the lower animals. Only he seems to have drawn the line in the wrong place. The line should really be drawn between those beings who use symbols and those who do not. If any animals do use symbols, they come above it; and if any human beings do not, they fall below it, even though they happen to walk on two legs.

8. My argument for the existence of other minds is an argument from language (in a wide sense of that word). It may,

however, be objected that I have considered only the *informative* function of language. But of course language is not merely informative. It also has what is called an *emotive* function. This again may be subdivided. In so far as it gives vent to the emotional or conative attitude of the speaker—gives vent to it, not describes it—language may be called *expressive*. In so far as it is designed to arouse the emotions of others, or to influence their actions, it may be called *evocative*. Now many would hold that in the language of everyday life (and it is this, not the language of science or philosophy, which concerns our present inquiry), the emotive function is quite as important as the informative, or, indeed, much more so. Would it not be very naïve to suppose that the main point of everyday language is to say things which are true or false? The main point of it surely is to express one's emotions and wishes, and to evoke those of others. Is it not this which makes language a *social* instrument? Or rather, since the word "instrument" suggests something which might conceivably be dispensed with and replaced by a substitute, let us say that language is the basis of society—a society is a set of minds which talk to one another. The contention then is that what makes it so is primarily its emotive function. Thus many who would agree that one's evidence for the existence of other minds comes from the perceiving and understanding of symbols would nevertheless complain that I have been approaching the problem from the wrong end. For I have been considering only the informative function of language, whereas according to them it is the emotive function which is of primary importance.

Now, of course, I agree that in any complete account of the nature and function of language great attention must be paid to the emotive side. But I am not concerned in this essay to suggest a theory of language, nor even the barest sketch of one. I am concerned simply with an *epistemological* problem: how the understanding of language gives each of us reason to believe in the existence of other minds. And for this purpose only the informative function of language is relevant. The reason for this is that one's access to another mind is not direct. One gets access to it indirectly by way of the *objects* which the other mind and oneself are aware of in common. If we like to speak of a "social relation" between one mind and another, then my contention is that this relation involves three terms, not two. It involves not merely the two minds, but also some object which they are both aware of. Or again: since I am never directly acquainted with another mind, my evidence for its existence can only be evidence for the existence of something satisfying a certain *description;* and the description must always contain a reference to some object or objects which we are aware of in common.

This primacy of the object is what makes the emotive function of language irrelevant to our present inquiry, however important it may be in other connections. Indeed, it is worse than irrelevant. If we allow it to intrude, we shall be involved in a vicious circle. For one can only understand the emotive aspect of an utterance (in that sense of the word "understand" which is here appropriate) if one has *already* got reason to think that the utterance was produced by a foreign mind. Once I have found out, by other means, that the foreign mind is there, I can get evidence that it has certain emotions and certain intentions, and I can discover certain rules for correlating these emotions and intentions with certain tones of voice and turns of phrase, as will be explained presently. But the evidence that it *is* there comes from the informative side of its utterances.

For what is the alternative? When people maintain that it is the emotive element in language which gives us our evidence for the existence of other minds, how are they going to work out this suggestion in detail? I think they must say that tone of voice, and likewise bodily bearing and facial conformation, *directly convey* to me the existence of foreign emotions and volitions. It is not enough to say that these features of utterances or of organisms "express" emotions or volitions, though doubtless they do. Your tone of voice may be ever so expressive. But the point is, how am I to *discover* that it is expressive, and what in particular it is expressive of? Why should I not be content to notice that the noise which this body utters has a peculiar raucous quality like the grating of a wheel, or a soft flowing quality like the sound of running water? And these facial grimaces—what makes me think that they are more than curious visible changes, like the flickering of a flame? No doubt these particular qualities of vocal noises do have what one may call a moving character. They give me so to speak a psycho-physical shake; and one may well suppose that the human organism has an innate tendency to be specially moved by them. But the fact that I myself am stirred by hearing a certain noise gives me no ground for inferring that someone else is feeling an emotion. Even if the emotion to which I am stirred happens to be just like the emotion which you felt when you uttered the noise, this does not help. It is not enough that there should in fact be a foreign mental state which my own mental state resembles—if indeed it does. For the question is, how am I to discover that there *is* this foreign mental state? So far this question has not been answered.

I can only think of one way in which it could be answered by those who hold that one's primary evidence for the existence of other minds comes from the emotive element in language. They must have recourse to a theory of "direct conveyance," as suggested above. They must say that the tone of a voice or the momentary configuration of a face enables me to be *directly aware* of the occurrence of a foreign emotion or volition. That is, they will have to hold that the experiencing of such-and-such auditory or visual qualities releases in me a certain cognitive capacity which cannot otherwise be exercised: a capacity for apprehending other minds, or their states, intuitively and immediately. They smuggle in this direct revelation under cover of the word "expressive," and so make their theory seem less paradoxical than it is. For it is really just a form of the Intuitive Theory, which was discussed earlier in this essay. The contention is that certain auditory or visual experiences—such as the hearing of a raucous tone of voice or the seeing of a facial grimace—enable me to perform an act of *extrospective acquaintance* whose object is a foreign emotion or volition. Perhaps the Intuitive Theory is more plausible in this form than in some others. But it is still open to fatal objections. How is it that I can be deceived by the voice or behavior of an actor, who expresses emotions which he does not actually feel, or for that matter by ordinary everyday hypocrisy? Might there not be a moving waxwork whose face made lifelike grimaces, and which uttered noises in an angry tone of voice?

It appears then that important as the emotive element in language may be, it cannot provide one with one's evidence for the existence of other minds. But it still remains to ask how one does learn that other minds experience emotions and volitions. The evidence so far considered, derived from the informative side of language, shows only that they are percipients and thinkers. In other words, how does one learn that there *is* an emotive element in most or all of the utterances which one hears and understands, and likewise in writing and gesture?

Let us first consider utterances expressive of volitions. How do I get my evidence that other minds experience volitions? It is because I first get evidence that they are entertaining certain thoughts, and then find that the objective world is being altered in such a way as to conform to those thoughts. For instance, I am seeing a door and I notice that it is open. I then hear the words "that the door has got to be shut." At present, we are assuming, the expressive element in language conveys nothing to me (we are trying to explain by what process it comes to do so). So at present I can make nothing of the words "has got to," nor yet of the determined tone in which they are said. It is just a curious auditory quality which the noises have. But I *can* understand the words "that door" and "be shut," both of which refer to certain objective entities which I am aware of: the one to a certain material thing which I observe, the other to an objective universal which I am familiar with. Thus they bring before my mind *a proposition,* the proposition "the door is shut." Now this is a piece of information. It tells me something new which I did not believe before; I did not believe it before, because I believed the contrary, and indeed I still do. So far, then, I have merely received a piece of false information; still it *is* information, and therefore gives me evidence of the existence of a foreign mind which is holding a false belief, or at least entertaining a false proposition. But now a curious thing happens. The organism from which the utterance emanated proceeds to move in such a way that the door *is* shut. The situation is so altered that the information which was false before is now made true. Here, then, I have got evidence of the occurrence of a foreign thought which *affects the objective world.* There was a thought with which the objective state of affairs did not correspond; and immediately afterwards the objective state of affairs is altered so that it does correspond with this thought. Apparently this thought has somehow brought about its own verification. It was false when first uttered, but it has altered the situation in such a way as to make itself true.

Normally this alteration comes about by the intermediation of certain movements in the organism from which the utterances proceeded; it gets up and shuts the door. But even if I observed no organism, I could still get evidence of the existence of a foreign volition. Let us reconsider our previous instance of a disembodied voice. Suppose I heard such voice saying, "Let there be a thunderstorm"; and suppose there promptly was a thunderstorm, although hitherto there had been no sign that any such event was likely to happen (the sky, we will assume, was perfectly clear at the moment when the utterance occurred). And suppose that there were many instances of this sort of thing, many occasions when this voice made an utterance conveying a proposition which was false at the time, but was followed by an objective change which verified it—a surprising change, which no previously observable feature in the situation made probable. I should then have good evidence for thinking that the voice proceeded from a foreign thinker whose thoughts could directly alter the objective world. Such "telekinetic" action of unembodied minds does not in fact happen. But there is no logical absurdity in it. And it is no more difficult to understand how a mind can directly cause changes in the atmosphere than to understand how it can directly cause changes in an organism, which after all is only a complex material object.

We now see how one discovers that certain utterances are expressive of volitions. If one is to discover this, the utterance which expresses the volition must also have an *informative* side. It must among other things propound a proposition, one which is at the moment false. I learn that it is expressive of a volition because of the effects by which it is followed. And when I recognize that a sentence is expressive of a volition without actually observing the physical change which fulfills it, I do so by noticing that it resembles other utterances which *have* been observed to have such effects. It resembles them in respect of tone of voice, or in grammatical structure (by containing verbs in the imperative mood), or in respect of the gestures which accompany it. So I conclude that it, like them, is probably followed by an objective change which verifies it.

Thus it is quite wrong to suppose that the utterance "directly conveys" a foreign volition. There is no question of an immediate and infallible revelation, giving me direct insight into the volition of another person. The "conveying" is a misleading name for an induction which I have to do for myself, by observing that noises uttered in a certain tone of voice are frequently followed by objective changes which verify the propositions they propound.

Let us now turn to utterances expressive of emotion. Emotions are intimately related to thinking on the one hand, to action on the other; and in virtue of these two relations, they are also intimately related to the objective world. Every emotion includes some thinking, and this thinking is not a mere accompaniment, but is an integral part of the emotion itself. The thinking may consist in holding a false belief, as when one is afraid of a purely imaginary danger. But even so, certain objective universals must be present to the mind; else there could be no belief, not even a false one. I may be afraid of a lion outside a door, when in fact there is no lion within miles. But in order to have this "groundless" fear, I must conceive of *lionhood* and *outsideness*. It follows that any utterance which completely expresses an emotion must also propound a proposition, true or false. If someone says in a horror-struck voice, "Oh! a snake!" he is incidentally making a statement which gives me information; the information is, that there is a snake in the immediate neighborhood. But how do I learn that the tone in which he speaks *is* a tone of horror? I answer, I learn it inductively. I discover by repeated observation that when an object is spoken of in that tone of voice, certain consequences are liable to follow. The objective situation is liable to change in a remarkable manner. The relation between the snake and the organism from which the noise proceeded does not usually remain what it was. The noise-making organism runs away, or strikes the snake with a stick. So when I hear that tone of voice again I conclude that such objective consequences are again likely to occur. We have seen that such utterances do propound propositions, and so give evidence of the occurrence of a foreign thought. But I have now found that when the utterance is in that tone of voice the foreign thought in question is a *tendentious* thought, one which tends to change the objective world in certain ways. And I can correlate differences in tone of voice (and in gesture or facial configuration) with different sorts of objective changes which are liable to follow. Thus I distinguish different sorts of tendentious thoughts, one tending to the avoidance of the object which the thought refers to, another tending to the pursuit of it, another to the destruction of it, and so on. And these are the different emotional attitudes.

It follows, and indeed is obvious in any case, that emotional attitudes and volitions are closely connected. Nevertheless, they are not expressed by the same sort of utterance. I discover that an utterance expresses a volition when I find that though false at the moment of its occurrence it results in an objective change which brings the facts into conformity with it. But utterances expressing emotions are related to subsequent objective changes in a more complex way than this. The objective change which follows varies with the specific quality of the utterance. This is not surprising. There is only one way of willing—setting yourself to bring into being the objective situation which you have thought of. But there are many different kinds of emotional attitude; one leads you to alter the objective world in one way, another in another way.

There are, however, certain emotional attitudes which appear not to influence conduct at all, and so do not affect the objective world; for instance, emotions about the past. How am I to discover that an emotion of this sterile kind is occurring in a foreign mind? The utterance which expresses it will indeed propound a proposition to me, and so give me evidence of the occurrence of a foreign thought. But it may seem that in this case the thought has no tendentiousness about it. To this I reply that if the foreign utterance really does express an emotion (and of course hypocrisy is always possible), then the thought of which it gives evidence *is* tendentious, though in rather a different way. Let us consider an emotion directed upon a historical character. Suppose that a man admires the Emperor Valentinian I. If he does, his thinking about that emperor does have effects, effects which it would not have if instead of admiring he disapproved of him. It does not affect the thinker's actions, but it does affect the course of his subsequent thoughts, and this will be revealed by subsequent utterances. We shall find, for instance, that he tends to talk about the good qualities of his hero rather than the bad ones: say, about his military efficiency rather than his atrocious bad temper. If we do not find this, we shall suspect that his utterance did not express emotion at all, but was merely a piece of hypocrisy. Thus in these cases the tendentious character of the thinking lies in the selective control which it exercises upon later think-

175

ings, in directing the thinker's attention upon one set of facts rather than another, and even causing him to ignore certain facts altogether. Thus we may say that in these cases, as in the others, the emotion reveals itself by its tendency to affect one's subsequent relations with objects: only "objects" must be understood to include thinkable objects as well as perceived ones, and "relations" must cover cognitive relations as well as practical ones.

# THE SIMPLICITY OF OTHER MINDS

PAUL ZIFF

BEING EPISTEMICALLY EBULLIENT about having a mind, one wonders about others. There is the doubtful, as they say, "privilege" of "direct access" to one's own mind, but the existence of that of the therefore possibly underprivileged other is supposed to remain another matter.

This "other minds" is a confusion, a confluence of questions, but there are principally these: I have a mind: do I know whether others do and if I do how do I?

1. I have a mind: do others? This question is backwards; turned right it reads: am I unlike others in having a mind?

Is the answer supposed to be difficult? That only I have a mind is nowadays not an unlikely but an at best altogether preposterous hypothesis, for altogether explicable reasons. (To suppose that a reasoned answer to this kind of question cannot be given, cannot coherently be asked for, is a curious dogma of the day.[1])

2. If only I have a mind, then I am a uniquely unique being. There is nothing unique in merely being unique: identical twins apart, all of us of course are unique in that each of us has

Reprinted by permission of the author and editor, from *The Journal of Philosophy*, XLII (1965), 575–584.

[1] See P. F. Strawson, *Individuals* (London: Methuen, 1959), p. 112.

a different genetic constitution; we may often share opinions, but rarely skin.[2] To be the only one with a mind would be another matter.

How could one conclude that one was unique in having a mind? The uniqueness of the individual with respect to skin grafts has been demonstrated over and again in the world's hospitals. Considerations in support of the conclusion that each of us (identical twins apart) has a unique genetic constitution may be adduced from various scientific disciplines and theories: from genetics, immunology, radiology.

Less than the first step in confirming the hypothesis that only I have a mind would be this: to find a conceivably relevant differential factor; unlike others, only I . . .

3. But what if there were no relevant factor? Suppose there were an other such that he and I were not only identical twins but alike in every determinable physiological feature; we were each complete chimeras. Further suppose we behaved in virtually identical ways, displayed the same capacities, manifested the same skills, and so forth. All this could conceivably be so. Then consider the hypothesis that only I have a mind.

Could the other one and I relevantly differ only in this: I do and he does not have a mind?

4. There may seem to be various options here: yes, no, and shades between, but not really, not today.

The hallmarks of a sound theory are here, as everywhere, coherence, completeness, and simplicity: coherence is in part a matter of unity but primarily a matter of consistency, and that, given the appropriate logical legerdemain, is not here especially difficult to attain; completeness is largely a matter of filling gaps, the articulation of theory by means of supporting and subsidiary hypotheses; perhaps parsimony and completeness are the simplest available indices of simplicity. I so gloss the obvious merely to remind you of these matters.

The question again then is: could the other one and I rele-

2 See P. B. Medawar, *The Uniqueness of the Individual* (New York: Basic Books, 1961), pp. 186ff.

vantly differ only in this: I do and he does not have a mind? Suppose we opt for yes. Then how do we account for the fantastic state of affairs? Why do I have a mind? Why doesn't he have a mind? Do minds just come and go in the universe? Did one just happen to alight in my head? Is there no bait for this bird?

Say yes or even maybe, and what else can one do but resolve to accept the relation, miraculous and inexplicable, between the mind and the body, anyone's of course? For it is not as though one has or is even likely to have any coherent theory of the mind in independence of the body. So there is nothing but no.

If no then if I am unique in having a mind then I must be unique in some further way. Of course I am: I am unlike others in that I alone have exactly the brain I have. There is certainly good reason to believe that no one ever has a brain exactly the same as anyone else's.

Shall I say that only I have a mind because only I have just the brain I do? If I argue that how shall I argue it? For why does having just the brain I do matter so much? What about my father, my mother, my children? If they don't have minds why don't they and if I do why do I?

What exactly is the difference between my brain and all others which makes such a difference? Or even roughly?

5. On the hypothesis that one is unique in having a mind, unless one has oneself been the subject of investigation, one is for the most part compelled to eschew reference to and reliance on the findings of psychologists, physiologists, biologists.

For if only I have a mind and if I have not myself been investigated, studied, examined, then though scientists may have discovered much, they are not likely to have discovered much directly concerned with the mind.

Evidently evidence is not easy to discover here. And almost anyone would soon find that the hypothesis that only he has a mind is hard to hold. And there is after all a more viable alternative.

6. I am not a uniquely unique being in being a being with a mind: others too have minds. But which? If we have minds then we have something else too. But what?

Those with a brain of course of the right sort and in the right shape. There is no problem, is there, of other brains? 'Are others brainless?' doesn't itch more than 'Are they legless?' even if it's not exactly as easy to scratch if it does. In a nutshell: there's their brain, being stimulated, responding, altogether well behaved, exemplary, but do they have a mind? To find the mind in the brain is the rub.

To talk about the mind is primarily a fancy way of talking about mental states and mental events (themselves fancy ways of talking). There is a relation between the mind and the brain; more carefully, there are relations between mental events and neurophysiological events, between mental states and neurophysiological states. The evidence for this is today overwhelming and, on the hypothesis that I am not unique in having a mind, here available to me.

7. The futility of the hypothesis that I am unique in having a mind provides important support for the counterthesis that others too have minds. But one is not restricted here to a *via negativa*. No hypothesis that stands up under investigation, consideration, stands alone. One holds another, and if they prove tenable in time all transmute from hypothesis to fact, anyway for a time. (And that childish facts continually decay in time to discarded hypotheses should prove no cause for dismay.)

To the hypothesis that my mind and my brain stand in significant relation I conjoin the hypothesis that my mind and my brain stand in this relation not because the mind is mine but because of what minds and brains are. And to these hypotheses I (as many others do) conjoin the hypothesis that among the others that have minds other animals are to be counted. (Possibly man is the only conjectural beast, but one can have a mind without being remarkably speculative.) But to say that horses, dogs, rats, cats, cows all have minds is not to deny that these beings may have qualitatively radically different experiences from men.

And to these hypotheses still others must of course be conjoined. What is in force and active here then is not a silly single hypothesis that there are other minds, this naively supposed to be somehow based on an unexplored analogy. Instead one is confronted with a complex conceptual scheme. The fact that there are other minds is an integral part of this scheme and at present essential to it.

8. A conceptual scheme such as this, commodious enough to encompass rats and others, draws support from a multitude of observations and experiments.

The efficacy of aspirin, mescal, opium is then an eloquent testimonial to the intimate relation between mind and body, provides confirmation for each of the conjoined hypotheses of the scheme, and so participates in the baptism of the existence of other minds as a fact.

Fat rats lend their weighty support: the urgent voluntary errand of the obese overeater may be owing to hypothalamic damage: "Control of feeding behavior in the hypothalamus is located in two 'feeding centers' in the lateral hypothalamus and two 'satiety' centers in the ventromedial hypothalamus. Destruction of the satiety centers resulted in overeating and obesity, whereas stimulation of these centers was followed by cessation of eating. Stimulation of the 'feeding centers,' on the other hand, led to eating, while their destruction produced a form of anorexia so intense that afflicted animals would starve to death in cages filled with food." [3]

And then the experiments of other rats further bolster our familiar scheme: "There are many indications that animals in problem-box situations experiment with many solutions. Thus one rat, in experiments with the inclined-plane box (Lashley

---

[3] Albert Stunkard, "Research on a Disease: Strategies in the Study of Obesity," in Robert Roessler and Norman S. Greenfield, eds., *Physiological Correlates of Psychological Disorder* (Madison: University of Wisconsin Press, 1962), p. 214.

and Franz, 1919), originally opened the box by an accidental fall from the roof of the restraining cage. For several trials thereafter she systematically climbed to the roof and let go, totaling more than 50 falls before the method was abandoned." [4]

9. That there are other minds is certainly a fact of the day, but it is flaccid stuff: we live in dark ages; our slack concepts crumble, our conceptual schemes are gapped with riddles. That there is a significant relation between the mind and the brain can today hardly be doubted, but precisely what that relation is is another matter presently not known.

Current attempts to identify mental states with cerebral states, mental events with cerebral events, can only be characterized as jejune and misguided: they reveal a fundamental failure of appreciation, a failure occasioned perhaps by a profound misconception of the conceptual situation. A mental event or state is not identical with, is not one and the same thing as, a cerebral or a neurophysiological event or state. This is seen at once once one sees and appreciates the differences between the relevant principles of individuation.

10. In offering a defense of "physicalism," Quine has claimed that "If there is a case for mental events and mental states, it must be just that the positing of them, like the positing of molecules, has some indirect systematic efficacy in the development of theory. But if a certain organization of theory is achieved by thus positing distinctive mental states and events behind physical behavior, surely as much organization could be achieved by positing merely certain correlative physiological states and events instead." [5] This ploy is worth considering, though readily countered, for it serves to underline the distinctiveness of mental states and events. But first the riposte: one might as poorly argue that if the positing of molecules has some indirect systematic efficacy in the development of theory,

[4] K. S. Lashley, *Brain Mechanisms and Intelligence* (New York: Dover, 1963), p. 135.

[5] W. V. O. Quine, *Word and Object* (New York: Wiley, 1960), p. 264.

surely as much organization could be achieved by positing merely certain correlative little objects instead. Quine adds: "The bodily states exist anyway; why add the others?" (264). Little objects exist anyway; why add mysterious little configurations?

For of course if there is a case for mental states and events, then no doubt, in some sense and as Quine claims, it must be that the positing of them, like the positing of molecules, has some systematic efficacy in the development of theory. But it doesn't follow that the positing of states and events of another kind and character need be similarly efficacious. Obviously, the positing of little objects of essentially the same kind and character as macro-objects would not only not contribute to the organization of quantum theory but would render it utterly incoherent.

What is the case for mental states and events? A minute part of it certainly is this: our psychological concepts are important explanatory devices; one can explain someone's tendency to group certain physiologically unlike stimulations together by saying that in each case he experiences the same feeling, in each case the same mental event occurs. By so saying one can avoid saying, what anyway presently appears to be positively untrue, that in each case the same physiological event occurs.

11. Consider a particular mental event, say that which occurs when one is stung by a bee: one experiences a sudden sharp pain, perhaps of relatively short duration, say one or two seconds. Can this particular mental event be identified with a particular cerebral event? Cerebral events are measured in milliseconds. "One of the big gaps in our knowledge, not filled either by physiology or by psychology, is an accurate time-space description of central nervous system electrical activity and behavior in the very short time-intervals. Psychologists tend to deal with long cumulative phenomena, the results of many billions of short-term events. The classical learning-motivation-drive studies illustrate the point; even perceptual-discrimination-motor-response experiments involve a long-term,

complex, spatial-temporal sequence of stimuli of unending variety from one millisecond to the next." [6]

If, instead of particular cerebral events, one were to attempt to identify mental events with particular collections of cerebral events, the move would be somewhat more plausible but still impossible. Consider a repeatable event, say the feeling of a feather touching one's arm: one first has that feeling at one time and then again at another time, each time the very same feeling. There is no reason to suppose that exactly the same collection of cerebral events recurred.

For first, it is nowadays reasonably clear that there is little reason to suppose that any sort of point-to-point relationship exists between the spot touched by the feather and a particular spot on the brain. "Stimulation of the skin at a specific spot will evoke responses in a much larger portion of the somatosensory cortex than the fraction of skin stimulated would lead one to expect on any simple point-to-point relationship." [7] Secondly, as ablation studies have shown over and over again, considerable portions of the brain may be excised without the loss of specific functions. Thus, in connection with patients who have undergone hemispherectomy, it is found that "Language, praxia and higher motor-sensory activities are usually preserved, whichever hemisphere is removed." [8] To suppose that exactly the same cerebral events recur if the same mental events recur subsequent to the hemispherectomy would seem to be a completely unwarranted supposition. More generally, any attempted identification of particular mental events with particular cerebral events or with particular collections of cerebral

[6] John C. Lilly, "Correlations between Neurophysiological Activity in the Cortex and Short-term Behavior in the Monkey," in Harry F. Harlow and Clinton N. Woolsey, eds., *Biological and Biochemical Bases of Behavior* (Madison: University of Wisconsin Press, 1958), p. 84.

[7] Clinton N. Woolsey, "Cortical Localization as Defined by Evoked Potential and Electrical Stimulation Studies," in Georges Schaltenbrand and Clinton N. Woolsey, eds., *Cerebral Localization and Organization* (Madison: University of Wisconsin Press, 1964), p. 17.

[8] Sixto Obrador, "Nervous Integration after Hemispherectomy in Man," in Schaltenbrand and Woolsey, *op. cit.*, pp. 144–145.

events or with particular collections of collections of cerebral events and so forth runs afoul of the well-known facts of functional plasticity: whether these be accounted for in terms of Lashley's "mass action" theory [9] or in terms of some current version of the standard Sherringtonian picture of central nervous integration,[10] they seem effectively to exclude from serious consideration all identity theories of mind-brain relationship.

12. Mental events cannot be identified with cerebral events. But to abandon an oversimple identity theory is not *ipso facto* to manufacture mysteries or substances. By the denial of identification we are not therewith saddled with multiple entities, double events. This duplicity of ontology is simply eliminable.

Any apple has of course a molecular constitution. So it has been said that "The atomic theory is all-encompassing in the physical world; it leaves no room for micro-objects *and* correlated macro-objects; the whole point is that a macro-object is a complex micro-structure and nothing more." [11] Brandt adds that "There is not similar compulsion to identify stabbing pains with states of the brain" (69). On the contrary: the compulsion is quite the same and to be resisted in either case.

I hold an apple in my hand; this apple is not identical with, is not one and the same thing as, a particular collection of molecules. That cannot possibly be so: I do not lose and acquire a new apple each time I toss it in air; yet the molecular constitution of my apple fluctuates from toss to toss: the collection constituting the apple at one toss is not identical with the collection constituting the apple at another toss. Unless the transitivity of identity is to be called into question, this is not a case of identity.

Then is my apple to be identified with a particular class of spatiotemporally ordered collections of molecules? But which collections? (Exactly how many hairs can a bald man have? Is

[9] See Lashley, *op. cit.*

[10] See R. W. Sperry, "Physiological Plasticity," in Harlow and Woolsey, *op. cit.*, pp. 401–424.

[11] Richard B. Brandt, "Doubts about the Identity Theory," in Sidney Hook, ed., *Dimensions of Mind* (New York: Collier, 1961), p. 69.

water $H_2O$? A glass of lake water is not a glass of $H_2O$. Isn't lake water water?) And one can bite an apple, but could one bite that class of spatiotemporally ordered collections of molecules? Or cut it in half? (Alternatively it is sometimes suggested that the apple is identical not with a particular collection of molecules but with a particular configuration of molecules. The switch from 'collection' to 'configuration' accomplishes nothing; the same problems remain: radically different principles of individuation are still involved.)

13. Apples can no more be identified with collections of molecules than mental events can be identified with cerebral events. But that does not mean that apples must be spiritual concomitants of collections of molecules. If there is no collection of molecules sporting in the neighborhood of a branch, then there is no apple dangling there.

To class something an apple is to employ a particular form of conceptualization; to class something a collection of molecules is to employ another. These two forms of conceptualization are two, not one, but they are not totally unrelated: in each case that which is conceived of is an entity of a sort. These two entities, so conceived, are neither one and the same entity nor yet exactly two different entities.

One of the simplest relations one could hope to find between entities would be that of identity: the entity conceived of as an alpha proves to be identical with, one and the same as, that conceived as a beta. Another simple relation would be that of difference: the entities conceived of are not only the same, but the existence of one is wholly independent, directly or indirectly, of the existence of the other. Between these two extremes there are innumerable cases, and there one finds apples and collections of molecules, minds and brains.

14. Psychophysiology is that relatively new branch of science concerned with determining the specific relations obtaining between mind and brain. Its task is to find and state dyadic translation functions, functions that take as arguments ordered pairs, one member of which ranges over psychological matters,

186

the other over physiological matters.[12] The function of a psychophysiological dyadic translation function is to coordinate psychological and physiological descriptions, referential expressions, and so forth, and so bridge the conceptual gap between these different forms of conceptualization.

An identity relation is a simple translation function serving to coordinate different descriptions at the same conceptual level. It is of no utility in connection with expressions exemplifying radically different forms of conceptualization. There is no reason to suppose that an identity function can be of any utility in psychophysiology: the forms of conceptualization employed there are too markedly different to allow any such easy interrelation.

15. There is a translation function that serves to coordinate our talk about apples with talk about collections and configurations of molecules. It is not a simple identity function.[13] It is complex and difficult to state. For, from the point of view of macro-entities, talk about micro-entities is inevitably excessively definite, exact, precise. A particular apple is not a particular class of spatiotemporally ordered collections of molecules, and even if it were, to bite an apple would not be to bite the class but rather to segment some member(s) of the class; but of course the members of such a class, namely collections of molecules, are not specifiable.[14]

Adequate translation functions are hard to come by in psychophysiology; in fact none are known. The reasons for this remarkable lack of knowledge are largely but not exclusively technological. Ablation and stimulation are the major methods of cerebral and neurophysiological research. The presently in-

---

[12] See Albert F. Ax, "Psychophysiological Methodology for the Study of Schizophrenia," in Roessler and Greenfield, *op. cit.*, pp. 29–44.

[13] See H. Putnam, "Minds and Machines," in Hook, *op. cit.*, pp. 155ff. Putnam's "theoretical identification" is, I believe, best thought of as a relatively complex translation function.

[14] See M. Black, *Problems of Analysis* (Ithaca: Cornell University Press, 1954), pp. 27ff., in connection with the nonexistence of rigidly demarcated classes.

superable problems posed by such techniques should be obvious: think of attempting to determine the functions of the various parts of a full-scale computer by examining the computer's output after removing bits of its mechanism or tampering with its input; and this greatly understates the problem. But the present state of technology is not the only significant difficulty in providing plausible psychophysiological translation functions.

16. Without peering overmuch, one can make out an unfortunate mentalistic conceptual scheme generally accepted today. One can discern an internally structured, albeit incoherent, set of concepts. There appears to be no end to tiresome talk of intentions, of motives, of direct awarenesses. It is this scheme that gives rise to the disembodied spirit, the death survivor, the telepath, the sufferer of ghostly agonies in the fireless flames of hell. Disembodied spirits not being choice physiological subjects, it need not be a source of astonishment that adequate translation functions are not at once available for all mentalistic concepts.

But fortunately conceptual decay is the order of the day. The current mentalistic scheme is gradually giving up the ghost. Our intellectual concepts, thinking, planning, experimenting, all are tottering; intelligence looks to be not importantly different from a trait of mechanical morons with lightninglike access to prodigious memories, computers. But no doubt pain and other plain concepts are likely to survive. And possibly in time, if the race lingers on, adequate translation functions will be found for the survivors.

# COMMENT

ALVIN PLANTINGA

With much of Ziff's interesting paper I have no quarrel. The identity theory, no doubt, is not compelling, and, while I don't share Ziff's disapproval of our "unfortunate" mentalistic conceptual scheme, this is for present purposes of little moment. More important is that Ziff seems, so far as I understand him, to give the traditional problem of other minds too short shrift. What he says on this head, however, is compressed and aphoristic; his arguments are sometimes merely adumbrated; I am by no means confident that I have grasped them. Hence my comments are a request for more light rather than a settled criticism.

"Do I know whether others have minds? and, if so, how do I?" The answer, says Ziff, is easy, the hypothesis that only he has a mind being nowadays preposterous. Why so? Ziff has two arguments. First, the hypothesis that only he (or I) has a mind is "futile"; for if I (or he) alone have a mind, then there must be some further relevant difference between me (or my body) and others: but no such differences can be found. And secondly, he says, there is much confirming evidence for our "conceptual scheme," a conjunction of hypotheses one conjunct of

Reprinted by permission of the author and editor, from *The Journal of Philosophy*, LXII (1965), 584–587.

189

which is that I am not unique in having a mind: so then this evidence confirms that conjunct.

But with respect to *what* is the hypothesis that only I have a mind futile? And what is the relevant evidence that confirms our conceptual scheme? Suppose we say *my total evidence* is a set of propositions of which $p$ is a member if *either* I know $p$ to be true and $p$ is merely about my own mind or physical objects (including human and animal bodies) and their behavior, *or* $p$ is a logical consequence of such propositions. (A necessary but not sufficient condition of $p$'s being merely about my own mind or physical objects is that it not entail the existence of mental states not my own.) Part of the problem of other minds, then, is the question whether we can show that it is more likely than not, on my total evidence, that I am not unique in having a mind.

Thus armed, let us return to Ziff's argument. *Why* must there be a relevant factor differentiating me or my body from others if only I have a mind? Couldn't there be a body like mine in the respects Ziff mentions but differing from it in being unminded? Couldn't I (or my body) have a mindless double? No, says Ziff, and he gives an argument for his conclusion. But just what is Ziff concluding? That it is *inconceivable* or *logically impossible* that I have a mindless double? This seems pretty clearly false, and the argument Ziff provides does not support it. That on what we all know to be true it is wildly improbable that I have a mindless double? This is doubtless so, but irrelevant to Ziff's further concerns. So the claim must be that *on my total evidence* it is vastly unlikely (or anyhow unlikely) that I have a mindless double. Why so? The essential premise seems to be

(A) If I had a mindless double, I would be unable to provide a sound (i.e., coherent, complete, and simple) theory explaining this fact.

But is (A) true? Despite Ziff's disarming disclaimer, it is no easy matter to explain simplicity, coherence, and completeness as applied to theories of the sort under consideration: consider the following "theory." There are just two minds, mine and Descartes' Evil Genius. The latter takes perverse pleasure in practical jokes of cosmic dimensions and has created me expressly to deceive me. He has also created a considerable array of mindless human bodies (among them my mindless double) that behave in pretty much the way one might expect minded human bodies to behave. He repeats this charade every seventy years or so with a different victim.

Does this "theory" explain the facts? Is it sufficiently coherent, simple, and complete? It is surely coherent; and it seems as simple as the theory that, for *each* of these bodies, there is a mind. As for completeness, no doubt suitable supplementary hypotheses can be adjoined to it. In short, I see no reason, or no very good reason, for thinking (A) true.

But suppose we concede this conclusion; suppose we grant that my total evidence contains or confirms the proposition that, if I alone have a mind, then I (or my body) must be unique in some further relevant respect. How does it follow that, on my total evidence, it is unlikely that I am unique in having a mind? I *am* unique in various further respects; no one else has these fingerprints, and only in my body do I, e.g., feel pain. And of many of the properties that distinguish me from others I cannot divest myself. It is no part of my total evidence that these properties are causally irrelevant to having a mind: how then am I to discover that they are? Accordingly, I find Ziff's first argument inconclusive.

Arguing, secondly, that on my total evidence the theory that others have minds is very probable, Ziff points out that this theory is one conjunct of a conjunction of hypotheses constituting what he calls a "conceptual scheme." Various conjuncts of this scheme, moreover, are confirmed by various parts of my evidence: which parts therefore confirm the entire scheme and each of its conjuncts. But the structure of this argument is not easy to discern. Possibly the suggestion is that this conceptual scheme is confirmed by any proposition confirming any conjunct of it, on the grounds that a conjunction is confirmed by any proposition that confirms any of its conjuncts; and possibly it is suggested that any proposition confirming the scheme confirms every conjunct of it, on the grounds that a proposition confirms the logical consequences of any proposition it confirms. But these two principles lead to trouble, entailing as they do that, if a proposition confirms any proposition, it confirms every proposition. Hence I do not know how the second argument is to be construed.

A crucial question here is this: can we show that no conceptual scheme inconsistent with the one we adopt is as probable as the latter on our total evidence? I do not say this cannot be shown; but I do not see how to show it.

# V

*Criteriological Argument*

# KNOWLEDGE OF OTHER MINDS

## *I*

I BELIEVE that the argument from analogy for the existence of other minds still enjoys more credit than it deserves, and my first aim will be to show that it leads nowhere. J. S. Mill is one of many who have accepted the argument and I take his statement of it as representative. He puts to himself the question, "By what evidence do I know, or by what considerations am I led to believe, that there exist other sentient creatures; that the walking and speaking figures which I see and hear, have sensations and thoughts, or in other words, possess Minds?" His answer is the following:

> I conclude that other human beings have feelings like me, because, first, they have bodies like me, which I know, in my own case, to be the antecedent condition of feelings; and because, secondly, they exhibit the acts, and other outward signs, which in my own case I know by experience to be caused by feelings. I am conscious in myself of a series of facts connected by an uniform sequence, of which the beginning is modifications of my body, the middle is feelings, the end is outward

Reprinted by permission of the author and Prentice-Hall, from *Knowledge and Certainty*, pp. 130–140. Copyright 1963.

demeanor. In the case of other human beings I have the evidence of my senses for the first and last links of the series, but not for the intermediate link. I find, however, that the sequence between the first and last is as regular and constant in those other cases as it is in mine. In my own case I know that the first link produces the last through the intermediate link, and could not produce it without. Experience, therefore, obliges me to conclude that there must be an intermediate link; which must either be the same in others as in myself, or a different one: I must either believe them to be alive, or to be automatons: and by believing them to be alive, that is, by supposing the link to be of the same nature as in the case of which I have experience, and which is in all other respects similar, I bring other human beings, as phenomena, under the same generalizations which I know by experience to be the true theory of my own existence.[1]

I shall pass by the possible objection that this would be very *weak* inductive reasoning, based as it is on the observation of a single instance. More interesting is the following point: Suppose this reasoning could yield a conclusion of the sort "It is probable that that human figure" (pointing at some person other than oneself) "has thoughts and feelings." Then there is a question as to whether this conclusion can *mean* anything to the philosopher who draws it, because there is a question as to whether the sentence "That human figure has thoughts and feelings" can mean anything to him. Why should this be a question? Because the assumption from which Mill starts is that he has *no criterion* for determining whether another "walking and speaking figure" does or does not have thoughts and feelings. If he had a criterion he could apply it, establishing with certainty that this or that human figure does or does not have feelings (for the only plausible criterion would lie in behavior and circumstances that are open to view), and there would be no call to resort to tenuous analogical reasoning that yields at best a probability. If Mill has no criterion for the existence of

[1] J. S. Mill, *An Examination of Sir William Hamilton's Philosophy*, 6th ed. (New York: Longmans, Green & Co., 1889), pp. 243–244.

feelings other than his own then in that sense he does not understand the sentence "That human figure has feelings" and therefore does not understand the sentence "It is *probable* that that human figure has feelings."

There is a familiar inclination to make the following reply: "Although I have no criterion of verification still I *understand,* for example, the sentence 'He has a pain.' For I understand the meaning of 'I have a pain,' and 'He has a pain' means that he has the *same* thing I have when I have a pain." But this is a fruitless maneuver. If I do not know how to establish that someone has a pain then I do not know how to establish that he has the *same* as I have when I have a pain.[2] You cannot improve my understanding of "He has a pain" by this recourse to the notion of "the same," unless you give me a criterion for saying that someone *has* the same as I have. If you can do this you will have no use for the argument from analogy: and if you cannot then you do not understand the supposed conclusion of that argument. A philosopher who purports to rely on the analogical argument cannot, I think, escape this dilemma.

There have been various attempts to repair the argument from analogy. Mr. Stuart Hampshire has argued[3] that its validity as a method of inference can be established in the following way: Others sometimes infer that I am feeling giddy from my behavior. Now I have direct, noninferential knowledge, says Hampshire, of my own feelings. So I can check inferences made about me against the facts, checking thereby the accuracy of the "methods" of inference.

All that is required for testing the validity of any method of factual inference is that each one of us should sometimes be in a position to confront the conclusions of the doubtful method of inference with what is known by him to be true indepen-

[2] "It is no explanation to say: the supposition that he has a pain is simply the supposition that he has the same as I. For *that* part of the grammar is quite clear to me: that is, that one will say that the stove has the same experience as I, *if* one says: it is in pain and I am in pain" (Ludwig Wittgenstein, *Philosophical Investigations* (New York: Macmillan, 1951), sec. 350).

[3] "The Analogy of Feeling," *Mind* (January, 1952), pp. 1–12.

dently of the method of inference in question. Each one of us is certainly in this position in respect of our common methods of inference about the feelings of persons other than ourselves, in virtue of the fact that each one of us is constantly able to compare the results of this type of inference with what he knows to be true directly and non-inferentially; each one of us is in the position to make this testing comparison, whenever he is the designated subject of a statement about feelings and sensations. I, Hampshire, know by what sort of signs I may be misled in inferring Jones's and Smith's feelings, because I have implicitly noticed (though probably not formulated) where Jones, Smith and others generally go wrong in inferring my feelings (*op. cit.*, pp. 4–5).

Presumably I can also note when the inferences of others about my feelings do not go wrong. Having ascertained the reliability of some inference-procedures I can use them myself, in a guarded way, to draw conclusions about the feelings of others, with a modest but justified confidence in the truth of those conclusions.

My first comment is that Hampshire has apparently forgotten the purpose of the argument from analogy, which is to provide some probability that "the walking and speaking figures which I see and hear, have sensations and thoughts" (Mill). For the reasoning that he describes involves the assumption that other human figures *do* have thoughts and sensations: for they are assumed to *make inferences* about me from *observations* of my behavior. But the philosophical problem of the existence of other minds *is* the problem of whether human figures other than oneself do, among other things, make observations, inferences, and assertions. Hampshire's supposed defense of the argument from analogy is an *ignoratio elenchi*.

If we struck from the reasoning described by Hampshire all assumption of thoughts and sensations in others we should be left with something roughly like this: "When my behavior is such and such there come from nearby human figures the sounds 'He feels giddy.' And generally I do feel giddy at the time. Therefore when another human figure exhibits the same behavior and I say 'He feels giddy,' it is probable that he does feel giddy." But the reference here to the sentence-like sounds coming from other human bodies is irrelevant, since I must not assume that those sounds express inferences. Thus the reasoning becomes simply the classical argument from analogy: "When my behavior is such and such I feel giddy; so probably when another human figure behaves the same way he feels the same way." This argument, again, is caught in the dilemma about the criterion of the *same*.

The version of analogical reasoning offered by Professor H. H. Price [4] is more interesting. He suggests that "one's evidence for the existence of other minds is derived primarily from the understanding of language" (p. 429). His idea is that if another body gives forth noises one understands, like "There's the bus," and if these noises give one new information, this "provides some evidence that the foreign body which uttered the noises is animated by a mind like one's own. . . . Suppose I am often in its neighborhood, and it repeatedly produces utterances which I can understand, and which I then proceed to verify for myself. And suppose that this happens in many different kinds of situations. I think that my evidence for believing that this body is animated by a mind like my own would then become very strong" (p. 430). The body from which these informative sounds proceed need not be a human body. "If the rustling of the leaves of an oak formed intelligible words conveying new information to me, and if gorse-bushes made intelligible gestures, I should have evidence that the oak or the gorse-bush was animated by an intelligence like my own" (p. 436). Even if the intelligible and informative sounds did not proceed from a body they would provide evidence for the existence of a (disembodied) mind (p. 435).

Although differing sharply from the classical analogical argument, the reasoning presented by Price is still analogical in

[4] "Our Evidence for the Existence of Other Minds," *Philosophy,* XIII (1938), 425–456.

form: I know by introspection that when certain combinations of sounds come from me they are "symbols in acts of spontaneous thinking"; therefore similar combinations of sounds, not produced by me, "probably function as instruments to an act of spontaneous thinking, which in this case is not my own" (p. 446). Price says that the reasoning also provides an *explanation* of the otherwise mysterious occurrence of sounds which I understand but did not produce. He anticipates the objection that the hypothesis is nonsensical because unverifiable. "The hypothesis is a perfectly conceivable one," he says, "in the sense that I know very well what the world would have to be like if the hypothesis were true—what sorts of entities there must be in it, and what sorts of events must occur in them. I know from introspection what acts of thinking and perceiving are, and I know what it is for such acts to be combined into the unity of a single mind . . ." (pp. 446–447).

I wish to argue against Price that no amount of intelligible sounds coming from an oak tree or a kitchen table could create any probability that it has sensations and thoughts. The question to be asked is: What would show that a tree or table *understands* the sounds that come from it? We can imagine that useful warnings, true descriptions and predictions, even "replies" to questions, should emanate from a tree, so that it came to be of enormous value to its owner. How should we establish that it understood those sentences? Should we "question" it? Suppose that the tree "said" that there was a vixen in the neighborhood, and we "asked" it "What is a vixen?," and it "replied," "A vixen is a female fox." It might go on to do as well for "female" and "fox." This performance might incline us to say that the tree understood the words, in contrast to the possible case in which it answered "I don't know" or did not answer at all. But would it show that the tree understood the words in the same sense that a person could understand them? With a person such a performance would create a presumption that he could make correct *applications* of the word in question; but not so with a tree. To see this point think of the normal teaching of words (e.g., "spoon," "dog," "red") to a child and how one decides whether he understands them. At a primitive stage of teaching one does not require or expect definitions, but rather that the child should *pick out* reds from blues, dogs from cats, spoons from forks. This involves his looking, pointing, reaching for and going to the right things and not the wrong ones. That a child says "red" when a red thing and "blue" when a blue thing is put before him is indicative of a mastery of those words *only* in conjunction with the other activities of looking, pointing, trying to get, fetching, and carrying. Try to suppose that he says the right words but looks at and reaches for the wrong things. Should we be tempted to say that he has mastered the use of those words? No, indeed. The disparity between words and behavior would make us say that he does not understand the words. In the case of a tree there could be no disparity between its words and its "behavior" because it is logically incapable of behavior of the relevant kind.

Since it has nothing like the human face and body it makes no sense to say of a tree, or an electronic computer, that it is looking or pointing at or fetching something. (Of course one can always *invent* a sense for these expressions.) Therefore it would make no sense to say that it did or did not understand the above words. Trees and computers cannot either pass or fail the tests that a child is put through. They cannot take them. That an object was a source of intelligible sounds or other signs (no matter how sequential) would not be enough by itself to establish that it had thoughts or sensations. How informative sentences and valuable predictions could emanate from a gorse-bush might be a grave scientific problem, but the explanation could never be that the gorse-bush has a mind. Better no explanation than nonsense!

It might be thought that the above difficulty holds only for words whose meaning has a "perceptual content" and that if we imagined, for example, that our gorse-bush produced nothing but pure mathematical propositions we should be justified in attributing thought to it, although not sensation. But suppose there was a remarkable "calculating boy" who could give right answers to arithmetical problems but could not apply numerals to reality in empirical propositions, e.g., he could not *count* any objects. I believe that everyone would be reluctant to say that he *understood* the mathematical signs and truths that he produced. If he could count in the normal way there would not be this reluctance. And "counting in the normal way" involves looking, pointing, reaching, fetching, and so on. That is, it requires the human face and body, and human behavior—or something similar. Things which do not have the human form, or anything like it, not merely do not but *cannot* satisfy the criteria for thinking. I am trying to bring out part of what Wittgenstein meant when he said, "We only say of a human being and what is like one that it thinks" (*Investigations*, sec. 360), and "The human body is the best picture of the human soul" (*ibid.*, p. 178).

I have not yet gone into the most fundamental error of the argument from analogy. It is present whether the argument is the classical one (the analogy between my body and other bodies) or Price's version (the analogy between my language and the noises and signs produced by other things). It is the mistaken assumption that *one learns from one's own case* what thinking, feeling, sensation are. Price gives expression to this assumption when he says: "I know from introspection what acts of thinking and perceiving are . . ." (*op. cit.*, p. 447). It is the most natural assumption for a philosopher to make and indeed seems at first to be the only possibility. Yet Wittgenstein has made us see that it leads first to solipsism and then to non-sense. I shall try to state as briefly as possible how it produces those results.

A philosopher who believes that one must learn what thinking, fear, or pain is "from one's own case," does not believe that the thing to be observed is one's behavior, but rather something "inward." He considers behavior to be related to the inward states and occurrences merely as an accompaniment or possibly an effect. He cannot regard behavior as a *criterion* of psychological phenomena: for if he did he would have no use for the analogical argument (as was said before) and also the priority given to "one's own case" would be pointless. He believes that he notes something in himself that he calls "thinking" or "fear" or "pain," and then he tries to infer the presence of the *same* in others. He should then deal with the question of what his criterion of the *same* in others is. This he cannot do because it is of the essence of his viewpoint to reject circumstances and behavior as a criterion of mental phenomena in others. And what else could serve as a criterion? He ought, therefore, to draw the conclusion that the notion of thinking, fear, or pain in others is in an important sense meaningless. He has no idea of what would count for or against it.[5] "That there should be thinking or pain other than my own is unintelligible," he ought to hold. This would be a rigorous solipsism, and a correct outcome of the assumption that one can know only from one's own case what the mental phenomena are. An equivalent way of putting it would be: "When I say 'I am in pain,' by 'pain' I mean a certain inward state. When I say '*He* is in pain,' by 'pain' I mean *behavior*. I cannot attribute pain to others *in the same sense* that I attribute it to myself."

Some philosophers before Wittgenstein may have seen the solipsistic result of starting from "one's own case." But I believe he is the first to have shown how that starting point destroys itself. This may be presented as follows: One supposes that one inwardly picks out something as thinking or pain and thereafter identifies it whenever it presents itself in the soul. But the question to be pressed is, Does one make *correct* identifications? The proponent of these "private" identifications has nothing to say here. He feels sure that he identifies correctly the occurrences in his soul; but feeling sure is no guarantee of being

---

[5] One reason why philosophers have not commonly drawn this conclusion may be, as Wittgenstein acutely suggests, that they assume that they have "an infallible paradigm of identity in the identity of a thing with itself" (*Investigations*, sec. 215).

right. Indeed he has no idea of what being *right* could mean. He does not know how to distinguish between actually making correct identifications and being under the impression that he does. (See *Investigations*, secs. 258–9.) Suppose that he identified the emotion of anxiety as the sensation of pain? Neither he nor anyone else could know about this "mistake." Perhaps he makes a mistake *every* time! Perhaps all of us do! We ought to see now that we are talking nonsense. We do not know what a *mistake* would be. We have no standard, no examples, no customary practice, with which to compare our inner recognitions. The inward identification cannot hit the bull's-eye, or miss it either, because there is no bull's-eye. When we see that the ideas of correct and incorrect have no application to the supposed inner identification, the later notion loses its appearance of sense. Its collapse brings down both solipsism and the argument from analogy.

## II

The destruction of the argument from analogy also destroys the *problem* for which it was supposed to provide a solution. A philosopher feels himself in a difficulty about other minds because he assumes that first of all he is acquainted with mental phenomena "from his own case." What troubles him is how to make the transition from his own case to the case of others. When his thinking is freed of the illusion of the priority of his own case, then he is able to look at the familiar facts and to acknowledge that the circumstances, behavior, and utterances of others actually are his *criteria* (not merely his evidence) for the existence of their mental states. Previously this had seemed impossible.

But now he is in danger of flying to the opposite extreme of behaviorism, which errs by believing that through observation of one's own circumstances, behavior, and utterances one can find out that one is thinking or angry. The philosophy of "from one's own case" and behaviorism, though in a sense opposites, make the common assumption that the first-person, present-tense psychological statements are verified by self-observation. According to the "one's own case" philosophy the self-observation cannot be checked by others; according to behaviorism the self-observation would be by means of outward criteria that are available to all. The first position becomes unintelligible; the second is false for at least many kinds of psychological statements. We are forced to conclude that the first-person psychological statements are not (or hardly ever) verified by self-observation. It follows that they have no verification at all; for if they had a verification it would have to be by self-observation.

But if sentences like "My head aches" or "I wonder where she is" do not express observations then what do they do? What is the relation between my declaration that my head aches and the fact that my head aches, if the former is not the report of an observation? The perplexity about the existence of *other* minds has, as the result of criticism, turned into a perplexity about the meaning of one's own psychological sentences about oneself. At our starting point it was the sentence "*His* head aches" that posed a problem; but now it is the sentence "*My* head aches" that puzzles us.

One way in which this problem can be put is by the question, "How does *one know when to say* the words 'My head aches'?" The inclination to ask this question can be made acute by imagining a fantastic but not impossible case of a person who has survived to adult years without ever experiencing pain. He is given various sorts of injections to correct this condition, and on receiving one of these one day, he jumps and exclaims, "Now I feel pain!" One wants to ask, "How did he *recognize* the new sensation as a *pain?*"

Let us note that if the man gives an answer (e.g., "I knew it must be pain because of the way I jumped") then he proves by that very fact that he has not mastered the correct use of the words "I feel pain." They cannot be used to state a *conclusion.* In telling us *how* he did it he will convict himself of a misuse. Therefore the question "How did he recognize his sensation?" requests the impossible. The inclination to ask it is evidence of our inability to grasp the fact that the use of this psychological sentence has nothing to do with recognizing or identifying or observing a state of oneself.

The fact that this imagined case produces an especially strong temptation to ask the "How?" question shows that we have the idea that it must be more difficult to give the right name of one's sensation *the first time*. The implication would be that it is not so difficult *after* the first time. Why should this be? Are we thinking that then the man would have a paradigm of pain with which he could compare his sensations and so be in a position to know right off whether a certain sensation was or was not a pain? But the paradigm would be either something "outer" (behavior) or something "inner" (perhaps a memory impression of the sensation). If the former then he is misusing the first-person sentence. If the latter then the question of whether he compared *correctly* the present sensation with the inner paradigm of pain would be without sense. Thus the idea that the use of the first-person sentences can be governed by paradigms must be abandoned. It is another form of our insistent misconception of the first-person sentence as resting somehow on the identification of a psychological state.

These absurdities prove that we must conceive of the first-person psychological sentences in some entirely different light. Wittgenstein presents us with the suggestion that the first-person sentences are to be thought of as similar to the natural nonverbal, behavioral expressions of psychological states. "My leg hurts," for example, is to be assimilated to crying, limping, holding one's leg. This is a bewildering comparison and one's first thought is that two sorts of things could not be more unlike. By saying the sentence one can make a *statement*; it has a *contradictory*; it is *true* or *false*; in saying it one *lies* or *tells the truth*; and so on. None of these things, exactly, can be said of crying, limping, holding one's leg. So how can there be any resemblance? But Wittgenstein knew this when he deliberately likened such a sentence to "the primitive, the natural, expressions" of pain, and said that it is "new pain-behavior" (*ibid.*, sec. 244). This analogy has at least two important merits: first, it breaks the hold on us of the question "How does one *know when to say* 'My leg hurts'?", for in the light of the analogy this will be as nonsensical as the question "How does one know when to cry, limp, or hold one's leg?"; second, it explains how the utterance of a first-person psychological sentence by another person can have *importance* for us, although not as an identification—for in the light of the analogy it will have the same importance as the natural behavior which serves as our preverbal criterion of the psychological states of others.

# WITTGENSTEIN'S
## *PHILOSOPHICAL INVESTIGATIONS*

NORMAN MALCOLM

*Ein Buch ist ein Spiegel; wenn ein Affe hineinguckt,
so kann freilich kein Apostel heraussehen.*

LICHTENBERG

An attempt to summarize the Investigations[1] would be neither successful nor useful. Wittgenstein compressed his thoughts to the point where further compression is impossible. What is needed is that they be unfolded and the connections between them traced out. A likely first reaction to the book will be to regard it as a puzzling collection of reflections that are sometimes individually brilliant, but possess no unity, present no system of ideas. In truth the unity is there, but it cannot be perceived without strenuous exertion. Within the scope of a review the connectedness can best be brought out, I think, by concentrating on some single topic—in spite of the fact that there are no separate topics, for each of the investigations in the book criss-crosses again and again with every other one. In the following I center my attention on Wittgenstein's

Reprinted by permission of the author and Prentice-Hall, from *Knowledge and Certainty*, pp. 96–129. Copyright 1963.

[1] Ludwig Wittgenstein, *Philosophical Investigations*, German and English on facing pages, tr. by G. E. M. Anscombe (New York: Macmillan, 1953).

treatment of the problem of how language is related to inner experiences—to sensations, feelings, and moods. This is one of the main inquiries of the book and perhaps the most difficult to understand. I am sufficiently aware of the fact that my presentation of this subject will certainly fail to portray the subtlety, elegance, and force of Wittgenstein's thinking and will probably, in addition, contain positive mistakes.

References to Part I will be by paragraph numbers, e.g. (207), and to Part II by page numbers, e.g. (p. 207). Quotations will be placed within double quotation marks.

*Private language.* Let us see something of how Wittgenstein attacks what he calls "the idea of a private language." By a "private" language is meant one that not merely is not but *cannot* be understood by anyone other than the speaker. The reason for this is that the words of this language are supposed to "refer to what can only be known to the person speaking; to his immediate private sensations" (243). What is supposed is that I "*associate* words with sensations and use these names in descriptions" (256). I fix my attention on a sensation and establish a connection between a word and the sensation (258).

It is worth mentioning that the conception that it is possible and even necessary for one to have a private language is not eccentric. Rather it is the view that comes most naturally to anyone who philosophizes on the subject of the relation of words to experiences. The idea of a private language is presupposed by every program of inferring or constructing the 'external world' and 'other minds.' It is contained in the philosophy of Descartes and in the theory of ideas of classical British empiricism, as well as in recent and contemporary phenomenalism and sense-datum theory. At bottom it is the idea that there is only a contingent and not an *essential* connection between a sensation and its outward expression—an idea that appeals to us all. Such thoughts as these are typical expressions of the idea of a private language: that I know only from my *own* case what the word 'pain' means (293, 295); that I can only *believe* that someone else is in pain, but I *know* it if I am (303); that another person cannot have *my* pains (253); that I can undertake to call *this* (pointing inward) 'pain' in the future (263); that when I say 'I am in pain' I am at any rate justified *before myself* (289).

In order to appreciate the depth and power of Wittgenstein's assault upon this idea you must partly be its captive. You must feel the strong grip of it. The passionate intensity of Wittgenstein's treatment of it is due to the fact that he lets this idea take possession of him, drawing out of himself the thoughts and imagery by which it is expressed and defended—and then subjecting those thoughts and pictures to fiercest scrutiny. What is written down represents both a logical investigation and a great philosopher's struggle with his own thoughts. The logical investigation will be understood only by those who duplicate the struggle in themselves.

One consequence to be drawn from the view that I know only from my *own* case what, say, 'tickling' means is that "I know only what *I* call that, not what anyone else does" (347). I have not *learned* what 'tickling' means, I have only called something by that name. Perhaps others use the name differently. This is a regrettable difficulty; but, one may think, the word will still work for me as a name, provided that I apply it consistently to a certain sensation. But how about 'sensation'? Don't I know only from my *own* case what *that* word means? Perhaps what I call a "sensation" others call by another name? It will not help, says Wittgenstein, to say that although it may be that what I have is not what others call a "sensation," at least I have *something*. For don't I know only from my own case what "having something" is? Perhaps my use of *those* words is contrary to common use. In trying to explain how I gave 'tickling' its meaning, I discover that I do not have the right to use any of the relevant words of our common language. "So in the end when one is doing philosophy one gets to the point where one would like just to emit an inarticulate sound" (261).

Let us suppose that I did fix my attention on a pain as I pronounced the word 'pain' to myself. I think that thereby I established a connection between the word and the sensation. But I did not establish a connection if subsequently I applied that word to sensations other than pain or to things other than sensations, e.g., emotions. My private definition was a success only if it led me to use the word correctly in the future. In the present case, 'correctly' would mean '*consistently* with my own definition'; for the question of whether my use agrees with that of others has been given up as a bad job. Now how is it to be decided whether I have used the word consistently? What will be the difference between my having used it consistently and its *seeming* to me that I have? Or has this distinction vanished? "Whatever is going to seem right to me is right. And that only means that here we can't talk about 'right'" (258). If the distinction between 'correct' and 'seems correct' has disappeared, then so has the concept *correct*. It follows that the 'rules' of my private language are only *impressions* of rules (259). My impression that I follow a rule does not confirm that I follow the rule, unless there can be something that will prove my impression correct. And the something cannot be another impression —for this would be "as if someone were to buy several copies of the morning paper to assure himself that what it said was true" (265). The proof that I am following a rule must appeal to something *independent* of my impression that I am. If in the nature of the case there cannot be such an appeal, then my private language does not have *rules*, for the concept of a rule requires that there be a difference between 'He is following a rule' and 'He is under the impression that he is following a rule'—just as the concept of understanding a word requires that there be a difference between 'He understands this word' and 'He thinks that he understands this word' (cf. 269).

'Even if I cannot prove and cannot know that I am correctly following the rules of my private language,' it might be said, 'still it *may* be that I am. It has *meaning* to say that I am. The supposition makes sense: you and I *understand* it.' Wittgenstein has a reply to this (348–353). We are inclined to think that we know what it means to say 'It is five o'clock on the sun' or 'This congenital deaf-mute talks to himself inwardly in a vocal language' or 'The stove is in pain.' These sentences produce pictures in our minds, and it *seems* to us that the pictures tell us how to *apply* them—that is, tell us what we have to look for, what we have to do, in order to determine whether what is pictured is the case. But we make a mistake in thinking that the picture contains in itself the instructions as to how we are to apply it. Think of the picture of blindness as a darkness in the soul or in the head of the blind man (424). There is nothing wrong with it *as a picture*. "But *what* is its application?" What shall count for or against its being said that this or that man is blind, that the picture applies to him? The *picture* doesn't say. If you think that you understand the sentence 'I follow the rule that *this* is to be called "pain"' (a rule of your private language), what you have perhaps is a picture of yourself checking off various feelings of yours as either being *this* or not. The picture appears to solve the problem of how you determine whether you have done the 'checking' right. Actually it doesn't give you even a hint in that direction; no more than the picture of blindness provides so much as a hint of *how* it is to be determined that this or that man is blind (348–353, 422–426, p. 184).

One will be inclined to say here that one can simply *remember* this sensation and by remembering it will know that one is making a consistent application of its name. But will it also be possible to have a *false* memory impression? On the private-language hypothesis, what would *show* that your memory impression is false—or true? Another memory impression? Would this imply that memory is a court from which there is no appeal? But, as a matter of fact, that is *not* our concept of memory.

> Imagine that you were supposed to paint a particular colour "C," which was the colour that appeared when the chemical substances X and Y combined.—Suppose that the colour struck

212

you as brighter on one day than on another; would you not sometimes say: "I must be wrong, the colour is certainly the same as yesterday"? This shews that we do not always resort to what memory tells us as the verdict of the highest court of appeal [56].

There is, indeed, such a thing as checking one memory against another, e.g., I check my recollection of the time of departure of a train by calling up a memory image of how a page of the time-table looked—but "this process has got to produce a memory which is actually *correct*. If the mental image of the time-table could not itself be *tested* for correctness, how could it confirm the correctness of the first memory?" (265).

I have a language that is really private (i.e., it is a logical impossibility that anyone else should understand it or should have any basis for knowing whether I am using a particular name consistently), my assertion that my memory tells me so and so will be utterly empty. 'My memory' will not even mean —my memory *impression*. For by a memory impression we understand something that is either accurate or inaccurate; whereas there would not be, in the private language, any *conception* of what would establish a memory impression as correct, any conception of what 'correct' would mean here.

*The same.* One wants to say, 'Surely there can't be a difficulty in knowing whether a feeling of mine is or isn't the *same* as the feeling I now have. I will call this feeling "pain" and will thereafter call the *same* thing "pain" whenever it occurs. What could be easier than to follow that rule?' To understand Wittgenstein's reply to this attractive proposal we must come closer to his treatment of rules and of what it is to follow a rule. (Here he forges a remarkably illuminating connection between the philosophy of psychology and the philosophy of mathematics.) Consider his example of the pupil who has been taught to write down a cardinal number series of the form '0, n, 2n, 3n . . .' at an order of the form '+n,' so that at the order '+1' he writes down the series of natural numbers (185). He has successfully done exercises and tests up to the number 1,000. We then ask him to continue the series '+2' beyond 1,000; and he writes 1,000, 1,004, 1,008, 1,012. We tell him that this is wrong. His instructive reply is, "But I went on in the same way" (185). There was nothing in the previous explanations, examples and exercises that made it *impossible* for him to regard that as the continuation of the series. Repeating *those* examples and explanations won't help him. One must say to him, in effect, 'That isn't what we *call* going on in the *same* way.' It is a fact, and a fact of the kind whose importance Wittgenstein constantly stresses, that it is *natural* for human beings to continue the series in the manner 1,002, 1,004, 1,006, given the previous training. But that is merely what it is—a fact of human nature.

One is inclined to retort, 'Of course he can misunderstand the instruction and misunderstand the order '+2'; but if he *understands* it he must go on in the right way.' And here one has the idea that "The understanding itself is a state which is the *source* of the correct use" (146)—that the correct continuation of the series, the right application of the rule or formula, springs from one's understanding of the rule. But the question of whether one understands the rule cannot be divorced from the question of whether one will go on in that one particular way that we call 'right.' The correct use is a criterion of understanding. If you say that knowing the formula is a state of the mind and that making this and that application of the formula is merely a *manifestation* of the knowledge, then you are in a difficulty: for you are postulating a mental apparatus that explains the manifestations, and so you ought to have (but do not have) a knowledge of the construction of the apparatus, quite apart from what it does (149). You would like to think that your understanding of the formula determines in advance the steps to be taken, that when you understood or meant the formula in a certain way "your mind as it were flew ahead and took all the steps before you physically arrived at this or that one" (188). But how you meant it is not independent of how in fact you use it. "We say, for instance, to someone who uses a sign unknown to us: 'If by 'x!2' you mean $x^2$, then you get *this* value for $y$, if you mean $2x$, *that* one!—Now ask yourself: how does one *mean* the one thing or the other by 'x!2'?" (190). The answer is that his putting down *this* value for $y$ shows whether he meant the one thing and not the other: "*That* will be how meaning it can determine the steps in advance" (190). How he meant the formula determines his subsequent use of it, only in the sense that the latter is a criterion of how he meant it.

It is easy to suppose that when you have given a person the order 'Now do the *same* thing,' you have pointed out to him the way to go on. But consider the example of the man who obtains the series 1, 3, 5, 7 . . . by working out the formula $2x + 1$ and then asks himself, "Am I always doing the same thing, or something different every time?" (226). One answer is as good as the other, it doesn't matter which he says, so long as he continues in the right way. If we could not observe his work, his mere remark 'I am going on in the same way' would not tell us what he was doing. If a child writing down a row of 2's obtained '2, 2, 2' from the segment '2, 2' by adding '2' once, he might deny that he had gone on in the *same* way. He might declare that it would be doing the same thing only if he went from '2, 2' to '2, 2, 2, 2' in *one* jump, i.e., only if he *doubled* the original segment (just as it doubled the original single '2'). That could strike one as a *reasonable* use of 'same.' This connects up with Wittgenstein's remark: "If you have to have an intuition in order to develop the series 1 2 3 4 . . . you must also have one in order to develop the series 2 2 2 2 . . ." (214). One is inclined to say of the latter series, 'Why, all that is necessary is that you keep on doing the *same* thing.' But isn't this just as true of the other series? In both cases one has already *decided* what the correct continuation is, and one calls that continuation, and no other, 'doing the same thing.' As Wittgenstein says: "One might say to the person one was training: 'Look, I always do the same thing: I . . .'" (223). And then one proceeds to show him what 'the same' *is*. If the pupil does

ESSAYS ON OTHER MINDS

not acknowledge that what you have shown him is the *same*, and if he is not persuaded by your examples and explanations to carry on as you wish him to—then you have reached bedrock and will be inclined to say "This is simply what I do" (217). You cannot give him more reasons than you yourself have for proceeding in that way. Your reasons will soon give out. And then you will proceed, without reasons (211).

*Private rules.* All of this argument strikes at the idea that there can be such a thing as my following a rule in my private language—such a thing as naming something of which only I can be aware, 'pain,' and then going on to call the same thing, 'pain,' whenever it occurs. There is a charm about the expression 'same' which makes one think that there cannot be any difficulty or any chance of going wrong in deciding whether *A* is the *same* as *B*—as if one did not have to be *shown* what the 'same' is. This may be, as Wittgenstein suggests, because we are inclined to suppose that we can take the identity of a thing *with itself* as "an infallible paradigm" of the *same* (215). But he destroys this notion with one blow: "Then are two things the same when they are what *one* thing is? And how am I to apply what the *one* thing shows me to the case of two things?" (215).

The point to be made here is that when one has given oneself the private rule 'I will call this same thing "pain" whenever it occurs,' one is then free to do anything or nothing. That 'rule' does not point in any direction. On the private-language hypothesis, no one can teach me what the correct use of 'same' is. I shall be the sole arbiter of whether this is the *same* as that. What I choose to call the 'same' will *be* the same. No restriction whatever will be imposed upon my application of the word. But a sound that I can use *as I please* is not a *word*.

How would you teach someone the meaning of 'same'? By example and practice: you might show him, for instance, collections of the same colors and same shapes and make him find and produce them and perhaps get him to carry on a certain ornamental pattern uniformly (208). Training him to form collections and produce patterns is teaching him what Wittgenstein calls "techniques." Whether he has mastered various techniques determines whether he understands 'same.' The exercise of a technique is what Wittgenstein calls a "practice." Whether your pupil has understood any of the rules that you taught him (e.g., the rule; this is the 'same' color as that) will be shown in his practice. But now there cannot be a 'private' practice, i.e., a practice that cannot be exhibited. For there would then be no distinction between believing that you have that practice and having it. 'Obeying a rule' is itself a practice. "And to *think* one is obeying a rule is not to obey a rule. Hence it is not possible to obey a rule 'privately'; otherwise thinking one was obeying a rule would be the same thing as obeying it" (202; cf. 380).

If I recognize that my mental image is the 'same' as one that I had previously, how am I to know that this public word 'same' describes what I recognize? "Only if I can express my recognition in some other way, and if it is possible for someone else to teach me that 'same' is the correct word here" (378). The notion of the private language doesn't admit of there being 'some other way.' It doesn't allow that my behavior and circumstances can be so related to my utterance of the word that another person, by noting my behavior and circumstances, can discover that my use of the word is correct or incorrect. Can I discover this for myself, and how do I do it? That discovery would presuppose that I have a conception of correct use which comes from outside my private language and against which I measure the latter. If this were admitted the private language would lose its privacy and its point. So it isn't admitted. But now the notion of 'correct' use that will exist within the private language will be such that if I *believe* that my use is correct then it is correct; the rules will be only impressions of rules; my 'language' will not be a language, but merely the impression of a language. The most that can be said for it is that I *think* I understand it (cf. 269).

*Sensations of others.* The argument that I have been out-lining has the form of *reductio ad absurdum*: postulate a 'private' language; then deduce that it is not *language*. Wittgenstein employs another argument that is an external, not an internal, attack upon private language. What is attacked is the assumption that once I know from my *own* case what pain, tickling, or consciousness is, then I can transfer the ideas of these things to objects outside myself (283). Wittgenstein says:

> If one has to imagine someone else's pain on the model of one's own, this is none too easy a thing to do: for I have to imagine pain which I *do not feel* on the model of the pain which I *do feel*. That is, what I have to do is not simply to make a transition in imagination from one place of pain to another. As, from pain in the hand to pain in the arm. For I am not to imagine that I feel pain in some region of his body. (Which would also be possible.) [302]

The argument that is here adumbrated is, I think, the following: If I were to learn what pain is from perceiving my own pain then I should, necessarily, have learned that pain is something that exists only when *I* feel pain. For the pain that serves as my paradigm of pain (i.e., my own) has the property of existing only when *I* feel it.[2] That property is essential, not

[2] [This is an error. Apparently I fell into the trap of assuming that if two people, A and B, are in pain, the pain that A feels must be *numerically* different from the pain that B feels. Far from making this assumption, Wittgenstein attacks it when he says: "In so far as it makes *sense* to say that my pain is the same as his, it is also possible for us both to have the same pain" (*op. cit.*, 253). There is not some sense of "same pain" (*numerically* the same) in which A and B *cannot* have the same pain. "Today I have that same backache that you had last week" is something we say. "Same" means here, answering to the same description. We attach no meaning to the "question" of whether the backache you had and the one I have are or are not "numerically" the same.

A more correct account of Wittgenstein's point in sec. 302 is the following: A proponent of the privacy of sensations rejects circumstances and behavior as a criterion of the sensations of others, this being essential to his viewpoint. He does not need (and could not have) a criterion for the existence of pain that he feels. But surely he will need a criterion for the existence of pain that *he* does *not* feel. Yet he cannot have one and still hold to the

accidental; it is nonsense to suppose that the pain I feel could exist when I did not feel it. So if I obtain my *conception* of pain from pain that I experience, then it will be part of my conception of pain that *I* am the only being that can experience it. For me it will be a *contradiction* to speak of *another's* pain. This strict solipsism is the necessary outcome of the notion of private language. I take the phrase "this is none too easy" to be a sarcasm.

One is tempted at this point to appeal to the 'same' again: "But if I suppose that someone has a pain, then I am simply supposing that he has just the same as I have so often had" (350). I will quote Wittgenstein's brilliant counterstroke in full:

> That gets us no further. It is as if I were to say: "You surely know what 'It is 5 o'clock here' means; so you also know what 'It's 5 o'clock on the sun' means. It means simply that it is just the same time there as it is here when it is 5 o'clock."—The explanation by means of *identity* does not work here. For I know well enough that one can call 5 o'clock here and 5 o'clock there "the same time," but what I do not know is in what cases one is to speak of its being the same time here and there.
>
> In exactly the same way it is no explanation to say: the supposition that he has a pain is simply the supposition that he has the same as I. For *that* part of the grammar is quite clear to me: that is, that one will say that the stove has the same experience as I, *if* one says: it is in pain and I am in pain [350].

*Expressions of sensation.* Wittgenstein says that he destroys "houses of cards" ("Luftgebäude": 118) and that his aim is to show one how to pass from disguised to obvious nonsense (464). But this is not all he does or thinks he does. For he says

privacy of sensation. If he sticks to the latter, he ought to admit that he has not the faintest idea of what would count for or against the occurrence of sensations that he does not feel. His conclusion should be, not that it is a contradiction, but that it is unintelligible to speak of the sensations of others. (There is a short exposition of Wittgenstein's attack on the idea that we learn what sensation is *from our own case*, in "Knowledge of Other Minds" in *Knowledge and Certainty*; see pp. 136–138.)]

that he changes one's *way of looking at things* (144). What is it that he wishes to substitute for that way of looking at things that is represented by the idea of private language? One would *like* to find a continuous exposition of his own thesis, instead of mere hints here and there. But this desire reflects a misunderstanding of Wittgenstein's philosophy. He rejects the assumption that he should put forward a *thesis* (128). "We may not advance any kind of theory" (109). A philosophical problem is a certain sort of confusion. It is like being lost; one can't see one's way (123). Familiar surroundings suddenly seem strange. We need to command a view of the country, to get our bearings. The country is well known to us, so we need only to be *reminded* of our whereabouts. "The work of the philosopher consists in assembling reminders for a particular purpose" (127). "The problems are solved, not by giving new information, but by arranging what we have always known" (109). When we describe (remind ourselves of) certain functions of our language, what we do must have a definite bearing on some particular confusion, some "deep disquietude" (111), that ensnares us. Otherwise our work is irrelevant—to *philosophy*. It is philosophically pointless to formulate a general theory of language or to pile up descriptions for their own sake. "This description gets its light, that is to say its purpose—from the philosophical problems" (109). Thus we may not complain at the absence from the *Investigations* of elaborate theories and classifications.

Wittgenstein asks the question "How do words *refer* to sensations?" transforms it into the question "How does a human being learn the meaning of the names of sensations?" and gives this answer: "Words are connected with the primitive, the natural expressions of the sensation and used in their place. A child has hurt himself and he cries; and then the adults talk to him and teach him exclamations and, later, sentences. They teach the child new pain-behaviour" (244). Wittgenstein must be talking about how it is that a human being learns to refer with words to his *own* sensations—about how he learns to use

'I am in pain'; not about how he learns to use 'He is in pain.' What Wittgenstein is saying is indeed radically different from the notion that I learn what 'I am in pain' means by fixing my attention on a 'certain' sensation and calling it 'pain.' But is he saying that what I do instead is to fix my attention on my *expressions* of pain and call them 'pain'? Is he saying that the word 'pain' means crying? "On the contrary: the verbal expression of pain replaces crying and does not describe it" (244). My words for sensations are used *in place of* the behavior that is the natural expression of the sensations; they do not *refer* to it.

Wittgenstein does not expand this terse reminder. He repeats at least once that my words for sensations are "tied up with my natural expressions of sensation" (256) and frequently alludes to the importance of the connection between the language for sensations and the behavior which is the expression of sensation (e.g., 288, 271). The following questions and objections will arise:

(1) What shows that a child has made this 'tie up'? I take Wittgenstein to mean that the child's utterances of the word for a sensation must, in the beginning, be frequently concurrent with some nonverbal, natural expression of that sensation. This concomitance serves as the criterion of his understanding the word. Later on, the word can be uttered in the absence of primitive expressions. ('It hurts' can be said without cries or winces.)

(2) In what sense does the verbal expression 'replace' the nonverbal expression? In the sense, I think, that other persons will react to the child's mere words in the same way that they previously reacted to his nonverbal sensation-behavior; they will let the mere words serve as a *new* criterion of his feelings.

(3) I feel inclined to object: 'But has the child *learned* what the words *mean*? Hasn't he merely picked up the *use* of the word from his parents?' My objection probably arises from assimilating the learning of the meaning of words to the labeling of bottles—a tendency that is easily decried but not easily

resisted. 'Learning *ought* to consist in attaching the right name to the right object,' I should like to say (cf. 26). The example of 'the beetle in the box' is pertinent here (see 293). The aim of this fantasy is to prove that attending to a private object can have nothing to do with learning words for sensations. Suppose you wanted to teach a child what a tickling feeling is. You tickle him in the ribs, and he laughs and jerks away. You say to him, 'That's what the feeling of tickling is.' Now imagine he felt something that you can't know anything about. Will this be of any interest to you when you decide from his subsequent use of the word 'tickling' whether he understands it? Others understand the word too. If each one has something that only he can know about, then all the somethings may be different. The something could even be nothing! Whatever it is, it can have no part in determining whether the person who has it understands the word. "If we construe the grammar of the expression of sensation on the model of 'object and name' the object drops out of consideration as irrelevant" (293, cf. 304).

My previous objection could be put like this: the teaching and learning of names of sensations cannot stop at the mere expressions of sensation; the names must be brought *right up* to the sensations themselves, must be applied *directly* to the sensations! Here we can imagine Wittgenstein replying, "Like *what*, e.g.?" as he replies to an analogous objection in a different problem (191). In *what* sense is Wittgenstein denying that names are applied directly to sensations? Do I have a model of what it would be to apply the name 'directly'? No. I have this picture—that learning the meaning of 'pain' is applying the sign 'pain' to pain itself. I have that picture, to be sure, but what does it teach me, what is its "application"? When shall I say that what it pictures has taken place, i.e., that someone has learned the meaning of 'pain'? It doesn't tell me; it is *only* a picture. It cannot conflict with, cannot refute, Wittgenstein's reminder of what it is that determines whether a child has learned the word for a sensation.

(4) Wittgenstein says that the verbal expressions of sensation

can take the place of the nonverbal expressions and that in learning the former one learns "new pain-behavior." This seems to mean that the words (and sentences) for sensations are related to sensations in the same way as are the primitive expressions of sensations. I am inclined to object again. I want to say that the words are used to *report* the occurrence of a sensation and to inform others of it. The natural expressions, on the contrary, are not used to inform others; they are not 'used' at all; they have no purpose, no function; they *escape* from one. But I have oversimplified the difference, because (a) a sentence can be forced from one, can escape one's lips ('My God, it hurts!'), and (b) a natural expression of sensation can be used to inform another, e.g., you moan to let the nurse know that your pain is increasing (you would have suppressed the moan if she hadn't entered the room), yet the moan is genuine. Perhaps my objection comes to this: I don't *learn* to moan; I do learn the words. But this is the very distinction that is made by saying that moaning is a "natural," a "primitive," expression of sensation.

It is a mistake to suppose that Wittgenstein is saying that the utterance 'My leg hurts' is *normally called* an 'expression of sensation.' (Of course it isn't. For that matter, only a facial expression, not a groan, is called an '*expression* of pain.' But this is of no importance.) He is not reporting ordinary usage, but drawing our attention to an *analogy* between the groan of pain and the utterance of those words. The important similarity that he is trying to bring to light (here I may misinterpret him) is that the verbal utterance and the natural pain-behavior are each (as I shall express it) 'incorrigible.'[3] A man cannot be in *error* as to whether he is in pain; he cannot say 'My leg hurts' by mistake, anymore than he can groan by mistake. It is senseless to suppose that he has wrongly identified a tickle as pain

[3] [I try to explain the notion of "incorrigibility," as I understand it, in "Direct Perception" in *Knowledge and Certainty* (see pp. 77–86). I concentrate there on the seeing of after-images, but with appropriate changes the notion carries over to bodily sensations.]

or that he falsely believes that it is in his leg when in fact it is in his shoulder. True, he may be undecided as to whether it is best described as an 'ache' or a 'pain' (one is often hard put to give satisfactory descriptions of one's feelings); but his very indecision *shows* us what his sensation is, i.e., something between an ache and a pain. His hesitant observation, 'I'm not sure whether it is a pain or an ache,' is itself an *expression* of sensation. What it expresses is an indefinite, an ambiguous sensation. The point about the incorrigibility of the utterance 'I'm in pain' lies behind Wittgenstein's reiterated remark that 'I *know* I'm in pain' and 'I don't know whether I'm in pain' are both senseless (e.g., 246, 408).[4] Wherever it is *meaningless* to speak of 'false belief,' it is also meaningless to speak of 'knowledge'; and wherever you cannot say 'I don't know . . .' you also cannot say 'I know. . . .' Of course, a philosopher can say of me that I *know* I am in pain. But "What is it supposed to mean—except perhaps that I *am* in pain?" (246).[5]

There are many 'psychological' sentences, other than sentences about sensations, that are incorrigible, e.g., the *truthful* report of a dream is a criterion for the occurrence of the dream and, unless some other criterion is introduced, "the question cannot arise" as to whether the dreamer's memory deceives him (pp. 222–223). If one who has a mental image were asked whom the image is of, "his answer would be decisive," just as it would be if he were asked whom the drawing represents that he has just made (p. 177). When you say 'It will stop soon' and are asked whether you *meant* your pain or the sound of the piano-tuning, your truthful answer *is* the answer (666–684).

When Wittgenstein says that learning the words for sensations is learning "new pain-behavior" and that the words "re-

---

[4] It is interesting to note that as long ago as 1930 Wittgenstein had remarked that it has no sense to speak of *verifying* "I have a toothache." (See G. E. Moore, "Wittgenstein's Lectures in 1930–33," *Mind*, LXIII (January, 1954), 14.)

[5] [In "A Definition of Factual Memory" in *Knowledge and Certainty*, I mention a sense in which an adult person (but not an infant or a dog) can be said to know that he has a pain (see p. 239).]

place" the natural expressions, he is bringing to light the arresting fact that my sentences about my present sensations have the same logical status as my outcries and facial expressions. And thus we are helped to "make a radical break with the idea that language always functions in one way, always serves the same purpose: to convey thoughts—which may be about houses, pains, good and evil, or anything else you please" (304).

This is not to deny that first-person sentences about sensations may, in other respects, be more or less like natural expressions of sensation. Wittgenstein's examples of the use of 'I am afraid' (pp. 187–188) show how the utterance of that sentence can be a cry of fear, a comparison, an attempt to tell someone how I feel, a confession, a reflection on my state of mind, or something in between. "A cry is not a description. But there are transitions. And the words 'I am afraid' may approximate more, or less, to being a cry. They may come quite close to this and also be *far* removed from it" (p. 189). The words 'I am in pain' "may be a cry of complaint, and may be something else" (p. 189); and 'it makes me shiver' may be a "shuddering reaction" or may be said "as a piece of information" (p. 174). If we pursue these hints, it is not hard to construct a list of examples of the use of the words 'My head hurts,' in which the variety is as great as in Wittgenstein's list for 'I am afraid.' E.g., compare 'Oh hell, how my head hurts!' with 'If you want to know whether to accept the invitation for tonight then I must tell you that my head hurts again.' In one case the sentence 'My head hurts' belongs to an exclamation of pain, not in the other. In saying that in *both* cases it is an 'expression' of pain, Wittgenstein stretches ordinary language and in so doing illuminates the hidden continuity between the utterance of that sentence and—expressions of pain.

*Criterion.* That the natural pain-behavior and the utterance 'It hurts' are each incorrigible is what makes it possible for each of them to be a criterion of pain. With some reluctance I will undertake to say a little bit about this notion of 'criterion,' a most difficult region in Wittgenstein's philosophy. Perhaps the best way to elucidate it is to bring out its connection with *teaching* and *learning* the use of words. "When I say the ABC to myself, what is the criterion of my doing the same as someone else who silently repeats it to himself? It might be found that the same thing took place in my larynx and in his. (And similarly when we both think of the same thing, wish the same, and so on.) But then did we learn the use of the words, 'to say such-and-such to oneself,' by someone's pointing to a process in the larynx or the brain?" (376). Of course we did not, and this means that a physiological process is not our 'criterion' that *A* said such-and-such to himself. Try to imagine, realistically and in detail, how you would teach someone the meaning of 'saying the ABC silently to oneself.' This, you may think, is merely psychology. But if you have succeeded in bringing to mind what it is that would show that he *grasped* your teaching, that he *understood* the use of the words, then you have elicited the 'criterion' for their use—and that is not psychology. Wittgenstein exhorts us, over and over, to bethink ourselves of how we learned to use this or that form of words or of how we should teach it to a child. The purpose of this is not to bring philosophy down to earth (which it does), but to bring into view those features of someone's circumstances and behavior that *settle* the question of whether the words (e.g., 'He is calculating in his head') rightly apply to him. Those features constitute the 'criterion' of calculating in one's head. It is logically possible that someone should have been born with a knowledge of the use of an expression or that it should have been produced in him by a drug; that his knowledge came about by way of the normal process of teaching is not necessary. What is necessary is that there should be something on the basis of which we *judge* whether he *has* that knowledge. To undertake to describe this may be called a 'logical' investigation, even though one should arrive at the description by reflecting on that logically inessential process of teaching and learning.

If someone says, e.g., 'I feel confident . . . ,' a question can arise as to whether he understands those words. Once you admit the untenability of 'private ostensive definition' you will see that there must be a *behavioral* manifestation of the feeling of confidence (579). There must be behavior against which his words 'I feel confident . . . ,' can be checked, if it is to be possible to judge that he does not understand them. Even if you picture a feeling of confidence as an "inner process," still it requires "outward criteria" (580).

Wittgenstein contrasts 'criterion' with 'symptom,' employing both words somewhat technically. The falling barometer is a 'symptom' that it is raining; its looking like *that* outdoors (think how you would teach the word 'rain' to a child) is the 'criterion' of rain (354). A process in a man's brain or larynx might be a symptom that he has an image of red; the criterion is "what he says and does" (377, 376). What makes something into a symptom of *y* is that experience teaches that it is always or usually associated with *y*; that so-and-so is the criterion of *y* is a matter, not of experience, but of "definition" (354). The satisfaction of the criterion of *y* establishes the existence of *y* beyond question. The occurrence of a symptom of *y* may also establish the existence of *y* 'beyond question'—but in a different sense. The observation of a brain process may make it certain that a man is in pain—but not in the same way that his pain-behavior makes it certain. Even if physiology has established that a specific event in the brain accompanies bodily pain, still it *could* happen (it makes sense to suppose) that a man was not in pain although that brain event was occurring. But it will not make sense for one to suppose that another person is not in pain if one's criterion of his being in pain is satisfied. (Sometimes, and especially in science, we *change* our criteria: "what to-day counts as an observed concomitant of a phenomenon will to-morrow be used to define it" [79].)

The preceding remarks point up the following question: Do the propositions that describe the criterion of his being in pain *logically imply* the proposition 'He is in pain'? Wittgenstein's answer is clearly in the negative. A criterion is satisfied *only in certain circumstances.* If we come upon a man exhibiting violent pain-behavior, couldn't something show that he is not in pain? Of course. For example, he is rehearsing for a play; or he has been hypnotized and told, 'You will act as if you are in pain, although you won't be in pain,' and when he is released from the hypnotic state he has no recollection of having been in pain; or his pain-behavior suddenly ceases and he reports in apparent bewilderment that it was as if his body had been possessed—for his movements had been entirely involuntary, and during the 'seizure' he had felt no pain; or he has been narrowly missed by a car and as soon as a sum for damages has been pressed into his hand, his pain-behavior ceases and he laughs at the hoax; or . . . , etc. The expressions of pain are a criterion of pain in *certain* "surroundings," not in others (cf. 584).

Now one would like to think that one can still formulate a logical implication by taking a description of his pain-behavior and conjoining it with the negation of every proposition describing one of those circumstances that would count against saying he is in pain. Surely, the conjunction will logically imply 'He is in pain'! But this assumes there is a *totality* of those circumstances such that if none of them were fulfilled, and he was also pain-behaving, then he *could not but* be in pain (cf. 183). There is no totality that can be exhaustively enumerated, as can the letters of the alphabet. It is quite impossible to list six or nine such circumstances and then to say 'That is all of them; no other circumstances can be imagined that would count against his being in pain.' The list of circumstances has no 'all,' in that sense; the list is, not infinite, but *indefinite.* Therefore, entailment-conditions cannot be formulated; there are none.

The above thought is hard to accept. It is not in line with our *ideal* of what language should be. It makes the 'rules' for the use of 'He is in pain' too vague, too loose, not really *rules.* Wittgenstein has deep things to say about the nature of this 'ideal': "We want to say that there can't be any vagueness in logic. The idea now absorbs us, that the ideal *'must'* be found in reality. Meanwhile we do not as yet see *how* it occurs there, nor do we understand the nature of this 'must.' We think it must be in reality; for we think we already see it there" (101). "The strict and clear rules of the logical structure of propositions appear to us as something in the background—hidden in the medium of the understanding" (102). "The more narrowly we examine actual language, the sharper becomes the conflict between it and our requirement. (For the crystalline purity of logic was, of course, not a *result of investigation*: it was a requirement.)" (107). What we need to do is to remove from our noses the logical glasses through which we look at reality (103). We must study our language as it is, without preconceived ideas. One thing this study will teach us is that the criteria for the use of third-person psychological statements are not related to the latter by an entailment-relation.

Wittgenstein suggests that propositions describing the fulfillment of behavioral criteria are related to third-person psychological statements in the way that propositions describing sense-impressions are related to physical-object statements (compare 486 and p. 180). It does not *follow* from the propositions describing my sense-impressions that there is a chair over there (486). The relation cannot be reduced to a *simple* formula (p. 180). *Why* doesn't it follow? Wittgenstein does not say, but the reason would appear to be of the same sort as in the example of 'He is in pain.' The propositions describing my sense-impressions would have to be conjoined with the proposition that I am not looking in a mirror, or at a painted scenery, or at a movie film, or . . . , etc. Here too there cannot be an exhaustive enumeration of the negative conditions that would have to be added to the description of sense-impressions *if* 'There's a chair over there' *were* to be logically implied.

The puzzling problem now presents itself: if it does not *follow* from his behavior and circumstances that he is in pain, then how can it ever be *certain* that he is in pain? "I can be as

ESSAYS ON OTHER MINDS

*certain* of someone else's sensations as of any fact," says Wittgenstein (p. 224). How can this be so, since there is not a definite set of six or eight conditions (each of which would nullify his pain-behavior) to be checked off as not fulfilled? It looks as if the conclusion ought to be that we cannot 'completely verify' that he is in pain. This conclusion is wrong, but it is not easy to see why. I comprehend Wittgenstein's thought here only dimly. He says:

> A doctor asks: "How is he feeling?" The nurse says: "He is groaning." A report on his behaviour. But need there be any question for them whether the groaning is really genuine, is really the expression of anything? Might they not, for example, draw the conclusion "If he groans, we must give him more analgesic"—without suppressing a middle term? Isn't the point the service to which they put the description of behaviour [p. 179]?

One hint that I take from this is that there can be situations of real life in which a question as to whether someone who groans is pretending, or rehearsing, or hypnotized, or . . . , simply does not exist. "Just try—in a real case—to doubt someone else's fear or pain" (303). A doubt, a question, would be rejected as absurd by anyone who knew the actual surroundings. 'But might there not be still further surroundings, unknown to you, that would change the whole aspect of the matter?' Well, we go only *so* far—and then we are certain. "Doubting has an end" (p. 180). Perhaps we can *imagine* a doubt; but we do not take it seriously (cf. 84). Just as it becomes certain to us that there is a chair over there, although we can imagine a *possible* ground of doubt. There is a concept of certainty in these language-games only because we stop short of what is conceivable.

"But, if you are *certain*, isn't it that you are shutting your eyes in face of doubt?'—They are shut" (p. 224). This striking remark suggests that what we sometimes do is draw a boundary around *this* behavior in *these* circumstances and say 'Any additional circumstances that might come to light will be irrelevant to whether this man is in pain.' Just as we draw a line and say 'No further information will have any bearing on whether there is a chair in the corner—that is settled.' If your friend is struck down by a car and writhes with a broken leg, you do not think: Perhaps it was prearranged in order to alarm me; possibly his leg was anesthetized just before the 'accident' and he isn't suffering at all. Someone *could* have such doubts whenever another person was ostensibly in pain. Similarly: "I can easily imagine someone always doubting before he opened his front door whether an abyss did not yawn behind it; and making sure about it before he went through the door (and he might on some occasion prove to be right)—but that does not make me doubt in the same case" (84).

The man who doubts the other's pain may be neurotic, may 'lack a sense of reality,' but his reasoning is perfectly sound. *If* his doubts are true then the injured man is *not* in pain. His reaction is abnormal but not illogical. The certainty that the injured man is in pain (the normal reaction) ignores the endless doubts that *could* be proposed and investigated.

And it is important to see that the abnormal reaction *must* be the exception and not the rule. For if someone *always* had endless doubts about the genuineness of expressions of pain, it would mean that he was not using *any criterion* of another's being in pain. It would mean that he did not accept anything as an *expression* of pain. So what could it mean to say that he even had the *concept* of another's being in pain? It is senseless to suppose that he has this concept and yet always doubts.

*Third-person sensation-sentences.* Wittgenstein assimilates first-person, not third-person, sensation-sentences as *expressions* of sensation. I will say one or two things more about his conception of the use of third-person sensation-sentences.
(1) "Only of a living human being and what resembles (behaves like) a living human being can one say: it has sensations; it sees; is blind; hears; is deaf; is conscious or unconscious"

(281). The *human* body and *human* behavior are the *paradigm* to which third-person attributions of consciousness, sensations, feelings are related. (The use of first-person sensation-sentences is governed by *no* paradigm). Thus there cannot occur in ordinary life a question as to whether other human beings ever possess consciousness, and I can have this question when I philosophize only if I forget that I use that paradigm in ordinary life. It is by analogy with the human form and behavior that I attribute consciousness (or unconsciousness) to animals and fish: the more remote the analogy the less sense in the attribution. (Just as it is by analogy with our ordinary language that anything is called 'language') (494). In order to imagine that a pot or a chair has thoughts or sensations one must give it, in imagination, something like a human body, face, and speech (282, 361). A child says that its doll has stomach-ache, but this is a "secondary" use of the concept of pain. "Imagine a case in which people ascribed pain *only* to inanimate things; pitied *only* dolls!" (282; cf. 385, p. 216). Wittgenstein means, I think, that this is an impossible supposition because we should not want to say that those people *understood* ascriptions of pain. If they did not ever show pity for human beings or animals or expect it for themselves, then their treatment of dolls would not be *pity*.

(2) My criterion of another's being in pain is, first, his behavior and circumstances and, second, his words (after they have been found to be connected in the right way with his behavior and circumstances). Does it follow that my interest is in his behavior and words, not in his pain? Does 'He is in pain' *mean* behavior? In lectures Wittgenstein imagined a tribe of people who had the idea that their slaves had no feelings, no souls—that they were automatons—despite the fact that the slaves had human bodies, behaved like their masters, and even spoke the same language. Wittgenstein undertook to try to give sense to that idea. When a slave injured himself or fell ill or complained of pains, his master would try to heal him. The master would let him rest when he was fatigued, feed him when he

was hungry and thirsty, and so on. Furthermore, the masters would apply to the slaves our usual distinctions between genuine complaints and malingering. So what could it mean to say that they had the idea that the slaves were automatons? Well, they would *look* at the slaves in a peculiar way. They would observe and comment on their movements *as if* they were machines. ('Notice how smoothly his limbs move.') They would discard them when they were worn and useless, like machines. If a slave received a mortal injury and twisted and screamed in agony, no master would avert his gaze in horror or prevent his children from observing the scene, any more than he would if the ceiling fell on a printing press. Here is a difference in 'attitude' that is not a matter of believing or expecting different facts.

So in the *Investigations,* Wittgenstein says, "My attitude towards him is an attitude towards a soul. I am not of the *opinion* that he has a soul" (p. 178). I do not *believe* that the man is suffering who writhes before me—for to what facts would a 'belief' be related, such that a change in the facts would lead me to alter it? I *react* to his suffering. I look at him with compassion and try to comfort him. If I complain of headache to someone and he says 'It's not so bad,' does this prove that he believes in something *behind* my outward expression of pain? "His attitude is a proof of his attitude. Imagine not merely the words 'I am in pain' but also the answer 'It's not so bad' replaced by instinctive noises and gestures" (310). The thought that behind someone's pain-behavior is the pain itself does not enter into our use of 'He's in pain,' but what does enter into it is our sympathetic, or unsympathetic, reaction to him. The fact that the latter does enter into our use of that sentence (but might not have) gives sense to saying that the sentence 'He is in pain' does not just *mean* that his behavior, words, and circumstances are such and such—although these are the criteria for its use.

When he groans we do not *assume*, even tacitly, that the groaning expresses pain. We fetch a sedative and try to put him at ease. A totally different way of reacting to his groans would be to make exact records of their volume and frequency—and do nothing to relieve the sufferer! But our reaction of seeking to comfort him does not involve a presupposition, for, "Doesn't a presupposition imply a doubt? And doubt may be entirely lacking" (p. 180).

*Form of life.* The gestures, facial expressions, words, and activities that constitute pitying and comforting a person or a dog are, I think, a good example of what Wittgenstein means by a "form of life." One could hardly place too much stress on the importance of this latter notion in Wittgenstein's thought. It is intimately related to the notion "language-game." His choice of the latter term is meant to "bring into prominence the fact that the *speaking* of language is part of an activity, or of a form of life" (23; cf. 19). If we want to understand any concept we must obtain a view of the human behavior, the activities, the natural expressions, that surround the words for that concept. What, for example, is the concept of *certainty* as applied to *predictions?* The nature of my certainty that fire will burn me comes out in the fact that "Nothing could induce me to put my hand into a flame" (472). That reaction of mine to fire shows the *meaning* of certainty in this language-game (474). (Of course, it is *different* from the concept of certainty in, e.g., mathematics. "The kind of certainty is the kind of language-game" [p. 124].) But is my certainty justified? Don't I need reasons? Well, I don't normally think of reasons, I can't produce much in the way of reasons, and I don't feel a need of reasons (cf. 477). Whatever was offered in the way of reasons would not strengthen my fear of fire, and if the reasons turned out to be weak I still wouldn't be induced to put my hand on the hot stove.

As far as 'justification' is concerned, "What people accept as a justification—is shewn by how they think and live" (325). If we want to elucidate the concept of justification we must take note of what people *accept* as justified; and it is clearly shown in our lives that we accept as justified both the certainty that fire will burn and the certainty that this man is in pain—even without reasons. Forms of life, embodied in language-games, teach us what justification is. As philosophers we must not attempt to justify the forms of life, to give reasons for *them*—to argue, for example, that we pity the injured man because we believe, assume, presuppose, or know that in addition to the groans and writhing, there is pain. The fact is, we pity him! "What has to be accepted, the given, is—so one could say— *forms of life*" (p. 226). What we should say is: "*This language-game is played*" (654).

From this major theme of Wittgenstein's thought one passes easily to another major theme—that "Philosophy simply puts everything before us, and neither explains nor deduces anything" (126). "It leaves everything as it is" (124).

*Strawson's criticism.* Mr. Peter Strawson's critical notice [6] of the *Investigations* contains misunderstandings that might obtain currency. To Strawson it appears that, for Wittgenstein, "no word whatever stands for or names a special experience," [7] "no words name sensations (or 'private experiences'); and in particular the word 'pain' does not." [8] Wittgenstein "has committed himself to the view that one cannot sensibly be said to recognize or identify anything, unless one uses *criteria*; and, as a consequence of this, that one cannot recognize or identify sensations." [9] His "obsession with the *expression* of pain" leads him "to deny that sensations can be recognized and bear names." [10] Wittgenstein is hostile to "the idea of what is not observed (seen, heard, smelt, touched, tasted), and in particular to the idea that what is not observed can in any sense be

[6] "Critical Notice: *Philosophical Investigations*," *Mind*, LXIII (January, 1954), 70–99. (References to Strawson will be placed in footnotes, references to Wittgenstein will remain in the text.)
[7] P. 83.
[8] P. 84.
[9] P. 86.
[10] P. 87.

recognized or described or reported" [11]—although at one place in the book (p. 189) "it looks as if he were almost prepared to acknowledge" that 'I am in pain' "may be just a report of my sensations." [12] His "prejudice against 'the inner'" lead him to deny that it is possible for a person to report the words that went through his mind when he was saying something to himself in his thoughts.[13] Strawson attributes Wittgenstein's errors not only to prejudice and, possibly, to "the old verificationist horror of a claim that cannot be checked," [14] but also to various confusions and muddles.[15]

It is important to see how very erroneous is this account of Wittgenstein. The latter says, "Don't we talk about sensations every day, and give them names?" and then asks, "How does a human being learn the names of sensations?—of the word 'pain' for example?" (244) So Wittgenstein does not deny that we *name* sensations. It is a howler to accuse Wittgenstein of "hostility to the idea of what is not observed" ("observed" apparently means 'perceived by one of the five senses') and of "hostility to the idea that what is not observed can in any sense be recognized or described or reported." [16] Dreams and mental pictures are not observed, in Strawson's sense; yet Wittgenstein discusses *reports* of dreams (p. 222; also p. 184) and *descriptions* of mental pictures (e.g., 367). Consider this general remark: "Think how many different kinds of things are called 'description': description of a body's position by means of its co-ordinates; description of a facial expression; *description of a sensation of touch*; of a mood" (24, my italics). And at many places in the *Investigations*, Wittgenstein *gives* descriptions of various sensations, although sensations are not observed, in Strawson's sense. Strawson's belief that Wittgenstein thinks that "one cannot sensibly be said to recognize or identify any-

[11] P. 90.
[12] P. 94.
[13] P. 91.
[14] P. 92.
[15] See p. 86 and p. 98.
[16] P. 90.

thing, unless one uses criteria," [17] is proved false by the remarks about mental images: I have *no* criterion for saying that two images of mine are the same (377); yet there is such a thing as *recognition* here, and a correct use of 'same' (378). How can it be maintained that Wittgenstein has a prejudice against 'the inner' when he allows that in our ordinary language a man *can* write down or give vocal expression to his "inner experiences—his feelings, moods, and the rest—for his private use"? (243). Wittgenstein does not deny that there are *inner* experiences any more than he denies that there are *mental* occurrences. Indeed, he gives examples of things that he calls "*seelische Vorgänge*," e.g., "a pain's growing more or less," and in contrast with which a thing like *understanding a word* is not, he argues a "*seelischen Vargang*" (154). Either to deny that such occurrences exist or to claim that they cannot be named, reported, or described is entirely foreign to Wittgenstein's outlook. For what would the denial amount to other than an attempt to "reform language," which is not his concern? It may *look* as if he were trying to reform language, because he is engaged in "giving prominence to distinctions which our ordinary forms of language easily make us overlook" (132). For example, Wittgenstein suggests that when we think about the philosophical problem of sensation the word 'describe' *tricks* us (290). Of course he does not mean that it is a mistake to speak of 'describing' a sensation. He means that the similarity in "surface grammar" (664) between 'I describe my sensations' and 'I describe my room' may mislead, may cause us to fail "to call to mind the differences between the language-games" (290).

Strawson rightly avers, "To deny that 'pain' is the name of a (type of) sensation is comparable to denying that 'red' is the name of a colour." [18] I suppose that, conversely, to affirm that 'pain' is the name of a sensation is like affirming that 'red' is the name of a color, and also that 'o' is the name of a number. This classification tells us nothing of philosophical interest.

[17] P. 86.
[18] P. 87.

What we need to notice is the *difference* between the way that
'o' and '2,' say, function, although both are 'names of numbers'
(think how easily one may be tempted to deny that o is a number), and the difference between the way 'red' and 'pain'
function, although both are 'names.' "We call very different
things 'names'; the word 'name' is used to characterize many
different kinds of use of a word, related to one another in many
different ways" (38). To suppose that the uses of 'pain' and
'red,' as *names,* are alike is just the sort of error that Wittgenstein wants to expose. If one thinks this, one will want to by-
pass the *expression* of pain and will wonder at Wittgenstein's
'obsession' with it. Not that Strawson does by-pass it, but he
seems to attach the wrong significance to it. He appears to
think that the fact that there is a characteristic pain-behavior
is what makes possible a *common* "language of pain," and he
seems to imply that if we did not care to have a *common* language of pain each of us would still be able to name and describe his pains in "a private language-game," even if there
were no characteristic pain-behavior.[19] It looks as if he thinks
that with his private language he could step between pain and
its expression, and apply names to the bare sensations themselves (cf. 245).

For Strawson the conception of a private language possesses
no difficulty. A man "might simply be struck by the recurrence
of a certain sensation and get into the habit of making a certain
mark in a different place every time it occurred. The making of
the marks would help to impress the occurrence on his memory."[20] Just as, I suppose, he might utter a certain sound each
time a cow appeared. But we need to ask, what makes the
latter sound a *word,* and what makes it the word for *cow?* Is
there no difficulty here? Is it sufficient that the sound is uttered
when and only when a cow is present? Of course not. The
sound might refer to anything or nothing. What is necessary is

[19] See pp. 84–88.
[20] P. 85.

that it should play a part in various activities, in calling, fetching, counting cows, distinguishing cows from other things and pictures of cows from pictures of other things. If the sound has no fixed place in activities ("language-games") of this sort, then it isn't a word for *cow*. To be sure, I can sit in my chair and talk about cows and not be engaged in any of those activities—but what makes my words *refer* to cows is the fact that I have already mastered those activities; they lie in the background. The kind of way that 'cow' refers is the kind of language-game to which it belongs. If a mark or sound is to be a word for a *sensation* it, too, must enter into language-games, although of a very different sort. What sort? Well, such things as showing the location of the sensation, exhibiting different reactions to different intensities of stimulus, seeking or avoiding causes of the sensation, choosing one sensation in preference to another, indicating the duration of the sensation, and so on. Actions and reactions of that sort constitute the sensation-behavior. They are the "outward criteria" (580) with which the sign must be connected if it is to be a sign for a sensation *at all*, not merely if it is to be a sign in a *common* language. In the mere supposition that there is a man who is "struck by the recurrence of a certain sensation" and who gets into the habit of "making a certain mark in a different place every time it occurred," no ground *whatever* has been given for saying that the mark is a sign for a sensation. The necessary surroundings have not been supplied. Strawson sees no problem here. He is surprised that "Wittgenstein gives himself considerable trouble over the question of how a man would *introduce* a name for a sensation into this private language." [21] It is as if Strawson thought: There is no difficulty about it; the man just *makes* the mark refer to a sensation. How the man does it puzzles Strawson so little that he is not even inclined to feel that the connection between the name and the sensation is queer, occult (cf. 38)—which it would be, to say the least, if

[21] *Ibid.*

the name had no fixed place in those activities and reactions that constitute sensation-behavior, for that, and not a magical act of the mind, is what *makes* it refer to a sensation.

The conception of private language that Wittgenstein attacks is not the conception of a language that only the speaker does understand, but of a language that no other person *can* understand (243). Strawson thinks that Wittgenstein has not refuted the conception of a private language but has only shown that certain conditions must be satisfied if a common language is to exist. Strawson appears to believe (I may misunderstand him) that each of us not only can have but does have a private language of sensations, that if we are to understand one another when we speak of our sensations there must be criteria for the use of our sensation-words, and that therefore the words with which we *refer* to our sensations must, in addition, contain "allusions" either to behavior or to material substances that are "associated" with the sensations.[22] The allusions must be to things that can be perceived by us all. By virtue of this the use of sensation-words can be taught and misuses corrected, and so those words will belong to a common language. There is another feature of their use (namely, their reference) that cannot be taught. Thus sensation-words will have both a public and a private meaning. Strawson's view appears to be accurately characterized by Wittgenstein's mock conjecture: "Or is it like this: the word 'red' means something known to everyone; and in addition, for each person, it means something known only to him? (Or perhaps rather: it *refers* to something known only to him.)" (273)

But if my words, *without* these allusions, can refer to my sensations, then what is alluded to is only *contingently* related to the sensations. Adding the "allusions to what can be seen and touched"[23] will not help one little bit in making us understand one another. For the behavior that is, for me, contingently associated with 'the sensation of pain' may be, for you,

[22] P. 86.
[23] *Ibid.*

contingently associated with 'the sensation of tickling'; the piece of matter that produces in you what you call 'a metallic taste' may produce in me what, if you could experience it, you would call 'the taste of onions'; my 'sensation of red' may be your 'sensation of blue'; we do not know and cannot know whether we are talking about the same things; we cannot *learn* the essential thing about one another's use of sensation-words—namely, their reference. The language in which the private referring is done cannot be turned into a common language by having something grafted on to it. Private language cannot be the understructure of the language we all understand. It is as if, in Strawson's conception, the sensation-words were supposed to perform two functions—to refer and to communicate. But if the reference is incommunicable, then the trappings of allusion will not communicate it, and what they do communicate will be irrelevant.

Strawson's idea that expressions like 'jabbing pain,' 'metallic taste,' mean something known to everyone and, in addition, for each person, refer to something known only to him, is responsible, I believe, for his failure to understand Wittgenstein on the topic of recognizing and identifying sensations. There is *a* sense of 'recognize' and 'identify' with respect to which Wittgenstein does deny that we can recognize or identify our own sensations, feelings, images. Consider, for example, that although a man understands the word 'alcohol' he may fail to identify the alcohol in a bottle as alcohol, because the bottle is marked 'gasoline' or because the cork smells of gasoline; or, although he understands 'rabbit' and is familiar with rabbits, he may fail to recognize a rabbit as a rabbit, taking it for a stump instead; or, he may be in doubt and say, 'I don't know whether this is alcohol,' 'I'm not sure whether that is a rabbit or a stump.' But can a man who understands the word 'pain' be in doubt as to whether he has pain? Wittgenstein remarks:

> If anyone said "I do not know if what I have got is a pain or something else," we should think something like, he does not know what the English word "pain" means; and we should

241

explain it to him.—How? Perhaps by means of gestures, or by pricking him with a pin and saying: "See, that's what pain is!" This explanation, like any other, he might understand right, wrong, or not at all. And he will show which he does by his use of the word, in this as in other cases.

If he now said, for example: "Oh, I know what 'pain' means; what I don't know is whether *this*, that I have now, is pain"— we should merely shake our heads and be forced to regard his words as a queer reaction which we have no idea what to do with [288].

That a man wonders whether what he has is pain can only mean that he does not understand the word 'pain'; he cannot both understand it and have that doubt. Thus there is a sense of 'identify' that has no application to sensations. One who understands the word 'alcohol' may fail to identify *this* as alcohol or may be in doubt as to its identity or may correctly identify it. These possibilities have no meaning in the case of pain. There is not over and above (or underneath) the understanding of the word 'pain' a further process of correctly identifying or failing to identify *this* as pain. There would be if Strawson's conception was right. But there is not, and this is why "That expression of doubt ['Oh, I know what 'pain' means; what I don't know is whether *this*, that I have now, is pain'] has no place in the language-game" (288). (Strawson does not have, but in consistency should have, an inclination to dispute this last remark of Wittgenstein's.)[24] The fact that there is no *further* process of identifying a particular sensation is a reason why "the object drops out of consideration as irrelevant" when "we construe the grammar of the expression of sensation on the model of 'object and name'" (293)—a remark that Strawson misunderstands as the thesis that "no words name sensations." [25] If my use of a sensation-word satisfies the normal outward criteria and if I truthfully declare that I have that sensation, then I *have* it—there is not a further problem of my apply-

[24] See p. 85.
[25] P. 84.

Wittgenstein's Philosophical Investigations

ing the word right or wrong within myself. If a man used the word 'pain' in accordance with "the usual symptoms and presuppositions of pain" then it would have no sense to suppose that perhaps his memory did not retain *what* the word 'pain' refers to, "so that he constantly called different things by that name" (271). If my use of the word fits those usual criteria there is not an added problem of whether I accurately pick out the objects to which the word applies. In this sense of 'identify,' the hypothesis that I identify my sensations is "a mere ornament, not connected with the mechanism at all" (270).

It does not follow nor, I think, does Wittgenstein mean to assert that there is *no* proper use of 'identify' or 'recognize' with sensations. He acknowledges a use of 'recognize' with mental images, as previously noted. It would be a natural use of language, I believe, if someone who upon arising complained of an unusual sensation were to say, 'Now I can identify it! It is the same sensation that I have when I go down in an elevator.' Wittgenstein, who has no interest in reforming language, would not dream of calling this an incorrect use of 'identify.' He attacks a philosophical use of the word only, the use that belongs to the notion of the private object. In this example of a non-philosophical use, if the speaker employed the rest of the sensation-language as we all do, and if his behavior in this case was approximately what it was when he was affected by the downward motion of an elevator, then his declaration that he was feeling the elevator-sensation would be decisive; and also his declaration that it was *not* the elevator-sensation would be decisive. It is *out of the question* that he should have made a mistake in identifying the sensation. His identification of his sensation is an *expression* of sensation (in Wittgenstein's extended sense of this phrase). The identification is 'incorrigible.' We have here a radically different use of 'identify' from that illustrated in the examples of alcohol and rabbit.

The philosophical use of 'identify' seems to make possible the committing of *errors* of identification of sensations and inner experiences. The idea is that my sensation or my image is an object that I cannot show to anyone and that I identify it and from it derive its description (374). But if this is so, why cannot my identification and description go wrong, and not just sometimes but always? Here we are in a position to grasp the significance of Wittgenstein's maneuver: "Always get rid of the idea of the private object in this way: assume that it constantly changes, but that you do not notice the change because your memory constantly deceives you" (p. 207). We are meant to see the *senselessness* of this supposition: for what in the world would *show* that I was deceived constantly or even once? Do I look again—and why can't I be deceived that time, too? The supposition is a knob that doesn't turn anything (cf. 270). Understanding this will perhaps remove the temptation to think that I have something that I cannot show to you and from which I derive a knowledge of its identity. This is what Wittgenstein means in saying that when I related to another what I just said to myself in my thoughts " 'what went on within me' is not the point at all" (p. 222). He is not declaring, as Strawson thinks, that I cannot report what words went through my mind.[26] He is saying that it is a report "whose truth is guaranteed by the special criteria of truthfulness" (p. 222). It is *that* kind of report. So it is not a matter of trying faithfully to observe something within myself and of trying to produce a correct account of it, of trying to do something at which I might unwittingly fail.

The influence of the idea of the private object on Strawson's thinking is subtly reflected, I believe, in his declaration that a metallic taste is "quite certainly recognizable and identifiable in itself" and in his remark that "if the question 'What is the criterion of identity here?' is pushed, one can only answer: 'Well, the taste itself' (cf. 'the sensation itself')."[27] Strawson realizes that we don't identify a sensation by means of criteria

[26] See pp. 90, 91.
[27] P. 86.

(e.g., a metallic taste by means of the metallic material that produces it). He is inclined to add that we identify it by 'the sensation itself.' This seems to me to misconstrue the 'grammar' of 'identify' here. It may be to the point to consider again the comparison of colors and sensations. Wittgenstein says, "How do I know that this colour is red?—It would be an answer to say 'I have learned English'" (381). One thing this answer does is to deny that I have *reasons* for saying that this color before me is red. We might put this by saying that I identify it as red by 'the color itself,' not by anything else. The cases of red and pain (or metallic taste) so far run parallel. Equally, I don't have reasons for saying that this color is red or that this sensation is pain. But it *can* happen that I should fail to identify this color correctly, even though I have learned English (e.g., the moonlight alters its appearance). Here the parallel ends. Nothing can alter the 'appearance' of the sensation. Nothing counts as mistaking its identity. If we assimilate identifying sensations to identifying colors, because in neither instance reasons are relevant, we conceal the philosophically more important difference. To insist that the parallel is perfect, that one identifies sensations in the same sense that one identifies colors, is like saying that "there must also be something boiling in the pictured pot" (297). Identifying one's own sensation is nothing that is either in error or *not* in error. It is not, in *that* sense, *identifying*. When I identify my sensation, I do not *find out* its identity, not even from 'the sensation itself.' My identification, one could say, *defines* its identity.

We use a man's identification of his sensation as a criterion of what his sensation is. But this is a *dependent* criterion. His verbal reports and identifications would not *be* a criterion unless they were grounded in the primitive sensation-behavior that is the primary and independent criterion of his sensations. If we cut out human behavior from the language-game of sensations (which Strawson does in defending the 'private language-game') one result will be that a man's identifying a sensation as the 'same' that he had a moment before will no longer be a criterion of its being the same. Not only the speaker but *no one* will have a criterion of identity. Consequently, for no one will it have any meaning to speak of a man's being "struck by the *recurrence* of a certain sensation." [28]

[28] P. 85, my italics.

# SYMPOSIUM: OTHER MINDS

## JOHN WISDOM AND J. L. AUSTIN

*I—by John Wisdom*

"To return to Françoise . . . if then in my anger at the thought
of being pitied by her I tried to pretend that on the contrary
I had scored a distinct success, my lies broke feebly on the
wall of her respectful but obvious unbelief. . . . For she knew
the truth."—Proust.

". . . it was she who first gave me the idea that a person
does not (as I had imagined) stand motionless and clear before our eyes with his merits, his defects, his plans, his intentions with regard to ourself exposed on his surface, like a garden at which, with all its borders spread out before us, we
gaze through a railing, but is a shadow, which we can never
succeed in penetrating, of which there can be no such thing
as direct knowledge, with respect to which we form countless
beliefs, based upon his words and sometimes upon his actions,
though neither word nor actions can give us anything but
inadequate and as it proves contradictory information—a
shadow behind which we can alternately imagine, with equal
justification, that there burns the flame of hatred and of
love."—Proust.

Reprinted by permission of the editor, from *Proceedings of the Aristotelian
Society*, XX (supplementary volume) (1946), 122–187. Copyright 1946 by the
Aristotelian Society.

Sometimes, looking out the window with someone, we see what he sees, hear what he hears, and feel how he is feeling. And some people, it is said, sometimes do this when the other person is far away. Remembering this we may wonder how we ever came to ask "Do we know, and how do we know, the thoughts and feelings of another?" Then we remember how we came to the doubt by calling seeing what he sees as we look out of the window, not "seeing what is in his mind" but "seeing the objects he sees," the laurels in the rain, and thinking of this, speaking of this, not as "seeing what is before his mind" but as "seeing in our mind images which tell us of the objects and correspond closely to the images in his mind which tell him of the objects," or, cutting out the objects, we speak of this seeing what he sees as "seeing in our mind images corresponding to images in his mind," or, cutting out his images, we speak of "seeing in our mind images from which we guess at later images in our mind" which later images we call "the confirmation of our guess at what he's seeing." Once we've done this, we shall describe in the same way seeing telepathically what he sees. This too we shall call "guessing from shadows now at shadows to come" and be half sick of shadows. And when this web is woven, it's hard to be free of it, though it's we who wove it.

When I began a course of lectures this year with the question "What are mental facts?" at once someone protested "But how do we know there are any?" which comes to "How do we know when a man's angry, or when a dog smells a rat?" So I said "You might as well ask 'How do we know when a kettle's boiling?' Surely we know water's boiling when we see it bubbling?"

"But that's different" someone said, meaning of course that the way a creature's growls are a reason for thinking him angry, or his smiles for thinking him pleased is different from the way the bubbling of water is a reason for thinking it boiling.

And no doubt it is different. Bubbles tell us water's boiling because we've so often made tea, or rather, bubbles tell us water's boiling, partly because bubbles are part of boiling, and partly because bubbles have been associated in our experience with the other parts of boiling. Now if anger were, like boiling, just a pattern of physical incidents, then a dog's growls would be a reason for thinking him angry and about to bite in the very way that bubbles in water are a reason for believing that it's boiling and will make tea. But anger is more than the pattern of physical incidents which others observe when a creature's angry. And so the reason for thinking him angry is more complicated than the reason for thinking he's growling and that if you move he'll fly at you. Conversely, the reason is more complicated, and so the conclusion is too. We know a creature's angry not merely by looking at what he's doing and remembering what usually follows, like the doctor anticipating the course of a disease he never felt and which, if you like, the patient too cannot feel. On the contrary, we know a creature's angry by the way we feel as we look at him and the way we have felt when we have acted rather as he is acting. And since the reason for thinking a creature angry involves all this, thinking it involves it too, and therefore "He is angry" is not a description merely of the creature's physical state like the words "It's boiling" are of water's physical state.

Many people will say here "Well of course! We all know 'He's angry,' unlike 'It's boiling,' refers not merely and even not at all, to the physical state of the creature it's about; it refers primarily to his inward state, to the state of the soul or mind which resides in his body."

And no doubt they are entirely right. Entirely. The trouble is that what they say provides no answer to the questions "How does one know of another creature that he's angry? Does one know?" It's not that what they say does not suggest an answer. It does and that a bad one. For it suggests the answer "We know the state of the soul in a body which isn't ours in the way we know the state of the inhabitant of a house we never enter—by analogy." And this won't do at all.

In the first place, when one argues from the lights behind

249

the blinds and the clatter of the cups that the people opposite are having tea, this is based not merely on having noticed in one's own house a connection between these things, but also upon having observed this connection in the houses of others which one has entered. Without this support the argument would be much feebler, and much feebler still had one never stepped outside one's own front door. And now the whole falsity of this comparison begins to dawn on us. For it's not merely that a condition fulfilled in the case of inference from the outward state of a house or a motor car or a watch to its inward state is not fulfilled in the case of inference from a man's outward state to his inward state; it is that we do not know what it would be like for this condition to be fulfilled, what it would be like to observe the state of the soul which inhabits another body. And it follows that knowing what in me accompanies the drawing of my sword is not related to my knowing what in my neighbor accompanies the drawing of his sword as knowing what in my house accompanies the drawing of the blinds is related to knowing what in my neighbor's house accompanies the drawing of the blinds.

It is the breakdown of this comparison, it is the failure of the answer "We know the thoughts and feelings of others by analogy" which has tempted some to the desperate paradox "We know a man's angry like we know a kettle's boiling— from the steam we guess at bubbles and the rest, and from bubbles and the rest it's a deduction that it's boiling. In the same way, from a face we guess at hidden tears and then distress is a deduction." For though this comparison too is defective, giving as it does too simple a model for the logic of thoughts and feelings, it has the great merit of bringing out how misleading is the old model so embedded in our language, the model of the house and its inhabitant, the outward sign and the inward state. The old model suggests that even were we in no doubt as to what a man had done and the circumstances in which he had done it and in no doubt as to what he would do next, we might still be in doubt as to how he felt, in the way we might be in doubt as to what was going on inside a machine although we knew all about its outside and what it would do next. And the new comparison, though defective, begins to show us how inappropriate is this suggestion.

Can we find another comparison which shall combine the merits of the old with the merits of the new? Can we say for example that we know the feelings of another like we know the weight of thistledown, of what's too light for us to feel, or like we know the power of another creature or thing? This comparison has in it something of the comparison to the house we can't enter. For we speak of weight we can't feel by analogy with weight we can, we use the words "weighs this" "weighs that," and we justify our metaphor, support our conclusion, by analogy. Indeed we might suddenly feel that what analogy suggests is perhaps not so and that we never really know the weight of things we can't feel. But here we instantly realize that the doubt is not a doubt, because our conclusion as to weight is not a conclusion but purely deductive, because given the premises all is over bar the calculation and there is no finding the conclusion wrong or right.

Of course the words "finding, feeling the weight of what can't be felt" could be so used that we could easily imagine doing this. We might come to feel the weight of thistledown, only then it would no longer be light as air, and so no longer thistledown. We might come to feel the weight of things the weight of which we can not now feel, but then they'd no longer be things the weight of which we couldn't feel. We shall soon see what lies in the future, but by then it won't lie in the future. We can imagine a man doing what we now can seldom do, something which people have called "looking into the future." This man doesn't examine seeds and with his experience predict the crop we may anticipate, he gazes in a glass and sees the flowers of the future. If this is to be called "looking into the future" then when someone says we can't see into the future what he refers to is the familiar fact that few of us can do this. But if this sort of thing is rejected as being no more than seeing the shadows the future casts upon the present, then indeed we can not know the future.

Likewise we can imagine a man doing what we now can seldom do, something which people have called "looking into the mind of another." This man doesn't examine present symptoms and predict how the patient will go on. He sees scenes in a glass or in his mind's eye and knows they are what another sees, he feels distress and knows that another is in distress. If this is to be called seeing what another sees or feeling what he feels, if this would be real knowledge of the thoughts and feelings of another, then when someone says "We can not know the feeling of others" what he refers to is the familiar fact that few of us can do this. But if this sort of thing is rejected as being no more than seeing the shadows of what is in another's mind upon the walls of our own, or as making two minds one, or as making what is seen partly public, and so no longer mental, then indeed we can not know the thoughts and feelings of another. Once more the Agnostic is entirely right—like he was about what lies in the future. Once more what he says is true, necessarily true, because it's a tautology in that natural development of language which its proof encourages us to adopt—a tautology but fortunately a pathological one and so illuminating.

2. "But," someone will say, "the objects in the mind of Mr. So-and-so are different, since someone observes them." Mr. So-and-so does. And when we talk of really knowing what they are, we are not talking of knowing the unknowable, but simply of knowing them in the way Mr. So-and-so knows them.

We know things in the future and the weight of things, the weight of which we cannot feel by "deductive analogy"— "deductive" because the conclusion doesn't go beyond what supports it, "analogy" because from like cases we argue to the case before us. But the hypothesis of feelings in others which we can't feel is not like the hypothesis of weight we can't feel, not even like the hypothesis of unconscious feelings, feelings which no one can feel.

These hypotheses, it is true, are like that of feelings in others in that it is wrong to describe them as mere picturesque redescriptions of the phenomena in the cases they are used to explain. Nevertheless, for these hypotheses we may well bring out the confusion there is in questioning the existence of the unobservable entities they involve, by calling them *"connecting descriptions."* A hypothesis of this sort, it is true, is not established merely by ascertaining the phenomena in the case which calls for it, since the connection, the analogy, must be established too. But the more these two jobs are done the less does one who questions the hypothesis ask a question. With the objects before the mind of Mr. So-and-so it's different. For these someone can observe. Mr. So-and-so can. It might seem for a moment that "Mr. So-and-so has a cold" or "Has Mr. So-and-so a cold?" mean nothing to us once we know how he's sneezing and are confident he'll cough. But they mean much more to Mr. So-and-so. And therefore, since we speak his language, they must mean much more to us. So the old comparison of the casket none can open but the owner, of the house with the closed doors and mock windows, is after all the best and the "soul a ghost we are never quick enough to see."

Undoubtedly there's something in all this. There's something wrong with the comparison of mental things to the utterly "unobservables." But what? And must we lose the ground we had gained and go back to gazing at the windows of the house that's haunted?

When counsel claims that what his client sells is a cordial, or like a cordial, we may come at the cash value of his engaging description by recalling the reasons he has offered for it— how sweet, how pleasing in appearance, is what his client sells —like the old cordials. Undoubtedly like the old cordials. At the same time his client's product may differ from the old cordials in features which in certain connections are very important.

Now what are the likenesses between the logic of claims about the contents of caskets and the logic of expressions of thoughts and feelings, statements about thoughts and feelings? And are they incompatible with those differences which the Behaviorist emphasizes in his crude way as important in meeting metaphysical doubt about thoughts and feelings, differences which I have tried to continue to emphasize in a less offensive way? What were the reasons offered us for saying "After all, what is going on in my neighbor's head is like what is going on in his house or the casket he won't open for me, and not like the weight of what I can't feel, which I cannot really know only because there's nothing which would be called really knowing it"?

The reasons were these. "He will have a cold" or "He will be in pain" or "He will see a dagger" mean more to the man they are about, it was said, than any story, however complete, of the symptoms of the predicted states; he can tell in a way others can't whether these predictions are fulfilled; he can check them by direct "observation." It seems an obvious inference that when these statements are made in the present tense he can tell by direct observation whether they are correct, and indeed there seems no need to *infer* this, for surely if one says to a man, rather oddly perhaps, "You are in pain," then doesn't he know how right one is in a way one doesn't oneself? It seems an obvious inference too from the fact that "He will be in pain" means more to him it is about than any prediction of his symptoms that it means more to the rest of us who speak the same language. And again there seems no need to infer this, for surely when a doctor says "Mr. So-and-so will be in pain in about an hour's time" he means to say of him what he means to say of himself when he says "I shall feel pain in about an hour's time"—a thing one might say after an operation before the anaesthetic had worn off. And this sentence means more to the speaker than any prediction of symptoms. And this more that it means is what the speaker can verify by observation. So when the speaker says of someone else "He will be in pain" he means to predict more than cries and moans and yet he means to predict the existence, not of something unobservable, but of something which will be observed and of the same sort as he himself has observed. So when we say we cannot really know the thoughts and feelings of another, we do not speak of something in principle unobservable like an unconscious feeling, or the weight of something still too light to feel, but of something unobservable like things done behind closed doors.

I believe that here in the fact that there is something that it is not self-contradictory for one man to know directly, while it is self-contradictory for others, we have a characteristic difficulty of the logic of the soul. Here is a feature of the assertions we make about the thoughts and feelings of others which leaves us still troubled about their logical propriety long after like troubles about other things have been removed. We have doubted the propriety of our confidence in the hypothetical entities of science, in the old and universal hypothesis of matter, in all assertions as to what is right and wrong, good and bad. These doubts come from taking the logic of these things to be like the logic of a taste we may lack, of a substance behind the shadows, of a mechanism we cannot see, and they go when we recognize the defects of these false models of the transcendental. But something about thoughts and feelings forces us back to the old model for them and makes them seem the least transcendental of all things. And yet here too the old model is unsatisfactory. There would be no difficulty were it not.

Before this impasse memory of other difficulties may encourage us. In the case of doubts about right and wrong when we found the model of the moral sense defective it was not that we found a new model which was faultless. When we grasped the essence of the variable, when we removed the mystery of the universe of discourse and the worlds of fiction, we didn't do so by saying what these were, thus making the variable still constant and the unreal real still. But neither did we in these cases show how different was the logic of these from what we wished to make it by producing a new comparison that was perfect. On the contrary we were satisfied by recognizing that these things had a logic all their own, that we could not stop at any of the comparisons on the way, although our destination could never have satisfied us without the journey. So in our present difficulty when someone tries to persuade us to go back we must remember why we started and critically examine his persuasions.

Let us examine a third time the argument which leads us back to thinking of our ignorance of the feelings of another as more than the temporary fact that we seldom or never know what a man's feelings are without seeing his face or hearing him speak and also as more than a timeless tautology like our ignorance of the future or the weight of what's too light to feel. The argument begins with "It will be admitted that 'He will be in pain' means more to the man it is about than any prediction of his symptoms," and it is not for nothing it *begins* with this. It does so because there is something about the way the sentence works on one person, the person it's about, which is different from the way it works on others and which makes it much more impossible to say that it means no more to him than a prediction of his symptoms than it is to say this of others who hear the sentence and are not by it led to expect pain but only sensations as of symptoms of pain. And no doubt it is this difference which is the source of the curious expression "means for him." An expression which becomes futile in view of the principle upon which the argument next relies, namely that what a sentence means to one man it must mean to everyone else who uses the same language.

Another odd thing strikes us. If we ask what more than symptoms it is that "He will be in pain" means to the man it is about, the answer is "A certain sensation." What sensation? Pain. But how can this be *part* of what is meant by a statement which is simply to the effect that he will have that sensation?

If in order to avoid the last paradox we say that "He will

be in pain" means nothing about symptoms to the man it is about, then are we to say that it means the same to the rest of us, and therefore nothing about how he will look? It is true that teaching the meaning of "He will be in pain" is not merely a matter of pointing out symptoms to the learner as in teaching the name of a mechanical disorder; it involves also saying to him when he is in pain "Now you are in pain," but nevertheless pointing out the symptoms is part of the teaching. And these two parts of the teaching are reflected in the understanding of "He will be in pain." It is true that it cannot be understood by one who has never felt pain any more than "smells of cheese" or "He smells cheese" can be understood by one who can't smell. But it is also true that it is not understood by one who does not understand how it is decided whether it is true or false, that is, by one who does not know the relevant symptoms. It is even more ridiculous to say that "He will be in pain" means nothing about how he will look than it is to say that "He will burst into tears" says nothing about how he will feel. For the latter sentence can be used even when his having felt quite cheerful is nothing against it. But take away all symptoms from the meaning of "He will be in pain" and immediately there is nothing we would call B's finding that C was right in saying "A will be in pain."

If, in order to avoid these paradoxes, we say that "He will be in pain" means one thing to the man it is about and another to everyone else, then this is paradoxical in itself and it leads to the following oddity. What does it mean to the man it is about and not to others? A certain sensation surely? In fact pain, his pain. And isn't this what is means to everyone? Doesn't it lead everyone to expect that he will be in pain? Doesn't it lead everyone to expect his pain, to expect pain? Clearly there is an ambiguity here. "So-and-so is expecting pain" may be used and most usually is used to mean that he is expecting to be in pain. But it may be used to mean merely that he is expecting that someone will be in pain. If we could set out the difference between these two processes we should set out the difference between the way "He will be in pain" works on the man it is about and the way it works on others. And this would show how it happens that it is absurd to talk of others checking the prediction in the way he checks it. Let us set down as unprovocatively as possible some of the main features of how such sentences as "I will be hungry," "You will be hungry," "He will be hungry" and "He is hungry," "You are hungry," and "I am hungry" work.

Suppose a mother says to a child "You will be hungry by 11 o'clock." Then (1a) the child will decide whether the prediction was correct by waiting with his eye on the clock till 11 A.M. and then if he begins to feel hungry saying "You were right, I am hungry," and if he does not feel hungry saying "You were wrong." It is at once apparent that what we have called his deciding whether the prediction was correct consists largely in having that sensation, being in that state, which was predicted in the statement about him. Is it any wonder that *others* cannot check *that* statement in *that* way? We may add under this head that he will not be surprised to find himself complaining that he is hungry or eating biscuits. (1b) Had his mother made the same prediction about his brother and not about himself he would again have waited with his eyes on the clock, only then he would not have waited for hunger but for symptoms in his brother. (2a) And this is what his brother will do in order to verify the prediction about him: I mean of course that the brother will wait for symptoms in the child, not in himself. (2b) Had his mother made the same prediction about his brother and not about himself, then his brother would have waited for hunger, I mean of course hunger in himself, that is, I mean would have anticipated feeling hungry. (3) When the clock reaches 11, the sentence "You will be feeling hungry at 11" ceases to tell the person it is about anything. In other words, "You, Alfred, are hungry" can tell the person to whom it is addressed nothing, but "He, Alfred, is hungry" can tell others much. This again shows up how much knowing, directly knowing, that a mental prediction is fulfilled in being in the mental state predicted.

It is no wonder that these facts lead to trouble when we try to sum them up in our usual logical notation.[1]

For in that notation a sentence must mean the same to any two people provided it is unambiguous and they are both using the same language. This implies of course that using "A will be hungry" either (1) means to A and the rest of us symptoms in A and only symptoms, or (2) means to A and the rest of us not only symptoms but also a certain sensation not of symptoms, or (3) means to A and the rest of us only a certain sensation.

Each of these alternatives illuminates a feature of the logic of sensations. But they are all paradoxes.

If we say that (1) "A will be hungry" means only symptoms both to A and to others so that his waiting for stomach sensations is no part of his learning the correctness of the prediction, we do not have to say that others can't learn its correctness in the way he can. But to refuse to call his waiting for a sensation of hunger and saying "You were right" or "You were wrong" according to whether he feels hungry or not "part of his learning whether the prediction was correct" is outrageous: and to say "A will see snakes" means to him nothing but symptoms does not do justice to the fact that "A will see snakes (hallucinatory)" works for him so very like "A will see snakes (real)": it does not do justice even to the way such a sentence works on others.

If on the other hand we say (2) that "A will be hungry" or "A will see snakes" means to A and to others not merely symptoms but also a sensation for A, or say (3) that it means both to A and to others nothing about symptoms but only a sensa-

---

[1] That is, when we try to describe the logic of private, singly observable, things with the notation suitable to describing the logic of public things. There is also trouble when we try to describe the logic of utterly unobservable things in the notation we have for describing the logic of universally observable things.

tion, then not only are these statements in themselves paradoxical but both imply that one can never really know the
thoughts and feelings of another. The proof, which is almost
the same for both, is as follows:

1. According to (2) A learns the correctness of "A will be
hungry at 11" simply by waiting for a feeling of hunger and
for symptoms in himself of this. According to (3) he learns the
correctness of the predictions simply on the basis of feeling
hungry.

2. A person, B, really knows the sensation of another, A,
only if he knows them in the way A knows them, that is, only
if he knows the correctness of a prediction as to A's sensations
in the way A knows it, that is, only if he learns its correctness
in the way A does.

3. Now when B hears a prediction such as "A will be hungry
at 11" either like A he waits for hunger (or for hunger and
symptoms in himself) and simply on this basis judges the prediction or he does not. If he does, he misinterprets the prediction as being about himself. If he does not, he learns its correctness not in the way A does.

Therefore a person, B, cannot learn the correctness of a
prediction about a person, A's, sensations in the way A himself does. Therefore no one really knows the sensations of
another.

The third part of this proof may be set out more fully as
follows: If when B hears someone say to A "Snakes at 6" he
doesn't wait for snakes but for symptoms in A, then he interprets the prediction correctly and checks it like we all would.
But then he doesn't check it like A would. If, on the other
hand, when B hears someone say "Snakes at 6" to A, he waits
for a sensation as of snakes, then either he takes the sensation
as of snakes (or the sensation and symptoms in himself) to
fulfill the prediction or he does not. If he does, then he misinterprets the prediction and therefore does not come to know its
correctness in the way A does. But if he does not, then either
he checks the prediction not in the way A does or he misinter-

prets the prediction. For if B, upon seeing snakes, does not look only for symptoms in A but looks for them in someone else or in everyone else, then he has misinterpreted "Snakes at 6" to mean "Snakes for C" or "Snakes for everyone!" that is, roughly, "Real Snakes." But if upon seeing snakes he looks only for symptoms in A in order to check the prediction, then he doesn't come to know its correctness like A does. Or does he? Some would say he does, since like A he waits for a sensation of snakes, and like A he looks for symptoms in A. Others would say he doesn't, because he doesn't look for symptoms in himself while A does look for symptoms in himself.

Shall we say that a man can't make the movement another makes, can't do what another does, because if A scratches his head then either B scratches his, A's, head too, and therefore he doesn't do what A does since he doesn't scratch his own head, or B scratches his, B's, head, and therefore again doesn't do what A does since A scratches A's head? Or shall we say that B does what A does if A scratches A's head and B scratches B's head? Or shall we say that B does what A does if A scratches A's head and B scratches A's head? These things are so simple that we can keep control of the notations and use or refuse the paradoxes without harm and at our convenience. With the notations for describing the peculiarities of sentences about sensations this is not so easy but it's possible. And in particular it's easy to see that if the case in which B knows A is hungry by feeling hungry himself and then finding symptoms in A is called "B's knowing A's sensation in the way A knows it," then the proof that we never know the mind of another can no longer be based entirely on self-evident premises but requires also the premise that in fact no one ever does know the sensation of another in the extraordinary telepathic way described. And when this premise is needed, immediately the conclusion diminishes from the paradox that we *can't* know the minds of others to the statement of fact that we *don't*.[2]

---

[2] I have here added to the first draft of this paper in response to Mr. Ayer's criticism that it was obscure.

For it becomes the statement that no one has telepathic knowledge of the mind of another. For it then *is* this statement put in the paradoxical and misleading form that no one knows, no one really knows, the mind of another.

The pure paradox that we *can* never know the mind of another emphasizes the differences between everything we do call or might be tempted to call one person's learning the correctness of a prediction about the mind of another and what we call a person's learning the correctness of a prediction about his own mind. It does this by using these differences to persuade us to call *nothing* knowing the correctness of a prediction about the mind of another in the way he knows it himself.

And this is easily done. For a person, A, is said to learn the correctness of a statement to the effect that he, A, will have a certain sensation largely by having that sensation, while another person's, B's, having that sensation is of course not called his learning the correctness of the statement about A. And if asked who knows best how a man feels, he himself or someone else, we readily answer "The man himself." It then remains only to call the way a man knows his own feeling, his own mind, the only real, direct, way of knowing his mind, and it follows at once that no one can have direct and real knowledge of the mind of another. Reached by this route, "We cannot know the mind of another" is a necessary truth in that natural development of ordinary language which its proof persuades us to adopt.

The statement of fact that we never *do* know the mind of another is also something of a paradox. For, of course, in the most usual use of words we do all sometimes know how a particular person is feeling although at times we do not, and it is only in a new sense of "knowing the mind of another," that we seldom or never do this although we can conceive of ourselves doing it quite often. The semi-paradox that we never *do* know the mind of another emphasizes how what is ordinarily called "knowing the mind of another" differs from a knowledge we may imagine ourselves to have, a knowledge which

Symposium: Other Minds

comes by having feeling or image or sensation just like that which we attribute to another and basing on this our beliefs about his mental state in the way we base on the images and feelings of memory our beliefs about the past. The semi-paradox emphasizes these differences by using them to persuade us to call only this imagined sort of knowledge, "real knowledge of the mind of another." This is easily done. For clearly such knowledge would be more like the knowledge a person has of his own mind than is our common knowledge which is based on what we can see of his face and what we can hear him say. And as we have noticed when considering the pure paradox there is in us all an inclination to call a man's knowledge of his own mind the best and most real knowledge of that mind.

Those who say "We never do really know the mind of another," having persuaded us to deny the title of "real knowledge" to what we ordinarily call by this name by holding up a new ideal knowledge to which we should confine the title, then remark that we seldom or never attain to this ideal. And they are quite right. We seldom or never do. It's a fact—a familiar fact.

When someone says, "We never know the mind of another" we need to ask him [3] whether (1) he wishes to say that the sort of thing we would ordinarily call "knowing the mind of another" doesn't happen—if so he makes in quite ordinary language a statement of fact which is false—or whether (2) he wishes to say that the particular sort of intimate, telepathic knowledge of another's mind which would give us knowledge of his mind comparable to our knowledge in memory of the past seldom or never occurs—if so he makes in a readily acceptable caricature of ordinary language a statement of fact which is true—or whether (3) he wishes to say that we cannot know the mind of another in exactly the way he does himself—if so, in a readily acceptable extreme caricature of ordinary language he makes a statement which is necessarily true, couldn't conceivably be false.

[3] Cf. A. J. Ayer, "The Terminology of Sense Data," *Mind* (October, 1945).

263

Nearly always the truth of the matter will be that the skeptical speaker is neither definitely doing one of these things nor definitely doing another. He is like a man who has moved a piece, a chessman perhaps, upon a board before us, but when we move in reply, explains that he is not playing exactly the game ordinarily played with the pieces he uses and that further he has not quite settled what modification of the ordinary game he plans to play. We shall not come to conclusions with him till this is settled. Is he making a statement of fact or is he making a statement which is necessarily true? He will resent this question for he will feel that with it we are trying either to force him to plod beside the scientist always subject to the vagaries of nature or to banish him to the *a priori* where blows indeed no wind of chance and *ipso facto* no breath of life. He is convinced that somehow he is revealing something about the world and yet making a statement which has all the necessity, all the immunity to chance, of a logical or mathematical statement.

So he may be. For a tautology may reveal something about the world. A tautology made without modifying ordinary language may do this. Still more may one like "Tigers burn bright in forests at night." To see the world we must connect things and as we connect them more or in a new way so we see old things anew. Even a logical statement, which by definition cannot involve any modification of linguistic inventions and which therefore in a sense cannot connect things in a new way, but can only underline connections already made, can reveal to us what we had not realized. Thus the equation "God exists" means "Something is divine" disconnects "God exists" from "God knows" and "God loves" and so breaks the power of an analogy suggested by the shape of sentences and very confusing, as we know, in certain connections. Still more can a metaphysical statement which may modify language, connect or disconnect things in a new way. And when the philosopher says "We can never know the mind of another" the proof he offers makes us realize that, when from a man's face or what he says we guess he's angry, we are not like one who from the outside of a house guesses that it is inhabited *and could make sure.*

Unfortunately the words "We cannot know the mind of another" also suggest that when from a man's face or words we guess at his feelings we *are* like one who from the outside of a house guesses that it is inhabited, but cannot make sure, because he can't unlock the door or because the windows, though seemingly transparent, are not or because he lacks the power of gazing in a crystal and so ascertaining what goes on behind closed doors. And thus the very words used to break the power of the analogy of the house and its inhabitant are in conformity with that analogy and encourage it.[4] This is why it is so very necessary to be clear as to whether one wishes to use them to make the scientific statement that we lack telepathic knowledge or to make the metaphysical and tautological statement aimed against the confusing analogy, embedded in our language, of the house and its inhabitant.

To sum up then: The words "We can not know the mind of another" or better "We can not really know the mind of another" may be used to reveal something about the world and at the same time to say something which can't be false. But this is not done, cannot be done, by making a statement of fact which has all the necessity of a tautology.

True, one who says "We cannot know the mind of another" may use these words to make the statement of fact that we lack telepathic knowledge and if he does he is making that statement in a modification of ordinary language in which it is

---

[4] This is characteristic of the expression of metaphysical advances. Thus to say "Matter does not exist" is to speak as if matter were something over and above sensations which is just what those who say it mean to deny. Schlick said that we now know that there are no such entities as numbers and thereby spoke as if they were things, though fabulous, the very way of speaking his statement was directed against. Wittgenstein did the same when he said "We have the idea that the meaning of a word is an object." The same habit lingers when we say "Material things are logical fictions," "Numbers and meanings are logical fictions."

necessarily true that we lack knowledge of the minds of others *unless we have telepathic knowledge*. But if so he is still making a statement which may at any time become false, because we may come to have the power we lack.

And again, one who says "We cannot know the mind of another" may use these words to make a statement which is necessarily true because made in a modification of ordinary language in which absolutely nothing is to be called "knowing the mind of another in the way he knows it himself" and absolutely nothing is to be called "knowing the mind of another" except knowing it in the way he knows it himself. But if the skeptical speaker is using words this way, then at once he is not making a statement of fact, he is not telling us of something we have missed. For then his statement that we can't know the mind of another has become like the statement that we can't possess the heart of another when we have decided that this description is not to be applied until that other has no desire apart from our own and is then still not to be applied because then that other is no longer other.

Once more then we reach the result that the words "the impossibility of knowing the mind of another" may stand either for something like the difficulty, or if you like, the impossibility of knowing the future from a crystal or for something like the impossibility of knowing the future just as we do the present, either for a prolonged accident or for a timeless necessity, either for a fact or a tautology, but not for something which is both. This is the result we reached [elsewhere]. The difference is that now we know the proof and therefore the point of the tautology and that now we can hold to it. We can now hold to it because we have seen how it is that, while there is one person for whom it is not impossible that he knows what is in the mind of a certain person, it is impossible for everyone else. For we have noticed how there is a language, and one we are half inclined to use, in which, while it is not self-contradictory to say that A knows the mind of A, it is self-contradictory to say of anyone other than A that he knows the mind of A.

3. But now alas, just when all seems well, a new whisper disturbs our complacency: "How *can* two people attach the same meaning to a statement, when the one can check it in a way in which it is impossible for the other to do so?" How *can* two people be concerned with the same proposition, the same fact, when the one can ascertain the truth of that proposition in a certain way, while it makes no sense to talk of the other ascertaining its truth in that way? This is the same difficulty, coming from the eccentric logic of sensations, as that we have just investigated. But one who puts the difficulty this way pretends to have another way out and leads us to a different destination. He says: "Face the difficulty at once and say that a sentence such as 'A will be hungry' means something different to A from what it means to the rest of us. You will then not be forced into admitting that we can never know the feelings of another. For you will be able to claim that we do know the statements we make about the feelings of another in the sense that *we* attach to them." It's not till later that we find that in order to preserve our knowledge we have followed a guide who leaves us in an isolation even more profound—not indeed among enemies whose words may be all lies but in a place where for ever there is beside our own voice only the chatter of the monkeys.

We have caught a glimpse of this person before. It was when we considered the paradoxes we have now worked till they are no longer paradoxes and noticed how they depended upon the principle "A sentence must mean the same to any two speakers unless it is ambiguous." He had then only a rather freakish air because he just hinted that we might deny this principle. Now he's becoming bolder. Is he a friend or an enemy?

When we dealt with the riddle "Can one man do what another man does?" we set out what makes paradoxical the answer "Yes" and in doing so set out what leads to the answer "No": and in setting out what makes paradoxical the answer "No," we set out what leads to the answer "Yes." Likewise in setting out the paradox involved in "A sentence must mean the same to any two speakers" and in "Mr. So-and-so will have a cold" means the same to any two speakers, we have set out what now seems to force us towards " 'Mr. So-and-so will have a cold' means more to him than to us," and therefore towards "A sentence need not mean the same to any two speakers." And if we now welcome this last paradox and set out what is involved in it, we shall see how we can still deny it and insist that "Mr. So-and-so will have a cold" means the same to him as to everyone else and that every sentence means the same to any two speakers of the same language.

Suppose someone says "We can't know what lies beyond the horizon." We reply "Don't be absurd. What you mean no doubt is that we can't know what's beyond the horizon like we can what's before us. And that's a tautology. For it's self-contradictory to talk of knowing the remote just as one knows the near." He may reply "But it can't be self-contradictory, because there may [5] be someone doing this, e.g., observing a fire in Fleet Street, at the very moment that one cannot oneself. And such a person is learning the truth of a statement with the same meaning as that one is wondering about. Now it cannot be sensible to talk of one person's knowing something in a certain way and absurd to talk of another person's knowing that thing in that way." Let us now meet this by saying that "Fire in Fleet Street" doesn't mean the same to people in different places. For this is true in a sense fatal to the Agnostic. And no harm is done if we are careful.

Imagine that people all over the country hear on the wireless "A fire is now raging in Fleet Street." Those in Fleet Street have a different and more direct means of checking this statement than those in Brighton or even those in Streatham. Those in Fleet Street have only to open their windows or their eyes, and they will be disappointed if upon doing so they see no

[5] This is one respect in which the puzzle about things in the distance differs from the puzzle about things in the soul. For things in the soul we may say *must* be known. Further the description of an event as Mr. So-and-so's anger tells who may know it but "Fire in Fleet Street" does not. . . .

flames. But the newspapermen on holiday by the sea will be astonished if they find the Front in flames. They may use their eyes of course and observe their editor mount a bus for the station, like people on the Euston road may watch the engines hurry from opposite St. Pancras' Church. But, unlike those on the spot, they cannot instantly, by opening their eyes, obtain sensations ultimately and overwhelmingly connected with the words "Fire in Fleet Street."

Let us say that the news means something different to listeners far from the scene from what it means to those who are there, and that it means to those at Brighton charred timbers and hurrying firemen in 60 minutes by the Southern Electric, to those in the Strand flames from the window, to watchers in Fleet Street nothing, since it tells them nothing.[6] Only if we say this, that the words have different meanings to listeners in different places, we must remember that they all speak the same language, that the case is not like that of people who being in different places speak a different dialect. On the contrary, were the news to have the same effects on a man in

---

[6] The peculiarity of a man's knowledge of his own sensations I have tried to bring out in "Other Minds VII," *Mind*, LII.

(a) The different meanings of "Big Ben points to 12" to persons, at different distances is given by "To a person 100 miles away this means Big Ben pointing to 2 o'clock in two turns of my clock with the speedometer at 50, to a person 50 miles away this means Big Ben pointing to 1 o'clock in one turn of my clock with the speedometer at 50, etc.," or by "This means to a person 100 miles away Big Ben pointing at 4 o'clock in 4 turns of my clock with the speedometer at 25, etc." These accounts of course are simplified and neglect grit in clocks and defective speedometers. The full account involves all the laws of nature, which once they are ascertained are put into the meanings of words. It is no miracle that they can then be pulled out again.

(b) The description of the different meanings of sentences about the distant can be given in terms of sentences about the present. The description of the different meanings of sentences about sensations can be given only in sentences about sensations. This leads people to fancy that these are being given a circular definition. But no definition is being given. The description of the use of general sentences cannot be given without the use of any such sentence. But this only means that we can't describe their use by a rule for providing substitutes. When we ask "What is the variable?" or "What is consciousness?" it is not that general or psychological sentences are unintelligible to us.

Brighton as it has on one in the Strand so as to give us some inclination to say that it means the same to him as it does to the man in the Strand, then we should say that the man in Brighton didn't understand English, that the words didn't mean the same to him as to the rest of us and therefore not the same as to the man in the Strand. We should say "The man in the Strand correctly understands them to mean a fire in Fleet Street, the man in Brighton incorrectly understands them to mean a fire in Brighton or a general fire, a fire everywhere. He attaches the wrong significance, or no significance to the spatial suffix 'Fleet Street' or 'here.'" In the same way if a man were to hear the words "Voices in Joan of Arc's ears" and then listen for voices, we should say that the words meant for him something different from what they mean for the rest of us and in that way something different from what they mean for Joan of Arc. We should say "He incorrectly takes the words 'Voices in Joan of Arc's ears' to mean voices in his own ears or public, real voices, voices in everyone's ears: he attaches the wrong significance, or no significance, to the personal suffix 'in Joan's ears,' in 'Joan's mind.'" Again we have asked "Does 'Voices in Joan of Arc's ears' mean more to Joan of Arc than it does to others, and if so what more does it mean?" The answer is "It doesn't mean more, any more than 'Fire in Fleet Street' means more to those on the spot than it does to others and consequently there is no answer to 'What more does it mean?'" except that it doesn't mean more. It follows at once that it is as misleading and wrong to say "'Voices in Joan's ears, pain in her heart' means nothing to Joan when she is already hearing the voices and feeling the pain, although it means something to others," as it is to say, "'Fire in Fleet Street,' means nothing to those already watching the fire, although it means something to others and what is more its meaning reaches a maximum just before a person reaches the spot." But although it is dangerous to say these things because in the usual meaning of "meaning" they are false, they are well worth saying in a modified meaning of "meaning," in which the meaning of a word to a particular person at a particular place at a particular time is a matter of what, if he knows the language, it must do to him then and there. For then these paradoxical statements about meaning something different, meaning more, meaning nothing, express what can otherwise be said only with another expression, such as "works differently for," "does more work for," "does nothing for," which expression is again liable to be misunderstood. It is liable to be misunderstood in the way "means more" is liable to be misunderstood, and although less liable to be misunderstood in this way, that is as attacking the truth that any sentence must mean the same to any two speakers of the same language, it is more liable to be misunderstood as referring merely to the fact that "Fire in Fleet Street" may mean more to a man whose business is there than it does to one whose business is elsewhere, that is, to unconventional, unsymmetrical differences. There is indeed at this juncture no substitute for luck and goodwill except industry—industrious description of the detailed differences between hearers and equally industrious description of the likenesses, and this will involve not merely a description of the use of the particular expression giving trouble such as "He hears voices," but also a description of other expressions in the same linguistic constellations, such as "I hear voices," "You are hearing voices," "You will hear voices," "Everyone will hear voices," "There will be voices," and at last the whole language.

And what point have these descriptions which are so apt to mislead or so laborious? None—unless we wish to answer the question with which we started "How do we know that a man is angry? Surely we do know this and yet how can we, since all we really know is how he frowns and growls?" But if we wish to free ourselves of that puzzling question and positively to gain that sort of new view of the world which a new language and a new grasp of language gives, then these dangerous or tedious descriptions are not merely useful but essential. For without referring to the facts we have dangerously described as sentences having different meanings for different people, we could not understand how true it is nor how it's true that no one can know what lies beyond the horizon or behind the windows of the soul. For without referring to these facts we could not understand how it is also true that, while one person may know these things, others cannot.

4. And it's not until we have understood these things that we ask "Why is it that familiar facts and truths have been so confusingly expressed?" Have we perhaps missed the deepest meaning of these metaphysical doctrines so absurd and so profound?

Virginia Woolf writes:

> Let us consider letters. Life would split asunder without them. "Come to tea, come to dinner, what's the truth of the story?, have you heard the news?, life in the capital is gay, the Russian dancers . . ." These are our stays and props. These lace our days together and make of life a perfect globe. And yet, and yet . . . when we go to dinner, when pressing fingertips we hope to meet somewhere soon, a doubt insinuates itself; is this the way to spend our days? the rare, the limited, so soon dealt out to us—drinking tea? dining out? And the notes accumulate. And the telephones ring. And everywhere we go wires and tubes surround us to carry the voices that try to penetrate before the last card is dealt and the days are over. "Try to penetrate," for as we lift the cup, shake the hand, express the hope, something whispers, Is this all? Can I ever know, share, be certain? Am I doomed all my days to write letters, send voices, which fall upon the tea-table, fade upon the passage, making appointments, while life dwindles, to come and dine? Yet letters are venerable: and the telephone valiant, for the journey is a lonely one, and if bound together by notes and telephones we went in company, perhaps—who knows?—we might talk by the way.[7]

This isolation which we may defeat but cannot vanquish, does it find voice in the old puzzle as to whether we really

[7] *Jacob's Room,* p. 91.

know what is in the mind of others? Does the contradiction in the philosopher's request for perfect knowledge of others reflect a conflict in the human heart which dreads and yet demands the otherness of others?

## II—*by J. L. Austin*

I feel that I agree with much, and especially with the more important parts, of what Mr. Wisdom has written, both in his present paper and in his beneficial series of articles on "Other Minds" and other matters. I feel ruefully sure, also, that one must be at least one sort of fool to rush in over ground so well trodden by the angels. At best I can hope only to make a contribution to one part of the problem, where it seems that a little more industry still might be of service. I could only wish it was a more central part. In fact, however, I did find myself unable to approach the center while still bogged down on the periphery. And Mr. Wisdom himself may perhaps be sympathetic towards a policy of splitting hairs to save starting them.

Mr. Wisdom, no doubt correctly, takes the "Predicament" to be brought on by such questions as "How do we know that another man is angry?" He also cites other forms of the question—"Do we (ever) know?," "Can we know?," "How can we know?" the thoughts, feelings, sensations, mind, &c., of another creature, and so forth. But it seems likely that each of these further questions is rather different from the first, which alone has been enough to keep me preoccupied, and to which I shall stick.

Mr. Wisdom's method is to go on to ask: *Is it like the way in which we know* that a kettle is boiling, or that there is a tea-party next door, or the weight of thistledown? But it seemed to me that perhaps, as he went on, he was not giving an altogether accurate account (perhaps only because too cursory a one) of what we should say if asked "How do you know?" these things. For example, in the case of the tea-party, to say we knew of it "by analogy" would at best be a very sophisticated answer (and one to which some sophisticates might prefer the phrase "by induction"), while in addition it seems incorrect because we don't, I think, claim to *know* by analogy, but only to *argue* by analogy. Hence I was led on to consider what sort of thing does actually happen when ordinary people are asked "How do you know?"

Much depends, obviously, on the sort of item it is about which we are being asked "How do you know?" and there are bound to be many kinds of cases that I shall not cover at all, or not in detail. The sort of statement which seems simplest, and at the same time not, on the face of it, unlike "He is angry," is such a statement as "That is a goldfinch" ("The kettle is boiling")—a statement of particular, current, empirical fact. This is the sort of statement on making which we are liable to be asked "How do you know?" and the sort that, at least sometimes, we say we don't know, but only believe. It may serve for a stalking-horse as well as another.

When we make an assertion such as "There is a goldfinch in the garden" or "He is angry," there is a sense in which we imply that we are sure of it or know it ("But I took it you *knew*," said reproachfully), though what we imply, in a similar sense and more strictly, is only that we *believe* it. On making such an assertion, therefore, we are directly exposed to the questions (1) "Do you *know* there is?" "Do you *know* he is?" and (2) "*How* do you know?" If in answer to the first question we reply "Yes," we may then be asked the second question, and even the first question alone is commonly taken as an invitation to state not merely *whether* but also *how* we know. But on the other hand, we may well reply "No" in answer to the first question: we may say "No, but I think there is," "No, but I believe he is." For the implication that I know or am sure is not strict: we are not all (terribly or sufficiently) strictly brought up. If we do this, then we are exposed to the question, which might also have been put to us without preliminaries, "Why do you believe that?" (or "What makes you think so?" "What induces you to suppose so?" &c.).

There is a singular difference between the two forms of

challenge: *"How* do you know?" and *"Why* do you believe?"
We seem never to ask *"Why* do you know?" or *"How* do you
believe?" And in this, as well as in other respects to be noticed
later, not merely such other words as "suppose," "assume," &c.,
but also the expressions "be sure" and "be certain," follow the
example of "believe," not that of "know."

Either question, "How do you know?" or "Why do you
believe?," may well be asked only out of respectful curiosity,
from a genuine desire to learn. But again, they may both be
asked as *pointed* questions, and, when they are so, a further
difference comes out. "How do you know?" suggests that perhaps you *don't* know it at all, whereas "Why do you believe?"
suggests that perhaps you *oughtn't* to believe it. There is no
suggestion [8] that you *ought* not to know or that you *don't*
believe it. If the answer to "How do you know?" or to "Why
do you believe?" is considered unsatisfactory by the challenger,
he proceeds rather differently in the two cases. His next riposte
will be, on the one hand, something such as "Then you *don't*
know any such thing," or "But that doesn't prove it: in that
case you don't really know it at all," and on the other hand,
something such as "That's very poor evidence to go on: you
oughtn't to believe it on the strength of that alone." [9]

The "existence" of your alleged belief is not challenged, but
the "existence" of your alleged knowledge *is* challenged. If we
like to say that "I believe," and likewise "I am sure" and "I am
certain," are descriptions of subjective mental or cognitive
states or attitudes, or what not, then "I know" is not that, or at
least not merely that: it functions differently in talking.

"But of course," it will be said, "'I know' is obviously more
than that, more than a description of my own state. If I *know,*
I *can't be wrong.* You can always show I don't know by show-

[8] But in special senses and cases, there is—for example, if someone has announced some top secret information, we can ask, "How do *you* know?" nastily.
[9] An interesting variant in the case of knowing would be "You *oughtn't to
say* (you've no business to say) you know it at all." But of course this is only
superficially similar to "You oughtn't to believe it": you ought *to say* you believe it, if you do believe it, however poor the evidence.

ing I am wrong, or may be wrong, or that I didn't know by showing that I might have been wrong. *That's* the way in which knowing differs even from being as certain as can be." This must be considered in due course, but first we should consider the types of answer that may be given in answer to the question "How do you know?"

Suppose I have said "There's a bittern at the bottom of the garden," and you ask "How do you know?" My reply may take very different forms:

(*a*) I was brought up in the fens.
(*b*) I heard it.
(*c*) The keeper reported it.
(*d*) By its booming.
(*e*) From the booming noise.
(*f*) Because it is booming.

We may say, roughly, that the first three are answers to the questions "How do you come to know?" "How are you in a position to know?" or "How do *you* know?" understood in different ways: while the other three are answers to "How can you tell?" understood in different ways. That is, I may take you to have been asking:

(1) How do I come to be in a position to know about bitterns?

(2) How do I come to be in a position to say there's a bittern here and now?

(3) How do (can) I tell bitterns?

(4) How do (can) I tell the thing here and now as a bittern?

The implication is that in order to know this is a bittern, I must have:

(1) been trained in an environment where I could become familiar with bitterns

(2) had a certain opportunity in the current case

(3) learned to recognize or tell bitterns

(4) succeeded in recognizing or telling this as a bittern.

(1) and (2) mean that my experiences must have been of cer-

tain kinds, that I must have had certain opportunities: (3) and (4) mean that I must have exerted a certain kind and amount of acumen.[10]

The questions raised in (1) and (3) concern our *past* experiences, our opportunities and our activities in learning to discriminate or discern, and, bound up with both, the correctness or otherwise of the linguistic usages we have acquired. Upon these earlier experiences depends how *well* we know things, just as, in different but cognate cases of "knowing," it is upon earlier experience that it depends how *thoroughly* or how *intimately* we know: we know a person by sight or intimately, a town inside out, a proof backwards, a job in every detail, a poem word for word, a Frenchman when we see one. "He doesn't know what love (real hunger) is" means he hasn't had enough experience to be able to recognize it and to distinguish it from other things slightly like it. According to how well I know an item, and according to the kind of item it is, I can recognize it, describe it, reproduce it, draw it, recite it, apply it, and so forth. Statements like "I know *very well* he isn't angry" or "You know *very well* that isn't calico," though of course about the current case, ascribe the excellence of the knowledge to past experience, as does the general expression "You are old enough to know better." [11]

By contrast, the questions raised in (2) and (4) concern the circumstances of the current case. Here we can ask "How *definitely* do you know?" You may know it for certain, quite positively, officially, on his own authority, from unimpeachable sources, only indirectly, and so forth.

---

[10] "I know, I *know*, I've seen it a hundred times, don't keep on telling me" complains of a superabundance of opportunity: "knowing a hawk from a handsaw" lays down a minimum of acumen in recognition or classification. "As well as I know my own name" is said to typify something I *must* have experienced and *must* have learned to discriminate.

[11] The adverbs that can be inserted in "How . . . do you know?" are few in number and fall into still fewer classes. There is practically no overlap with those that can be inserted in "How . . . do you believe?" (firmly, sincerely, genuinely, &c.).

Some of the answers to the question "How do you know?" are, oddly enough, described as "reasons for knowing" or "reasons to know," or even sometimes as "reasons why I know," despite the fact that we do not ask "Why do you know?" But now surely, according to the Dictionary, "reasons" should be given in answer to the question "Why?" just as we do in fact give reasons for believing in answer to the question "Why do you believe?" However there is a distinction to be drawn here. "How do you know that I. G. Farben worked for war?" "I have every reason to know: I served on the investigating commission": here, giving my reasons for knowing is stating how I come to be in a position to know. In the same way we use the expressions "I know *because* I saw him do it" or "I know *because* I looked it up only ten minutes ago": these are similar to "So it is: it *is* plutonium. How did you know?" "I did quite a bit of physics at school before I took up philology," or to "I ought to know: I was standing only a couple of yards away." Reasons for *believing* on the other hand are normally quite a different affair (a recital of symptoms, arguments in support, and so forth), though there are cases where we do give as reasons for believing our having been in a position in which we could get good evidence: "Why do you believe he was lying?" "I was watching him very closely."

Among the cases where we give our reasons for knowing things, a special and important class is formed by those where we cite authorities. If asked "How do you know the election is today?" I am apt to reply "I read it in *The Times*," and if asked "How do you know the Persians were defeated at Marathon?" I am apt to reply "Herodotus expressly states that they were." In these cases "know" is correctly used: we know "at second hand" when we can cite an authority who was in a position to know (possibly himself also only at second hand).[12]

[12] Knowing at second hand, or on authority, is not the same as "knowing indirectly," whatever precisely that difficult and perhaps artificial expression may mean. If a murderer "confesses," then, whatever our opinion of the worth of the "confession," we cannot say that "we (only) know indirectly that he did

The statement of an authority makes me aware of something, enables me to know something, which I shouldn't otherwise have known. It is a source of knowledge. In many cases, we contrast such reasons for knowing with other reasons for believing the very same thing: "Even if we didn't know it, even if he hadn't confessed, the evidence against him would be enough to hang him."

It is evident, of course, that this sort of "knowledge" is "liable to be wrong," owing to the unreliability of human testimony (bias, mistake, lying, exaggeration, &c.). Nevertheless, the occurrence of a piece of human testimony radically alters the situation. We say "We shall never know what Caesar's feelings were on the field of the battle of Philippi," because he did not pen an account of them: *if* he *had*, then to say "We shall never know" won't do in the same way, even though we may still perhaps find reason to say "It doesn't read very plausibly: we shall never *really* know the *truth*" and so on. Naturally, we are judicious: we don't say we know (at second hand) if there is any special reason to doubt the testimony: but there has to be *some* reason. It is fundamental in talking (as in other matters) that we are entitled to trust others, except in so far as there is some concrete reason to distrust them. Believing persons, accepting testimony, is the, or one main, point of talking. We don't play (competitive) games except in the faith that our opponent is trying to win: if he isn't, it isn't a game, but something different. So we don't talk with people (descriptively) except in the faith that they are trying to convey information.[13]

It is now time to turn to the question "How can you tell?" i.e., to senses (2) and (4) of the question "How do you know?"

---

it," nor can we so speak when a witness, reliable or unreliable, has stated that he saw the man do it. Consequently, it is not correct, either, to say that the murderer himself knows "directly" that he did it, whatever precisely "knowing directly" may mean.

[13] Reliance on the authority of others is fundamental too, in various special matters, for example, for corroboration and for the correctness of our own use of words, which we learn from others.

If you have asked "How do you know it's a goldfinch?" then I may reply "From its behavior," "By its markings," or, in more detail, "By its red head," "From its eating thistles." That is, I indicate, or to some extent set out with some degree of precision, those features of the situation which enable me to recognize it as one to be described in the way I did describe it. Thereupon you may still object in several ways to my saying it's a goldfinch, without in the least "disputing my facts," which is a further stage to be dealt with later. You may object:

(1)   But goldfinches *don't* have red heads

(1a)   But that's not a *goldfinch*. From your own description I can recognize it as a gold*crest*.

(2)   But that's not enough: plenty of other birds have red heads. What you say doesn't prove it. For all you know, it may be a woodpecker.

Objections (1) and (1a) claim that, in one way or another, I am evidently unable to recognize goldfinches. It may be (1a) —that I have not learned the right (customary, popular, official) name to apply to the creature ("Who taught you to use the word 'goldfinch'?") ; [14] or it may be that my powers of discernment, and consequently of classification, have never been brought sharply to bear in these matters, so that I remain confused as to how to tell the various species of small British birds. Or, of course, it may be a bit of both. In making this sort of accusation, you would perhaps tend not so much to use the expression "You don't know" or "You oughtn't to say you know" as, rather, "But that *isn't* a goldfinch (*goldfinch*)," or "Then you're wrong to call it a goldfinch." But still, if asked, you would of course deny the statement that I do know it is a goldfinch.

[14] Misnaming is not a trivial or laughing matter. If I misname I shall mislead others, and I shall also misunderstand information given by others to me. "Of course I knew all about his condition perfectly, but I never realized that was *diabetes*: I thought it was cancer, and all the books agree that's incurable: if I'd only known it was diabetes, I should have thought of insulin at once." Knowing *what a thing is* is, to an important extent, knowing what the name for it, and the right name for it, is.

It is in the case of objection (2) that you would be more inclined to say right out "Then you don't know." Because it doesn't prove it, it's not enough to prove it. Several important points come out here:

(*a*) If you say "That's not enough," then you must have in mind some more or less definite lack. "To be a goldfinch, besides having a red head it must also have the characteristic eye-markings": or "How do you know it isn't a woodpecker? Woodpeckers have red heads too." If there is no definite lack, which you are at least prepared to specify on being pressed, then it's silly (outrageous) just to go on saying "That's not enough."

(*b*) Enough is enough: it doesn't mean everything. Enough means enough to show that (within reason, and for present intents and purposes) it "can't" be anything else, there is no room for an alternative, competing, description of it. It does *not* mean, for example, enough to show it isn't a *stuffed* goldfinch.

(*c*) "*From* its red head," given as an answer to "How do you know?" requires careful consideration: in particular it differs very materially from "*Because* it has a red head," which is also sometimes given as an answer to "How do you know?," and is commonly given as an answer to "Why do you believe?" It is much more akin to such obviously "vague" replies as "From its markings" or "From its behavior" than at first appears. Our claim, in saying we know (i.e., that we can tell) is to *recognize*: and recognizing, at least in this sort of case, consists in seeing, or otherwise sensing, a feature or features which we are sure are similar to something noted (and usually named) before, on some earlier occasion in our experience. But, this that we see, or otherwise sense, is not necessarily *describable in words*, still less describable in detail, and in noncommittal words, and by anybody you please. Nearly everybody can recognize a surly look or the smell of tar, but few can describe them noncommittally, i.e., otherwise than as "surly" or "of tar": many can recognize, and "with certainty," ports of different vintages, models by different fashion houses, shades of green, motor-car makes from behind, and so forth, without being able to say "*how* they recognize them," i.e., without being able to "be more specific about it"—they can only say they can tell "by the taste," "from the cut," and so on. So, when I say I can tell the bird "from its red head," or that I know a friend "by his nose," I imply that there is something *peculiar* about the red head or the nose, something peculiar to goldfinches or to him, by which you can (always) tell them or him. In view of the fewness and crudeness of the classificatory words in any language compared with the infinite number of features which are recognized, or which could be picked out and recognized, in our experience, it is small wonder that we often and often fall back on the phrases beginning with "from" and "by," and that we are not able to *say*, further and precisely, *how* we can tell. Often we know things quite well, while scarcely able at all to say "from" what we know them, let alone what there is so very special about them. Any answer beginning "From" or "By" has, intentionally, this saving "vagueness." But on the contrary, an answer beginning "Because" is dangerously definite. When I say I know it's a goldfinch "because it has a red head," that implies that all I have noted, or needed to note, about it is that its head is red (nothing special or peculiar about the shade, shape, &c. of the patch): so that I imply that there is no other small British bird that has any sort of red head except the goldfinch.

(*d*) Whenever I say I know, I am always liable to be taken to claim that, in a certain sense appropriate to the kind of statement (and to present intents and purposes), I am able to *prove* it. In the present, very common, type of case, "proving" seems to mean stating what are the features of the current case which are enough to constitute it one which is correctly describable in the way we have described it, and not in any other way relevantly variant. Generally speaking, cases where I can "prove" are cases where we use the "because" formula: cases where we "know but can't prove" are cases where we take refuge in the "from" or "by" formula.

I believe that the points so far raised are those most genuinely and normally raised by the question "How do you know?" But there are other, further, questions sometimes raised under the same rubric, and especially by philosophers, which may be thought more important. These are the worries about "reality" and about being "sure and certain."

Up to now, in challenging me with the question "How do you know?" you are not taken to have *queried my credentials as stated,* though you have asked what they were: nor have you *disputed my facts* (the facts on which I am relying to prove it is a goldfinch), though you have asked me to detail them. It is this further sort of challenge that may now be made, a challenge as to the *reliability* of our alleged "credentials" and our alleged "facts." You may ask:

(1) But do you know it's a *real* goldfinch? How do you know you're not dreaming? Or after all, mightn't it be a stuffed one? And is the head really red? Couldn't it have been dyed, or isn't there perhaps an odd light reflected on it?

(2) But are you certain it's the *right* red for a goldfinch? Are you quite sure it isn't too orange? Isn't it perhaps rather too strident a note for a bittern?

These two sorts of worry are distinct, though very probably they can be combined or confused, or may run into one another: e.g., "Are you sure it's really red?" may mean "Are you sure it isn't orange?" or again "Are you sure it isn't just the peculiar light?"

*1. Reality.* If you ask me, "How do you know it's a real stick?" "How do you know it's really bent?" ("Are you sure he's really angry?"), then you are querying my credentials or my facts (it's often uncertain which) in a certain special way. In various *special, recognized* ways, depending essentially upon the nature of the matter which I have announced myself to

know, either my current experiencing or the item currently
under consideration (or uncertain which) may be abnormal,
*phoney*. Either I myself may be dreaming, or in delirium, or
under the influence of mescal, &c.: or else the item may be
stuffed, painted, dummy, artificial, trick, freak, toy, assumed,
feigned, &c.: or else again there's an uncertainty (it's left open)
whether *I* am to blame or *it* is—mirages, mirror images, odd
lighting effects, &c.

These doubts are all to be allayed by means of recognized
procedures (more or less roughly recognized, of course), appropriate to the particular type of case. There are recognized
ways of distinguishing between dreaming and waking (how
otherwise should we know how to use and to contrast the
words?), and of deciding whether a thing is stuffed or live, and
so forth. The doubt or question "But is it a *real* one?" has
always (*must* have) a special basis, there must be some "reason
for suggesting" that it isn't real, in the sense of some specific
way, or limited number of specific ways, in which it is suggested that this experience or item may be phoney. Sometimes
(usually) the context makes it clear what the suggestion is: the
goldfinch might be stuffed but there's no suggestion that it's
a mirage, the oasis might be a mirage but there's no suggestion
it might be stuffed. If the context doesn't make it clear, then I
am entitled to ask "How do you mean? Do you mean it may be
stuffed or what? *What are you suggesting?*" The wile of the
metaphysician consists in asking "It it a real table?" (a kind of
object which has no obvious way of being phoney) and not
specifying or limiting what may be wrong with it, so that I
feel at a loss "how to prove" it *is* a real one.[15] It is the use of
the word "real" in this manner that leads us on to the supposition that "real" has a single meaning ("the real world" "mate-

---

[15] Conjurers, too, trade on this. "Will some gentleman kindly satisfy himself
that this is a perfectly ordinary hat?" This leaves us baffled and uneasy: sheep-
ishly we agree that it seems all right, while conscious that we have not the least
idea what to guard against.

rial objects"), and that a highly profound and puzzling one. Instead, we should insist always on specifying with what "real" is being contrasted—"not what" I shall have to show it is, in order to show it is "real": and then usually we shall find some specific, less fatal, word, appropriate to the particular case, to substitute for "real."

Knowing it's a "real" goldfinch isn't in question in the ordinary case when I say I know it's a goldfinch: reasonable precautions only are taken. But when it *is* called in question, in *special* cases, then I make sure it's a real goldfinch in ways essentially similar to those in which I made sure it was a goldfinch, though corroboration by other witnesses plays a specially important part in some cases. Once again the precautions cannot be more than reasonable, relative to current intents and purposes. And once again, in the special cases just as in the ordinary cases, two further conditions hold good:

(*a*) I don't by any means *always* know whether it's one or not. It may fly away before I have a chance of testing it, or of inspecting it thoroughly enough. This is simple enough: yet some are prone to argue that because I *sometimes* don't know or can't discover, I *never* can.

(*b*) "Being sure it's real" is no more proof against miracles or outrages of nature than anything else is or, *sub specie humanitatis,* can be. If we have made sure it's a goldfinch, and a real goldfinch, and then in the future it does something outrageous (explodes, quotes Mrs. Woolf, or what not), we don't say we were wrong to say it was a goldfinch, *we don't know what to say.* Words literally fail us: "What would you have said?" "What are we to say now?" "What would *you* say?" When I have made sure it's a real goldfinch (not stuffed, corroborated by the disinterested, &c.) then I am *not* "predicting" in saying it's a real goldfinch, and in a very good sense I can't be proved wrong whatever happens. It seems a serious mistake to suppose that language (or most language, language about real things) is "predictive" in such a way that the future can always prove it wrong. What the future *can* always do, is to make us *revise our ideas* about goldfinches or real goldfinches or anything else.

Perhaps the normal procedure of language could be schematized as follows. First, it is arranged that, on experiencing a complex of features C, then we are to say "This is C" or "This is a C." Then subsequently, the occurrence either of the whole of C or of a significant and characteristic part of it is, on one or many occasions, accompanied or followed in definite circumstances by another special and distinctive feature or complex of features, which makes it seem desirable to revise our ideas: so that we draw a distinction between "This looks like a C, but in fact is only a dummy, &c." and "This is a real C (live, genuine, &c.)." *Henceforward,* we can only ascertain that it's a *real* C by ascertaining that the special feature or complex of features is present in the appropriate circumstances. The old expression "This is a C" will tend as heretofore to fail to draw any distinction between "real, live, &c." and "dummy, stuffed, &c." If the special distinctive feature is one which does not have to manifest itself in *any* definite circumstances (on application of some specific test, after some limited lapse of time, &c.) then it is not a suitable feature on which to base a distinction between "real" and "dummy, imaginary, &c." All we can then do is to say "Some Cs are and some aren't, some do and some don't: and it may be very interesting or important whether they are or aren't, whether they do or don't, but they're all Cs, real Cs, just the same." [16] Now if the special feature is one which must appear in (more or less) definite circumstances, then "This is a real C" is not necessarily predictive: we can, in favorable cases, make sure of it.[17]

[16] The awkwardness about some snarks being boojums.

[17] Sometimes, on the basis of the new special feature, we distinguish, not between Cs and real Cs, but rather between Cs and Ds. There is a reason for choosing the one procedure rather than the other: all cases where we use the "real" formula exhibit (complicated and serpentine) likenesses, as do all cases where we use "proper," a word which behaves in many ways like "real," and is no less nor more profound.

2. *Sureness and Certainty.* The other way of querying my credentials and proofs ("Are you sure it's the *right* red?") is quite different. Here we come up against Mr. Wisdom's views on "the peculiarity of a man's knowledge of his own sensations," for which he refers us to "Other Minds VII" (*Mind*, vol. lii, n.s., no. 207), a passage with which I find I disagree.

Mr. Wisdom there says that, excluding from consideration cases like "being in love" and other cases which "involve prediction," and considering statements like "I am in pain" which, in the requisite sense, do *not* involve prediction, then a man *cannot* "be wrong" in making them, in the most favored sense of being wrong: that is, though it is of course possible for him to *lie* (so that "I am in pain" may be false), and though it is also possible for him to *misname*, i.e., to use the word "pawn" say, instead of "pain," which would be liable to mislead others but would not mislead himself, either because he regularly uses "pawn" for "pain" or because the use was a momentary aberration, as when I call John "Albert" while knowing him quite well to be John—though it is possible for him to be "wrong" in these two senses, it is not possible for him to be wrong in the most favored sense. He says again that, with this class of statement (elsewhere called "sense-statements"), to know directly that one is in pain is "to say that one is, and to say it on the basis of being in pain": and again, that the peculiarity of sense-statements lies in the fact that "when they are correct and made by X, then X knows they are correct."

This seems to me mistaken, though it is a view that, in more or less subtle forms, has been the basis of a very great deal of philosophy. It is perhaps the original sin (Berkeley's apple, the tree in the quad) by which the philosopher casts himself out from the garden of the world we live in.

Very clearly detailed, this is the view that, at least and only in a certain favored type of case, I can "say what I see (or otherwise sense)" almost quite literally. On this view, if I were to say "Here is something red," then I might be held to imply or to state that it is really a red thing, a thing which would appear red in a standard light, or to other people, or tomorrow too, and perhaps even more besides: all which "involves prediction" (if not also a metaphysical substratum). Even if I were to say "Here is something which looks red," I might still be held to imply or to state that it looks red to others also, and so forth. If, however, I confine myself to stating "Here is something that looks red to me now," then at last I can't be wrong (in the most favored sense).

However, there is an ambiguity in "something that looks red to me now." Perhaps this can be brought out by italics, though it is not really so much a matter of emphasis as of tone and expression, of confidence and hesitancy. Contrast "Here is something that (definitely) *looks to me* (anyhow) red" with "Here is something that looks to me (something like) *red* (I should say)." In the former case I am quite confident that, however it may look to others, whatever it may "really be," &c., it certainly does look red to me at the moment. In the other case I'm not confident at all: it looks reddish, but I've never seen anything quite like it before, I can't quite describe it— or, I'm not very good at recognizing colors, I never feel quite happy about them, I've constantly been caught out about them. Of course, this sounds silly in the case of "red": red is so *very* obvious, we all know red when we see it, it's *unmistakable*.[18] Cases where we should not feel happy about red are not easy (though not impossible) to find. But take "magenta": "It looks rather like magenta to me—but then I wouldn't be too sure about distinguishing magenta from mauve or from heliotrope. Of course I know in a way it's purplish, but I don't really know whether to say it's magenta or not: I just can't be sure." Here, I am interested in ruling out consideration of how it looks to others (looks *to me*) or considerations about what its *real* color is (*looks*): what I am ruling out is *my being sure or certain* what it looks to me. Take tastes, or take sounds: these are so much better as examples than colors, because we

[18] And yet she always *thought* his shirt was white until she saw it against Tommy's Persil-washed one.

288

never feel so happy with our other senses as with our eyesight. Any description of a taste or sound or smell (or color) or of a feeling, involves (is) saying that it is like one or some that we have experienced before: any descriptive word is classificatory, involves recognition and in that sense memory, and only when we use such words (or names or descriptions, which come down to the same) are we knowing anything, or believing anything. But memory and recognition are often uncertain and unreliable.

Two rather different ways of being hesitant may be distinguished.

(*a*) Let us take the case where we are tasting a certain taste. We may say "I simply don't know what it is: I've never tasted anything remotely like it before. . . . No, it's no use: the more I think about it the more confused I get: it's perfectly distinct and perfectly distinctive, quite unique in my experience." This illustrates the case where I can find nothing in my past experience with which to compare the current case: I'm certain it's not appreciably like anything I ever tasted before, not sufficiently like anything I know to merit the same description. This case, though distinguishable enough, shades off into the more common type of case where I'm not quite certain, or only fairly certain, or practically certain, that it's the taste of, say, laurel. In all such cases, I am endeavoring to recognize the current item by searching in my past experience for something like it, some likeness in virtue of which it deserves, more or less positively, to be described by the same descriptive word: [19] and I am meeting with varying degrees of success.

(*b*) The other case is different, though it very naturally combines itself with the first. Here, what I try to do is to *savor* the current experience, to *peer* at it, to sense it vividly. I'm not sure it *is* the taste of pineapple: isn't there perhaps just *something* about it, a tang, a bite, a lack of bite, a cloying sensation,

---

[19] Or, of course, related to it in some other way than by "similarity" (in any ordinary sense of "similarity"), which is yet sufficient reason for describing it by the same word.

which isn't *quite* right for pineapple? Isn't there perhaps just a peculiar hint of green, which would rule out mauve and would hardly do for heliotrope? Or perhaps it is faintly odd: I must look more intently, scan it over and over: maybe just possibly there is a suggestion of an unnatural shimmer, so that it doesn't look quite like ordinary water. There is a lack of sharpness in what we actually sense, which is to be cured not, or not merely, by thinking, but by acuter discernment, by sensory discrimination (though it is of course true that thinking of other, and more pronounced, cases in our past experience can and does assist our powers of discrimination).[20]

Cases (*a*) and (*b*) alike, and perhaps usually together, lead to our being not quite sure or certain what it is, what to say, how to describe it: what our feelings really are, whether the tickling is painful exactly, whether I'm really what you'd call angry with him or only something rather like it. The hesitation is of course, in a sense, over misnaming: but I am not so much or merely worried about possibly misleading others as about misleading myself (the most favored sense of being wrong). I should suggest that the two expressions "being certain" and "being sure," though from the nature of the case they are often used indiscriminately, have a tendency to refer to cases (*a*) and (*b*) respectively. "Being certain" tends to indicate confidence in our memories and our past discernment, "being sure" to indicate confidence in the current perception. Perhaps this comes out in our use of the concessives "to be sure" and "certainly," and in our use of such phrases as "certainly not" and "surely not." But it may be unwise to chivvy language beyond the coarser nuances.

It may be said that, even when I don't know exactly how to describe it, I nevertheless *know* that I *think* (and roughly how confidently I think) it is mauve. So I do know *something*. But this is irrelevant: I *don't* know it's mauve, that it definitely looks to me now mauve. Besides, there are cases where I really

[20] This appears to cover cases of dull or careless or uninstructed perception, as opposed to cases of diseased or drugged perception.

don't know what I think: I'm completely baffled by it.

Of course, there are any number of "sense-statements" about which I can be, and am, completely sure. In ordinary cases ordinary men are nearly always certain when a thing looks red (or reddish, or anyhow reddish rather than greenish), or when they're in pain (except when that's rather difficult to say, as when they're being tickled): in ordinary cases an expert, a dyer or a dress designer, will be quite sure when something looks (to him in the present light) reseda green or nigger brown, though those who are not experts will not be so sure. Nearly always, if not quite always, we can be quite, or pretty, sure if we take refuge in a sufficiently *rough* description of the sensation: roughness and sureness tend to vary inversely. But the less rough descriptions, just as much as the rough, are all "sense-statements."

It is, I think, the problems of sureness and certainty, which philosophers tend (if I am not mistaken) to neglect, that have considerably exercised scientists, while the problem of "reality," which philosophers have cultivated, does not exercise them. The whole apparatus of measures and standards seems designed to combat unsureness and uncertainty, and concomitantly to increase the possible precision of language, which, in science, pays. But for the words "real" and "unreal" the scientist tends to substitute, wisely, their cash-value substitutes, of which he invents and defines an increasing number, to cover an increasing variety of cases: he doesn't ask "Is it real?" but rather "Is it denatured?" or "Is it an allotropic form?" and so on.

It is not clear to me what the class of sense-statements is, nor what its "peculiarity" is. Some who talk of sense-statements (or sense data) appear to draw a distinction between talking about simple things like red or pain, and talking about complicated things like love or tables. But apparently Mr. Wisdom does not, because he treats "This looks to me now like a man eating poppies" as in the same case with "This looks to me now red." In this he is surely right: a man eating poppies may be more "complex" to recognize, but it is often not appreciably more difficult than the other. But if, again, we say that non-sense-statements are those which involve "prediction," why so? True, if I say "This is a (real) oasis" without first ascertaining that it's not a mirage, then I do chance my hand: but if I *have* ascertained that it's not, and can recognize for sure that it isn't (as when I am drinking its waters), then surely I'm not chancing my hand any longer. I believe, of course, that it will continue to perform as (real) oases normally do: but if there's a *lusus naturae,* a miracle, and it doesn't, that wouldn't mean I was wrong, previously, to call it a real oasis.

With regard to Mr. Wisdom's own chosen formulae, we have seen already that it can't be right to say that the peculiarity of sense-statements is that "when they are correct, and made by X, then X knows they are correct": for X may *think,* without much confidence, that it tastes to him like Lapsang, and yet be far from certain, and then subsequently become certain, or more certain, that it did or didn't. The other two formulae were: "To know that one is in pain is to say that one is and to say it on the basis of being in pain" and that the only mistake possible with sense-statements is typified by the case where "knowing him to be Jack I call him 'Alfred,' thinking his name is Alfred or not caring a damn what his name is." The snag in both these lies in the phrases "on the basis of being in pain" and "knowing him to be Jack." "Knowing him to be Jack" means that I have recognized him as Jack, a matter over which I may well be hesitant and/or mistaken: it is true that I needn't recognize him *by name* as "Jack" (and hence I may call him "Alfred"), but at least I must be recognizing him correctly as, for instance, the man I last saw in Jerusalem, or else I *shall* be misleading *myself.* Similarly, if "on the basis of being in pain" only means "when I am (what would be correctly described as) in pain," then something more than merely *saying* "I'm in pain" is necessary for knowing I'm in pain: and this something more, as it involves recognition, may be hesitant and/or mistaken, though it is of course unlikely to be so in a case so comparatively obvious as that of pain.

Possibly the tendency to overlook the problems of recognition is fostered by the tendency to use a direct object after the word *know*. Mr. Wisdom, for example, confidently uses such expressions as "knowing the feelings of another (his mind, his sensations, his anger, his pain) in the way that *he* knows them." But, although we do correctly use the expressions "I know your feelings on the matter" or "He knows his own mind" or (archaically) "May I know your mind?" these are rather special expressions, which do not justify any general usage. "Feelings" here has the sense it has in "very strong feelings" in favor of or against something: perhaps it means "views" or "opinions" ("very decided opinions"), just as "mind" in this usage is given by the Dictionary as equivalent to "intention" or "wish." To extend the usage uncritically is somewhat as though, on the strength of the legitimate phrase "knowing someone's tastes," we were to proceed to talk of "knowing someone's sounds" or "knowing someone's taste of pineapple." If, for example, it is a case of *physical* feelings such as fatigue, we do not use the expression "I know your feelings."

When, therefore, Mr. Wisdom speaks generally of "knowing his sensations," he presumably means this to be equivalent to "knowing *what* he is seeing, smelling, &c.," just as "knowing the winner of the Derby" means "knowing *what won* the Derby." But here again, the expression "know what" seems sometimes to be taken, unconsciously and erroneously, to lend support to the practice of putting a direct object after *know*: for "what" is liable to be understood as a relative, = "that which." This is a grammatical mistake: "what" *can* of course be a relative, but in "know what you feel" and "know what won" it is an interrogative (Latin *quid,* not *quod*). In this respect, "I can smell what he is smelling" differs from "I can know what he is smelling." "I know what he is feeling" is not "There is an *x* which both I know and he is feeling," but "I know the answer to the question 'What is he feeling?'" And similarly with "I know what I am feeling": this does *not* mean that there is something which I am *both knowing and feeling.*

Expressions such as "We don't know another man's anger in the way he knows it" or "He knows his pain in a way we can't" seem barbarous. The man doesn't "know his pain": he feels (not knows) what he recognizes as, or what he knows to be, anger (not his anger), and he knows that he is feeling angry. Always assuming that he does recognize the feeling, which in fact, though feeling it acutely, he may not: "Now I know what it was, it was jealousy (or gooseflesh or angina). At the time I did not know at all what it was, I had never felt anything quite like it before: but since then I've got to know it quite well." [21]

Uncritical use of the direct object after *know* seems to be one thing that leads to the view that (or to talking as though) sensa, that is things, colors, noises, and the rest, speak or are labelled by nature, so that I can literally *say* what (that which) I *see:* it pipes up, or I read it off. It is as if sensa were *literally* to "announce themselves" or to "identify themselves," in the way we indicate when we say "It presently identified itself as a particularly fine white rhinoceros." But surely this is only a manner of speaking, a reflexive idiom in which the French, for example, indulge more freely than the English: sensa are dumb, and only previous experience enables *us* to identify them. If we choose to say that they "identify themselves" (and certainly "recognizing" is not a highly voluntary activity of ours), then it must be admitted that they share the birthright of all speakers, that of speaking unclearly and untruly.

*If I know I can't be wrong.* One final point about "How do you know?," the challenge to the user of the expression "I know," requires still to be brought out by consideration of the saying that "If you know you can't be wrong." Surely, if what

[21] There are, of course, legitimate uses of the direct object after *know*, and of the possessive pronoun before words for feelings. "He knows the town well," "He has known much suffering," "My old vanity, how well I know it!"—even the pleonastic "Where does he feel his ( = the) pain?" and the educative tautology "*He* feels *his* pain." But none of these really lends support to the metaphysical "He knows his pain (in a way we can't)."

has so far been said is correct, then we are often right to say we *know* even in cases where we turn out subsequently to have been mistaken—and indeed we seem always, or practically always, liable to be mistaken.

Now, we are perfectly, and should be candidly, aware of this liability, which does not, however, transpire to be so very onerous in practice. The human intellect and senses are, indeed, *inherently* fallible and delusive, but not by any means *inveterately* so. Machines are inherently liable to break down, but good machines don't (often). It is futile to embark on a "theory of knowledge" which denies this liability: such theories constantly end up by admitting the liability after all, and denying the existence of "knowledge."

"When you know you can't be wrong" is perfectly good sense. You are prohibited from saying "I know it is so, but I may be wrong," just as you are prohibited from saying "I promise I will, but I may fail." If you are aware you may be mistaken, you ought not to say you know, just as, if you are aware you may break your word, you have no business to promise. But of course, being aware that you may be mistaken doesn't mean merely being aware that you are a fallible human being: it means that you have some concrete reason to suppose that you may be mistaken in this case. Just as "but I may fail" does not mean merely "but I am a weak human being" (in which case it would be no more exciting than adding "D.V."): it means that there is some concrete reason for me to suppose that I shall break my word. It is naturally *always* possible ("humanly" possible) that I may be mistaken or may break my word, but that by itself is no bar against using the expressions "I know" and "I promise" as we do in fact use them.

At the risk (long since incurred) of being tedious, the parallel between saying "I know" and saying "I promise" may be elaborated.[22]

---

[22] It is the use of the expressions "I know" and "I promise" (first person singular, present indicative tense) alone that is being considered. "If I knew, I can't have been wrong" or "If she knows she can't be wrong" are not worry-

When I say "S is P," I imply at least that I believe it, and, if I have been strictly brought up, that I am (quite) sure of it: when I say "I shall do A," I imply at least that I hope to do it, and, if I have been strictly brought up that I (fully) intend to. If I only believe that S is P, I can add "But of course I may (very well) be wrong": if I only hope to do A, I can add "But of course I may (very well) not." When I only believe or only hope, it is recognized that further evidence or further circumstances are liable to make me change my mind. If I say "S is P" when I don't even believe it, I am lying: if I say it when I believe it but am not sure of it, I may be misleading but I am not exactly lying. If I say "I shall do A" when I have not even any hope, not the slightest intention, of doing it, then I am deliberately deceiving: if I say it when I do not fully intend to, I am misleading but I am not deliberately deceiving in the same way.

But now, when I say "I promise," a new plunge is taken: I have not merely announced my intention, but, by using this formula (performing this ritual), I have bound myself to others, and staked my reputation, in a new way. Similarly, saying "I know" is taking a new plunge. But it is *not* saying "I have performed a specially striking feat of cognition, superior, in the same scale as believing and being sure, even to being merely quite sure": for there *is* nothing in that scale superior to being quite sure. Just as promising is not something superior, in the same scale as hoping and intending, even to merely fully intending: for there *is* nothing in that scale superior to fully intending. When I say "I know," I *give others my word: I give others my authority for saying* that "S is P."

When I have said only that I am sure, and prove to have

---

ing in the way that "If I ('you') know I ('you') can't be wrong" is worrying. Or again, "I promise" is quite different from "he promises": if I say "I promise," I don't say I *say* I promise, I *promise,* just as if he says he promises, he doesn't say he says he promises, he promises: whereas if I say "he promises," I do (only) say he *says* he promises—in the other "sense" of "promise," the "sense" in which *I* say *I* promise, only *he* can say he promises. I *describe* his promising, but I *do* my own promising and he must do *his* own.

been mistaken, I am not liable to be rounded on by others in the same way as when I have said "I know." I am sure *for my part*, you can take it or leave it: accept it if you think I'm an acute and careful person, that's your responsibility. But I don't know "for my part," and when I say "I know" I don't mean you can take it or leave it (though of course you *can* take it or leave it). In the same way, when I say I fully intend to, I do so for my part, and, according as you think highly or poorly of my resolution and chances, you will elect to act on it or not to act on it: but if I say I promise, you are *entitled* to act on it, whether or not you choose to do so. If I have said I know or I promise, you insult me in a special way by refusing to accept it. We all *feel* the very great difference between saying even "I'm *absolutely* sure" and saying "I know": it is like the difference between saying even "I firmly and irrevocably intend" and "I promise." If someone has promised me to do A, then I am entitled to rely on it, and can myself make promises on the strength of it: and so, where someone has said to me "I know," I am entitled to say *I* know too, at second hand. The right to say "I know" is transmissible, in the sort of way that other authority is transmissible. Hence, if I say it lightly, I may be *responsible* for getting *you* into trouble.

If you say you *know* something, the most immediate challenge takes the form of asking "Are you in a position to know?": that is, you must undertake to show, not merely that you are sure of it, but that it is within your cognizance. There is a similar form of challenge in the case of promising: fully intending is not enough—you must also undertake to show that "you are in a position to promise," that is, that it is within your power. Over these points in the two cases parallel series of doubts are apt to infect philosophers, on the ground that I cannot foresee the future. Some begin to hold that I should never, or practically never, say I know anything—perhaps only what I am sensing at this moment: others, that I should never, or practically never, say I promise—perhaps only what is actually within my power at this moment. In both cases there is an obsession: if I know *I can't be wrong*, so I can't have the right to say I know, and if I promise *I can't fail*, so I can't have the right to say I promise. And in both cases this obsession fastens on my inability to make *predictions* as the root of the matter, meaning by predictions claims to know the future. But this is doubly mistaken in both cases. As has been seen, we may be perfectly justified in saying we know or we promise, in spite of the fact that things "may" turn out badly, and it's a more or less serious matter for us if they do. And further, it is overlooked that the conditions which must be satisfied if I am to show that a thing is within my cognizance or within my power are conditions, not about the future, but about *the present and the past*: it is not demanded that I do more than *believe* about the future.[23]

We feel, however, an objection to saying that "I know" performs the same sort of function as "I promise." It is this. Supposing that things turn out badly, then we say, on the one hand "You're proved wrong, so you *didn't* know," but on the other hand "You've failed to perform, although you *did* promise." I believe that this contrast is more apparent than real. The sense in which you "did promise" is that you did *say* you promised (did say "I promise"): and you did *say* you knew. That is the gravamen of the charge against you when you let us down, after we have taken your word. But it may well transpire that you never fully intended to do it, or that you had concrete reason to suppose that you wouldn't be able to do it (it might even be manifestly impossible), and in another "sense" of promise you *can't* then have promised to do it, so that you *didn't* promise.

Consider the use of other phrases analogous to "I know" and "I promise." Suppose, instead of "I know," I had said "I swear": in that case, upon the opposite appearing, we should say, exactly as in the promising case, "You *did* swear, but you were

[23] If "Figs never grow on thistles" is taken to mean "None ever have and none ever will," then it is implied that I *know* that none ever have, but only that I *believe* that none ever will.

wrong." Suppose again that, instead of "I promise," I had said "I guarantee" (e.g., to protect you from attack): in that case, upon my letting you down, you can say, exactly as in the knowing case "You *said* you guaranteed it, but you *didn't* guarantee it." [24] Can the situation perhaps be summed up as follows? In these "ritual" cases, the approved case is one where *in the appropriate circumstances*, I say a certain formula: e.g., "I do" when standing, unmarried or a widower, beside woman, unmarried or a widow and not within the prohibited degrees of relationship, before a clergyman, registrar, &c., or "I give" when it is mine to give, &c., or "I order" when I have the authority to, &c. But now, if the situation transpires to have been in some way not orthodox (I was already married: it wasn't mine to give: I had no authority to order), then we tend to be rather hesitant about how to put it, as heaven was when the saint blessed the penguins. We call the man a bigamist, but his second marriage was not a marriage, is null and void (a useful formula in many case for avoiding saying either "he did" or "he didn't"): he did "order" me to do it, but, having no authority over me, he *couldn't* "order" me: he did warn me it was going to change, but it wasn't or anyway I knew much more about it than he did, so in a way he couldn't warn me, didn't warn me.[25] We hesitate between "He didn't order me," "He had no right to order me," "He oughtn't to have said he ordered me," just as we do between "You didn't know," "You can't have known," "You had no right to say you knew" (these perhaps having slightly different nuances, according to what precisely it is that has gone wrong). But the essential factors

[24] "Swear," "guarantee," "give my word," "promise," all these and similar words cover cases both of "knowing" and of "promising," thus suggesting the two are analogous. Of course they differ subtly from each other; for example, *know* and *promise* are in a certain sense "unlimited" expressions, while when I swear I swear *upon* something, and when I guarantee I guarantee that, upon some adverse and more or less to be expected circumstance arising, I will take *some more or less definite action* to nullify it.

[25] "You can't warn someone of something that isn't going to happen" parallels "You can't know what isn't true."

are (*a*) You said you knew: you said you promised (*b*) You were mistaken: you didn't perform. The hesitancy concerns only the precise way in which we are to round on the original "I know" or "I promise."

To suppose that "I know" is a descriptive phrase is only one example of the *descriptive fallacy*, so common in philosophy. Even if some language is now purely descriptive, language was not in origin so, and much of it is still not so. Utterance of obvious ritual phrases, in the appropriate circumstances, is not *describing* the action we are doing, but *doing* it ("I do"): in other cases it functions, like tone and expression, or again like punctuation and mood, as an intimation that we are employing language in some special way ("I warn," "I ask," "I define"). such phrases cannot, strictly, *be* lies, though they can "imply" lies, as "I promise" implies that I fully intend, which may be untrue.

If these are the main and multifarious points that arise in familiar cases where we ask "How do you know that this is a case of so-and-so?," they may be expected to arise likewise in cases where we say "I know he is angry." And if there are, as no doubt there are, special difficulties in this case, at least we can clear the ground a little of things which are not special difficulties, and get the matter in better perspective.

As a preliminary, it must be said that I shall only discuss the question of feelings and emotions, with special reference to anger. It seems likely that the cases where we know that another man thinks that 2 and 2 make 4, or that he is seeing a rat, and so on, are different in important respects from, though no doubt also similar to, the case of knowing that he is angry or hungry.

In the first place, we certainly do say sometimes that we know another man is angry, and we also distinguish these occasions from others on which we say only that we *believe* he is angry. For of course, we do not for a moment suppose that we *always* know, of *all* men, whether they are angry or not, or that we could discover it. There are many occasions when I realize that I can't possibly tell what he's feeling: and there are many *types* of people, and many individuals too, with whom I (they being what they are, and I being what I am) never can tell. The feelings of royalty, for example, or fakirs or bushmen or Wykehamists or simple eccentrics—these may be very hard to divine: unless you have had a prolonged acquaintance with such persons, and some intimacy with them, you are not in any sort of position to know what their feelings are, especially if, for one reason or another, they can't or don't tell you. Or again, the feelings of some individual whom you have never met before—they might be almost anything: you don't know his character at all or his tastes, you have no experience of his mannerisms, and so on. His feelings are elusive and personal: people differ so much. It is this sort of thing that leads to the situation where we say "You never know" or "You never can tell."

In short, here even more than in the case of the goldfinch, a great deal depends on how familiar we have been in our past experience with this type of person, and indeed with this individual, in this type of situation. If we have no great familiarity, then we hesitate to say we know: indeed, we can't be expected to say (tell). On the other hand, if we *have* had the necessary experience, then we can, in favorable current circumstances, say we know: we certainly can recognize when some near relative of ours is angrier than we have ever seen him.

Further, we must have had experience also of the emotion or feeling concerned, in this case anger. In order to know what you are feeling, I must also apparently be able to imagine (guess, understand, appreciate) what you're feeling. It seems that more is demanded than that I shall have learned to discriminate displays of anger in others: I must also have been angry myself.[26] Or at any rate, if I have never felt a certain

---

[26] We say we don't know what it must feel like to be a king, whereas we do know what one of our friends must have felt when mortified. In this ordinary (imprecise and evidently not whole-hog) sense of "knowing what it

emotion, say ambition, then I certainly feel an *extra* hesitation in saying that his motive is ambition. And this seems to be due to the very special nature (grammar, logic) of feelings, to the special way in which they are related to their occasions and manifestations, which requires further elucidation.

At first sight it may be tempting to follow Mr. Wisdom, and to draw a distinction between (1) the physical symptoms and (2) the feeling. So that when, in the current case, I am asked "How can you tell he's angry?" I should answer "From the physical symptoms," while if *he* is asked how *he* can tell he's angry, he should answer "From the feeling." But this seems to be a dangerous over-simplification.

In the first place, "symptoms" (and also "physical") is being used in a way different from ordinary usage, and one which proves to be misleading.

"Symptoms," a term transferred from medical usage,[27] tends to be used only, or primarily, in cases where that of which there are symptoms is something undesirable (of incipient disease rather than of returning health, of despair rather than of hope, of grief rather than of joy): and hence it is more colorful than "signs" or "indications." This, however, is comparatively trivial. What is important is the fact that we never talk of "symptoms" or "signs" except *by way of implied contrast with inspection of the item itself.* No doubt it would often be awkward to have to say exactly where the signs or symptoms end and the item itself begins to appear: but such a division is always implied to exist. And hence the words "symptom" and

---

would be like" we do often know what it would be like to be our neighbor drawing his sword, whereas we don't know (can't even guess or imagine), really, what it would feel like to be a cat or a cockroach. But of course we don't ever "know" what in our neighbor accompanies the drawing of his sword in Mr. Wisdom's peculiar sense of "know what" as equivalent to "directly experience that which."

[27] Doctors nowadays draw a distinction of their own between "symptoms" and "(physical) signs": but the distinction is not here relevant, and perhaps not very clear.

"sign" have no use except in cases where the item, as in the case of disease, is liable to be *hidden*, whether it be in the future, in the past, under the skin, or in some other more or less notorious casket: and when the item is itself before us, we no longer talk of signs and symptoms. When we talk of "signs of a storm," we mean signs of an impending storm, or of a past storm, or of a storm beyond the horizon: we do *not* mean a storm on top of us.[28]

The words function like such words as "traces" or "clues." Once you know the murderer, you don't get any more clues, only what were or would have been clues: nor is a confession, or an eye-witness's view of the crime, a particularly good clue— these are something different altogether. When the cheese is not to be found or seen, then there may be traces of it: but not when it's there in front of us (though of course, there aren't, then, "no traces" of it either).

For this reason, it seems misleading to lump together, as a general practice, all the characteristic features of any casual item as "signs" or "symptoms" of it: though it is of course sometimes the case that some things which could in appropriate circumstances be called characteristics or effects or manifestations or parts or sequelae or what not of certain items may *also* be called signs or symptoms of those items in the appropriate circumstances. It seems to be this which is really wrong with Mr. Wisdom's paradox ("Other Minds III") about looking in the larder and finding "all the signs" of bread, when we see the loaf, touch it, taste it, and so on. Doing these things is not finding (some) signs of bread at all: the taste or feel of bread is not a sign or symptom of bread at all. What I might be taken

---

[28] There are some, more complicated, cases like that of inflation, where the signs of incipient inflation are of the same nature as inflation itself, but of a less intensity or at a slower tempo. Here, especially, it is a matter for decision where the signs or "tendencies" end and where the state itself sets in: moreover, with inflation, as with some diseases, we can in some contexts go on talking of signs or symptoms even when the item itself is fairly decidedly present, because it is such as not to be patent to simple observation.

to mean if I announced that I had found signs of bread in the larder seems rather doubtful, since bread is not normally casketed (or if in the bin, leaves no traces), and not being a transeunt event (impending bread &c.), does not have any normally accepted "signs": and signs, peculiar to the item, have to be more or less normally accepted. I might be taken to mean that I had found traces of bread, such as crumbs, or signs that bread had at one time been stored there, or something of the kind: but what I could *not* be taken to mean is that I had seen, tasted, or touched (something like) bread.

The sort of thing we do actually say, if the look is all right but we haven't yet tasted it, is "Here is something that looks like bread." If it turns out not to be bread after all, we might say "It tasted like bread, but actually it was only bread-substitute," or "It exhibited many of the characteristic features of bread, but differed in important respects: it was only a synthetic imitation." That is, we don't use the words "sign" or "symptom" at all.

Now, if "signs" and "symptoms" have this restricted usage, it is evident that to say that we only get at the "signs" or "symptoms" of anything is to imply that we never get at *it* (and this goes for "*all* the signs" too). So that, if we say that I only get at the *symptoms* of his anger, that carries an important implication. But *is* this the way we do talk? Surely we do not consider that we are never aware of more than *symptoms* of anger in another man?

"Symptoms" or "signs" of anger tend to mean signs of *rising* or of *suppressed* anger. Once the man has exploded, we talk of something different—of an expression or manifestation or display of anger, of an exhibition of temper, and so forth. A twitch of the eyebrow, pallor, a tremor in the voice, all these may be symptoms of anger: but a violent tirade or a blow in the face are not, they are the acts in which the anger is vented. "Symptoms" of anger are not, at least normally, contrasted with the man's own inner personal feeling of anger, but rather with the actual display of anger. Normally at least, where we have only symptoms to go upon, we should say only that we *believe* that the man is angry or getting angry: whereas when he has given himself away we say that we *know*.[29]

The word "physical" also, as used by Mr. Wisdom in contrast to "mental," seems to me abused, though I am not confident as to whether this abuse is misleading in the current case. He evidently does not wish to call a man's feelings, which he cites as a typical example of a "mental" event, *physical*. Yet this is what we ordinarily often do. There are many physical feelings, such as giddiness, hunger or fatigue: and these are included by some doctors among the physical signs of various complaints. Most feelings we do not speak of as either mental or physical, especially emotions, such as jealousy or anger itself: we do not assign them to the *mind* but to the *heart*. Where we do describe a feeling as mental, it is because we are using a word normally used to describe a physical feeling in a special transferred sense, as when we talk about "mental" discomfort or fatigue.

It is then, clear, that more is involved in being, for example, angry than simply showing the symptoms and feeling the feeling. For there is also the display or manifestation. And it is to be noted that the feeling is related in a unique sort of way to the display. When we are angry, we have an impulse, felt and/or acted on, to do actions of particular kinds, and, unless we suppress the anger, we do actually proceed to do them. There is a peculiar and intimate relationship between the emotion and the natural manner of venting it, with which,

[29] Sometimes, it is said, we use "I know" where we should be prepared to substitute "I believe," as when we say "I know he's in, because his hat is in the hall": thus "know" is used loosely for "believe," so why should we suppose there is a fundamental difference between them? But the question is, what exactly do we mean by "prepared to substitute" and "loosely"? We are "prepared to substitute" *believe* for *know* not as an *equivalent* expression but as a weaker and therefore preferable expression, in view of the seriousness with which, as has become apparent, the matter is to be treated: the presence of the hat, which would serve as a proof of its owner's presence in many circumstances, could only through laxity be adduced as a proof in a court of law.

having been angry ourselves, we are acquainted. The ways in which anger is normally manifested are *natural* to anger just as there are tones *naturally* expressive of various emotions (indignation, &c.). There is not normally taken to be [30] such a thing as "being angry" apart from any impulse, however vague, to vent the anger in the natural way.

Moreover, besides the natural expressions of anger, there are also the natural *occasions* of anger, of which we have also had experience, which are similarly connected in an intimate way with the "being angry." It would be as nonsensical to class these as "causes" in some supposedly obvious and "external" sense, as it would be to class the venting of anger as the "effect" of the emotion in a supposedly obvious and "external" sense. Equally it would be nonsensical to say that there are three wholly distinct phenomena, (1) cause or occasion, (2) feeling or emotion, and (3) effect or manifestation, which are related together "by definition" as all necessary to anger, though this would perhaps be less misleading than the other.

It seems fair to say that "being angry" is in many respects like "having mumps." It is a description of a whole pattern of events, including occasion, symptoms, feeling, and manifestation, and possibly other factors besides. It is as silly to ask "What, really, *is* the anger *itself*?" as to attempt to fine down "the disease" to some one chosen item ("the functional disorder"). That the man himself feels something which we don't (in the sense that he feels angry and we don't) is, in the absence of Mr. Wisdom's variety of telepathy,[31] evident enough, and incidentally nothing to complain about as a "predicament":

[30] A new language is naturally necessary if we are to admit unconscious feelings, and feelings which express themselves in paradoxical manners, such as the psychoanalysts describe.

[31] There is, it seems to me, something which does actually happen, rather different from Mr. Wisdom's telepathy, which does sometimes contribute towards our knowledge of other people's feelings. We do talk, for example, of "feeling another person's displeasure," and say, for example, "his anger could be felt," and there seems to be something genuine about this. But the feeling we feel, though a genuine "feeling," is *not*, in these cases, displeasure or anger, but a special *counterpart* feeling.

but there is no call to say that "that" ("the feeling") [32] *is* the *anger*. The pattern of events whatever its precise form, is, fairly clearly, peculiar to the case of "feelings" (emotions)—it is not by any means exactly like the case of diseases: and it seems to be this peculiarity which makes us prone to say that, unless we have had experience of a feeling ourselves, we cannot know when someone else is experiencing it. Moreover, it is our confidence in the general pattern that makes us apt to say we "know" another man is angry when we have only observed parts of the pattern: for the parts of the pattern are related to each other very much more intimately than, for example, newspapermen scurrying in Brighton are related to a fire in Fleet Street.[33]

The man himself, such is the overriding power of the pattern, will sometimes accept corrections from outsiders about his own emotions, i.e., about the correct description of them. He may be got to agree that he was not really angry so much as, rather, indignant or jealous, and even that he was not in pain, but only fancied he was. And this is not surprising, especially in view of the fact that he, like all of us, has primarily learned to use the expression "I am angry" of himself by (*a*) noting the occasion, symptoms, manifestation, &c., in cases where other persons say "I am angry" of *themselves*, (*b*) being told by others, who have noted all that can be observed about *him* on certain occasions, that "You are angry," i.e., that he should say "I am angry." On the whole, "mere" feelings or emotions, if there are such things genuinely detectable, are certainly very hard to be sure about, even harder than, say, tastes, which we already choose to describe, normally, only by their occasions (the taste of "tar," "of pineapple," &c.).

All words for emotions are, besides, on the vague side, in two ways, leading to further hesitations about whether we

[32] The "feelings," i.e., sensations, we can observe in ourselves when angry are such things as a pounding of the heart or tensing of the muscles, which cannot in themselves be justifiably called "the feeling of anger."

[33] It is therefore misleading to ask "How do I get from the scowl to the anger?"

"know" when he's angry. They tend to cover a rather wide and ill-defined variety of situations: and the patterns they cover tend to be, each of them, rather complex (though common and so not difficult to recognize, very often), so that it is easy for one of the more or less necessary features to be omitted, and thus to give rise to hesitation about what exactly we should say in such an unorthodox case. We realize, well enough, that the challenge to which we are exposed if we say we *know* is to *prove* it, and in this respect vagueness of terminology is a crippling handicap.

So far, enough has perhaps been said to show that most of the difficulties which stand in the way of our saying we know a thing is a goldfinch arise in rather greater strength in the case where we want to say we know another man is angry. But there is still a feeling, and I think a justified feeling, that there is a further and quite *special* difficulty in the latter case.

This difficulty seems to be of the sort that Mr. Wisdom raises at the very outset of his series of articles on "Other Minds." It is asked, might the man not exhibit all the symptoms (and display and everything else) of anger, even ad infinitum, and yet still *not* (*really*) *be* angry? It will be remembered that he there treats it, no doubt provisionally, as a difficulty similar to that which can arise concerning the reality of any "material object." But in fact, it has special features of its own.

There seem to be three distinguishable doubts which may arise:

1. When to all appearances angry, might he not really be laboring under some other emotion, in that, though he normally feels the same emotion as we should on occasions when we, in his position, should feel anger and in making displays such as we make when angry, in this particular case he is acting abnormally?

2. When to all appearances angry, might he not really be laboring under some other emotion, in that he normally feels, on occasions when we in his position should feel anger and when acting as we should act if we felt anger, some feeling

which we, if we experienced it, should distinguish from anger?

3. When to all appearances angry, might he not really be feeling no emotion at all?

In everyday life, all these problems arise in special cases, and occasion genuine worry. We may worry (1) as to whether someone is *deceiving* us, by suppressing his emotions, or by feigning emotions which he does not feel: we may worry (2) as to whether we are *misunderstanding* someone (or he us), in wrongly supposing that he does "feel like us," that he does share emotions like ours: or we may worry (3) as to whether some action of another person is really deliberate, or perhaps only involuntary or inadvertent in some manner or other. All three varieties of worry may arise, and often do, in connection with the actions of persons whom we know very well.[34] Any or all of them may be at the bottom of the passage from Mrs. Woolf: all work together in the feeling of loneliness which affects everybody at times.

None of these three special difficulties about "reality" arises in connection with goldfinches or bread, any more than the special difficulties about, for example, the oasis arise in connection with the reality of another person's emotions. The goldfinch cannot be assumed, nor the bread suppressed: we may be deceived by the appearance of an oasis, or misinterpret the signs of the weather, but the oasis cannot lie to us and we cannot misunderstand the storm in the way we misunderstand the man.

Though the difficulties are special, the ways of dealing with them are, initially, similar to those employed in the case of the goldfinch. There are (more or less roughly) established procedures for dealing with suspected cases of deception or of misunderstanding or of inadvertence. By these means we do very often establish (though we do not expect *always* to

---

[34] There is, too, a special way in which we can doubt the "reality" of our own emotions, can doubt whether we are not "acting to ourselves." Professional actors may reach a state where they never really know what their genuine feelings are.

establish) that someone is acting, or that we were misunderstanding him, or that he is simply impervious to a certain emotion, or that he was not acting voluntarily. These special cases where doubts arise and require resolving, are contrasted with the normal cases which hold the field [35] *unless* there is some special suggestion that deceit, &c., is involved, and deceit, moreover, of an intelligible kind in the circumstances, that is, of a kind that can be looked into because motive, &c., is specially suggested. There is no suggestion that I *never* know what other people's emotions are, nor yet that in particular cases I might be wrong for no special reason or in no special way.

Extraordinary cases of deceit, misunderstanding, &c. (which are themselves not the normal), do not, *ex vi termini*, ordinarily occur: we have a working knowledge of the occasions for, the temptations to, the practical limits of, and the normal types of deceit and misunderstanding. Nevertheless, they *may* occur, and there may be varieties which are common without our yet having become aware of the fact. If this happens, we are in a certain sense wrong, because our terminology is inadequate to the facts, and we shall have thenceforward to be more wary about saying we know, or shall have to revise our ideas and terminology. This we are constantly ready to do in a field so complex and baffling as that of the emotions.

There remains, however, one further special feature of the case, which also differentiates it radically from the goldfinch case. The goldfinch, the material object, is, as we insisted above, uninscribed and *mute*: but the man *speaks*. In the complex of occurrences which induces us to say we know another man is angry, the complex of symptoms, occasion, display, and the rest, a peculiar place is occupied by the man's own statement as to what his feelings are. In the usual case, we accept this statement without question, and we then say that we know (as it were "at second-hand") what his feelings are: though of course "at second-hand" here could not be used to imply that anybody

[35] "You cannot fool all of the people all of the time" is "analytic."

but he could know "at first-hand," and hence perhaps it is not in fact used. In unusual cases, where his statement conflicts with the description we should otherwise have been inclined to give of the case, we do not feel bound to accept it, though we always feel some uneasiness in rejecting it. If the man is an habitual liar or self-deceiver, or if there are patent reasons why he should be lying or deceiving himself on this occasion, then we feel reasonably happy: but if such a case occurred as the imagined one where a man, having given throughout life every appearance of holding a certain pointless belief, leaves behind a remark in his private diary to the effect that he never did believe it, then we probably should not know what to say.

I should like to make in conclusion some further remarks about this crucial matter of our believing what the man says about his own feelings. Although I know very well that I do not see my way clearly in this, I cannot help feeling sure that it is fundamental to the whole Predicament, and that it has not been given the attention it deserves, possibly just because it is so obvious.

The man's own statement is not (is not treated primarily as) a sign or symptom, although it can, secondarily and artificially, be treated as such. A unique place is reserved for it in the summary of the facts of the case. The question then is: "Why believe him?"

There are answers that we can give to this question, which is here to be taken in the general sense of "Why believe him ever?" not simply as "Why believe him this time?" We may say that the man's statements on matters other than his own feelings have constantly been before us in the past, and have been regularly verified by our own observations of the facts he reported: so that we have in fact some basis for an induction about his general reliability. Or we may say that his behavior is most simply "explained" on the view that he does feel emotions like ours, just as psychoanalysts "explain" erratic behavior by analogy with normal behavior when they use the terminology of "unconscious desires."

These answers are, however, dangerous and unhelpful. They are so obvious that they please nobody: while on the other hand they encourage the questioner to push his question to "profounder" depths, encouraging us, in turn, to exaggerate these answers until they become distortions.

The question, pushed further, becomes a challenge to the very possibility of "believing another man," in its ordinarily accepted sense, at all. What "justification" is there for supposing that there is another mind communicating with you at all? How can you know what it would be like for another mind to feel anything, and so how can you understand it? It is then that we are tempted to say that we only mean by "believing him" that we take certain vocal noises as signs of certain impending behavior, and that "other minds" are no more really real than unconscious desires.

This, however, is distortion. It seems, rather, that believing in other persons, in authority and testimony, is an essential part of the act of communicating, an act which we all constantly perform. It is as much an irreducible part of our experience as, say, giving promises, or playing competitive games, or even sensing colored patches. We can state certain advantages of such performances, and we can elaborate rules of a kind for their "rational" conduct (as the Law Courts and historians and psychologists work out the rules for accepting testimony). But there is no "justification" for our doing them as such.

*Final Note.* One speaker at Manchester said roundly that the real crux of the matter remains still that "I ought not to say that I know Tom is angry, because I don't introspect his feelings": and this no doubt is just what many people do boggle at. The gist of what I have been trying to bring out is simply:

1. *Of course* I *don't* introspect Tom's feelings (we should be in a pretty predicament if I did).

2. *Of course* I *do* sometimes know Tom is angry.

Hence

3. to suppose that the question "How do I know that Tom is angry?" is meant to mean "How do I introspect Tom's feelings?" (because, as we know, that's the sort of thing that knowing is or ought to be), is simply barking our way up the wrong gum tree.

# PERSONS

## P. F. STRAWSON

### I

In the *Tractatus* (5.631–5.641), Wittgenstein writes of the I which occurs in philosophy, of the philosophical idea of the subject of experiences. He says first: "The thinking, presenting subject—there is no such thing." Then, a little later: "*In an important sense* there is no subject." This is followed by: "The subject does not belong to the world, but is a limit of the world." And a little later comes the following paragraph: "There is [therefore] really a sense in which in philosophy we can talk non-psychologically of the I. The I occurs in philosophy through the fact that the 'world is my world.' The philosophical I is not the man, not the human body, or the human soul of which psychology treats, but the metaphysical subject, the limit—not a part of the world." These remarks are impressive, but also puzzling and obscure. Reading them, one might think: Well, let's settle for the human body and the human soul of which psychology treats, and which is a part of the world, and let the metaphysical subject go. But again

Reprinted by permission of the University of Minnesota Press, from Herbert Feigl, Michael Scriven, and Grover Maxwell, eds., *Minnesota Studies in the Philosophy of Science*, vol. II. Copyright 1958 by the University of Minnesota.

we might think: No, when I talk of myself, I do after all talk of that which has all of my experiences, I do talk of the subject of my experiences—and yet also of something that is part of the world in that it, but not the world, comes to an end when I die. The limit of *my* world is not—and is not so thought of by me—the limit of *the* world. It may be difficult to explain the idea of something which is both a subject of experiences and a part of the world. But it is an idea we have: it should be an idea we can explain.

Let us think of some of the ways in which we ordinarily talk of ourselves, of some of the things which we ordinarily ascribe to ourselves. They are of many kinds. We ascribe to ourselves *actions and intentions* (I am doing, did, shall do this); *sensations* (I am warm, in pain); *thoughts and feelings* (I think, wonder, want this, am angry, disappointed, contented); *perceptions and memories* (I see this, hear the other, remember that). We ascribe to ourselves, in two senses, position: *location* (I am on the sofa) and *attitude* (I am lying down). And of course we ascribe to ourselves not only temporary conditions, states, and situations, like most of these, but also enduring characteristics, including such physical characteristics as height, coloring, shape, and weight. That is to say, among the things we ascribe to ourselves are things of a kind that we also ascribe to material bodies to which we would not dream of ascribing others of the things that we ascribe to ourselves. Now there seems nothing needing explanation in the fact that the particular height, coloring, and physical position which we ascribe to ourselves, should be ascribed to *something or other;* for that which one calls one's body is, at least, a body, a material thing. It can be picked out from others, identified by ordinary physical criteria and described in ordinary physical terms. But it can seem, and has seemed, to need explanation that one's states of consciousness, one's thoughts and sensations, are ascribed *to the very same thing* as that to which these physical characteristics, this physical situation, is ascribed. Why are one's states of consciousness ascribed to the very same thing as certain corporeal characteristics, a certain physical situation, etc.? And once this question is raised, another question follows it, viz.: Why are one's states of consciousness ascribed to (said to be of, or to belong to) anything at all? It is not to be supposed that the answers to these questions will be independent of one another.

It might indeed be thought that an answer to both of them could be found in the unique role which each person's body plays in his experience, particularly his perceptual experience. All philosophers who have concerned themselves with these questions have referred to the uniqueness of this role. (Descartes was well enough aware of its uniqueness: "I am *not* lodged in my body like a pilot in a vessel.") In what does this uniqueness consist? Well, of course, in a great many facts. We may summarize some of these facts by saying that for each person there is one body which occupies a certain *causal* position in relation to that person's perceptual experience, a causal position which is in various ways unique in relation to each of the various kinds of perceptual experience he has; and—as a further consequence—that this body is also unique for him as an *object* of the various kinds of perceptual experience which he has. This complex uniqueness of the single body appears, moreover, to be a contingent matter, or rather a cluster of contingent matters; we can, or it seems that we can, imagine many peculiar combinations of dependence and independence of aspects of our perceptual experience on the physical states or situation of more than one body.

Now I must say, straightaway, that this cluster of apparently contingent facts about the unique role which each person's body plays in his experience does not seem to me to provide, *by itself*, an answer to our questions. Of course these facts explain *something*. They provide a very good reason why a subject of experience should have a *very special regard* for just one body, why he should think of it as unique and perhaps more important than any other. They explain—if I may be permitted to put it so—why I feel *peculiarly attached* to what

316

in fact I call my own body; they even might be said to explain why, granted that I am going to speak of one body as *mine*, I should speak of this body (the body that I do speak of as mine) as mine. But they do not explain why I should have the concept of *myself* at all, why I should ascribe my thoughts and experiences to *anything*. Moreover, even if we were satisfied with some other explanation of why one's states of consciousness (thoughts and feelings and perceptions) were ascribed to *something*, and satisfied that the facts in question sufficed to explain why the "possession" of a particular body should be ascribed to the *same* thing (i.e., to explain why a particular body should be spoken of as standing in some special relation, called "being possessed by" to that thing), yet the facts in question still do not explain why we should, as we do, ascribe certain corporeal characteristics not simply to the body standing in this special relation to the thing to which we ascribe thoughts, feelings, etc., but to the thing itself to which we ascribe those thoughts and feelings. (For we say "I am bald" as well as "I am cold," "I am lying on the hearthrug" as well as "I see a spider on the ceiling.") Briefly, the facts in question explain why a subject of experience should pick out one body from others, give it, perhaps, an honored name and ascribe to it whatever characteristics it has; but they do not explain why the experiences should be ascribed to any subject at all; and they do not explain why, if the experiences are to be ascribed to something, they *and* the corporeal characteristics which might be truly ascribed to the favored body, should be ascribed to the same thing. So the facts in question do not explain the use that we make of the word "I," or how any word has the use that word has. They do not explain the concept we have of a person.

## II

A possible reaction at this point is to say that the concept we have is wrong or confused, or, if we make it a rule not to say that the concepts we have are confused, that the usage we have, whereby we ascribe, or seem to ascribe, such different kinds of predicate to one and the same thing, is confusing, that it conceals the true nature of the concepts involved, or something of this sort. This reaction can be found in two very important types of view about these matters. The first type of view is Cartesian, the view of Descartes and of others who think like him. Over the attribution of the second type of view I am more hesitant; but there is some evidence that it was held, at one period, by Wittgenstein and possibly also by Schlick. On both of these views, one of the questions we are considering, namely "Why do we ascribe our states of consciousness to the very same thing as certain corporeal characteristics, etc.?" is a question which does not arise; for on both views it is only a linguistic illusion that both kinds of predicate are properly ascribed to one and the same thing, that there is a common owner, or subject, of both types of predicate. And on the second of these views, the other question we are considering, namely "Why do we ascribe our states of consciousness to anything at all?" is also a question which does not arise; for on this view, it is only a linguistic illusion that one ascribes one's states of consciousness at all, that there is any proper subject of these apparent ascriptions, that states of consciousness belong to, or are states of, anything.

That Descartes held the first of these views is well enough known. When we speak of a person, we are really referring to one or both of two distinct substances (two substances of different types), each of which has its own appropriate type of states and properties; and none of the properties or states of either can be a property or state of the other. States of consciousness belong to one of these substances, and not to the other. I shall say no more about the Cartesian view at the moment—what I have to say about it will emerge later on— except to note again that while it escapes one of our questions, it does not escape, but indeed invites, the other: "Why are one's states of consciousness *ascribed* at all, to *any* subject?"

The second of these views I shall call the "no-ownership" or "no-subject" doctrine of the self. Whether or not anyone has explicitly held this view, it is worth reconstructing, or constructing, in outline.[1] For the errors into which it falls are instructive. The "no-ownership" theorist may be presumed to start his explanations with facts of the sort which illustrate the unique causal position of a certain material body in a person's experience. The theorist maintains that the uniqueness of this body is sufficient to give rise to the idea that one's experiences can be ascribed to some particular individual thing, can be said to be possessed by, or owned by, that thing. This idea, he thinks, though infelicitously and misleadingly expressed in terms of ownership, would have some validity, would make some sort of sense, so long as we thought of this individual

[1] The evidence that Wittgenstein at one time held such a view is to be found in the third of Moore's articles in *Mind* on "Wittgenstein's Lectures in 1930–33" (*Mind*, 1955, especially pp. 13–14). He reportedly held that the use of "I" was utterly different in the case of "I have a tooth-ache" or "I see a red patch" from its use in the case of "I've got a bad tooth" or "I've got a match-box." He thought that there were two uses of "I" and that in one of them "I" was replaceable by "this body." So far the view might be Cartesian. But he also said that in the other use (the use exemplified by "I have a tooth-ache" as opposed to "I have a bad tooth"), the "I" *does not denote a possessor,* and that no ego is involved in thinking or in having tooth-ache; and referred with apparent approval to Lichtenberg's dictum that, instead of saying "I think," we (or Descartes!) ought to say "There is a thought" (i.e., "Es denkt").

The attribution of such a view to Schlick would have to rest on his article "Meaning and Verification," Pt. V (*Readings in Philosophical Analysis*, H. Feigl and W. Sellars, eds.). Like Wittgenstein, Schlick quotes Lichtenberg, and then goes on to say: "Thus we see that unless we choose to call our body the owner or bearer of the data [the data of immediate experience]—which seems to be a rather misleading expression—we have to say that the data have no owner or bearer." The full import of Schlick's article is, however, obscure to me, and it is quite likely that a false impression is given by the quotation of a single sentence. I shall say merely that I have drawn on Schlick's article in constructing the case of my hypothetical "no-subject" theorist, but shall not claim to be representing his views.

Lichtenberg's anti-Cartesian dictum is, as the subsequent argument will show, one that I endorse, if properly used. But it seems to have been repeated, without being understood, by many of Descartes' critics.

The evidence that Wittgenstein and Schlick ever held a "no-subject" view seems indecisive, since it is possible that the relevant remarks are intended as criticisms of a Cartesian view rather than as expositions of the true view.

thing, the possessor of the experiences, as the body itself. So long as we thought in this way, then to ascribe a particular state of consciousness to this body, this individual thing, would at least be to say something contingent, something that might be, or might have been, false. It might have been a misascription; for the experience in question might be, or might have been, causally dependent on the state of some other body; in the present admissible, though infelicitous, sense of "belong," it might have belonged to some other individual thing. But now, the theorist suggests, one becomes confused: one slides from this admissible, though infelicitous, sense in which one's experiences may be said to belong to, or be possessed by, some particular thing, to a wholly inadmissible and empty sense of these expressions; and in this new inadmissible sense, the particular thing which is supposed to possess the experiences is not thought of as a body, but as something else, say an ego.

Suppose we call the first type of possession, which is really a certain kind of causal dependence, "having$_1$," and the second type of possession, "having$_2$"; and call the individual of the first type "B" and the supposed individual of the second type "E." Then the difference is that while it is genuinely a contingent matter that *all my experiences are had$_1$ by B*, it appears as a necessary truth that *all my experiences are had$_2$ by E*. But the belief in E and in having$_2$ is an illusion. Only those things whose ownership is logically transferable can be owned at all. So experiences are not owned by anything except in the dubious sense of being causally dependent on the state of a particular body. This is at least a genuine relationship to a thing, in that they might have stood in it to another thing. Since the whole function of E was to own experiences in a logically non-transferable sense of "own," and since experiences are not owned by anything in that sense, for there is no such sense of "own," E must be eliminated from the picture altogether. It only came in because of a confusion.

I think it must be clear that this account of the matter, though it contains *some* of the facts, is not coherent. It is not coherent, in that one who holds it is forced to make use of that sense of possession of which he denies the existence, in presenting his case for the denial. When he tries to state the contingent fact, which he thinks gives rise to the illusion of the "ego," he has to state it in some such form as "All *my* experiences are had₁ by (uniquely dependent on the state of) body B." For any attempt to eliminate the "my," or some other expression with a similar possessive force, would yield something that was not a contingent fact at all. The proposition that *all* experiences are causally dependent on the state of a single body B, for example, is just false. The theorist means to speak of all the experiences *had by a certain person* being contingently so dependent. And the theorist cannot consistently argue that "all the experiences of person P" *means the same thing* as "all experiences contingently dependent on a certain body B"; for then his proposition would not be contingent, as his theory requires, but analytic. He must mean to be speaking of some class of experiences of the members of which it is in fact contingently true that they are all dependent on body B. And the defining characteristic of this class is in fact that they are "*my* experiences" or "the experiences *of* some person," where the sense of "possession" is the one he calls into question.

This internal incoherence is a serious matter when it is a question of denying what prima facie is the case: that is, that one does genuinely ascribe one's states of consciousness to something, viz., oneself, and that this kind of ascription is precisely such as the theorist finds unsatisfactory, i.e., is such that it does not seem to make sense to suggest, for example, that the identical pain which was in fact one's own might have been another's. We do not have to seek far in order to understand the place of this logically nontransferable kind of ownership in our general scheme of thought. For if we think of the requirements of identifying reference, in speech, to *particular* states of consciousness, or private experiences, we see that such particulars cannot be thus identifyingly referred to except as the states or experiences *of* some identified *person*. States, or experiences, one might say, *owe* their identity as particulars to the identity of the person whose states or experiences they are. And from this it follows immediately that if they can be identified as particular states or experiences at all, they must be possessed or ascribable in just that way which the no-ownership theorist ridicules, i.e., in such a way that it is logically impossible that a particular state or experience in fact possessed by someone should have been possessed by anyone else. The requirements of identity rule out logical transferability of ownership. So the theorist could maintain his position only by denying that we could ever refer to particular states or experiences at all. And *this* position is ridiculous.

We may notice, even now, a possible connection between the no-ownership doctrine and the Cartesian position. The latter is, straightforwardly enough, a dualism of two subjects (two types of subject). The former could, a little paradoxically, be called a dualism too: a dualism of one subject (the body) and one nonsubject. We might surmise that the second dualism, paradoxically so called, arises out of the first dualism, nonparadoxically so called; in other words, that if we try to think of that to which one's states of consciousness are ascribed as something utterly different from that to which certain corporeal characteristics are ascribed, then indeed it becomes difficult to see why states of consciousness should be ascribed, thought of as belonging to, anything at all. And when we think of this possibility, we may also think of another: viz., that both the Cartesian and the no-ownership theorist are profoundly wrong in holding, as each must, that there are two uses of "I" in one of which it denotes something which it does not denote in the other.

### III

The no-ownership theorist fails to take account of all the facts. He takes account of some of them. He implies, correctly, that the unique position or role of a single body in one's experience is not a sufficient explanation of the fact that one's experiences, or states of consciousness, are ascribed to something which *has* them, with that peculiar nontransferable kind of possession which is here in question. It may be a necessary part of the explanation, but it is not, by itself, a sufficient explanation. The theorist, as we have seen, goes on to suggest that it is perhaps a sufficient explanation of something else: viz., of our confusedly and mistakenly *thinking* that states of consciousness are to be ascribed to something in this special way. And this suggestion, as we have seen, is incoherent: for it involves the denial that someone's states of consciousness are anyone's. We avoid the incoherence of this denial, while agreeing that the special role of a single body in someone's experience does not suffice to explain why that experience should be ascribed to anybody. The fact that there is this special role does not, by itself, give a sufficient reason why what we think of as a subject of experience should have any use for the conception of himself as such a subject.

When I say that the no-ownership theorist's account fails through not reckoning with all the facts, I have in mind a very simple but, in this question, a very central, thought: viz., that it is a necessary condition of one's ascribing states of consciousness, experiences, to oneself, in the way one does, that one should also ascribe them (or be prepared to ascribe them) to others who are not oneself.[2] This means not less than it says.

[2] I can imagine an objection to the unqualified form of this statement, an objection which might be put as follows. Surely the idea of a uniquely applicable predicate (a predicate which *in fact* belongs to only one individual) is not absurd. And, if it is not, then surely the most that can be claimed is that a necessary condition of one's ascribing predicates of a certain class to one individual (oneself) is that one should be prepared, or ready, on appropriate occasions, to ascribe them to other individuals, and hence that one should have a conception of what those appropriate occasions for ascribing them would be; but not, necessarily, that one should actually do so on any occasion.

The shortest way with the objection is to admit it, or at least to refrain from disputing it; for the lesser claim is all that the argument strictly requires, though it is slightly simpler to conduct it on the basis of the larger claim. But it is well to point out further that we are not speaking of a single predicate, or merely of some group or other of predicates, but of the whole of an

It means, for example, that the ascribing phrases should be used in just the same sense when the subject is another, as when the subject is oneself. Of course the thought that this is so gives no trouble to the nonphilosopher: the thought, for example, that "in pain" means the same whether one says "I am in pain" or "He is in pain." The dictionaries do not give two sets of meanings for every expression which describes a state of consciousness: a first-person meaning, and a second- and third-person meaning. But to the philosopher this thought has given trouble; indeed it has. How could the sense be the same when the method of verification was so different in the two cases—or, rather, when there *was* a method of verification in the one case (the case of others) and not, properly speaking, in the other case (the case of oneself)? Or, again, how can it be right to talk of *ascribing* in the case of oneself? For surely there can be a question of ascribing only if there is or could be a question of identifying that to which the ascription is made? And though there may be a question of identifying the one who is in pain when that one is another, how can there be such a question what that one is oneself? But this last query answers itself as soon as we remember that we speak primarily to others, for the information of others. In one sense, indeed, there is no question of my having to *tell who it is* who is in pain, when I am. In another sense I may have to *tell who it is*, i.e., to let others know who it is.

What I have just said explains, perhaps, how one may properly be said to ascribe states of consciousness to oneself, given that one ascribes them to others. But how is it that one can

---

enormous class of predicates such that the applicability of those predicates or their negations determines a major logical type of category of individuals. To insist, at this level, on the distinction between the lesser and the larger claims is to carry the distinction over from a level at which it is clearly correct to a level at which it may well appear idle or, possibly, senseless.

The main point here is a purely logical one: the idea of a predicate is correlative with that of a range of distinguishable individuals of which the predicate can be significantly, though not neccessarily truly, affirmed.

ascribe them to others? Well, one thing is certain: that *if* the things one ascribes states of consciousness to, in ascribing them to others, are thought of as a set of Cartesian egos to which *only* private experiences can, in correct logical grammar, be ascribed, *then* this question is unanswerable and this problem insoluble. If, in identifying the things to which states of consciousness are to be ascribed, private experiences are to be all one has to go on, then, just for the very same reason as that for which there is, from one's own point of view, no question of telling that a private experience is one's own, there is also no question of telling that a private experience is another's. All private experiences, all states of consciousness, will be mine, i.e., no one's. To put it briefly: one can ascribe states of consciousness to oneself only if one can ascribe them to others; one can ascribe them to others only if one can identify other subjects of experience; and one cannot identify others if one can identify them *only* as subjects of experience, possessors of states of consciousness.

It might be objected that this way with Cartesianism is too short. After all, there is no difficulty about distinguishing bodies from one another, no difficulty about identifying bodies. And does not this give us an indirect way of identifying subjects of experience, while preserving the Cartesian mode? Can we not identify such a subject as, for example, "the subject that stands to that body in the same special relation as I stand to this one"; or, in other words, "the subject of those experiences which stand in the same unique causal relation to body N as *my* experiences stand to body M"? But this suggestion is useless. It requires me to have noted that *my* experiences stand in a special relation to body M, when it is just the right to speak of *my* experiences at all that is in question. (It requires me to have noted that *my* experiences stand in a special relation to body M; but it requires me to have noted this as a condition of being able to identify other subjects of experience, i.e., as a condition of having the idea of myself as a subject of experience, i.e., as a condition of thinking of any experience as *mine*.)

So long as we persist in talking, in the mode of this explanation, of experiences on the one hand, and bodies on the other, the most I may be allowed to have noted is that experiences, *all* experiences, stand in a special relation to body M, that body M is unique in just this way, that this is what makes body M unique among bodies. (This "most" is, perhaps, too much—because of the presence of the word "experiences.") The proffered explanation runs: "Another subject of experience is distinguished and identified as the subject of those experiences which stand in the same unique causal relationship to body N as *my* experiences stand to body M." And the objection is: "But what is the word 'my' doing in this explanation? (It could not get on without it.)"

What we have to acknowledge, in order to begin to free ourselves from these difficulties, is the *primitiveness* of the concept of a person. What I mean by the concept of a person is the concept of a type of entity such that *both* predicates ascribing states of consciousness *and* predicates ascribing corporeal characteristics, a physical situation, etc. are equally applicable to a single individual of that single type. And what I mean by saying that this concept is primitive can be put in a number of ways. One way is to return to those two questions I asked earlier: viz., (1) why are states of consciousness ascribed to anything at all? and (2) why are they ascribed to the very same thing as certain corporeal characteristics, a certain physical situation, etc.? I remarked at the beginning that it was not to be supposed that the answers to these questions were independent of each other. And now I shall say that they are connected in this way: that a necessary condition of states of consciousness being ascribed at all is that they should be ascribed to the *very same things* as certain corporeal characteristics, a certain physical situation, etc. That is to say, states of consciousness could not be ascribed at all, *unless* they were ascribed to persons, in the sense I have claimed for this word. We are tempted to think of a person as a sort of compound of two kinds of subject—a subject of experiences (a pure consciousness, an ego), on the one hand, and a subject of corporeal attributes on the other.

Many questions arise when we think in this way. But, in particular, when we ask ourselves how we come to frame, to get a use for, the concept of this compound of two subjects, the picture—if we are honest and careful—is apt to change from the picture of two subjects to the picture of one subject and one nonsubject. For it becomes impossible to see how we could come by the idea of different, distinguishable, identifiable subjects of experiences—different consciousnesses—*if this idea is thought of as logically primitive,* as a logical ingredient in the compound idea of a person, the latter being composed of two subjects. For there could never be any question of assigning an experience, as such, to any subject other than oneself; and therefore never any question of assigning it to oneself either, never any question of ascribing it to a subject at all. So the concept of the pure individual consciousness—the pure ego— is a concept that cannot exist; or, at least, cannot exist as a primary concept in terms of which the concept of a person can be explained or analyzed. It can only exist, if at all, as a secondary, nonprimitive concept, which itself is to be explained, analyzed, in terms of the concept of a person. It was the entity corresponding to this illusory primary concept of the pure consciousness, the ego-substance, for which Hume was seeking, or ironically pretending to seek, when he looked into himself, and complained that he could never discover himself without a perception and could never discover anything but the perception. More seriously—and this time there was no irony, but a confusion, a Nemesis of confusion for Hume—it was this entity of which Hume vainly sought for the principle of unity, confessing himself perplexed and defeated; sought vainly because there is no principle of unity where there is no principle of differentiation. It was this, too, to which Kant, more perspicacious here than Hume, accorded a purely formal ("analytic") unity: the unity of the "I think" that accompanies all my perceptions and therefore might just as well accompany none. And finally it is this, perhaps, of which Wittgenstein spoke when he said of the subject, first, that there is no such thing, and, second, that it is not a part of the world, but its limit.

So, then, the word "I" never refers to this, the pure subject. But this does not mean, as the no-ownership theorist must think and as Wittgenstein, at least at one period, seemed to think, that "I" in some cases does not refer at all. It refers, because I am a person among others. And the predicates which would, *per impossible,* belong to the pure subject if it could be referred to, belong properly to the person to which "I" does refer.

The concept of a person is logically prior to that of an individual consciousness. The concept of a person is not to be analyzed as that of an animated body or of an embodied anima. This is not to say that the concept of a pure individual consciousness might not have a logically secondary existence, if one thinks, or finds, it desirable. We speak of a dead person— a body—and in the same secondary way we might at least think of a disembodied person, retaining the logical benefit of individuality from having been a person.[3]

## IV

It is important to realize the full extent of the acknowledgment one is making in acknowledging the logical primitiveness of the concept of a person. Let me rehearse briefly the stages of the argument. There would be no question of ascribing one's own states of consciousness, or experiences, to anything, unless one also ascribed states of consciousness, or experiences, to other individual entities of the same logical type as that thing to which one ascribes one's own states of consciousness. The condition of reckoning oneself as a subject of such predicates is that one should also reckon others as subjects of such predicates. The condition, in turn, of this being possible, is that one should be able to distinguish from one another (pick out,

[3] A little further thought will show how limited this concession is. But I shall not discuss the question now.

identify) different subjects of such predicates, i.e., different individuals of the type concerned. And the condition, in turn, of this being possible is that the individuals concerned, including oneself, should be of a certain unique type: of a type, namely, such that to each individual of that type there *must* be ascribed, or ascribable, *both* states of consciousness *and* corporeal characteristics. But this characterization of the type is still very opaque and does not at all clearly bring out what is involved. To bring this out, I must make a rough division, into two, of the kinds of predicates properly applied to individuals of this type. The first kind of predicate consists of those which are also properly applied to material bodies to which we would not dream of applying predicates ascribing states of consciousness. I will call this first kind M-predicates: and they include things like "weighs 10 stone," "is in the drawing room," and so on. The second kind consists of all the other predicates we apply to persons. These I shall call P-predicates. And P-predicates, of course, will be very various. They will include things like "is smiling," "is going for a walk," as well as things like "is in pain," "is thinking hard," "believes in God," and so on.

So far I have said that the concept of a person is to be understood as the concept of a type of entity such that *both* predicates ascribing states of consciousness *and* predicates ascribing corporeal characteristics, a physical situation, etc. are equally applicable to an individual entity of that type. And all I have said about the meaning of saying that this concept is primitive is that it is not to be analyzed in a certain way or ways. We are not, for example, to think of it as a secondary kind of entity in relation to two primary kinds, viz., a particular consciousness and a particular human body. I implied also that the Cartesian error is just a special case of a more general error, present in a different form in theories of the no-ownership type, of thinking of the designations, or apparent designations, of persons as *not* denoting precisely the same thing, or entity, for all kinds of predicate ascribed to the entity designated. That is, if we are to avoid the general form of this error we must *not* think of "I" or "Smith" as suffering from type-ambiguity. (If we want to locate type-ambiguity somewhere, we would do better to locate it in certain predicates like "is in the drawing room," "was hit by a stone," etc., and say they mean one thing when applied to material objects and another when applied to persons.)

This is all I have so far said or implied about the meaning of saying that the concept of a person is primitive. What has to be brought out further is what the implications of saying this are as regards the logical character of those predicates in which we ascribe states of consciousness. And for this purpose we may well consider P-predicates in general. For though not all P-predicates are what we should call "predicates ascribing states of consciousness" (for example, "going for a walk" is not), they may be said to have this in common, that they imply the possession of consciousness on the part of that to which they are ascribed.

What then are the consequences of this view as regards the character of P-predicates? I think they are these. Clearly there is no sense in talking of identifiable individuals of a special type, a type, namely, such that they possess both M-predicates and P-predicates, unless there is in principle some way of telling, with regard to any individual of that type, and any P-predicate, whether that individual possesses that P-predicate. And, in the case of at least some P-predicates, the ways of telling must constitute in some sense logically adequate kinds of criteria for the ascription of the P-predicate. For suppose in no case did these ways of telling constitute logically adequate kinds of criteria. Then we should have to think of the relation between the ways of telling and what the P-predicate ascribes (or a part of what it ascribes) always in the following way: we should have to think of the ways of telling as *signs* of the presence, in the individual concerned, of this different thing (the state of consciousness). But then we could only know that the way of telling was a sign of the presence of the different thing ascribed by the

P-predicate, by the observation of correlations between the two. But this observation we could each make only in one case, namely, our own. And now we are back in the position of the defender of Cartesianism, who thought our way with it was too short. For what, now, does "our own case" mean? There is no sense in the idea of ascribing states of consciousness to oneself, or at all, unless the ascriber already knows how to ascribe at least some states of consciousness to others. So he cannot (or cannot generally) argue "from his own case" to conclusions about how to do this; for unless he already knows how to do this, he has no conception of *his own case*, or any *case* (i.e., any subject of experiences). Instead, he just has evidence that pain, etc. may be expected when a certain body is affected in certain ways and not when others are.

The conclusion here is, of course, not new. What I have said is that one ascribes P-predicates to others on the strength of observation of their behavior; and that the behavior criteria one goes on are not just signs of the presence of what is meant by the P-predicate, but are criteria of a logically adequate kind for the ascription of the P-predicate. On behalf of this conclusion, however, I am claiming that it follows from a consideration of the conditions necessary for any ascription of states of consciousness to anything. The point is not that we must accept this conclusion in order to avoid skepticism, but that we must accept it in order to explain the existence of the conceptual scheme in terms of which the skeptical problem is stated. But once the conclusion is accepted, the skeptical problem does not arise. (And so with the generality of skeptical problems: their statement involves the pretended acceptance of a conceptual scheme and at the same time the silent repudiation of one of the conditions of its existence. This is why they are, in the terms in which they are stated, insoluble.) But this is only half the picture about P-predicates.

Now let us turn to the other half. For of course it is true, at least of some important classes of P-predicates, that when one ascribes them to oneself, one does not do so on the strength of observation of those behavior criteria on the strength of which one ascribes them to others. This is not true of all P-predicates. It is not, in general, true of those which carry assessments of character and capability: these, when self-ascribed, are in general ascribed on the same kind of basis as that on which they are ascribed to others. And of those P-predicates of which it is true that one does not generally ascribe them to oneself on the basis of the criteria on the strength of which one ascribes them to others, there are many of which it is also true that their ascription is liable to correction by the self-ascriber on this basis. But there remain many cases in which one has an entirely adequate basis for ascribing a P-predicate to oneself, and yet in which this basis is quite distinct from those on which one ascribes the predicate to another. (Thus one says, reporting a present state of mind or feeling: "I feel tired, am depressed, am in pain.") How can this fact be reconciled with the doctrine that the criteria on the strength of which one ascribes P-predicates to others are criteria of a logically adequate kind for this ascription?

The apparent difficulty of bringing about this reconciliation may tempt us in many directions. It may tempt us, for example, to deny that these self-ascriptions are really ascriptions at all; to *assimilate* first-person ascriptions of states of consciousness to those other forms of behavior which constitute criteria on the basis of which one person ascribes P-predicates to another. This device seems to avoid the difficulty; it is not, in all cases, entirely inappropriate. But it obscures the facts, and is needless. It is merely a sophisticated form of failure to recognize the special character of P-predicates (or at least of a crucial class of P-predicates). For just as there is not (in general) one primary process of learning, or teaching oneself, an inner private meaning for predicates of this class, then another process of learning to apply such predicates to others on the strength of a correlation, noted in one's own case, with certain forms of behavior, so—and equally—there is not (in general) one primary process of learning to apply such predicates to others on the strength of behavior criteria, and then another process of acquiring the secondary technique of exhibiting a new form of behavior, viz., first-person P-utterances. Both these pictures are refusals to acknowledge the unique logical character of the predicates concerned.

Suppose we write "Px" as the general form of propositional function of such a predicate. Then according to the first picture, the expression which primarily replaces "x" in this form is "I," the first-person singular pronoun; its uses with other replacements are secondary, derivative, and shaky. According to the second picture, on the other hand, the primary replacements of "x" in this form are "he," "that person," etc., and its use with "I" is secondary, peculiar, not a true ascriptive use. But it is essential to the character of these predicates that they have both first- and third-person ascriptive uses, that they are both self-ascribable otherwise than on the basis of observation of the behavior of the subject of them, and other-ascribable on the basis of behavior criteria. To learn their use is to learn both aspects of their use. In order to *have* this type of concept, one must be both a self-ascriber and an other-ascriber of such predicates, and must see every other as a self-ascriber. And in order to *understand* this type of concept, one must acknowledge that there is a kind of predicate which is unambiguously and adequately ascribable *both* on the basis of observation of the subject of the predicate *and* not on this basis (independently of observation of the subject): the second case is the case where the ascriber is also the subject. If there were no concepts answering to the characterization I have just given, we should indeed have no philosophical problem about the soul; but equally we should not have *our* concept of a person.

To put the point—with a certain unavoidable crudity—in terms of one particular concept of this class, say, that of depression, we speak of behaving in a depressed way (of depressed behavior) and also of feeling depressed (of a feeling of depression). One is inclined to argue that feelings can be felt, but not observed, and behavior can be observed, but not felt, and that therefore there must be room here to drive in a logical wedge. But the concept of depression spans the place where one wants to drive it in. We might say, in order for there to be such a concept as that of X's depression, the depression which X has, the concept must cover both what is felt, but not observed, by X and what may be observed, but not felt, by others than X (for all values of X). But it is perhaps better to say: X's depression *is* something, one and the same thing, which is felt but not observed by X and observed but not felt by others than X. (And, of course, what can be observed can also be faked or disguised.) To refuse to accept this is to refuse to accept the structure of the language in which we talk about depression. That is, in a sense, all right. One might give up talking; or devise, perhaps, a different structure in terms of which to soliloquize. What is not all right is simultaneously to pretend to accept that structure and to refuse to accept it, i.e., to couch one's rejection in the language of that structure.

It is in this light that we must see some of the familiar philosophical difficulties in the topic of the mind. For some of them spring from just such a failure to admit, or fully appreciate, the character which I have been claiming for at least some P-predicates. It is not seen that these predicates could not have either aspect of their use (the self-ascriptive and the non-self-ascriptive) without having the other aspect. Instead, one aspect of their use is taken as self-sufficient, which it could not be, and then the other aspect appears as problematical. And so we oscillate between philosophical skepticism and philosophical behaviorism. When we take the self-ascriptive aspect of the use of some P-predicates (say, "depressed") as primary, then a logical gap seems to open between the criteria on the strength of which we say that another is depressed, and the actual state of depression. What we do not realize is that if this logical gap is allowed to open, then it swallows not only his depression, but our depression as well. For if the logical gap exists, then depressed behavior, however much there is of it, is no more than a sign of depression. And it can become a sign of depression only because of an observed correlation between it and depression. But whose depression? Only mine, one is tempted to say. But if *only* mine, then *not* mine at all. The skeptical position customarily represents the crossing of the logical gap as at best a shaky inference. But the point is that not even the syntax of the premises of the inference exists if the gap exists.

If, on the other hand, we take the other-ascriptive uses of these predicates as self-sufficient, we may come to think that all there is in the meaning of these predicates, as predicates, is the criteria on the strength of which we ascribe them to others. Does this not follow from the denial of the logical gap? It does not follow. To think that it does is to forget the self-ascriptive use of these predicates, to forget that we have to do with a class of predicates to the meaning of which it is essential that they should be both self-ascribable and other-ascribable to the same individual, when self-ascriptions are not made on the observational basis on which other-ascriptions are made, but on another basis. It is not that these predicates have two kinds of meaning. Rather, it is essential to the single kind of meaning that they do have that both ways of ascribing them should be perfectly in order.

If one is playing a game of cards, the distinctive markings of a certain card constitute a logically adequate criterion for calling it, say, the Queen of Hearts; but, in calling it this, in the context of the game, one is also ascribing to it properties over and above the possession of those markings. The predicate gets its meaning from the whole structure of the game. So it is with the language which ascribes P-predicates. To say that the criteria on the strength of which we ascribe P-predicates to others are of a logically adequate kind for this ascription is not to say that all there is to the ascriptive meaning of these predicates is these criteria. To say this is to forget that they are P-predicates, to forget the rest of the language-structure to which they belong.

## V

Now our perplexities may take a different form, the form of the question "But how can one ascribe to oneself, not on the basis of observation, *the very same thing* that others may have, on the basis of observation, a logically adequate reason for ascribing to one?" And this question may be absorbed in a wider one, which might be phrased: "How are P-predicates possible?" or "How is the concept of a person possible?" This is the question by which we replace those two earlier questions, viz.: "Why are states of consciousness ascribed at all, ascribed to anything?" and "Why are they ascribed to the very same thing as certain corporeal characteristics, etc.?" For the answer to these two initial questions is to be found nowhere else but in the admission of the primitiveness of the concept of a person, and hence of the unique character of P-predicates. So residual perplexities have to frame themselves in this new way. For when we have acknowledged the primitiveness of the concept of a person and, with it, the unique character of P-predicates, we may still want to ask what it is in the natural facts that makes it intelligible that we should have this concept, and to ask this in the hope of a nontrivial answer.[4] I do not pretend to be able to satisfy this demand at all fully. But I may mention two very different things which might count as beginnings or fragments of an answer.

And, first, I think a beginning can be made by moving a certain class of P-predicates to a central position in the picture. They are predicates, roughly, which involve doing something, which clearly imply intention or a state of mind or at least consciousness in general, and which indicate a characteristic pattern, or range of patterns, of bodily movement, while not indicating at all precisely any very definite sensation or experience. I mean such things as "going for a walk," "furling a rope," "playing ball," "writing a letter." Such predicates have the

---

[4] I mean, in the hope of an answer which does not *merely* say: Well, there are people in the world.

interesting characteristic of many P-predicates that one does not, in general, ascribe them to oneself on the strength of observation, whereas one does ascribe them to others on the strength of observation. But, in the case of these predicates, one feels minimal reluctance to concede that what is ascribed in these two different ways is the same. And this is because of the marked dominance of a fairly definite pattern of bodily movement in what they ascribe, and the marked absence of any distinctive experience. They release us from the idea that the only things we can know about without observation, or inference, or both, are private experiences; we can know also, without telling by either of these means, about the present and future movements of a body. Yet bodily movements are certainly also things we can know about by observation and inference.

Among the things that we observe, as opposed to the things we know without observation, are the movements of bodies similar to that about which we have knowledge not based on observation. It is important that we understand such observed movements; they bear on and condition our own. And in fact we understand them, we interpret them, only by seeing them as elements in just such plans or schemes of action as those of which we know the present course and future development without observation of the relevant present movements. But this is to say that we see such movements (the observed movements of others) as *actions*, that we interpret them in terms of intention, that we see them as movements of individuals of a type to which also belongs that individual whose present and future movements we know about without observation; that we see others, as self-ascribers, not on the basis of observations, of what we ascribe to them on this basis.

Of course these remarks are not intended to suggest how the "problem of other minds" could be solved, or our beliefs about others given a general philosophical "justification." I have already argued that such a "solution" or "justification" is impossible, that the demand for it cannot be coherently stated. Nor are

337

these remarks intended as a priori genetic psychology. They are simply intended to help to make it seem intelligible to us, at this stage in the history of the philosophy of this subject, that we have the conceptual scheme we have. What I am suggesting is that it is easier to understand how we can see each other (and ourselves) as persons, if we think first of the fact that we act, and act on each other, and act in accordance with a common human nature. "To see each other as persons" is a lot of things; but not a lot of separate and unconnected things. The class of P-predicates that I have moved into the center of the picture are not unconnectedly there, detached from others irrelevant to them. On the contrary, they are inextricably bound up with the others, interwoven with them. The topic of the mind does not divide into unconnected subjects.

I spoke just now of a common human nature. But there is also a sense in which a condition of the existence of the conceptual scheme we have is that human nature should not be common, should not be, that is, a community nature. Philosophers used to discuss the question of whether there was, or could be, such a thing as a "group mind." And for some the idea had a peculiar fascination, while to others it seemed utterly absurd and nonsensical and at the same time, curiously enough, pernicious. It is easy to see why these last found it pernicious: they found something horrible in the thought that people should cease to have toward individual persons the kind of attitudes that they did have, and instead have attitudes in some way analogous to those toward groups; and that they might cease to decide individual courses of action for themselves and instead merely participate in corporate activities. But their finding it pernicious showed that they understood the idea they claimed to be absurd only too well. The fact that we find it natural to individuate as persons the members of a certain class of what might also be individuated as organic bodies does not mean that such a conceptual scheme is inevitable for any class of beings not utterly unlike ourselves.

Might we not construct the idea of a special kind of social

world in which the concept of an individual person has no
employment, whereas an analogous concept for groups does
have employment? Think, to begin with, of certain aspects of
actual human existence. Think, for example, of two groups of
human beings engaged in some competitive but corporate activity, such as battle, for which they have been exceedingly
well trained. We may even suppose that orders are super-
fluous, though information is passed. It is easy to imagine that,
while absorbed in such activity, the members of the groups
make no references to individual persons at all, have no use for
personal names or pronouns. They do, however, refer to the
groups and apply to them predicates analogous to those predicates ascribing purposive activity which we normally apply to
individual persons. They may, *in fact,* use in such circumstances the plural forms "we" and "they"; but these are not
genuine plurals, they are plurals without a singular, such as
we use in sentences like these: "We have taken the citadel,"
"We have lost the game." They may also refer to elements in
the group, to members of the group, but exclusively in terms
which get their sense from the parts played by these elements
in the corporate activity. (Thus we sometimes refer to what
are in fact persons as "stroke" or "tackle.")

When we think of such cases, we see that we ourselves, over
a part of our social lives—not, I am thankful to say, a very
large part—do operate conceptual schemes in which the idea
of the individual person has no place, in which its place is
taken, so to speak, by that of a group. But might we not think
of communities or groups such that this part of the lives of
their members was the dominant part—or was the whole? It
sometimes happens, with groups of human beings, that, as *we*
say, their members think, feel, and act "as one." The point I
wish to make is that a condition for the existence, the use, of
the concept of an individual person is that this should happen
*only sometimes.*

It is absolutely useless to say, at this point: But all the same,
even if this happened all the time, every member of the group

would have an individual consciousness, would be an individual subject of experience. The point is, once more, that there is no sense in speaking of the individual consciousness just as such, of the individual subject of experience just as such: for there is no way of identifying such pure entities.[5] It is true, of course, that in suggesting this fantasy, I have taken our concept of an individual person as a starting point. It is this fact which makes the useless reaction a natural one. But suppose, instead, I had made the following suggestion: that each part of the human body, each organ and each member, had an individual consciousness, was a separate center of experiences. This, in the same way, but more obviously, would be a useless suggestion. Then imagine all the intermediate cases, for instance these. There is a class of moving natural objects, divided into groups, each group exhibiting the same characteristic pattern of activity. Within each group there are certain differentiations of appearance accompanying differentiations of function, and in particular there is one member of each group with a distinctive appearance. Cannot one imagine different sets of observations which might lead us, in the one case, to think of the particular member as the spokesman of the group, as its mouthpiece; and in the other case to think of him as its mouth, to think of the group as a single *scattered* body? The point is that as soon as we adopt the latter way of thinking then we want to drop the former; we are no longer influenced by the human analogy in its first form, but only in its second; and we no longer want to say: "Perhaps the members have consciousness." To understand the movement of our thought here, we need only remember the startling ambiguity of the phrase "a body and its members."

## VI

I shall not pursue this attempt at explanation any further. What I have been mainly arguing for is that we should acknowledge

---

[5] More accurately: their identification is necessarily secondary to the identification of persons.

the logical primitiveness of the concept of a person and, with this, the unique logical character of certain predicates. Once this is acknowledged, certain traditional philosophical problems are seen not to be problems at all. In particular, the problem that seems to have perplexed Hume [6] does not exist— the problem of the principle of unity, of identity, of the particular consciousness, of the particular subject of "perceptions" (experiences) considered as a primary particular. There is no such problem and no such principle. If there were such a principle, then each of us would have to apply it in order to decide whether any contemporary experience of his was his or someone else's; and there is no sense in this suggestion. (This is not to deny, of course, that one *person* may be unsure of his own identity in some way, may be unsure, for example, whether some particular action, or series of actions, had been performed by him. Then he uses the same methods (the same in principle) to resolve the doubt about himself as anyone else uses to resolve the same doubt about him. And these methods simply involve the application of the ordinary criteria for *personal* identity. There remains the question of what exactly these criteria are, what their relative weights are, etc.; but, once disentangled from spurious questions, this is one of the easier problems in philosophy.)

Where Hume erred, or seems to have erred, both Kant and Wittgenstein had the better insight. Perhaps neither always expressed it in the happiest way. For Kant's doctrine that the "analytic unity of consciousness" neither requires nor entails any principle of unity is not as clear as one could wish. And Wittgenstein's remarks (at one time) to the effect that the data of consciousness are not owned, that "I" as used by Jones, in speaking of his own feelings, etc., does not refer to what "Jones" as used by another refers to, seem needlessly to flout the conceptual scheme we actually employ. It is needlessly paradoxical to deny, or seem to deny, that when Smith says "Jones has a pain" and Jones says "I have a pain," they are talking about the

[6] Cf. the Appendix to the *Treatise of Human Nature*.

same entity and saying the same thing about it, needlessly paradoxical to deny that Jones can *confirm* that he has a pain. Instead of denying that self-ascribed states of consciousness are really ascribed at all, it is more in harmony with our actual ways of talking to say: For each user of the language, there is just one person in ascribing to whom states of consciousness he does not need to use the criteria of the observed behavior of that person (though he does not necessarily not do so); and that person is himself. This remark at least respects the structure of the conceptual scheme we employ, without precluding further examination of it.

# VI

*Direct Access*

# SENSATIONS, RAW FEELS,
## AND OTHER MINDS

E. M. ZEMACH

## A

I⊤ IS POSSIBLE to discern three main types of answers commonly
given to the question about the nature of sensations. The first
is the classical "private access" theory, according to which I
(and *only* I) can sense my own pain, while the pains of others
can never be subject to direct inspection by me. The presence
of overt pain behavior may inductively confirm the hypothesis
that the body thus behaving is besouled and subject to a sensation of pain, but I can never be sure that such pain really exists.
I can feel only my own pain, and every pain I feel is necessarily
my own. One token of this view is Cartesian dualism, but it is
also adopted by most kinds of interactionism, epiphenomenalism, and their ilk. One of the notorious consequences of this
theory is, that it makes the problem of Other Minds practically
insoluble. Do the other humanoids have minds like my own,
do they experience raw feelings similar to mine? The question remains logically unanswerable. The argument from anal-

Reprinted by permission of the author and editor, from *The Review of
Metaphysics*, XX (1966), 317–340.

ogy was often shown to be very tenuous,[1] and one is therefore driven to accept the conclusion (actually drawn at one time by Wittgenstein[2]) that sensation words must mean one thing in the context of egocentric sentences and quite another thing when the subject of the sentence is other than I. But if this is the case, mentalistic attributes *proper* are only I-ascriptive: that is, it would be a logical howler to apply them to anything other than myself; grammar thus forces me to adopt a position similar to that of the solipsist.

The opposition to the "private access" theories is generally offered by some version (behavioristic or materialistic) of the identity theory. These theories maintain that it is not logically impossible to envisage a physicalistic language containing no mentalistic terms whatsoever, yet which adequately replaces our present way of speaking about sensations, raw feels, and their like. If such replacement, or translation, of the "manifest image"[3] of our human world is possible, then, clearly, the problem of other minds entirely disappears. If statements about feeling hatred, seeing red, etc., may be translated into, or replaced by, statements which refer to overt behavior and dispositions to behave (on the behavioristic view) or (on the materialistic view) to statements which only mention brain cells and movements of neurons, there must be an independent method of verification, open to the competent scientist, of all such statements. Thus there is no "privileged access" to sensations of the subject, no special status for first person reports, and hence no problem about the "minds" of others.

But, so it seems to me, the project of such translation or replacement is misguided in principle. It is impossible to learn a language—any language—unless the learner is acquainted

[1] Cf. J. L. Austin, "Other Minds," *Proceedings of the Aristotelian Society,* Supp. Vol. XX (1946); N. Malcolm, "Knowledge of Other Minds," *Journal of Philosophy,* LV (1958); P. F. Strawson, *Individuals* (London, 1959), pp. 101ff.

[2] G. E. Moore, *Philosophical Papers* (New York, 1962), p. 301.

[3] Cf. Wilfrid Sellars, *Science, Perception, and Reality* (New York, 1963), pp. 4ff. and *passim.*

with some attributes to which some of the predicates of the learned language refer. Every language that has any descriptive value must presuppose an ability on the part of the student to recognize *which* state of affairs, *which* quality, or *which* particular is referred to by this or that linguistic expression. This ability to recognize and discriminate is absolutely fundamental, and without it all languages are quite useless.[4] It is clear that, if people are supposed to use a language properly and intelligently, they must know when they should describe some situation they encounter by statement *a*, and when it is the case that statement *b* is proper. This precondition of meaningfulness must apply to all languages, whether "scientistic" or not, notwithstanding whether these languages include names of everyday objects or whether they recognize only "theoretical" entities such as electrons and genes. That is, even if we adopt Rorty's[5] scientistic language, a language entirely expurgated of mentalistic expressions, sensations will still be essential in order to discriminate and make this language apply to anything. Although in this language, instead of reporting a pain, I shall make a complicated statement about the position of my, say, C-fibers, if this claim is to be made noninferentially (as Rorty insists it must), then it is necessary that I should be acquainted with some sensation, Q, which will be just the peculiar sensation I have when my C-fibers fire. And, clearly, Q must be quite different from the sensation P, that is, the sensation I have when my retina is shelled by D-type photons. To make a long story short, I must be able to tell feeling pain from seeing red. Only when I have learned to recognize and identify these sensations shall I be able to make any use of Rorty's (or any other) language. Our reliance upon sensations is not impugned by the fact that our language might not have any names for them. Most sensations we daily encounter are

[4] The *genetic* question, whether concepts are actually derived by abstraction from such attributes, is beside the point here.

[5] Cf. Richard Rorty, "Mind-Body Identity, Privacy, and Categories," *The Review of Metaphysics*, XIX (1966), 24–54.

nameless even in present day English, and are referred to by means of the objects which habitually occasion them. Nobody, to my knowledge, has ever tried to draw an ontological line between the named and nameable, arguing that only the former, but not the latter, do genuinely exist. Thus, although sensation terminology may be expunged from the *object* language if we cease to speak about sensing pain and only refer to C-fibers firing, sensation words will crop up again in the *metalanguage,* where questions like "how do you know that your C-fibers fire" must be answered. We could have obtained the same effect, without all the scientistic paraphernalia, by speaking, e.g., of feeling a splinter driven into one's finger, rather than use a special name to refer to the sensation thus occasioned.

The identity theorist might argue now that, after all, many simple machines can sort out objects, i.e., make distinctions and discriminations without our ascribing "awareness" to them. Similarly, might not a child be trained to react in a certain verbal way to a stimulation of his C-fibers without his being "aware" of anything? Now it is true that such a process is actually referred to by many psychologists as "a process of learning," but I doubt whether we are allowed to assimilate to it the process of conscious learning in humans without prejudging the whole issue. For to answer our objection by claiming that we are mistaken in supposing that there is anything like being aware of a certain quality, will be to *presuppose* the materialistic thesis, i.e., the vacuity of our common experience of being conscious or aware of objects and sense qualities. The identity theorist cannot *start out* by claiming that the reports we make of our experiences report actually *nothing,* i.e., that they are *no* reports at all, since if he does this there is nothing for him to explain, and the identity theory becomes a vacuous tautology.

Typically the identity theorist does not hold this position. What he claims is that what *seems to us* to be a mental occurrence is *really* a physical occurrence. Although the C-fibers do

348

not have the property Q (that is, pain) *formaliter*, Q is still the way in which a stimulation of those fibers *appears* to me. But the employment of such argument amounts to a complete surrender. First of all, it admits the category of persons as an irreducible element of the final explanation: or else, who is that "me" which it mentions? Secondly, using the term "appear," it acknowledges that the category of "appearing to," and hence the having of sensations and their discriminative recognition, is also irreducible. The reduction scheme for Q, "There is something, P, which *we* sense as Q" (or—"which *only appears* as Q") cannot be applied to appearing itself, i.e., to that which is discriminated by sensing. The statement "There is something, P, which *we* sense as sensing" could not obviously be used to eliminate the term "sensing" from our language, since the term "sense" must be *used* in the reduction scheme itself.

A third theory which stands roughly in the middle between the two extremes (the Private Access and the Identity Theory), is Strawson's theory of P-predicates. A P-predicate, according to Strawson, "is a kind of predicate which is unambiguously and adequately ascribable *both* on the basis of observation of the subject of the predicate *and* not on this basis, i.e., independently of observation of the subject" (*Individuals*, p. 108). According to Strawson, outward symptoms of depression reflected in the behavior of a person are as much primary features of one's depression as the raw feel of depression felt by the depressed person. This duality of critera for ascription of P-predicates, viz., observation for third person ascriptions and immediate, noninferential sensing for first person ascriptions, is exactly what makes these predicates what they are. This is, at least, what Strawson claims. But actually he does very little in order to convince us that P-predicates are really irreducible. One's obvious suspicion is, then, that P-predicates are hybrid, systematically ambiguous terms, since they are used in two entirely different ways. Strawson warns us that if we distinguish between these two uses of P-predicates, that is, between overt behavior (such as the clutching of one's foot) and the immediate "raw feel" of pain, and divide this concept in two, we are likely to fall into the most undesirable position of having to choose between behaviorism and Cartesianism. But although we might agree with Strawson that neither of these positions is tenable, this in itself does not constitute a convincing reason to adopt his way out. It is possible, of course, to claim that one and the same thing has a set of characteristics, A, as well as another, entirely different set of characteristics B. But in order to maintain such a position we must have some positive evidence for believing that it is really so. Because, clearly enough, if there is no such evidence, we have no reason to take A and B as revealing aspects of the same thing. If we only happen to use the word "P" with respect to both A and B, we should be rather inclined to regard "P" as a systematically ambiguous word.

And what is true of attributes can also be said about criteria. The fact that different spectators may have to use different criteria in order to ascertain whether or not a certain predicate is applicable in given situations is not, in itself, enough indication that the said predicate is systematically ambiguous. A blind man would use one criterion to determine whether there is a clock in the room, while his friend, the deaf man, *must* use a totally different criterion for the same purpose; yet there is no question of the term "clock" being used ambiguously by the blind man and the deaf man. We must remember, however, that if "clock" is to be nonambiguously used it is necessary that the blind man would insist that the deaf man's criterion, as well as his, *may* be used to determine whether the object examined is a clock or not. That is, he should be ready to withdraw, or at least reconsider, his own pronouncement on this matter if he has good reasons to believe that the requirements set by the other criterion were *not* met. Now this is exactly a feature which P-predicates notoriously lack. It was often pointed out that no report based upon observations of my overt behavior (even if we allow an extension of this term, so that it will cover changes in the nervous system as well) is going to change my mind about the question whether I am in pain or not. This is to say that in our case a user of one criterion may actually *ignore* the findings of the user of the second criterion. Now this ignoring is precisely the most typical sign of a linguistic ambiguity. Using a criterion (say, acceptance of money deposits) to determine what is a bank, I can afford to disregard results achieved through the use of another criterion (say, delimiting a river) only if I consider the term "bank" ambiguous. We may conclude, thus, that in the case of P-predicates we have not only a double criterion but an actual ambiguity.[6]

In a very interesting paper on this question G. Iseminger [7] argues that the only way to understand Strawson's position concerning P-predicates is by dissociating the concept of meaning from the concept of criteria. The *meaning* of a P-predicate is one and the same, although the *criteria* for its application may be (necessarily) dual. Strawson's example for this divorce of meaning and criterion, which Iseminger considers very helpful, runs as follows: "The distinctive markings of a certain card constitute a logically adequate criterion for calling it, say, the Queen of Hearts; but in calling it this, in the context of the game, one is ascribing to it properties over and above the possession of these markings. The predicate gets its meaning from the whole structure of the game" (*Individuals*, p. 110). Now, if this example is supposed to show how a meaning may be something over and above its criteria of application, then it is, I believe, grossly misguided. The term "Queen of Hearts" is used here in a double sense. First, it is used to name a card of a certain shape and size; second, it is used to name a certain role in a certain specific game of cards. These two meanings are quite independent of each other: the said card may be used

---

[6] For another discussion of this problem, see R. B. Freed and J. A. Fodor, "Pains, Puns, Persons and Pronouns," *Analysis*, XXII (1961), 6–9; Donald S. Mannison, "On the Alleged Ambiguity of Strawson's P-predicates," *Analysis*, XXIII (1962), 3–5; J. A. Fodor and R. B. Freed, "Some Types of Ambiguous Tokens," *Analysis*, XXIV (1963), 19–23.

[7] "Meaning, Criteria, and P-predicates," *Analysis*, XXIV (1963), 11–18.

in a totally different role, and the said role may be played by a different card. Having certain well-known markings is *not* "a logically adequate criterion" that the card actually plays the *role* "Queen of Hearts," and nothing short of an observation of the way this card is used in the game would constitute such an adequate criterion. The same goes, of course, for the first sense of the term "Queen of Hearts." In either case, meaning is *never* distinct from criteria of application.

Strawson's thesis is, in fact, quite ambiguous at this point. It might be interpreted as follows: "There is something, call it 'Depression,' which has both the set of properties A and the set of properties B." I have tried to argue that this view, although not self-contradictory, is extremely unlikely, since we have no evidence whatsoever that A and B, which belong in two entirely different logical categories (raw feels and behavior of physical bodies), are first order properties of the same entity, viz., depression. But there is another interpretation of Strawson's position, an interpretation favored in some of his formulations, which claims, roughly, that X's depression is a certain quality, one and the same quality, which is felt, but not observed, by X, and observed, but not felt, by people other than X. But this view is surely logically invalid. On this view the same *quality* which is felt by X may be observed by Y. It means that the raw feel, depression, which is sensed by X may be *observed* by Y, and that the overt behavior which is observed by Y may be *felt* by X. But this certainly looks like a logical howler.

What Strawson has to say at this point is, probably, a warning that to regard "depression" as ambiguous is "to refuse to accept the *structure* of the language in which we talk" (*ibid.*, p. 109). But this argument does not help. First of all, it is simply not true that we use one and the same word, e.g., "depression," to refer both to X's outward demeanor and to the kind of feeling he has. We clearly do speak about X's behavior as a "sign" of X's being depressed, etc. But even if Strawson *were* right on this point, I do not see how noting an ambiguity of an English word is tantamount to a metaphysical revision of the structure of language.

The theory we seem to need is a theory which will allow us to regard sense-properties as what we experience them to be, and yet will not make them into Wittgenstein's "beetle in the box," private objects which do not admit of inter-subjective inspection and verification. But how is such a theory possible?

## B

Speaking about pains, thoughts, and similar "entities," Strawson claims: "Such particulars cannot be thus identifyingly referred to except as the states or experiences *of* some identified *person*. States, or experiences . . . owe their identity as particulars to the identity of the person whose states or experiences they are. From this, it follows immediately that if they can be identified as particular states or experiences at all, they must be possessed or ascribable . . . in such a way that it is logically impossible that a particular state or experience in fact possessed by someone should have been possessed by anyone else" (*Individuals*, p. 97). This claim is often seconded in the literature.[8]

But is this view really justified? Is it absolutely necessary for us to refer to pains, etc., *only* as "states or experiences of some identified person"? Let us consider, for example, the case of a sense-property like the color *red*. We certainly do say, do we not, that two different people may notice that a certain dress is red (and not, say, brown)? They have both seen the *same* sense-property, although, of course, *a*'s seeing red is a different event than *b*'s seeing red. In common discourse we refer to colors, sounds, and to similar sense-qualities as *intentional* objects, which may be inspected by several, independent observ-

---

[8] Cf. A. J. Ayer, *The Foundations of Empirical Knowledge* (London, 1940), pp. 138–139; "The barriers that prevent us from enjoying one another's experiences are not natural but logical. . . . It is not conceivable that there should be people who were capable of having one another's pains." Cf. also Jerome Shaffer, "Persons and Their Bodies," *Philosophical Review*, LXXV (1966), 66ff.

ers. Both you and I may hear the noise of the approaching car: non-Berkeleyians will not hesitate to say that both of us heard the same noise, as both of us may see the same color. Noises and colors are *not* individuals: yet I do not think that Strawson or his followers will wish to argue that they "cannot be identifyingly referred to except as the states or experiences *of* some identified *person*." This view, i.e., the view that no statement about the sensible qualities of things can be made without the rider "it was X's experience that . . . ," commonly known as phenomenalism, was—of course—actually maintained by a great many philosophers in this century, but I do not think that Strawson, or most of his followers, are advocating this view or trying to maintain that all sentences about sense-properties are actually covered up protocol-sentences. Therefore, if I understand correctly, what Strawson holds is not that all, but that only some sense-properties, i.e., instances of those properties commonly known as "tertiary," owe their identity *not* to those things whose properties they are, but to the identity of the persons discerning them.[9] To put it roughly, this is the view that the adjectives "boring," "painful," "ticklish," etc.—perhaps also adjectives like "smooth" or "hot"—should not be construed as properties of things, but as states of the percipient. It is this proto-Humean theory of private objects which is responsible, to my mind, for the entire notion of "private access," and probably for the major part of the philosophical mess created around the seemingly insoluble problem of "other minds." Our first task is, therefore, to dispose of the theory which maintains that sizes and colors are "public," but pains, for some reason, are "private."

Suppose there is, in the next room, a red, electrically charged piece of metal which buzzes faintly. If *a* enters the room he is

[9] Cf. *Individuals*, pp. 42ff. Strawson holds that the ostensive expressions "this pain" "really do contain an implicit reference to a particular person"; it is "a kind of shorthand for 'the pain I am suffering.'" On the other hand, " 'this tree,' used of a particular tree, may be spoken to anybody by anybody, in the appropriate surrounding, without change of identificatory force. No implicit reference to a particular *person* is essential."

able to see the red color of this piece of metal; if he draws
nearer he can hear the noise; if he touches it he can feel a mild
electric shock. If *b* enters the same room, and if *b* is a normal
human percipient, he will be able to register the same three
qualities of the piece of metal. Of course, *a*'s getting the shock
is not *b*'s getting the shock—these are two separate events—
but neither is *a*'s hearing the noise or seeing the color the same
as *b*'s. This is precisely the logic of patent, observable qualities
of things, that there may be many events of perceiving and
noticing them. This suggestion, however, seems to run against
our regular way of speaking: If I touch a flame and get burned,
I do not say that the *flame* aches; this I do not deny. But even
in this case I ascribe the pain to some material thing, viz., my
finger. On the other hand we *do* generally ascribe some "tertiary" properties to some other situations, facts, and things—we
say that this situation is dangerous, this word is harsh, this fact
is painful, or this piece of music is melancholy. Very often we
shuttle between intentionalistic and nonintentionalistic ways
of speaking about sense-qualities (cf., e.g., "It looks red to
*me!*"). I see, therefore, no logical impediment to regard all
sense qualities, secondary and tertiary alike, as properties of
*material things*, where "material things" may be interpreted as
including both external objects and parts of our own bodies
(thus I accept expressions like "my leg hurts" *literally*). I suggest, therefore, that the alleged distinction between primary,
secondary, and tertiary properties be disregarded. (This distinction might have, though, some other significance, a *range-
significance*, as we shall see in the following.) [10]

I have just claimed that all raw feels may be construed as
qualities of public, material objects. But have I not missed

[10] A recent interpretation of Wittgenstein's *Philosophical Investigations*
ascribes to Wittgenstein much the same view, viz., the view that though raw
feels are in no way reducible to overt behavior, they are not private entities
(John W. Cook, "Wittgenstein on Privacy," *Philosophical Review*, LXXIV
(1965), 281–314). This view, however, differs from mine in that it holds
sensation-words to be universals, like "gait" or "build" (and not particular
qualities of material things, as I believe they are).

somehow the most difficult case, the case of internal feelings? What about my private toothache? Can it be felt, or sensed, by anybody else beside myself? Should I not say that the toothache I have is distinct from a toothache which might be felt by anyone else?

Greek mythology has it, that the three sisters of Fate, the *Parcae*, have only one eye and one tooth among them. Whenever one of the three desires to nibble on something, she has to ask for the tooth from the sister holding it at the moment; when she desires to observe her surroundings, she asks for the eye. Now suppose the tooth develops a cavity, or that the eye becomes inflamed. Whenever one of the sisters borrows the tooth, she feels a certain pain, i.e., a toothache, and whenever she removes it the pain ceases. I suggest that in such circumstances it would be natural for the sisters to identify the pain by referring to it as a quality inherent in the tooth, which each of them may come to know when she puts the tooth on. The tooth feels smooth, cool, and painful. These are the tooth's properties, which might be felt by anyone who puts it on. The three sisters are, no doubt, very well acquainted with this particular pain and they probably discuss *it* quite often. Would it be sensible to say that, "really," each of the three sisters has a different toothache, but that the three toothaches are of the same kind? Of course it would not be *wrong* to say so, only one has to remember that by speaking in this way he has switched to a phenomenalistic mode of speech. There is nothing wrong in speaking of "my sight of the table" and giving up the kind of language which involves countenancing the overt properties of material things, only one must be aware what is at stake here: The question about the existence or nonexistence of a *logical* private access is really the question about whether we should, or should not, consider speaking in protocol sentences as the sole legitimate way of conversing. After Ryle and Austin, I do not think one has to take such a suggestion seriously.

Am I suggesting, then, that it is possible for some man other than myself—say, my doctor—to feel the pain I have in my leg?

In a way, the answer is Yes. But I shall postpone the defense of this positive answer to the next section. At the moment, all I am saying is that it is not logically impossible for him to do so. If he only could extend a nerve and plug it into an outlet in my central nervous system, he could easily hearken to my pain by feeling it, as he does now hearken to noises in my heart by attaching a stethoscope to my chest. And note, it is not even the case that his sensation and mine must be of the same *kind*; it is certainly conceivable that, in order not to make the medical profession extremely unattractive, we should let the doctor feel the pain, only in somewhat reduced intensity. I do not think that thereby the pain he feels will cease to be the same one felt by me. I may say, may I not, that Tom and I have heard the same explosion, or have seen the same glaring light, only he, being much closer to the place where the bomb fell, heard (or saw) it much more intensely. Both the doctor and I can, thus, feel the torn muscle (in the distinctive human way of noticing material things) through the appearance of a sense-quality—in this case, the sense-quality, "pain." The divergence between ways of talking about various sensations should not hypnotize us into seeing philosophical distinctions where they do not exist. The fact that our earth is enveloped by air makes it possible for any two people to see the same red book, but the structure of our nervous system makes it technically impossible to feel the same aching leg. But it is easy to imagine a reversal of these conditions. If the atmosphere of this planet were to have been attached, in big drops, to every material body and *cling* to it, you would have to hook up your atmosphere to mine in order to see my injured leg or hear my sobbing voice, and this might be physically impossible. What we now call "overt" behavior would be, on that planet, a prototype of privacy, a beetle in the box. But, assuming the possibility of nerve connections, finding out that someone got hurt would be no problem: air or no air, the pain would be felt clearly enough by, say, some relative, and a doctor could be rushed to treat the wound.

I have mentioned before range-differences between qualities: this distinction, I believe, is a sound one, but it is entirely empirical. The presence of air on this earth, for example, makes it easy for most of us to detect things by their colors and shapes. On these circumstances, colors do occupy the widest of all quality ranges. The situation is, of course, quite different from our canine friends who would rather use smells as their most encompassing quality range. One could imagine that if they used a language, colors would be treated in it mostly in a non-intentional, phenomenalistic way, allowing for the private idiosyncrasies of particular dogs (as we allow for human idiosyncrasies in matters of taste, etc.). The distinction is, on the whole, a pragmatic one. The difference in ranges between different types of qualities should be explained by the biologist and the sociologist, not the philosopher.

## C

But our task is not finished yet. Unfortunately, the minute we say that feeling someone else's pain is impossible, albeit only empirically so, the question of other minds raises its ugly head. What does it matter *what* makes it impossible for me to have first hand knowledge about the other's feelings? *I* cannot tell whether there is anybody else who is able to sense raw feels the way I do, says the solipsist. In order to quell his doubts we have to show not only that on some science-fiction conditions it would be possible to share pains with another person, but that in some sense, such first hand knowledge of the sensations of other persons is a real fact. To do this we have to go one level deeper and inquire, this time, not about the sameness conditions of *properties*, but about the conditions of sameness for *things*.

P. T. Geach, in his *Mental Acts*, gives the following account of such sameness: "It is meaningless to say without qualification that the baby, the youth, the adult, and the old man are 'the same,' or 'the same thing,' and that this is what justifies us in calling them by the same name; nor yet is it a matter for our

358

free decision whether or not they are deemed 'the same.' 'The same' is a fragmentary expression, and has no significance unless we say or mean 'the same X,' where 'X' represents a general term . . . the identity of a thing always consists in its being the same X, e.g., the same *man*." With this account I wish fully to concur. In a more recent article Joseph Margolis [11] brings up the same issue again and draws, more or less, the same conclusion: It is possible for us to say that the man Dracula and a certain bat are "the same" since they are the same *something*— the same vampire. We cannot say, e.g., that they are the same *man*, since a bat is not a man, and we certainly cannot say that they are the same *simpliciter,* since, certainly, there is a great difference indeed between a bat and a man. This conclusion I would like to adopt and extend. It has, I think, a considerable importance for the philosophy of mind in general, and for the problem dealt with in the present paper in particular.

Let me start with a sort of a Wittgensteinian fable. There is a tribe whose language resembles ours in many respects; only they seem to use the term "person" in the following way: Until puberty the child is considered to be one person, and an entirely different person after his initiation rites have taken place. Initiation, in this culture, is considered as the death of one person and the birth of another, quite different from the first—who is thereafter referred to as "his deceased father." No adult is considered responsible in any way for what "his father," i.e., the child he has been, might have done. Now an anthropologist using a Strawsonian concept of person (which we may call "S-person") and not the tribe's concept (which we may call "T-person") may, of course, say that a certain person (i.e., S-person) who was called before puberty "Ababu" is now renamed "Bulubu." But it would be a bad mistake for him to say that Bulubu was once referred to as "Ababu." "Bulubu" is a name of a T-person, and the T-person Bulubu had no former

[11] Joseph Margolis, "Dracula the Man: An Essay in the Logic of Individuation," *International Philosophical Quarterly*, IV (1964), 541–549.

name. Using names of T-persons, one has to abide by the grammar of the concept "T-person," and, according to our fable, it is incorrect to say of any T-person that he had a former name. It should be remembered that the sentence "Ababu and Bulubu are just one and the same entity" is not even true or false, but simply incomplete: "entity" here functions as a concept-variable, since we have yet to know which *kind* of entity is here intended. If it is an S-person the sentence is true, but if the intended substituend is a T-person, the sentence is false.

Our anthropologist might protest that such analysis is absurd: *either* Strawson is right and the tribe is wrong *or else* Strawson is wrong and the tribe is right about what does and what does not constitute a criterion for personal identity, but it cannot be the case that they are both right. In the following pages I shall refer to this view as "atomistic." The atomist is the philosopher who believes that there must be one and only one way to distinguish between persons. Once *the* correct method is reached, what shall be found will be absolutely discrete, substance-like monads: primary persons. Although atomists like Leibniz and P. F. Strawson might disagree about the nature of these fundamental persons, they do not doubt that there is just one absolute way in which the concept of "person" might be defined. Atomism, then, is the thesis that it is possible to discover *the* true criterion for sameness of persons in general. This position I take to be utterly false. It seems that there are several possible criteria for personal identity, and every one of them, as well as many of their combinations, may be taken as defining *a* concept—a *different* concept—of a person.

Let us take, for example, the criterion of bodily continuity, regarded as *the* criterion for personal sameness by P. F. Strawson, B. A. O. Williams, G. C. Nerlich, and others.[12] I certainly

---

[12] B. A. O. Williams, "Personal Identity and Individuation," *Proceedings of Aristotelian Society*, LVII (1956–57), 239; G. C. Nerlich, "Sameness, Difference and Continuity," *Analysis*, XVIII (1958), 144–149; G. C. Nerlich, " 'Continuity' Continued," *Analysis*, XXI (1960), 117; Terence Penelhum,

do not wish to deny that this criterion *may* be used to determine personal identity. That is, we *may* slice up our world into S-persons. According to this way of making distinctions, Dr. Jekyll and Mr. Hyde, or Ababu and Bulubu, would indeed be the same persons, respectively. I do not see, however, why there should be any objection to adopt the concept of a T-person as well. In fact, given the set of beliefs and physical surroundings of our mythical tribe, the concept of a T-person will be able to do all the jobs done by the concept of an S-person, and better. It is not difficult to imagine a world in which the concept of S-person will be quite useless. One example for such a science-fiction cosmos is given us by Wittgenstein in the *Blue Book*.[13] Another example is offered by J. M. Shorter,[14] who describes a universe in which all available facts are such that transmigration of souls becomes a reasonable nomological generalization. It is obvious that in such circumstances, although we *might* yet stick to S-persons (i.e., to bodily continuity as *the* criterion for personal identity), it would be wiser, simpler, and more intuitive to avail ourselves of other concepts of person, i.e., of other criteria for personal identity.

Such criteria may be based upon one's ability to have memories about oneself: e.g., it can be maintained that if I remember that I have been in $P_1$ at $T_1$, then I am the same person as the man who has actually been in $P_1$ at $T_1$. Another, slightly different, criterion might be the following: $(x)$ $(y)$ $(x = y) \equiv$ Remembers $(x, p)$ & Involved in $(y, p)$ & Remembers $(x, x = y)$. Or take the criterion of knowing, or being able to perform, certain things (e.g., if I know what *a* thought, or where *a* buried the gold, then I must be the same person as *a*),

"Analysis Problem," *Analysis*, XVII (1957), 123–124; Terence Penelhum, "Personal Identity, Memory, and Survival," *Journal of Philosophy*, LVI (1959), 902ff.; B. A. O. Williams, "Bodily Continuity and Personal Identity—A Reply," *Analysis*, XXI (1960), 43–48.

[13] Ludwig Wittgenstein, *The Blue and Brown Book* (Oxford, 1960), p. 61.

[14] "More about Bodily Continuity and Personal Identity," *Analysis*, XXII (1962), 79–85.

etc. For certain world-states (e.g., if memory claims of people are, as a rule, never countered by opposing memory claims of others) these criteria will suffice, and the persons thus identified might be called M (for "Mind" or "Memory") persons. On other world-states, where conflicting memory-claims are rather common, we might wish to supplement these criteria by, say, a demand for mental continuity, i.e., a continuity between the thoughts of *a* at any given moment and *b*'s thoughts at the next moment *if a* is deemed identical with *b*. Another possible supplementation is the condition that a = b iff for every moment t such that *a* is at t, there is a moment t + 1, which immediately follows t, such that *b* is at t + 1, and *a* has a set of memories, hopes and wishes M, and *b* has almost (the degree of this "almost" is subject to stipulation) the same set M. Similar criteria may easily be contrived. What is important, however, is not the offered criteria themselves, but the fact that every one of them is subject to change, supplementation, or cancellation. For example, we might remove the condition of awareness of being identical with a former temporal slice of oneself on certain conditions, regard certain memories as *false* if they contradict many other memories of many other people, etc. We might even add a different *kind* of criterion, e.g., that of bodily continuity, to the M-criteria. But again—S. Shoemaker's position [15] to the contrary—we are never *obligated* to do so. It is most important to realize that (1) *many* criteria do a fair job of defining what a person might be taken to be—that is, they capture some of our intuitions concerning this notion—and that, at the same time, (2) *no* criterion or combination of criteria is necessary and sufficient for this task. It is impossible to state a criterion of personal identity which will have sharp boundaries and would operate equally well under all imaginable conditions. I think that several criteria might be very useful for giving sense to *a* concept of person, but I deny that any of them captures "the" meaning of this concept "itself."

[15] S. Shoemaker, "Personal Identity and Memory," *Journal of Philosophy*, LVI (1959), 868–902.

I have already mentioned P. F. Strawson as a proponent of atomism. His famous solution to the problem of other minds stands and falls with a certain version of atomism, viz., the view that being embodied is a necessary condition for personal identification. In his laconic formulation, "One can ascribe states of consciousness to oneself only if one can ascribe them to others. One can ascribe them to others only if one can identify other subjects of experience. And one cannot identify others if one can identify them *only* as subjects of experience." Hence, persons *must* be endowed with bodies; the concept "body" *must* be an important part of the concept "person" and *must* enter into every possible definition of this concept. Now I cannot understand how Strawson can claim that no identification of bodiless entities is ever possible after having written the brilliant chapter on "Sounds" (the second chapter of *Individuals*), in which he does precisely this, i.e., creates a model of identifiable bodiless entities. But even leaving sounds aside, it is not difficult to think up a hundred and one ways of identifying such individuals (angels, spirits, demons, and their like). I may communicate with them, say, telepathically and recognize each such spiritual individual by his peculiar manner of thinking (his "cognitive style"), by the kind of things he tells me, or else I might simply ask him to identify himself. But can there not be *two* disembodied spirits whose cognitive styles, etc. will be quite similar? How can I be sure that I am not mistaking one of these spiritual twins for his sibling? The answer is that I cannot be *absolutely* sure, but I do not see why I have to be *that* sure in order to maintain that I am conversing today with the same angel who appeared to me yesterday. Can I be *absolutely* sure that the friend I am talking to right now is the same one with whom I started to argue five minutes ago? Perhaps the former friend disappeared and another, just like him in all respects, took his place instantaneously? But this assumption is idle and rather foolish. Why should I think that my friend has suddenly disappeared? What reasonable arguments can be brought up to make such radical hypothesis worth considering? There are none—and this is quite enough assurance both for me and for Strawson. Now why should I suppose (if there are *no reasons whatsoever* to suppose so apart from the vacuous "perhaps") that I have fallen victim to some private joke of two identical angel-twins? As long as all the facts I can glean indicate that I am dealing with the *same* disembodied spirit on several occasions, the mere baseless suspicion of a possible universal hoax cannot seriously be used as an argument against the possibility of bodiless existence.

I do not see, then, any good reason against using M-criteria to determine our position in questions of personal identity. Should a beggar claiming to be Napoleon reincarnated be considered the same person as Napoleon if he has vivid memories concerning all Napoleon's experiences, possesses his exact character, etc.? I think the question calls for a conceptual *decision*. Our beggar is certainly not the same S-person as Napoleon, since, of course, Napoleon has died, and his body disintegrated. Operating within the framework of S-persons, we would thus conclude that the beggar is only very much *like* Napoleon. But there might be excellent reasons (say, if this phenomenon would occur quite frequently) to use a different concept of person, a D- (for "Dibbuk") person, such that the beggar will be the same D-person as Napoleon. Every Christian would certainly like to be able to say that it was Lazarus himself who was raised from the dead, and not that somebody else, similar to Lazarus in many respects, came suddenly into being (this, I believe, must be Williams' conclusion).

But what, asks Williams, should we say if there would be *two* beggars exactly resembling Napoleon, instead of just one? Should we say that Napoleon had bifurcated? If the beggar *a* is identical with Napoleon and the beggar *b* is identical with Napoleon, then *a* is identical with *b*, although *a* and *b* are contemporary—and this, according to Williams, is logically impossible. This trial-case shows, he claims, that the use of M-criteria is misguided in principle, even in case we have just one Napoleonizing beggar. Most of Williams' adversaries (such as R. C. Coburn [16] and J. M. Shorter [17]) granted the logical impossibility of the trial-case (that *a* and *b* be identical though contemporaneous) but tried to drive a logical wedge between this conclusion and the rejection of M-criteria in general. My objection is quite different. I see nothing sacrosanct about the spatial contiguity of persons, and should the necessity arise to speak, *à la* Quine, about scattered or bifurcated individuals (B-persons), I can think of no reason why we should hesitate to do so. Why should one's body be just in one piece? One might object, however, that if we have *two* beggars claiming to be Napoleon, then each of them must have his separate sensations, emotions, and hopes. Is it not the case that each of them has his own particular pain, for example? But this stumbling stone for regarding two M-persons as one B-person was already removed, I believe, in the previous section. We have seen that the form "x senses y" may be interpreted as either intentional or not. If we do interpret it as intentional, then we *can* say that the beggars do feel the *same* pain, the *same* sensations and hopes, and there will be no numerical multiplicity of similar experiences which will make it neces-sary to stipulate the existence of two distant subjects of these experiences. If we prefer, though, to speak in a nonintentional manner, i.e., about the *having* of the pain rather than about the pain had, then the decision how many persons are having the pain is dependent upon our decision as to what kind of persons we choose to recognize. And, if it be B- rather than M-persons, we shall have no basis whatever to speak about more than one having of a pain, by one B-person.

But this is surely mad! Have we not previously agreed that if the two beggars report a sensation of pain, there are *two* pangs of pain, i.e., two events of having-a-pain? Yes and No. The question, how many pangs of pain occurred, has no factual, obvious answer, since it depends upon the criterion we use for

[16] *Analysis*, XX (1960), 117ff.
[17] *Ibid.*

counting pain-events. *No* such criterion is simply "given," and
we can devise one that suits our special purposes. E.g., when I
am in pain for five minutes, how many pain-events should I
number? One? Five? Or perhaps five million! Suppose I am
in dire pain for five minutes. After that the pain ceases for a
short while and then starts again; it is very weak during the first
minute, but soon recovers its full previous strength. How many
pain-events should I count? Two? Three? Or perhaps just one
(discontinuous) event? Again, the decision is up to us. The
situation is basically the same with our two beggars: Once we
have decided to regard them as just one B-beggar, there is no
reason why we should not go on and similarly count their pain-
events as one. Also, if it is possible (and doubtless it *is* possible) for one M-person to undergo more than one pain-event,
we may also admit that two separate pain-events had taken
place without thereby endangering our commitment to the
unity of the B-beggar. Pain and person do not have to agree
in number.

Cases of bifurcation, or fission, are by no means peculiar to
M-persons. Even B. A. O. Williams is well aware of this fact:
one can easily imagine S-persons splitting in two like amoebae.
But since Williams refuses to acknowledge *any* B-persons he
must say that even in case of bodily continuous entities which
multiply by fission "the resultant items are not, in the strict
sense, spatio-temporally continuous with the original." [18] It is
not quite clear what the phrase "in the strict sense" is doing
in this sentence. But, if I understand Williams correctly, this
phrase is *not* hinting at a possibility of distinguishing between
a "strict-sense" and a "non-strict-sense" of identity. Williams'
view is, I think, that the splitting of the original body dis-
qualifies *all* the resultant parts to be considered as identical
with the original body. This position I find very strange. One
of its strangest results is that after I clip my nails or get a hair-
cut, I am not anymore the person I was before I so recklessly
entered the fatal barber shop. "In the strict sense" I am not

[18] *Analysis*, XXI (1961), 48.

"spatio-temporally continuous with the original." Take another case: suppose that, on planet Alpha, expectant mothers give birth by fission. Clearly, only one of the resultant parts will resemble, in all details, the mother. The other one would be a baby. But Williams would not let the happy mother come home with her newborn son. For the person who was pregnant before the birth (fission) would no longer exist after the birth (fission), and according to the ordinary logic of the mother-son relation, this relation could not be said to hold.

Normally, however, we would not refuse to regard one or more of the parts of a bifurcated entity as identical with the original entity. Our hesitation in the case of the two beggars is due not to their spatial noncontiguity, but to the fact that they are both sentient beings. But, as I have tried to show earlier, in case their mental lives are exactly similar, then there is no reason for such hesitation. (Whether such exact similarity is possible or not is unimportant.) At this point, however, we get to the crux of the matter: Suppose these men are not *exactly* like each other in all respects. Could we not loosen our criteria a little bit for the identity of B-persons? After all, considering criteria for S-identity we allowed for physical bodily change, and M-identity is not forfeited by changes of character or mentality. Indeed, I think we should be liberal even here and admit some nonuniformity within B-identity as well. But if this is the case, would it not be possible to regard two people, such as husband and wife (and perhaps their children as well) as being the same person? At first blush this sounds rather fantastic, but getting used to the idea is, after all, not so difficult. Consider Bulubu's amazement when he learns that, according to our way of splitting up persons, he is considered to be the same person as Ababu, his "father," just because he inherited the latter's body and some scanty recollections about the poor child's (that is, Ababu's) life! If it is not ludicrous for a grown man to point to the picture of a baby and say "That's me!" or refer to its experiences as "mine," I do not see why it should be so shocking if we try to expand the concept of personal

367

identity in another direction, that is, not in time, but, so to speak, in space.

A natural reaction to such a suggestion would be to try and stress the difference between "real" persons and the "fake," "merely linguistic" persons which I have here conjured up. One is likely to say, for example, this: "When I am in pain I know it noninferentially, with absolute certainty. It is ridiculous to suggest that I shall have to consult the doctor or the morning paper in order to find out whether I am in pain or not. But on your suggestion this is exactly what may happen—since a family or a whole community might be considered as one person, it would make sense to read in the paper, or to hear from a friend, that 'I' (that is, some part or other of this mega-person) am in pain!" Let us consider this argument closely. Is it really the case that *every* attribution of "feeling pain" to a person by the same person is infallible and noninferential? Obviously not. I may seem to remember having suffered intense pain on a certain (past) occasion, when in fact I was subject to no such inconvenience. On the other hand, I may infer (e.g., from something I have written at that time) that on the said occasion I greatly suffered, although this experience was utterly forgotten.

The doubts of our adversary are not likely yet to subside. After all, one does feel that he *is* the person who underwent the experience x a few minutes ago! But to say this is (1) to claim infallibility for memory, or at least to regard information acquired by way of remembering as having a special status, and (2) to assume that we are using the term "person" univocally. Neither of these assumptions is true. It is possible to have erroneous memories, and it is also possible, as Wittgenstein has shown, to use concepts which lack sharp boundaries. The "same" concept may be understood by different people as embodying different, irreconcilable rules when used in borderline cases. The various concepts of personal identity, those we tacitly assume and those which we might use should a certain eventuality arise, do *overlap*. They have, one might say, blurred edges and they shade into each other quite naturally and imperceptibly. The atomist is the one who cannot stand this untidy state of affairs, and tries to "regiment" our concepts in such a way that he will be able to see "ultimate" persons lying next to each other, clear and distinct like gems. This passion for metaphysical order is typical of Leibniz, Whitehead, and Strawson alike. But the price they have to pay for the neatness of their world-picture is really exorbitant. They are left with an insoluble problem of solipsism.

On the other hand, if we reject atomism, the problem of other minds will immediately loose much of its bite. If persons do overlap, there is no insurmountable barrier between an absolute *me* and absolute, alien *others*. This was seen very clearly by Hegel, who said that if we insist on finding the absolute, atomic, indivisible "I" we shall have to countenance a pure nothing. The present split of a second in which immediate awareness is supposed to occur should be divided and redivided out of existence in order to find the pure present. Both Wittgenstein and Hegel would agree that it is impossible neatly to distinguish the element of pure noninferential witnessing of something as something from the linguistic rules, memories, and anticipations which this witnessing presupposes. The search for the ultimate "I" leads us nowhere. Pure immediacy is an ideal limit, not a Whiteheadian building-brick of the real world, an actual entity inside which time stands still to let a pure ego find itself within fixed boundaries. Hegel, I think, was justified in maintaining that the "I" is an ideal limit, not an atom of experience. Once we come to see that, we have, I think, to grant Hegel a further point: that there is no hard and fast limit for the ego's expansion: a single moment, the last ten years, a life span, the lives of a master and his slave, a family, a class, or a nation—they all may be considered as persons in their own way. I beg to differ from Hegel where he states that there is a certain historical succession among these person-concepts, such that the more encompassing ones must come into predominance at a later period. I do not know how a certain language-game using one variety of person-concepts comes to prevail over others, or why it yields its place to other games at a later date. Although I believe that our choice of these concepts is culture-dependent, it does not seem as if cultures are temporally arranged as Hegel thought they are. The distinction between persons is therefore, I think, a matter of language, not of history. This is why it seems to me that the category of personal identity does not simply expand, with each new version enclosing the former, like a series of Chinese boxes. There are many *different* concepts of personal identity, and they greatly *overlap*. In spite of this divergence from Hegel's word in his *Phenomenology of Spirit*, however, I believe that the answer I propose to give the question "How do I know that there are other persons beside me?" is basically Hegelian (a Linguistic-Hegelian answer, if you wish): "Because the term 'I' ranges, already, over many entities which could otherwise be referred to as 'others,' and because the term 'others' ranges over entities which could—from another point of view—be regarded as parts of myself."

# INTERSUBJECTIVE KNOWLEDGE

KENNETH GALLAGHER

## *"Other Minds"*

The epistemological problem of the existence of other selves is both easier and harder to solve than is the more general problem of the existence of "objects" other than ourselves. It is at once apparent that our conviction that there are other selves asserts considerably more than does the mere conviction of an objective world in general. For in asserting that other selves exist, we are not merely asserting that objects exist, but that other *subjects* exist. When speaking of objects we do not at first experience in any urgent way the need to conceive the "inside" of these objects; an object is, so to speak, all "outside." This is especially true in the case of an inanimate thing like a stone or a mountain; we do not proceed by conceiving these things as there "for themselves" in the way a conscious subject is.[1] But the assertion that other selves exist does immediately entail the belief that there is more to certain entities than the corporeal front which they present to perception. This being

Reprinted by permission of Sheed and Ward, from *The Philosophy of Knowledge*, pp. 251–275. Copyright 1964.

[1] This is not to say that eventually a problem of this kind will not arise in respect to objects, since in some analogous way they too must be conceived as "subjects."

sitting across from me on the subway train is not only a rather complicated kind of bodily object; he is also, I am sure, a subject. Maybe I am only observing his "outside," his bodily behavior, but I am sure that there is an "inside," a conscious experience similar to my own.

On reflection, however, the justification for this assurance may strike us as hard to come by. For is not subjectivity just what is most private, most intimate, most noncommunicable of all things? Surely I know that I exist as a subject, for I am in a privileged position with respect to my own experience: I *am* my own "inside." But this "inside" of mine, my interior consciousness, is, one would think, available for me alone. No one is present to my consciousness in the way that I am. No one can read my mind—my consciousness is that which is concealed from the probing scrutiny of others. My body is observable by others, but not my mental processes. In the same way, one might think that if there really are other subjects, still their subjectivity is just as concealed from me as my subjectivity is from them. Then how can I be sure that there are other selves if I do not directly observe them? Can I possibly *directly* experience any subjectivity besides my own? We would be inclined to say no. But then, whence do I derive the assurance of the existence of such subjectivities? From one standpoint this problem is manifestly more perplexing than the problem of other "objects," since it adds a completely new dimension to my claim to make contact with what is other than myself.

Yet from another standpoint it is easier to get at than the more general problem. Even though I may be perplexed as to how I can be certain that other selves exist, I do not seem to experience much difficulty with the *meaning* of the assertion that they do. That is, I have a perfectly good notion of what it means to exist as a self, and I experience no great barrier in conceiving what it would *mean* for other selves to exist. This is in sharp contrast to the difficulty I feel when I try to imagine the independent existence of a cloud, a leaf, a stone, an atom, or a lump of earth. I may be convinced that these things do exist independently, but I am very confused as to what it "feels" like to exist in this way. There is no such obstacle in grasping the meaning of the existence of other selves for the mode of existence here asserted is the mode of existence which I myself actually experience. We stand, then, in a peculiarly ambiguous condition of assurance and uncertainty in respect to this question.

The question is not a particularly old one in the history of philosophy, and it may first be dealt with in the form of the "problem of other minds," which was first posed by John Stuart Mill and which has become what might be called the traditional form of this question. Let it be noted that the problem of "other minds" is significantly, though subtly, different from the problem of "other selves." A mind is conceived specifically as the interior psychic concomitant of a bodily process. If my retina is stimulated by a light-wave, I may perceive the color red; or if the tympanum of my ear is set vibrating by a sound-stimulus, I may hear a shrill noise. Any witness may observe the stimuli and my outward reactions, and a physiologist may even observe and measure my neural and cortical reactions; but no witness may observe my conscious perception of red or shrill. That is available to me alone. What is true in the case of sensations is apparently even more true in the case of emotions or thoughts: I may be "observed" in a fit of pique or a brown state, but this observation is restricted to my grimaces and bodily postures, and does not extend to an awareness of what I am feeling and thinking.

This line of reflection led Mill to his problem of why, if it is true that we cannot directly observe the interior life of consciousness of another, we ever can be said to "know" that other minds really exist. His answer is the "analogy" argument, which was once standard but has lately lost favor.[2] The circumstances

[2] For criticism of the analogy argument, see Max Scheler, *The Nature of Sympathy*, trans. by Peter Heath, intro. by Werner Stark (New Haven: Yale University Press, 1954), pp. 239ff.; John Wisdom, *Other Minds* (Oxford:

of the situation are this: Only outward behavior is available for observation, and it must therefore be that outward behavior gives us the basis for our inference in respect to the inner concomitant. This is possible because in one instance, our own life, we have a privileged access to the inner concomitant. We then proceed by this reasoning: In my own case I realize that certain bodily processes are accompanied by inner conscious processes (unified under the term "mind") and therefore I decide that when I observe these bodily processes in others, I may infer that they are accompanied by mental processes not directly observable by me. My certainty that others exist is a product of an analogical inference which sets out from my own existence and its known connection with my bodily actions.[3]

Now in spite of an initial plausibility, this view is open to various objections which rather conclusively refute it, and which have more or less led to its abandonment. Of these objections, we will mention only two. First of all, there is what might be called the "mirror argument," which has been very frequently employed against it.[4] What Mill has contended is that I argue to the consciousness of others by supplying a missing link in a chain of analogy which begins with my own behavior, a patent fallacy. In order for me to argue that behind the bared teeth and squinting eyes which I now observe in this face confronting me there is a feeling of kindness and good humor, I would, on Mill's terms, have had to observe my own inner feelings as united to similar outward conduct: I would have had to observe myself smiling. But that, of course, I do not do. I don't know how I look when I smile, or am angry, or embarrassed, or sad. In my own case, I have the inner feel-

---

Blackwell, 1952), pp. 68ff., pp. 194ff.; Louis Arnauld Reid, *Ways of Knowledge and Experience* (London: Allen & Unwin, 1961), pp. 237ff.; W. Wylie Spencer, *Our Knowledge of Other Minds* (New Haven: Yale University Press, 1930), pp. 55ff.

[3] John Stuart Mill, *An Examination of Sir William Hamilton's Philosophy,* Chapt. XII.

[4] See Scheler, *op. cit.,* p. 240; Reid, *op. cit.,* p. 238; Spencer, *op. cit.,* p. 67.

ing but not the outer view. If I wanted to have the outer view of myself in the grip of these emotions, I would have to observe my facial and bodily contortions in a mirror—hardly a standard procedure. Therefore I do not comprehend that certain bodily behavior is the sign of another mind by comparing it to my own bodily behavior, for the simple reason that this is a comparison I could not possibly make, never having observed my own behavior.

Secondly, it can be shown that if I did proceed by analogical inference in this way, such an inference could never give me the *other*. Mill suggests that I *derive* my knowledge of the other by this means, but this is impossible. Unless I already had an awareness of the other, then the best I could do by means of an analogy would be to argue that behind a certain bodily facade was *my own* consciousness. That is, beginning with this proportion: this sort of bodily behavior is accompanied by my consciousness, then whenever I met this sort of bodily behavior, I would infer that it is accompanied by my consciousness. For the analogy to be strict, there would have to be some middle term that could serve as a sign of the presence of another; but if *behavior* is the middle term, then I only know what behavior signifies in the case when both the sign and the signified are present—my own conscious experience. Therefore, behavior signifies my consciousness, and it could only validate an inference to *my* consciousness. Nor could we claim that we must distinguish between *my* behavior and the *other's* behavior, for that is just what is in question: the behavior is supposed to be the basis for my awareness of another self, and I cannot begin by assuming that I already know it to be the behavior of another self.

This reasoning seems to be sufficient to deprive the argument from analogy of any claim to explain the origin of our knowledge of other selves. This is not to say that analogical inference in a broad sense may not be frequently used in interpreting others' conduct, but it cannot explain our awareness of the other as such, since it already presumes this awareness. We note already that the approach to the problem of other selves taken by this argument presumes that this knowledge is not primary, that it is the product of some sort of inference. There is no need to take much cognizance of this belief in its most aggravated form, the contention that the only things directly given to consciousness are bundles of discrete sense data, and that everything else is a matter of construction or interpretation. This view itself is an assumption, and a very shaky one. It will help to begin with the confidence that much more can be given to direct experience than the sense-datum theorist or the phenomenalist will admit.

Actually, anyone beginning with the phenomenalist viewpoint has a literally impossible task in reaching another self. On the phenomenalist's assumption, only transitory and discrete sense data are available to consciousness. Given this assumption, even the *meaning* of the assertion that other selves exist becomes doubtful. If, on the phenomenalist's basis, an "object" is simply a logical construction out of a set of sense data, then so is a subject. What it would mean to reach another self as a logical construct is very hard to imagine. Not only would this construct be indistinguishable from the object-construct, but it would have independent reality only in the meaningless Pickwickian sense of all phenomenalist "objects."

Yet, even if we start with the expectation that much more can be directly given to us in experience than impoverished sense data, there is still a very special difficulty in wondering how another mind can be directly given. Here we may consult the exhaustive and entertaining presentation of the problem which was made by John Wisdom.[5] Wisdom's difficulty comes down to this: Once we have made the plausible distinction between the inside and the outside of experience (mind and body), how can we ever be sure that any outside is the sign of any inside? That is, if we distinguish between any emotional state and its bodily expression, and say that the second is observable while the first is not, how, given this split, can the

[5] Wisdom, *op. cit.*, p. 84.

376

second ever be taken as a sure sign of the presence of the first?
For example, I might hold as an obvious fact that the pain
which I *feel* is not to be identified with the gnashing teeth,
rolling eyes, and clenched fists which manifest this pain outwardly. What I mean by saying that I am in pain is my ex-
cruciating, nonoutward feeling. So with gaiety, delight, sorrow,
disappointment, anxiety, or any psychic state—we may distinguish the mental state from the bodily manifestation.

Then, says Wisdom, what possible guarantee do I have that
this bodily state in another corresponds in him to a mental state
such as it would correspond to in me? I *assume* it does, but do
I know that it does? Since I don't observe his emotional state,
it always seems at least logically conceivable that it is very
different from what it would be in me, given similar bodily
manifestations. Here I see someone rolling his eyes, clenching
his fists, and screaming, and I say he is in pain. But how do I
know that this is not the way in which he expresses delight? I
don't observe his felt pain, I only infer it. Similarly, a mother
playing with her baby may observe what she takes to be all
the outward signs of joy: laughter, waving arms, gurgling. Yet
can she be logically certain that these particular gesticulations
are not the manner in which this particular being expresses his
grief? Isn't it conceivable that the mother is inflicting the
tortures of the damned upon her baby and that he is expressing it in this unfortunate manner which misleads his doting
parent? Obviously, this sort of question here bears on the accuracy with which we can read the inner life of the other
and not on the question of how we can know that there *is*
another there. Yet it could be easily generalized, for we might
think of the misreading being extended without limit, so that
we could misread as conscious responses what were only the
responses of an automaton.

The bizarre character of such reflection inevitably forces the
suspicion that there must be something fundamentally wrong
with posing the problem of other selves quite in this way. No
doubt the mind-body distinction is valid, and no doubt there is

an irreducible difference between mental and physical processes. Yet to treat the body as a kind of facade behind which
the existence and nature of mind has to be verified seems to get
things off on the wrong foot. We might try to recover a certain
balance even within this framework by suggesting a "king and
three sages" type of inference to other minds. Perhaps, one
might hold, we do not infer immediately to the inside of others,
but go through our own. That is, I can infer that the other
understands *my* inner life. This could happen somewhat as
follows: Suppose I am in a position where someone is causing
me pain, let us say a dentist drilling my teeth. Eyes tearing and
blinking, knuckles white, face contorted, I finally complain
that it hurts. I may reason as follows: if he understands by the
word "pain" what I understand by it, he will do what I would
do if I understood what he meant by the word "pain" and he
told me that I was hurting him. The dentist stops drilling. I
then infer that he and I mean the same thing by the word
pain. If he thought that by "pain" or "hurting" I meant pleasure
or delight, he would smile cheerfully and keep blasting away.
The fact that he doesn't indicates that the word "pain" signifies a reality about which he and I feel the same. The example,
of course, could be extended to take in not only pain but
pleasure, joy, sorrow, and so forth. What happens is not that I
infer how another feels, but that I infer how he would act if
he knows how I feel.[6]

Suppose, while still remaining within this general assumption
of an "indirect" knowledge of others, we try to situate the problem of "other minds" against a wider background. The child
certainly becomes aware of the existence of others before he

[6] The example given here includes language, whose crucial importance is
clear. But it might be proved without bringing in language at all. If I merely
wish the dentist would stop, yet refrain from saying anything, while my physical symptoms are identical, and if he actually does stop, I infer that he understands *my* physical symptoms. He does what I would wish him to do if he
understood my inner life. Does this prove that I can read *his* inner life? At
least it shows a certain mutuality between us which, I might assume, could just
as well run from my side to his.

makes the distinction between mind and body: he knows himself as a member of a class of which there are other members. Subsequently, one may suggest, he realizes that he has a "mind" and he wonders whether his natural belief that the other members of the class likewise do is well founded. How might he assure himself of this? [7] One route to this assurance might be the *responsive* character which distinguishes the behavior of certain objects of my experience from others. The child crying for the rattle he has just hurled from him elicits no response from the bars of his play-pen or from the carpet, but a human being nearby may retrieve it for him. There is thus built up the realization of a close connivance between this behavior and his wishes. His reaching out finds response in one case and not in another. There is a reciprocity which is missing elsewhere. Some might insist that these responses are still physical, that the other is doing what I would do with my own body if I could—and that hence this approach does not give us another mind. The fact that this is a true response of the other and not an extension of my own will is brought forcibly home in the instances where the response is of rivalry or resistance.

Further, there are cases where the response called for and elicited is not just another physical act; sometimes I require collaboration in a fully conscious process, and then the response becomes evidence for a fully conscious respondent. Some activities call into play our full nature as human beings, and those who are able to respond and cooperate in such acts evince thereby the presence of other minds. It is the other who actually calls us forth into full self-consciousness. The parents playing with the child are not opaque "others" to an already conscious individual; they are instruments by which the individual is brought to consciousness. *Their* response is implicated in *his* consciousness. As this consciousness expands, it expands in reciprocity with the other: in friendship, in common endeavors,

[7] The ensuing remarks owe much to the discussion of Spencer, *op. cit.*, pp. 20–48, who makes many interesting and instructive points on this issue.

in shared enthusiasms, the other responds to me in my entirety as a human entity, and therefore his entirety is present in his response. We now approach the realization that it is not quite right to think of the "mind" of the other as concealed behind a bodily facade. If our self comes-to-consciousness, then the respondents in this process of coming-to-consciousness are already present as minds. Mind, then, is at the boundary of the self and the other: it is a revelation of the other as well as the self. The primary manifestation of this, of course, is language, which is a perfectly "open" reality. Human consciousness finds itself in language. Then in finding itself it does not find only itself.

The objection may be raised that this awareness of others as respondents does not explain our rich and detailed awareness of *individual* selves, since it is rather indiscriminate and generalized. The point is valid enough, but the question may also be asked how we know our own selves as individual and unique beings. It is too easily assumed that the meaning of "I" is clear, but the meaning of "thou" is obscure. The truth may rather be that the profound meaning of "I" is equally hidden, that here, too, the revelation is a reciprocal one. Perhaps I only become "I" in the encounter with "thou" and perhaps apart from that encounter the only referent I have for "I" is a tatterdemalion succession of psychic states. Many modern philosophers have come to believe that this is the case. If something of the sort is true, then the problem is not of "other minds" or even of "other selves" but just the problem of "persons." Not even "other persons," for if these philosophers are right, the category of person already includes a reference to the other, and for one who knows himself as a person, there cannot be a problem of other persons.

## Direct Knowledge of the Other

Before following up the suggestion contained in the preceding sentence, it will be interesting to inspect some views which make the transition to it easier. The primary drawback to the approaches outlined above is that they regard our awareness of "other minds" as indirect. Even where an attempt is made to avoid the errors of the "analogy" explanation, the assumption continues to be that the reality of other minds is not an immediate datum but is known through an inference of some sort. Now one way of undercutting this whole difficulty is obviously to make the opposite assumption—to assume that the other is given directly and does not have to be argued to at all. This alternative may strike us as outlandish if we are accustomed to conceiving experience in terms of "sense perception." But in equating experience with "sense experience" we tend to forget that we could be led rather quickly to a *reductio ad absurdum*. For if only what is given immediately "to" the senses is a primary datum, then the only primary data are the discrete and multiple snippets of color, sound, scent, and so forth. On this view, not only must we say that we don't perceive other selves directly, but also that we don't even perceive tables, chairs, or trees directly: we don't perceive "things" at all. With this, the epistemological bark is once again stranded in the backwaters of phenomenalism. Actually the plight of phenomenalism is extremely grave, for if the only hard datum is the discrete sensory immediate, then it becomes extremely difficult to see how the entire *past* does not disappear from the catalog of the immediately known, and with it the continuing personal identity of the knower. Once the circle is broken and the suspicion dawns that direct perception may include much more than "sense data" it will not seem such an implausible claim that we may know other selves directly.

One philosopher who pressed this claim was Max Scheler.[8] Scheler's thesis was that *expression* was a primary datum and that as such it was the direct revelation of the other self. It is nonsense to say that we infer the existence of the other analogically, for the child who recognizes and responds to the warmth and friendliness of his mother's face is completely incapable of such an inference. Rather, the warmth and kindliness are ex-

[8] *Op. cit.*, p. 239.

pressive phenomena, just as much directly given as the color of the mother's hair or the size of her face. What we perceive are not "bodies" or "minds" but integral wholes: our distinction between the "body" and the "self" of the other post-dates this primary perception. Once we break out of the bonds of an empiricism which is essentially unfaithful to experience, we will see that our primary experience is that of configurational unities. Therefore, there is no problem of how I infer the reality of a mind behind a bodily facade, since I only arrive at calling this thing a "body" by *subtracting* something from the original experience. By adopting a certain attitude, I can see the bared teeth and squinting eyes as purely a physiological facade; but from a different posture, I see a smile. I cannot "compose" the smile out of "purely physiological" features, for the smile is not accessible from the mental stance in which I am able to identify something as a "purely physiological feature." [9] Neither can I break it down into physiological elements. The smile is an original phenomenon of expressiveness.

Scheler goes even further. His contention is that, far from it being "self-evident" that I cannot experience another's experience, it is perfectly natural for me to do so.[10] The apparent impossibility of it is assumed because I think too exclusively with reference to another's bodily states when thinking of his "experience." [11] It is true that I cannot feel his pain or experience his sensation of seeing or hearing. As part of the bodily complex, these are tied to the purely private nature of the bodily complex. But the situation changes in regard to the higher spiritual states, the emotions proper. There is no reason why I cannot experience another's grief or joy. I do not "argue" to these or infer their presence behind a corporeal facade. In some cases we may even speak, says Scheler, of *one* emotion shared by two selves. A father and mother standing together by the body of their dead child have their grief in common.

[9] *Ibid.*, pp. 261–262.
[10] *Ibid.*, pp. 244–247.
[11] *Ibid.*, p. 254.

There are not here simply two consciousnesses, but two consciousnesses sharing one identical sorrow. They experience it as "our sorrow." [12] In the face of such experiences, the problem of "other minds" loses all standing.

Similarly, Scheler adduces the nature of *sympathy* as a patent example of reaching the experience of the other. Sympathy is somewhat different from the parents' shared grief, for I may sympathize with another's grief without actually feeling that grief myself. My sympathy in another's grief (or joy) cannot be regarded as an original revelation of the existence of the other, for the act of sympathy already presupposes knowledge of the reality of that with which I am in sympathy.[13] But sympathy is an irreducibly given experience and its existence is a standing rebuttal to those who declare that the experience undergone by another is sealed off to me. Sympathy exists precisely because of the accessibility of the emotion of the other for me; consequently, it is a testimony to that accessibility. My commiseration with another's grief or rejoicing in his joy is consequent upon the transparence of his emotional consciousness for my own.[14]

Another philosopher who reaches the other directly and without any sort of inference is Jean-Paul Sartre. His views are fashioned in a metaphysical context peculiar to himself, but possess a value by no means restricted to that context. Where Scheler concentrates upon our experience of sympathy, Sartre finds the presence of the other most piercingly revealed in the experience of *shame*. It is not too much to say that for him our experience of shame *is* the experience of the other. Actually Sartre begins his analysis by regarding consciousness as a hyper-isolated knower. Proceeding by a strict act/object analysis of consciousness, he arrives at his now famous distinction

[12] *Ibid.*, pp. 12–13.

[13] *Ibid.*, p. 8.

[14] To make this viewpoint stand up, Scheler must show that sympathy actually does have this intentional reference to the other and that it is not reducible to elements which do not require this interpretation. This he does on pp. 37–50.

between the *en-soi* and the *pour-soi*, into which we may follow him just far enough for our present purposes.[15] Consciousness breaks down into awareness (*pour-soi*) and object of awareness (*en-soi*). The primary fact about awareness is that it is *not* its object. The primary fact about the object is that it excludes whatever is introduced by awareness. We then begin with a dichotomy between two different modes of being: being as awareness and being as the object of awareness. The first Sartre calls being-for-itself (*pour-soi*) and the second being-in-itself (*en-soi*). All negation is introduced into reality by consciousness: consciousness *is not* its object; its pure being-for-itself and not-being-its-object is the source of all negation. The in-itself which is purely *other* than consciousness escapes all negations and is conceived by Sartre as a massive self-identity, a kind of solid block of being.

All this is mentioned in order to lead up to the revelation of the other, as Sartre conceives it. Consciousness, the for-itself, exists as a kind of pure spontaneity which faces the inert passivity of the in-itself like a god in splendid isolation. All the world is a stage and it is the solitary player. In fact, as the solitary actor (the in-itself is inert), it confers the character of being a stage upon the in-itself. It *makes* a world wherein it can act. This is what Sartre calls the "project" of consciousness, by which it constitutes the arena in which it disports. But now, in a typically flamboyant manner, Sartre introduces the jarring presence of the other. The other's presence announces itself as my shame.[16] Suppose, says Sartre, I am engaged in some reprehensible activity, say kneeling down and looking through a keyhole. In this situation, the for-itself is a pure spontaneous looking-at an object; at this moment it projects its world in an absolutely autonomous way. Its frivolity is like the extreme of a fiat which constitutes its world and its own freedom. Suddenly, while I am in this ridiculous posture, I hear footsteps

[15] Jean-Paul Sartre, *Being and Nothingness*, pp. lxiv–lxix, 21–24, 73–79, *passim*.

[16] *Ibid.*, pp. 221–222, 259–263.

round the corner and look up to see two contemptuous eyes peering down at me. At once, my world collapses. Now I am not viewer but viewed. I feel myself looked at, and my autonomy and spontaneity ooze away. I am no longer a for-itself, but *for-another*. I feel the muscles in my jaws tighten, my mouth dry up, my body become a ludicrous and unwieldy bulk—I feel myself congealing to the rigidity of the in-itself. The other is the gorgon's head which turns me to stone.

Shorn of all specifically Sartrean trimmings, this is still a powerful example of what would be meant by the direct experience of the other. This is no inference, no argument by analogy. The other is there as directly as my shame. His presence is so directly felt that it causes my own to shrivel. Far from having to *argue* to his existence from my own, I would give anything to be freed from this utterly obtrusive presence, so that I might gather up the pieces of my own shattered existence.[17]

With these two examples as beginnings, it will occur to many that this approach could be broadened to include various other instances. What sympathy and shame do is to distill into a very pure form a quality which is widely, though more weakly, present in experience. We need only think of such states as admiration, loyalty, expectation, or anxiety, or such conditions as loneliness or boredom, which are testimonies in reverse to the reality of the other. Much could be done to show that these experiences are phenomenologically unintelligible except in relation to another self. Loneliness is an especially clear example of this. The experience of loneliness is built upon the experience of the other, but the experience of the other is now absent. Reference to the other is to such a degree an ontological dimension of the self that in the complete absence of all others,

[17] We need not follow Sartre into the consequences which he drew from such cases. He became so obsessed with the "look" as the revelation of the other that in his thought, human relations become a mutual "staring-down" process, the "other" is consistently regarded as either a threat or an opportunity for appropriation, and the whole positive side of intersubjectivity is largely lost.

my being is still turned towards the absent. There is no possibility of explaining this inferentially or of reducing it to different terms. This consideration was in Scheler's mind when he declared that an imaginary Robinson Crusoe who had never in all his life perceived any beings of his own kind would still be said to know the thou and possess the notion of community.[18] Scheler's position is that the knowledge of the nature of community and the existence of the thou in general is an *a priori* factor, given as an irreducible background to any encounter with individual persons—given, one might say, as a structural component of the human person. The sphere of the thou is just as essentially and irreducibly a sphere of the fundamental being of man as is the sphere of the "external world." Seen in this light, the human person *is* a reference to a thou, and his coming to self-consciousness is mediated by this reference and impossible without it.

## I and Thou

The most promising area of escape from the problem of "other selves" seems to lie in the direction of suppressing the assumption upon which it rests. This is the assumption that the intelligibility contained in the "I" is anterior to that contained in the "thou." If this is not so, if on the contrary the meaning of "I" is a function of the "thou," then it is clearly inconsistent for the I to raise the question of the existence of the thou. Among the philosophers who press for this solution, the most prominent name in the last century was that of Josiah Royce. According to Royce, the self was through and through a *social* entity: whatever meaningful content I have for the word "I," I build up out of an original experience of relationship. "I am not first self-conscious and then secondarily conscious of my fellow. On the contrary, I am conscious of myself, on the whole, as in relation to some real or ideal fellow, and apart from my consciousness of my fellow, I have only secondary and derived

[18] *Op. cit.,* pp. 234–235.

states and habits of self-consciousness." [19] And again: "Speaking in psychological terms, one can say that our finite self-consciousness is no primitive possession at all but is the hard-earned outcome of the contract between the being capable of becoming rational and the rationally disposed world in which he slowly learns to move." [20] The individual does not first know himself as a rational conscious being and then search about to discover whether, behind external appearances, there are other beings like him. Rather, his gradually developing explicit consciousness of himself as a rational, conscious being is an interpretive awareness of himself as a focal point in a social whole. Rational consciousness is essentially social; all philosophical questions are raised by rational consciousness, and it is therefore barren to raise as a rational issue the existence of other selves. In this outlook, Royce is true and inspired by the earlier idealism of Hegel, from whom the whole conception of the social nature of consciousness ultimately seems to derive. But his idealism finds echoes in quite different sorts of thinkers, such as the somewhat behavioristically oriented American philosopher, G. H. Mead, who was long preoccupied with this issue and sums up his feelings in the declaration that "It is impossible to conceive of a self arising outside of social experience." [21]

Martin Buber and Gabriel Marcel speak a different idiom from that of Royce, but the conception of the self as social is the cornerstone of their thought. Much of the point of this thought will be missed unless it is understood that they do not treat the self as an already realized entity which remains identical throughout the gamut of its experiences. The self is es-

[19] Josiah Royce, *Studies of Good and Evil* (New York: Appleton, 1898), p. 201. See also *The World and the Individual*, 2nd series (New York: Macmillan, 1900), pp. 245–277.

[20] *Ibid.*, p. 207.

[21] George H. Mead, *Mind, Self and Society*, ed. by Charles W. Morris (Chicago: University of Chicago Press, 1934), p. 140. See the interesting comparative study of Mead and Buber done by Paul E. Pfuetze, *The Social Self* (New York: Bookman Associates, 1954).

sentially a creative category: it is something which exists and is achieved in the order of freedom. Marcel and Buber locate the full potentiation of the self in its encounter with the thou, and it is in their discovery and exploration of the unique nature of this encounter that their contribution to the discussion consists. Others have emphasized the social character of the self in more general terms, but Marcel and Buber put their stress upon the singular character of the thou.[22] Whatever the "I" is, it is as unique; whatever establishes the "I" in its uniqueness establishes it in its authentic being. Whatever questions are posed about the other are either posed by a generalized "I" (say, an epistemological subject-in-general, or a social self) or by the "I" in all its uniqueness. Many have had a tendency to approach the problem of "other selves" from the side of a merely generalized "I." Marcel and Buber drive towards the unique and unrepeatable "I" and attack the problem in terms of it. But what they discover is that the unique and unrepeatable "I" only knows itself as such in the face of a "thou." Apart from my relation to the "thou," I am not aware of myself as a unique self at all—I am a mere bundle of sensations, series of experiences, or logical thinking subject. Here is a paradoxical discovery: the unique is a category of communion. If I want to say "I" in the most intense and fully realized way, I must say "thou." The unique dimension of existence represented by the "I" only emerges to consciousness in so far as there is an encounter with a "thou."

This means that my full experience of selfhood does not have priority over others, but is a co-emergent of communion. If anything, it is the other who has priority: the thou gives me to myself. What Marcel and Buber have discovered is the thou as an original dimension of existence. They make a fundamental

[22] A convenient place to meet Buber's thought on this is *I and Thou*, trans. by Ronald Smith (New York: Scribner's, 1958), esp. pp. 3ff. This "I-thou" theme is scattered through Marcel's whole work, but special reference may be made to *The Mystery of Being*, I, 176ff., *Metaphysical Journal*, pp. 219ff., and *Du refus à l'invocation*, pp. 50–52.

distinction between an "I-it" relation and an "I-thou" relation. They make this as an ontological distinction, and not merely a psychological one: that is, we cannot represent things as though there is one identical "I" variously related to others, but existing in the same ontological manner through the various relations. Rather the "I" is a relational category, and its status in being varies with its relation: the "I" of the "I-it" relation is ontologically different from the "I" of the "I-thou" relation.[23]

Certainly we may see what is meant by saying that an "I" which was reflexively conscious of itself in an "I-it" relation would not be conscious at the same ontological level as the "I" which was reflexively conscious in the "I-thou" relation. What this amounts to, then, is that the thou introduces us to a new dimension of being. In my relation with another person, being is revealed to me in a manner in which it is not revealed in any relation with a nonpersonal reality. "Things" or "objects" are not there for me in the way in which a thou is there. They are always to a certain extent "absent"—truncated, alien presences. Only in a personal encounter do I undergo the full experience of presence; and this is a twofold assertion: only in a personal encounter am I really present to myself, through the presence of a thou. Self-presence and the presence of a thou are two sides of one coming-to-presence which is the creative achievement of human communion.

This must not be taken to mean that wherever I am as a matter of fact dealing with a human person, I actually do encounter a thou. The tragedy of the human condition is exactly that the experience of the thou is so fugitive and tenuous. Clearly the "presence" spoken of here does not refer to simply physical presence. The table or chair is "with" me in that sense. Other human beings who are occupying the same region of space with me do not automatically become "thou's": my fellow workers in the office, the people sitting across from me on the subway, or standing shoulder to shoulder in the elevator, even those with whom I am ostensibly "talking" can

[23] Buber, *op. cit.*, pp. 3, 12.

be mere "absent thirds." The genuine experience of the thou is a relatively rare and privileged one. That is why Marcel will concentrate on such experiences as love, hope, or fidelity, which are thematically centered on the thou in the fullness of his presence. It is in experiences like these that the full ontological originality of the thou can be appreciated.

For the thou to whom I am related in love cannot be grasped in the manner of a thing "about which" I speak. He is precisely incommensurate with all descriptive language. Love does not bear on a "content" or a characterizable object. The beloved being is not a repository of certain predicates in which I can summarize the foundation for my affection.[24] Love bears on an uncharacterizable presence. It opens me to the mystery of the singular. Precisely in so far as a being is beloved, he is beyond all inventory which I could take of him to explain why he is beloved. Objects can be characterized; objects can be given predicates; in fact an "object" (in the sense of Buber and Marcel) just is the presumed structure upon which I can hang my set of predicates. But that which I characterize, that to which I assign predicates, is always that "about which" I am speaking: it is spoken of in the third person. A "thou" is not that about which I speak, but the one to whom I speak: it is addressable only in the second-person. Presence, second-personness, cannot be approached from the side of objectified structure. It therefore represents an original revelation of being, a revelation which is inaccessible by any other route.

This last remark will help in answering a question which is bound to come up at this point: in what sense can the experience of the thou be called "knowledge"? It may be thought that I have added very little to my store of expressible information through the experience of love or fidelity, and there may be the renewed suspicion that these are only psychologically interesting states of an individual subject. Now it may be allowed at the outset that if knowledge is identified with "information," this objection is well taken. For all information

[24] *Ibid.*, p. 17.

bears on "objects," and a thou is not an object but a presence. All information, too, is conceived as transmittable through the ordinary channels of language to any properly equipped observer: but the truth of the thou is not transmittable to an observer at all, but to the "I" which is co-present with it, and which is a participant, not an observer. Nevertheless there is a defense for continuing to use the word "knowledge" here. First of all, "knowledge" can be extended to take in the *ground* of a propositional statement, and in this sense any original source of evidence is freighted with cognitional value. Here, the I-thou experience clearly qualifies: the *only* way to know another person in his singularity is to *love* him, and hence love is cognitional. But further, to the extent that this experience can be *expressed* at all, its expression can be said to acquire the status of knowledge in so far as it is an instrument by which thought regains the experience and recognizes the revelation inherent in it. Not transmittability, but *expressibility* may be taken as the hallmark of knowledge. With this proviso, it is not hard to assign various cognitional aspects to the I-thou relation.

As has been seen, it is a revelation of a new dimension of being, inaccessible in any other way. The "thou" is ontologically unique and cannot be reduced either to an object or to a projection of the self. The uncharacterizable presence which I discover in love, hope, or fidelity, reveals something to me which cannot be revealed to sense perception, logical thought, or objectified knowledge. To the extent that I succeed in expressing this unique dimension of being, I may be said to know what I could not otherwise know and therefore this expression is undoubtedly a sort of knowledge of being.

In what sense can it be viewed as knowledge of the *single* one? [25] That is, what do I know of the thou whom I love which I would not otherwise know? Here we must tread carefully. In one sense, I don't know anything more. That is, since the thou is not known as a characterizable object, I don't add to my aggregate of "facts" about him through love. The thou can-

[25] *Ibid.*, pp. 62–63.

not be reached as a toting up of traits, and therefore reaching the thou does not increase my objective knowledge about him. Yet, this must be emended. For surely, let us say, a young man who loves a girl "knows" her in a way that others do not. Far from being blind, love is rather a principle of knowledge. Still, he does not "know her better" in the sense that he has been impelled to study her personality more closely and observe features which others might just as well observe but don't bother to. He knows her in a manner that only one who loves her can know her. For her "being" or her "person" is not an already realized objective reality viewed by him from a more advantageous perspective: it is a creative category. The boy's love is the creative invocation of her being: it is a participation in the mystery of her uniqueness. He does not simply see better traits which are already actually there: he calls forth perfections which are virtual in her—and virtual in the order of freedom.[26] Her beauty, her charm, her goodness are not for him the same traits available for others: they are assimilated into the mystery of her uniqueness and appeal to him as revelation of that mystery. His response is a hope, a summons. Naturally love is impelled to declare itself, for the declaration makes more instant the qualities which it perceives. Love desires to call forth perpetually the beauty which its privileged vision sees, to bring to birth what is already born. This is true not only of the love between man and woman, but equally and perhaps more plainly true of other sorts of love. Aristotle made the same point, albeit intermittently, in respect to friendship. Consider, too, the love of parent for child, where these features are thematic. The mother and father, in going out towards the person of their child, know themselves to be going out towards a being which is largely virtual and latent; they are enraptured by a singularity which they are conspiring to bring into being. Nothing could better illustrate the twofold character of love as both creation and response. My love calls forth the being of the other; but I love the other because I have found in him a

[26] This is so even if his love is unrequited or unproclaimed.

being which I desire to call forth into the approval of my love.

Do I in this manner "know" his uniqueness? If this means, can I enumerate what makes him unique, the answer must be "no." Enumeration cannot reach the unique; for enumeration adds up "properties," and properties are always multipliable. Objectified thought, or indeed conceptual thought, must fall short of the singular. But I reach his uniqueness in the only way it can be reached—in the same way that he reaches it. For this person does not know his own uniqueness "objectively." His way of being present to himself cannot be reduced to an aggregate of traits; he does not know himself as a "what," but as inexpressible presence. But what quickens this presence and unfolds its fullness is the encounter with a thou. Thus the unique "I" stands at the boundary of giving and receiving. Love knows the unique because it is a creator of the unique.

As a consequence, there is another way in which the "I-thou" relation is cognitional; it is an instrument for my self-knowledge. The encounter with the thou is not only a revelation of the thou, but a revelation of myself. As we have seen, the "I" of the "I-thou" relation is met only within this relation. In relation to the thou I know something about myself that I could not otherwise know. Obviously this does not mean that I can enumerate more attributes of myself. But the uncharacterizable presence of the thou is also a revelation of an abyss of existence within myself. The whole "I-thou" experience is, so to speak, bottomless. It occurs in a realm that is transcendent in relation to objectified knowledge. In so far as I belong to this experience, I belong to a realm of being which is specifically inexhaustible. That is why Marcel will say "To love a person is to say to him, 'Thou at least shalt not die.' " [27] This is not to be understood as some kind of objective information which I have come across; it is simply the translation into language of the experience of presence with which communion is flooded. It will do no good to say that nevertheless he *will* die since all things come to an end, for the prophetic affirmation of love is

[27] *The Mystery of Being*, II, 62.

precisely a proclamation that the beloved as beloved is exempt from the penalties of thingness. The thou is not a thing. That is why the "I-thou" relation can provide the basis for a privileged kind of knowledge.

Only to the extent that I can affirm myself as spirit, as transphenomenal, can I be said to have "knowledge" of the "immortality of the soul" (which is a rather unsatisfactory objectified phrase). Then the experiences which enable me to grasp the unique meaning of non-thingified personal existence occupy a crucial position for this sort of knowledge. The traditional "proof" for the immortality of the soul (as simple and spiritual) proceeds as if we could have an objective grasp of the soul as a special sort of thing with attributes implying natural immortality. But once the soul is approached in the objectified mode of thought, we are in danger of coming to rest in an implication of concepts. At best we have proved that the soul is a repository or an efficient cause of universal ideas and that thus it is immaterial. But an "it" which is not material is a rather negative notion and rather vulnerable to the formalist reduction of Kant. The positive intelligibility of existing as a person, rather than a thing, is given in the experience of communion. Only a thought which clings to communion remains attached to the meaning which makes the affirmation of immortality possible. It is not an object called the soul which is immortal; it is "we" who are immortal. We, here together, bound in love, we grant and bestow the mutual tokens of immunity from death. Immortality is not a consequence implicit in the concept of "immateriality," it is a promise spoken to those existing in communion. Love, in being a revelation of the thou, is also a revelation of my self, and the transphenomenal character of my being. How do I affirm this? Only so far as I participate in communion. Love is "the actual refusal to treat itself as subjective." It is charged with cognitive potentialities to the precise extent that it is love. Only a reflection which plunges into communion can make this affirmation, which is why communion is a source of knowledge.

Finally, for the same reason, in the opinion of both Marcel and Buber, the "I-thou" relation is cognitive in yet another way. The abyss of existence is revealed to subjectivity and subjectivity is revealed to communion. As a member of a spiritual communion I move in a realm of an open presence. The finite thou is always to some extent also a thing, but the aura of the inexhaustible which surrounds communion is an intimation of an unfailing presence which sustains it. The light of the Absolute Thou is shed across human communion.[28] The transcendent is present to our experience as *intimation,* and this intimation is made to communion. The thou calls us beyond our isolated egos, and in calling summons us to a presence which founds a new being; but back of the discrete appeals which scattered selves fling out to us, there is the absolute appeal to found ourselves in a realm where love and fidelity make unassailable sense. For both Marcel and Buber, the I-thou relation is thus the avenue to the transcendent, and the proper name of God is Absolute Thou.

Once again we may ask whether all this should be called "knowledge," assuming that we grant value to the description of experience herein recounted. It is not knowledge that is accessible to "anyone at all"—but then this may be too narrow an idea of knowledge. It is knowledge which is available, if Marcel and Buber are right, to one who belongs to the I-thou relation and whose thought rejoins that relation. To the extent that they succeed in expressing this thought, they have raised the experience to a cognitive status; to the extent that this experience gives us a privileged access to an otherwise unavailable realm, it is a privileged sort of knowledge.

[28] Buber, *op. cit.,* p. 75; Marcel, *Du refus à l'invocation,* pp. 179, 218.

# BIBLIOGRAPHY

For extensive bibliographies of books and articles dealing with issues related to the other minds problem, consult A. J. Ayer, ed., *Logical Positivism* (New York: The Free Press, 1959), pp. 381–446; V. C. Chappell, ed., *The Philosophy of Mind* (Englewood Cliffs, N.J.: Prentice-Hall, 1962), pp. 173–178; Harold Morick, ed., *Wittgenstein and the Problem of Other Minds* (New York: McGraw-Hill, 1967), pp. 227–231; and John O'Connor, ed., *Modern Materialism: Readings on the Mind-Body Identity* (New York: Harcourt, Brace and World, 1969), pp. 285–289.

## Books

Buber, Martin. *The Knowledge of Man.* New York: Harper and Row, 1965.

Locke, D. B. *Myself and Others: A Study in Our Knowledge of Minds.* Oxford: Clarendon Press, 1968.

MacMurray, John. *Persons in Relation.* New York: Harper and Brothers, 1961.

Plantinga, Alvin. *God and Other Minds.* Ithaca, N.Y.: Cornell University Press, 1967.

Sartre, Jean-Paul. *Being and Nothingness.* Translated and with an introduction by Hazel E. Barnes. London: Methuen, 1957.

Sayre, Kenneth M. *Consciousness: A Philosophic Study of Minds and Machines.* New York: Random House, 1969.

Scheler, Max. *The Nature of Sympathy.* Translated by Peter Heath with introduction by Werner Stark. New Haven: Yale University Press, 1954.

Spencer, W. Wylie. *Our Knowledge of Other Minds.* New Haven: Yale University Press, 1930.

Wisdom, John. *Other Minds.* Oxford: Basil Blackwell, 1952.

## Articles

Albritton, Rogers. "On Wittgenstein's Use of the Term 'Criterion.' " *Journal of Philosophy,* LVI (1959).

Alexander, P. "Other People's Experiences." *Proceedings of the Aristotelian Society,* LI (1950–51).

Aune, Bruce. "The Problem of Other Minds." *Philosophical Review,* LXX (1961).

———. "On Thought and Feeling." *Philosophical Quarterly,* XIII (1963).

Ayer, A. J. "One's Knowledge of Other Minds." *Theoria,* XI (1953).

Baier, Kurt. "Pains." *Australasian Journal of Philosophy,* XL (1962).

Buck, R. "Non-Other Minds," in R. J. Butler, ed., *Analytical Philosophy.* New York: Barnes and Noble, 1962.

Castaneda, Hector-Neri. "Criteria, Analogy, and Knowledge of Other Minds." *Journal of Philosophy,* LIX (1962).

———. "On the Logic of Attributions of Self-Knowledge to Others." *Philosophical Review,* LXV (1968).

Chappell, V. C. "Myself and Others." *Analysis Supplement,* XXIII (1963).

Duhrssen, Alfred. "Philosophic Alienation and the Problem of Other Minds." *Philosophical Review,* LXX (1963).

Evans, J. L. "Knowledge and Behavior." *Proceedings of the Aristotelian Society,* LIV (1953–54).

Fulton, J. S. "Our Knowledge of One Another." *Philosophical Review,* LI (1942).

Gregory, J. C. "Some Tendencies of Opinion in Our Knowledge of Other Minds." *Philosophical Review,* XXXI (1921).

Hamlyn, D. W. "Behaviour." *Philosophy,* XXVIII (1953).

Hartland-Swann, John. "The Logic of 'Knowing Jones.' " *Philosophical Studies,* VIII, nos. 1–2 (January–February, 1957).

Jones, J. R. "Our Knowledge of Other Persons." *Philosophy,* XXV (1950).

## Bibliography

Jorgensen, J. "Remarks Concerning the Concept of Mind and the Problem of Other People's Minds." *Theoria*, XV (1949).

Karalis, Nicholas. "Knowledge of Other Minds." *Review of Metaphysics*, IX (1955–56).

Long, Douglas C. "The Philosophical Concept of a Human Body." *Philosophical Review*, LXXIII (1964).

Long, Thomas. "Two Conceptions of Wittgenstein's Criteria." *Philosophical Quarterly*, XXXIX (1966).

Meiland, J. W. "Meaning, Identification and Other Minds." *Australian Journal of Psychology and Philosophy*, XLII (1964).

Meller, W. W. "Three Problems about Other Minds." *Mind*, LXV (1956).

Mukherji, S. R. "The Problem of Other Minds." *Philosophical Quarterly of India*, XXXIX, no. 1 (April, 1966).

Narveson, Anne H. "Evidential Necessity and Other Minds." *Mind*, LXXV (1966).

Pap, A. "Other Minds and the Principle of Verifiability." *Revue internationale de philosophie*, V (1951).

Plantinga, Alvin. "Things and Persons." *Review of Metaphysics*, XIV (March, 1961).

Polanyi, Michael. "Tacit Knowing: Its Bearing on Some Problems of Philosophy." *Reviews of Modern Physics*, XXXIV, no. 4 (October, 1962).

Price, H. H. "Our Knowledge of Other Minds." *Proceedings of the Aristotelian Society*, XXXII (1931–32).

Rollins, C. D. "Professor Ayer's Query on 'Other Minds.'" *Analysis*, VIII (1947–48).

Rorty, Richard. "Mind-Body Identity, Privacy, and Categories." *Review of Metaphysics*, XIX (1965).

Schuetz, Alfred. "Scheler's Theory of Intersubjectivity." *Philosophy and Phenomenological Research*, II (1942).

Sellars, Wilfrid. "Empiricism and the Philosophy of Mind," in Herbert Feigl and Michael Scriven, eds., *Minnesota Studies in the Philosophy of Science*, vol. I. St. Paul: University of Minnesota Press, 1956.

———. "Mind, Meaning and Behavior." *Philosophical Studies*, III, no. 6 (December, 1952).

Shearn, M. "Other People's Sense-Data." *Proceedings of the Aristotelian Society*, L (1949–50).

Steinkraus, Warren. "Berkeley's Wisdom on Other Minds." *Philosophical Forum*, XV (1958).

Stern, Kenneth. "Private Language and Skepticism." *Journal of Philosophy*, LX (1965).

Suresh. "Knowing What Others Feel." *Philosophical Quarterly of India*, XXXV, no. 1 (April, 1962).

Thalberg, Irving. "Other Times, Other Places, Other Minds." *Philosophical Studies*, XX, nos. 1–2 (January–February, 1969).

Thomson, J. F. "The Argument from Analogy and Our Knowledge of Other Minds." *Mind*, LX (1951).

Urban, W. M. "Knowledge of Other Minds and the Problem of Meaning and Value." *Philosophical Review*, XXVI (1917).

Van de Vate, Jr., Dwight. "Other Minds and the Uses of Language." *American Philosophical Quarterly*, III, no. 3 (July, 1966).

———. "Strawson's Concept of a Person." *Southern Journal of Philosophy*, VII, no. 1 (Spring, 1969).

Watling, John. "Ayer on Other Minds." *Theoria*, XX (1954).

Weinberg, J. "Our Knowledge of Other Minds." *Philosophical Review*, LX (1946).

Wellman, Carl. "Our Criteria for Third-Person Psychological Sentences." *Journal of Philosophy*, LVIII (1961).

———. "Wittgenstein's Conception of a Criterion." *Philosophical Review*, LXXI (1962).

Whiteley, C. A. "Behaviorism." *Mind*, LXX (1961).

# INDEX

Behaviorism (*continued*)
tique of, 126; critique of peripheralistic, 126
Behavioristic theory, 138-139; critique of, 254-255
Belief: knowledge and, 274-275
Bodily pain: conditions for determining, 29
Body: associated with mind, 7; human, 314; perceptual experience related to human, 316; causally related to mind, 316; behavior of physical, 352
Brain, 180
Buber, Martin, 387

Carnap, Rudolf, xv, 126n
Cartesian dualism, 345
Cartesianism, x, 318-350 *passim;* critique of, 324-325, 329-330
Central states: xvii; neurophysiological nature of, 127
Cerebral events, 183
Cerebral states: mental states and, 121
Certainty, 287-309 *passim*
Character: physicalization of properties, 95-101
Chinese ideographs, 147
Coburn, R. C., 365
Coherence, xix
Coherence argument, 64; critique of, 190-192
Communication: language and, 20; central to other minds problem, 139-140; voluntary and involuntary, 139-140
Communication situations, 139-143
Communion, 394-395
Consciousness: ascription to objects, 321-328 *passim*
Cook, John W., 355n
Copernicus, 72
Criteria: meaning and, 351
Criteriological argument, xx; critique of, xxiii
Criterion, 196-197; Wittgenstein's use of, 225-233; contrasted with symptom, 227; of pain behavior, 232-233; for sensation-words, 244-246

Darwin, Charles, 72

Deceit: methods for correcting, 310
Deception: determining, 15-16
Definition: private ostensive, 227
Descartes, René, xix, 5, 22, 33, 163, 167, 191, 209, 316, 318, 319n; and private language, 209
Description, 169
Direct access theory. *See* Direct insight theory
Direct insight theory, xxiii-xxvi, 134-139, 170-171, 177; critique of, xxv-xxvi, 135, 137-139, 252; extrospective acquaintance with, 134-135; not supported by mental telepathy, 135-136; variations of, 135-137; as two-term relation, 169
Direct knowledge: critique of, 122
Disembodied minds, 188
Disposition: physicalization of properties, 95
Doubt, Cartesian, 163n
Dreams: psychological sentences about, 224

Ego: as logically nonprimitive, 327
Egocentric particulars: place of in common language, 125-126
Einstein, Albert, 80
Emotions, 174-175, 300; symptoms of, 304; venting of, 305-306
Empiricism, British, 209
Epiphenomenalism, 345
Epistemological idealism: argument for, 33
Epistemological realism: reasonableness of, 60-62
Error: basis for, 294-295
Evidence, 9; for knowledge claims, 276; and reasons, 278; and authority, 278-279
Experience: direct access to other minds, 382-383
Expression: as revelation of other minds, 381

Fear: learned from "one's own case," 202
Feelings: statements about, 11; directly known, 11-12; and physical symptoms, 302; and self, 315; as material objects, 355-356; and protocol sentences, 356; as logically

Materialism, 6

Mathematics, 141

Matter: as dead, 4

Mead, George H., 387

Meaning: identity of, 267-273; and criteria, 351

Memory: and private language, 212-213; and personal identity, 361-362

Mental: contrasted with physical, 305

Mental events, xi, xvii; related to neurophysiological states, 180; as physical events, 248-249; as critique of physical events, 249; as inward, 249-250; as unobservables, 252-253; meaning of, 257-258; prediction of, 258-259

Mental facts, 248

Mental images, 212; on identifying, 243

Mental states: first-person confirmation of, xvii; unobservability of others', 24; determined by observation, 24-25; beliefs about as probable, 30; evidence for beliefs about, 30-31; and cerebral states, 121; direct confirmation of, 129

Mental telepathy: as objection to physicalism, 84-86

M-predicates, 329-342 passim

Metaphysics, 70, 80

Mill, John Stuart, ix, 195, 196, 197, 373-375

Mind: space-time structure of, 3; causally related to body, 316; group, 338-339

Mind-body relation, x

Minds: evidence for disparity among, 122; lower animals, 166

Models: of the transcendental, 255

Moore, G. E., 224, 319n, 346n

Naming: misnaming and, 280

Negation: introduced by consciousness, 384

Neutral monism, 125

Nietzsche, Friedrich, 72

Noises: parrots and symbolic, 148-149; symbolic as mental instruments, 157-158

Objects: ascription of consciousness to, 321-328 passim

Old Testament, 146

Ordinary language, 265

Organism, observable, 146-147

Other: as contextual term, 19

Other minds: statements about as contextual, 21-23; source of problem, 119; criteria for knowledge claims, 121; evidence for existence of, 151; problem of misconceived, 377-378; awareness of as indirect, 381; awareness of as direct, 381-395 passim; knowledge of as non-inferential, 381-385

Other minds problem: how arises, 12; meaning of, 12-13; commonsense answer to, 13; formulation of, 119, 177, 248, 256, 273, 371-372; and philosophical therapy, 123; critique of philosophical therapeutic approach to, 123-124; and first-person psychological sentences, 203-207; elimination of, 204; as insoluble, 337; escape from, 386-387

Pain: determined by observation, 24-25; evidence for bodily, 38-39; learned from "one's own case," 202; paradigm of sensation, 206

Pap, A., 125n, 128

Parrots, 148-149

Past: on testing statements about, 16; how problem arises, 16-18; as contextual term, 18-19

Perry, R. B., 128

Person: as two substances, 318; concept of as primitive, 326-342 passim; and P-predicates, 329; and M-predicates, 329-342 passim; critique of Strawson's version, 363-364; as limit, 369

Phenomenalism, x, 125; and private language, 209; and other minds problem, 376

Phenomenology, 73

Physical: contrasted with mental, 305

Physical behavior, xi

Physicalism, 124, 346; thesis of, 70; emotional resistance to, 72-73; defense of, 182

Physical language: universal, 69; universal and subjective, 70; relation to psychological language, 71

# Index

Physics, 4-5, 78; and general laws, 74

Physiology: undeveloped state of, 81; as objection to physicalism, 81-82

Plantinga, Alvin, xiii, 45

Plato, 22

Poincaré, J. H., 80

P-predicates: characteristics of, 329-335; criteria for ascription of, 331, 349; as first-person utterances, 332-333; as other-ascriptive, 334; as systematically ambiguous, 350-351

Present: as contextual term, 18

Price, H. H., xviii, xix, 199-204 *passim*

Principles, synthetic a priori, 129

Privacy, 124-125, 259n; absolute, 122-123; relative, 123; problem of, 354-370 *passim*

Private language, x, xix, 238-240; and sense-datum theory, 209; and Descartes, 209; and phenomenalism, 209; rules of, 211; and memory, 212-213; and knowing, 295-300

Pronouns: function of, 17-18; use of, 20

Properties: psychological and physical, 95-97; primary, secondary, and tertiary, 355-358

Protocol language, 70, 90

Protocol sentences, 71, 77, 354; testing with reference to, 80

Psychology, 78; describes physical occurrences, 69; sentences of translatable into physical language, 71; laws of translatable into physical language, 72; gestalt, 75; metaphysical orientation of, 81; intuitive, 89-94; demands made on, 94; physicalization of concepts in, 94-101; as physical science, 99-100, 109; critique of introspective, 101-108; critique of physicalism, 102-103

Psychophysical interrelations, 75

Psychophysiology: task of, 186-187

Quine, W. V. O., 127, 182-183, 365

Raw feels, 352

Reality, 283-294 *passim;* procedures for determining, 284-285; and deceit, 308-309

Relations, causal, xi, xii

Rorty, Richard, 346-349

Royce, Josiah, 386

Rule: and private language, 211, 216-217; Wittgenstein on linguistic, 213-217; and understanding, 214

Russell, Bertrand, xii, 22, 129, 145

Ryle, G., 356

Sameness: of statements, 20

Sartre, Jean-Paul, 383-385

Scheler, Max, 373n, 381-383

Schilpp, P. A., 110

Schlick, M., 318, 319n

Scriven, Michael, 109, 314n

Self: ways of talking about, 315; "no-ownership" doctrine of, 318-326; critique of "no-ownership" doctrine, 320-326; Hume and, 327; as a unity, 341; as social, 387-395 *passim*

Self-consciousness: growth of, 378-380

Sensations, xvii; cause of, 5; expressions of, 219-225; how words refer to, 220-221; description of, 235-237; logic of, 259-261; knowledge of, 293-294; and self, 315; critique of private access theory, 345-346; critique of identity theory, 346-349; P-predicate theory of, 349-353; as mental states, 353; as tertiary, 354; identity of, 354; as private, 354; direct accessibility of others', 358

Sensation-sentences: third-person, 231-234; human behavior as paradigms of third-person, 232-233

Sensation-words: and language-games, 239

Sense-data, 291-292; as private, 164, 165; and other minds, 376-377

Sense-datum theory: and private language, 209

Sentences: general psychological, 73; singular and general, 73; inductively established general, 75; about one's own mind, 75; about other minds, 75; about physical objects and other minds, 75-76; singular, 75-76; translatability of psychological into physical, 108-

405

# NOTES ON CONTRIBUTORS

J. L. Austin (1911–60) was White's Professor of Moral Philosophy at Oxford University. *How To Do Things with Words, Philosophical Papers* (published posthumously), and *Sense and Sensibilia* are his major publications.

Rudolf Carnap (1891–    ) is a German-born philosopher who came to the United States in 1936. From 1936 to 1952 he taught at the University of Chicago. From 1954 until his retirement in 1961 he was professor of philosophy at the University of California, Los Angeles. His major writings include *The Logical Syntax of Language* and *Meaning and Necessity.*

Herbert Feigl (1902–    ) is professor of philosophy at the University of Minnesota and has been visiting professor of philosophy at the University of California, Berkeley. His major works are *Readings in Philosophical Analysis* and *Minnesota Studies in the Philosophy of Science,* vols. I, II, and III.

Kenneth Gallagher (1922–    ) is associate professor of philosophy at Fordham University. He is the author of *The Philosophy of Gabriel Marcel.*

Stuart Hampshire (1914–    ) is Fellow of All Souls College,

Oxford University, and has written *Spinoza, The Freedom of the Individual,* and *Thought and Action.*

Norman Malcolm (1911–   ) is professor of philosophy at the Sage School of Philosophy, Cornell University. Among his publications are *Ludwig Wittgenstein: A Memoir* and *Knowledge and Certainty.*

Alvin Plantinga (1932–   ) is professor of philosophy at Calvin College and has been visiting professor at University of Chicago, University of Michigan, and Harvard University. *God and Other Minds* is his major publication.

H. H. Price (1899–   ) has held teaching positions at Magdalen and Trinity Colleges, Oxford, and University of Liverpool. At the time of his retirement he was Wykeham Professor of Logic at Oxford University. *Perception* and *Thinking and Experience* are among his major works.

Bertrand Russell (1872–1970), lecturer in philosophy at University of Cambridge and Fellow of Trinity College, Oxford. Author, politician, statesman. Among his major works are *Principia Mathematica* (with A. N. Whitehead), *Our Knowledge of the External World,* and *Logic and Knowledge.*

Michael Slote (1941–   ) is assistant professor of philosophy at Columbia University. His most important work is *Reason and Scepticism.*

P. F. Strawson (1919–   ), Fellow of University College, Oxford, is well known for his work, *Individuals.*

John Wisdom (1904–   ) is professor of philosophy at the University of Cambridge. Beside his work *Other Minds,* he has published *Philosophy* and *Psycho-Analysis, Paradox and Discovery,* and *Problem of Mind and Matters.*

E. M. Zemach (1935–   ) has held positions at Yale University, New York State University at Stony Brook, and is currently teaching at the Hebrew University of Jerusalem. His published work has been primarily in epistemology and philosophy of mind.

Paul Ziff (   –   ) is professor of philosophy at the University of North Carolina. Among his important works are *Philosophic Turnings* and *Semantic Analysis.*